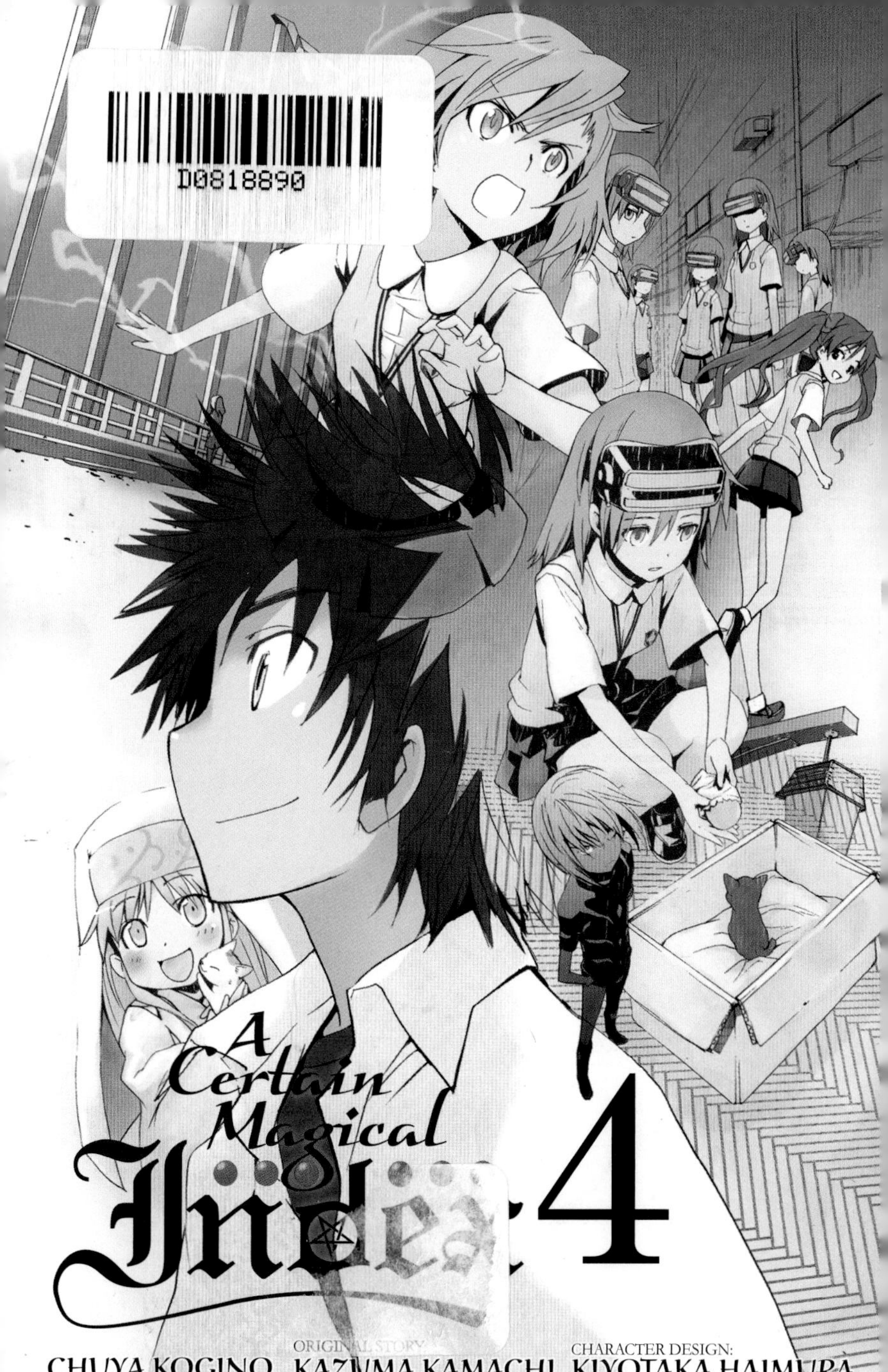

A Certain Magical Index 4

CHUYA KOGINO
ORIGINAL STORY: KAZUMA KAMACHI
CHARACTER DESIGN: KIYOTAKA HAIMURA

A CERTAIN MAGICAL INDEX 4 TABLE OF CONTENTS

Index Librorum Prohibitorum

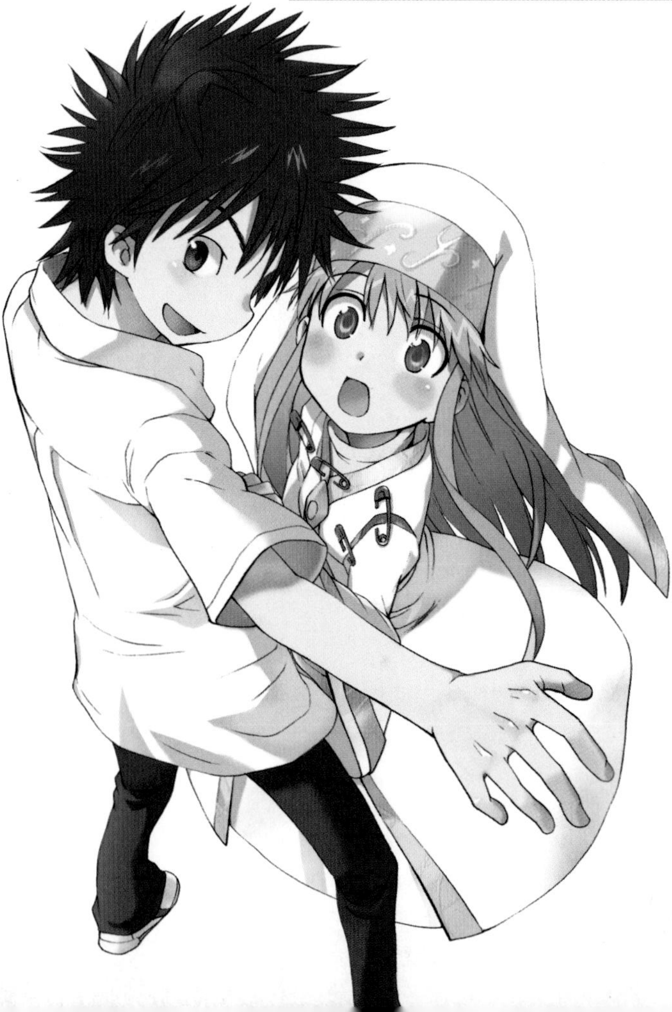

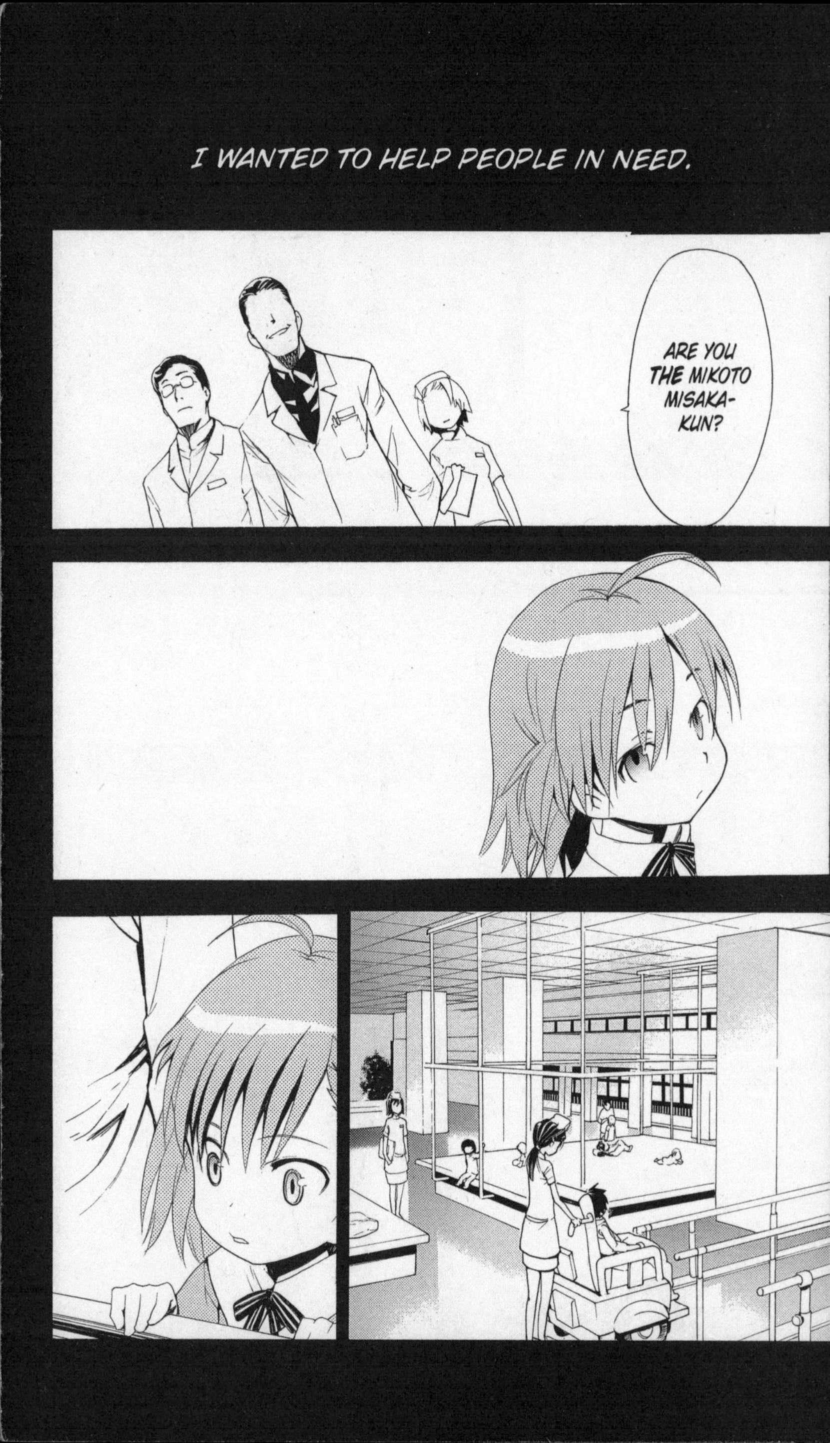
I WANTED TO HELP PEOPLE IN NEED.
ARE YOU THE MIKOTO MISAKA-KUN?

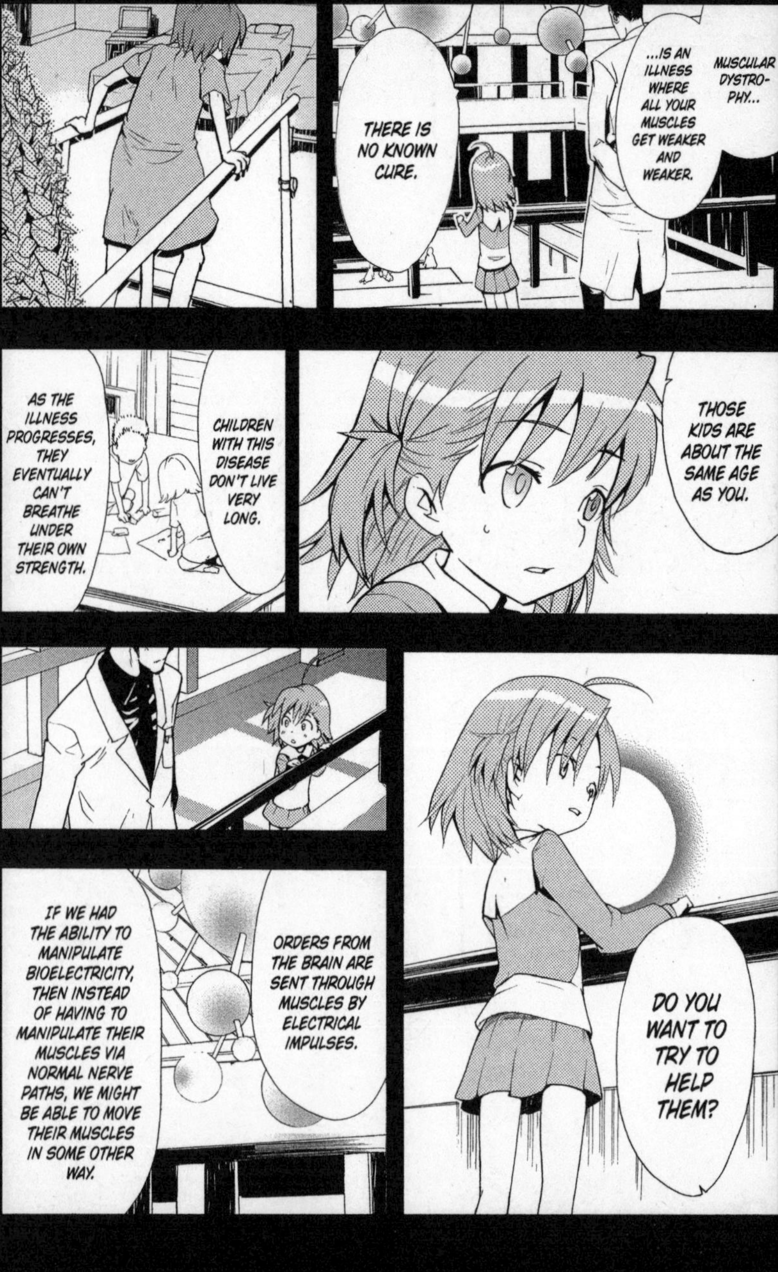
MUSCULAR DYSTROPHY...
...IS AN ILLNESS WHERE ALL YOUR MUSCLES GET WEAKER AND WEAKER.
THERE IS NO KNOWN CURE.
THOSE KIDS ARE ABOUT THE SAME AGE AS YOU.
CHILDREN WITH THIS DISEASE DON'T LIVE VERY LONG.
AS THE ILLNESS PROGRESSES, THEY EVENTUALLY CAN'T BREATHE UNDER THEIR OWN STRENGTH.
DO YOU WANT TO TRY TO HELP THEM?
ORDERS FROM THE BRAIN ARE SENT THROUGH MUSCLES BY ELECTRICAL IMPULSES.
IF WE HAD THE ABILITY TO MANIPULATE BIOELECTRICITY, THEN INSTEAD OF HAVING TO MANIPULATE THEIR MUSCLES VIA NORMAL NERVE PATHS, WE MIGHT BE ABLE TO MOVE THEIR MUSCLES IN SOME OTHER WAY.

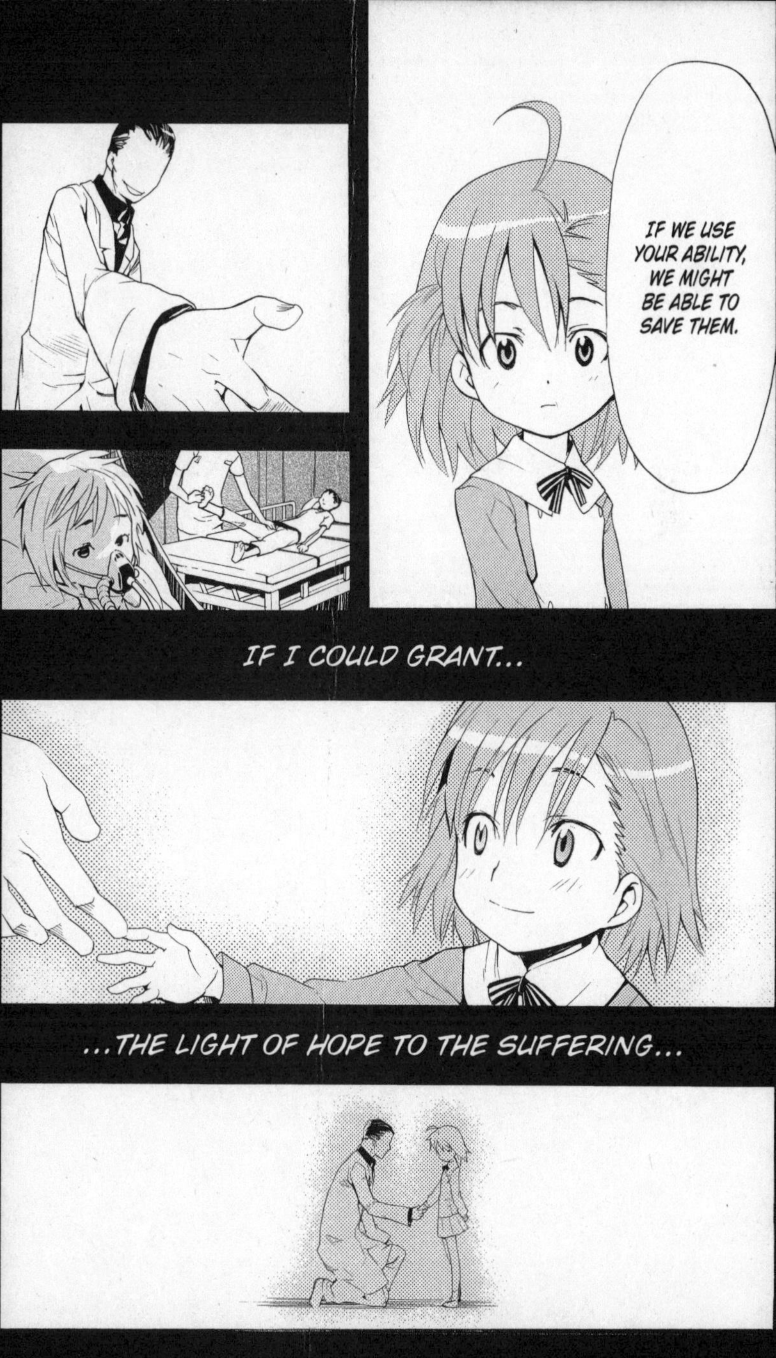
IF WE USE YOUR ABILITY, WE MIGHT BE ABLE TO SAVE THEM.
IF I COULD GRANT...
...THE LIGHT OF HOPE TO THE SUFFERING...

#16 - REPORT ②

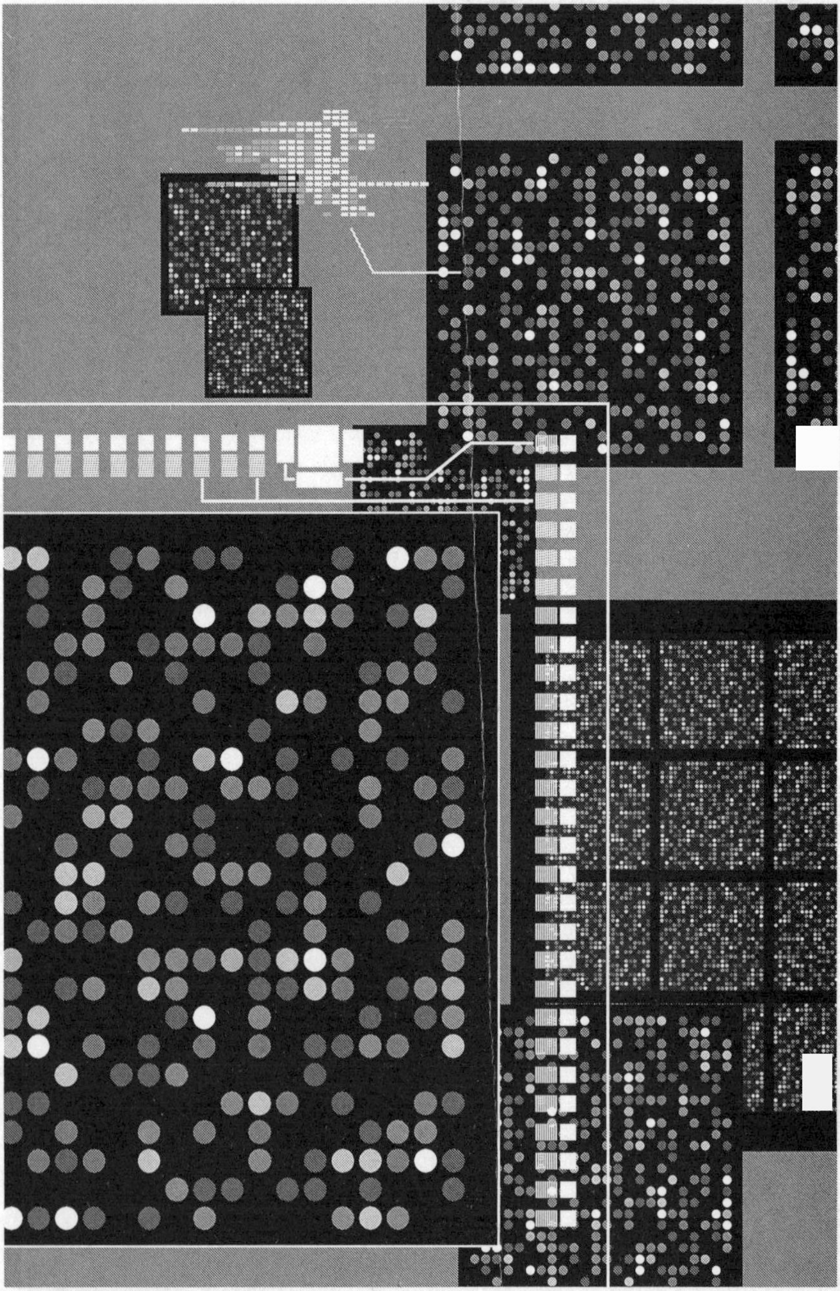

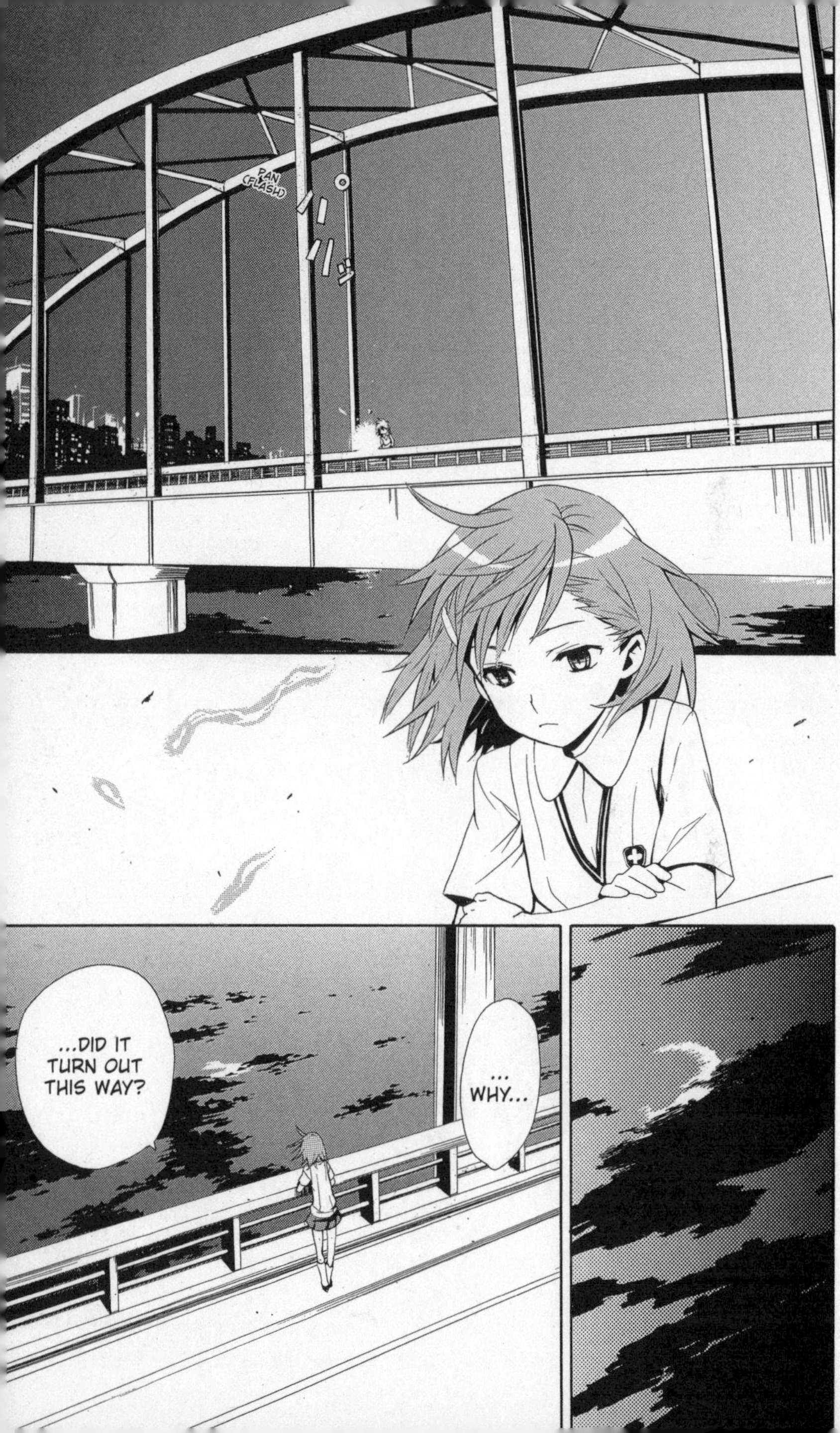
PAN (FLASH)
... WHY...
...DID IT TURN OUT THIS WAY?

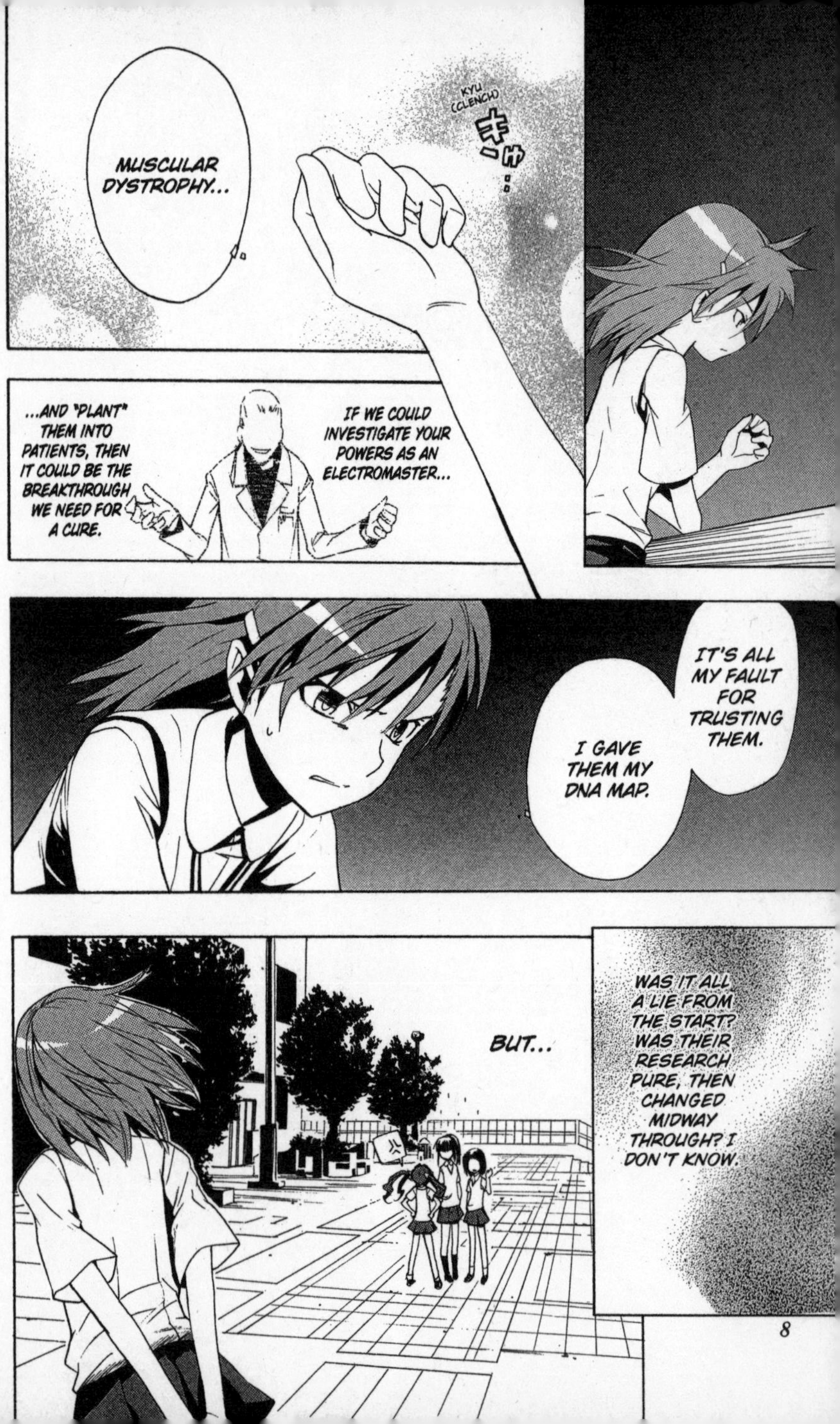
KYU (CLENCH)
MUSCULAR DYSTROPHY...
IF WE COULD INVESTIGATE YOUR POWERS AS AN ELECTROMASTER...
...AND "PLANT" THEM INTO PATIENTS, THEN IT COULD BE THE BREAKTHROUGH WE NEED FOR A CURE.
IT'S ALL MY FAULT FOR TRUSTING THEM.
I GAVE THEM MY DNA MAP.
WAS IT ALL A LIE FROM THE START? WAS THEIR RESEARCH PURE, THEN CHANGED MIDWAY THROUGH? I DON'T KNOW.
BUT...

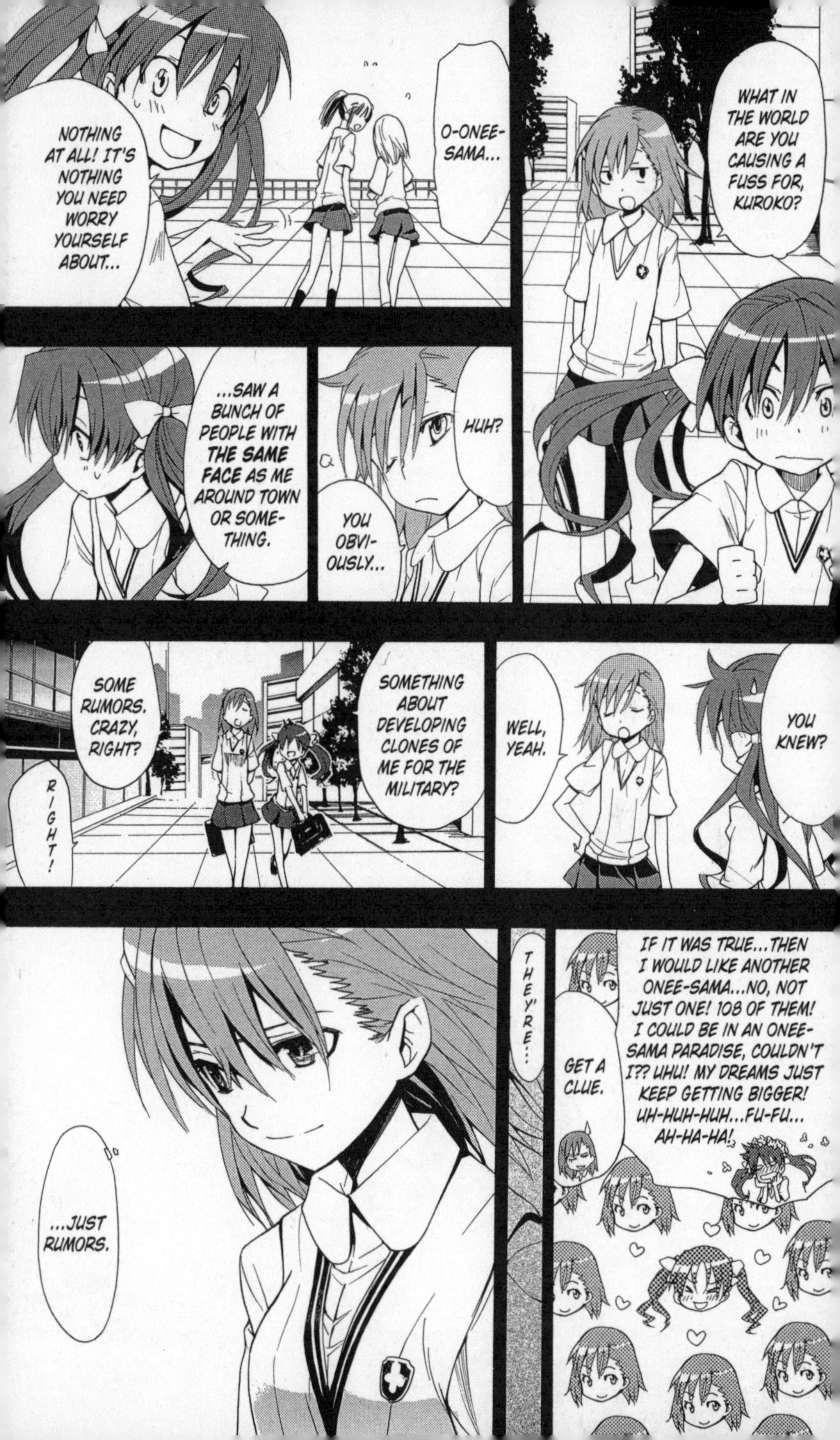
WHAT IN THE WORLD ARE YOU CAUSING A FUSS FOR, KUROKO?
O-ONEE-SAMA...
NOTHING AT ALL! IT'S NOTHING YOU NEED WORRY YOURSELF ABOUT...
HUH?
YOU OBVIOUSLY...
...SAW A BUNCH OF PEOPLE WITH THE SAME FACE AS ME AROUND TOWN OR SOMETHING.
YOU KNEW?
WELL, YEAH.
SOMETHING ABOUT DEVELOPING CLONES OF ME FOR THE MILITARY?
SOME RUMORS. CRAZY, RIGHT?
RIGHT!
IF IT WAS TRUE...THEN I WOULD LIKE ANOTHER ONEE-SAMA...NO, NOT JUST ONE! 108 OF THEM! I COULD BE IN AN ONEE-SAMA PARADISE, COULDN'T I?? UHU! MY DREAMS JUST KEEP GETTING BIGGER! UH-HUH-HUH...FU-FU... AH-HA-HA!
THEY'RE...
GET A CLUE.
...JUST RUMORS.

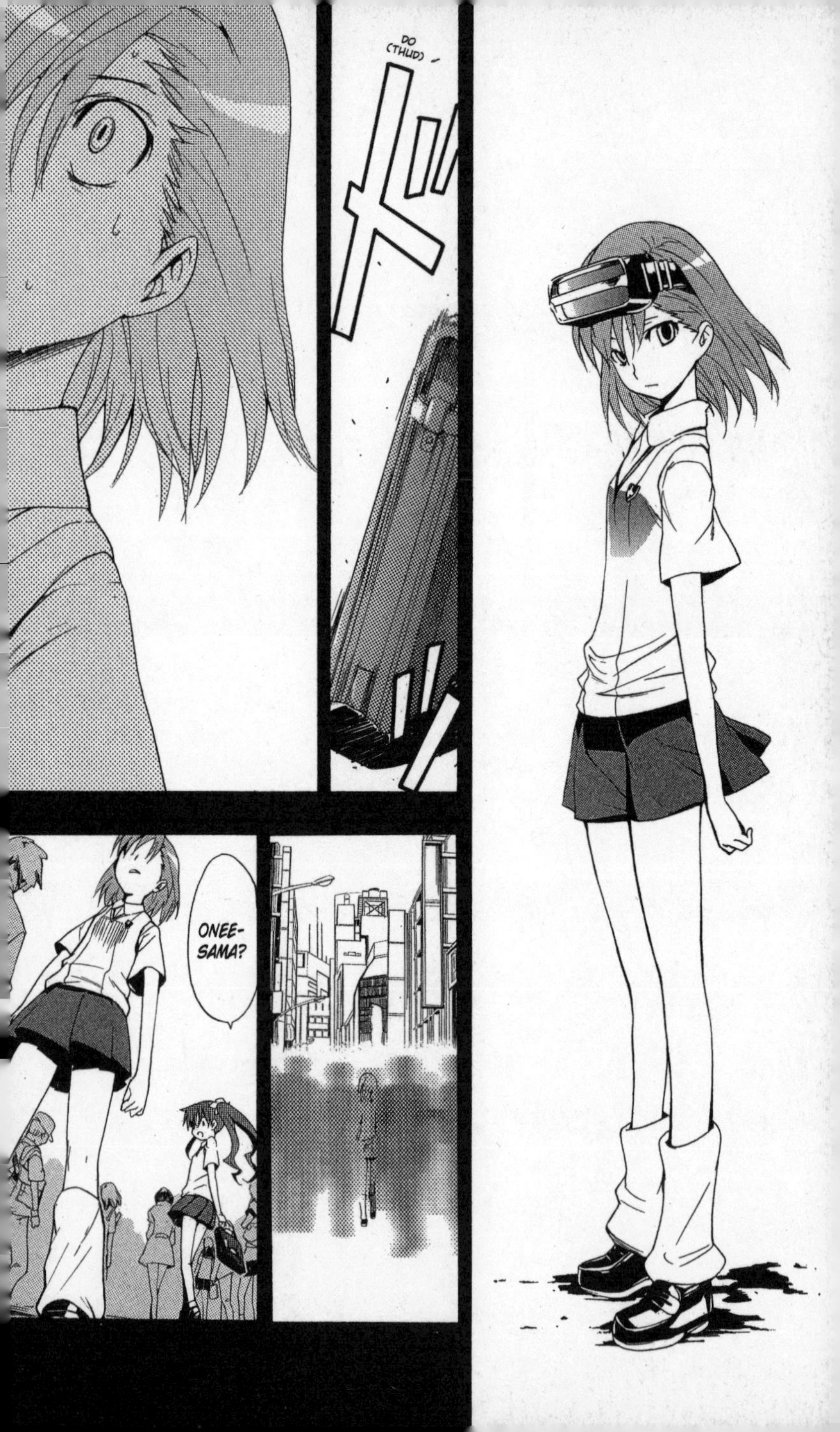
DO (THUD)
ONEE-SAMA?

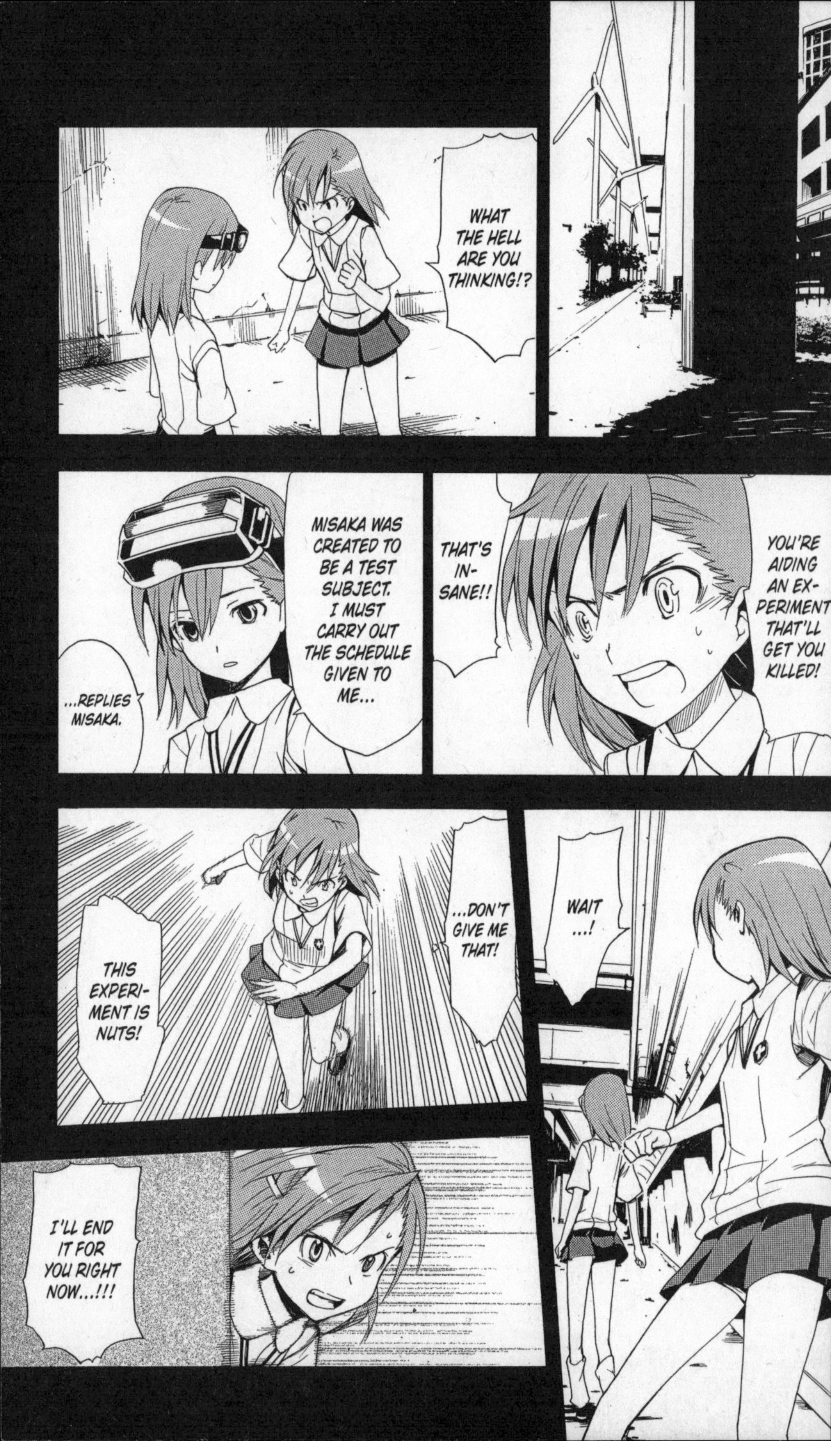
WHAT THE HELL ARE YOU THINKING!?
YOU'RE AIDING AN EXPERIMENT THAT'LL GET YOU KILLED!
THAT'S INSANE!!
MISAKA WAS CREATED TO BE A TEST SUBJECT. I MUST CARRY OUT THE SCHEDULE GIVEN TO ME...
...REPLIES MISAKA.
WAIT ...!
...DON'T GIVE ME THAT!
THIS EXPERIMENT IS NUTS!
I'LL END IT FOR YOU RIGHT NOW...!!!

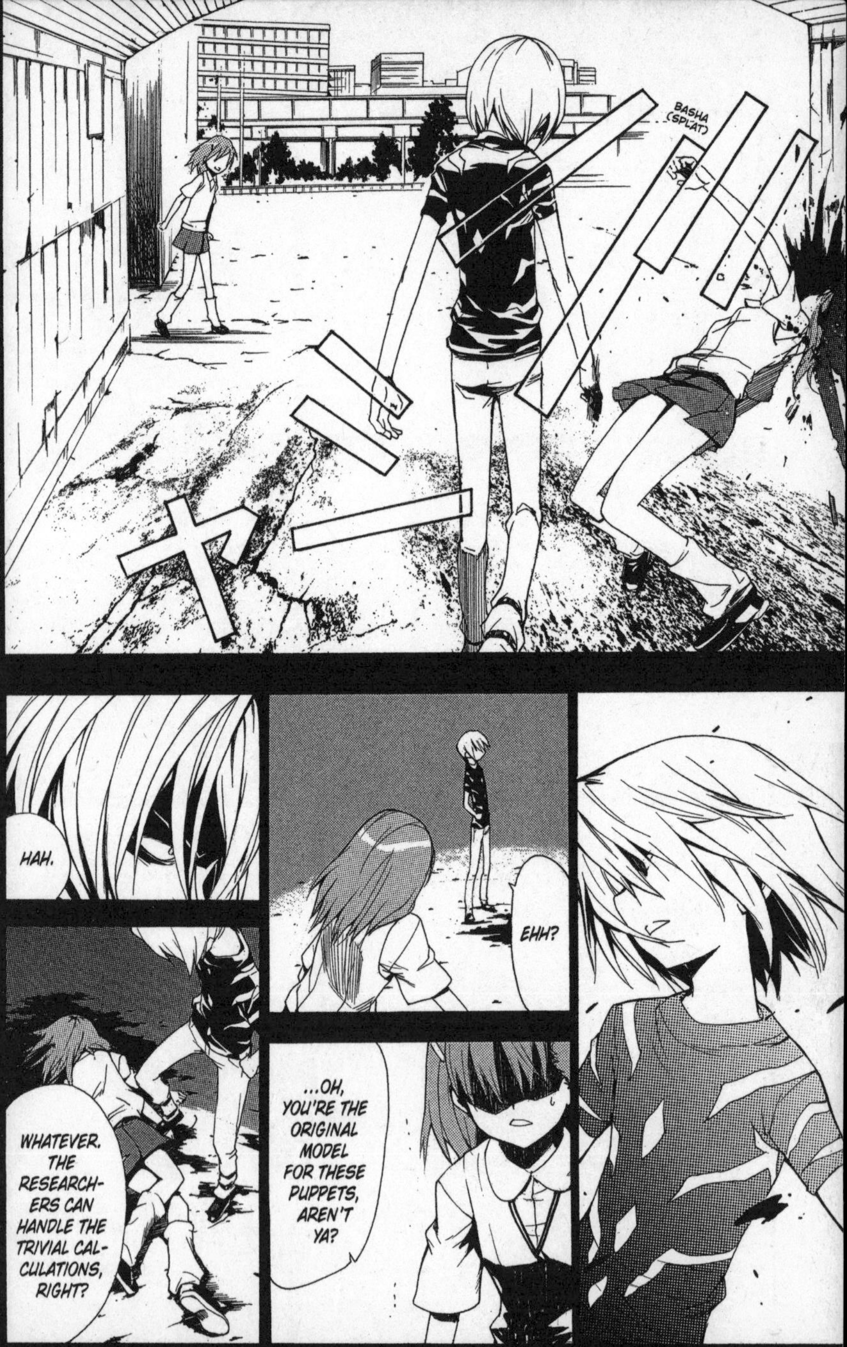
BASHA (SPLAT)
EHH?
...OH, YOU'RE THE ORIGINAL MODEL FOR THESE PUPPETS, AREN'T YA?
HAH.
WHATEVER. THE RESEARCHERS CAN HANDLE THE TRIVIAL CALCULATIONS, RIGHT?

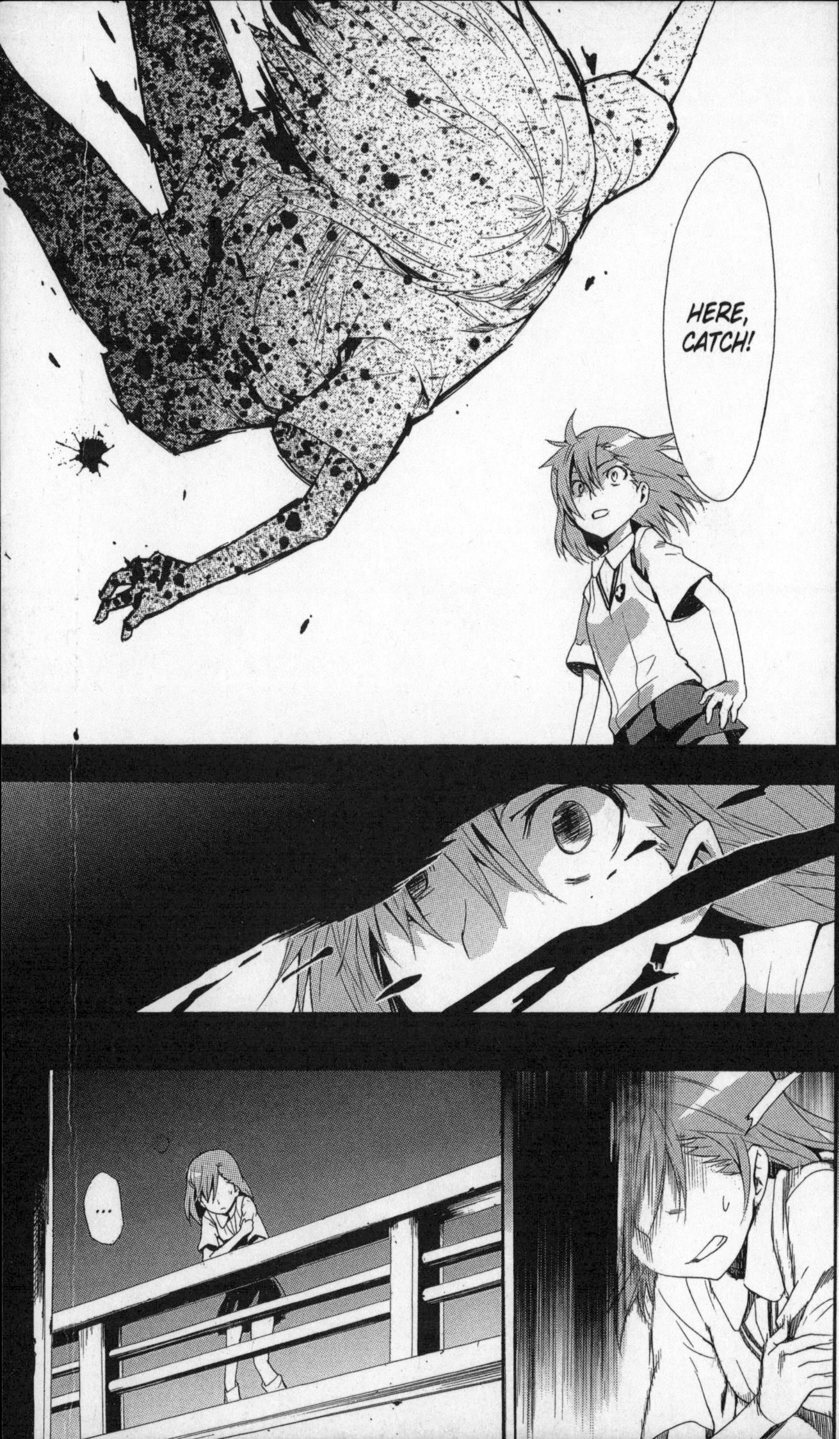
HERE, CATCH!
...

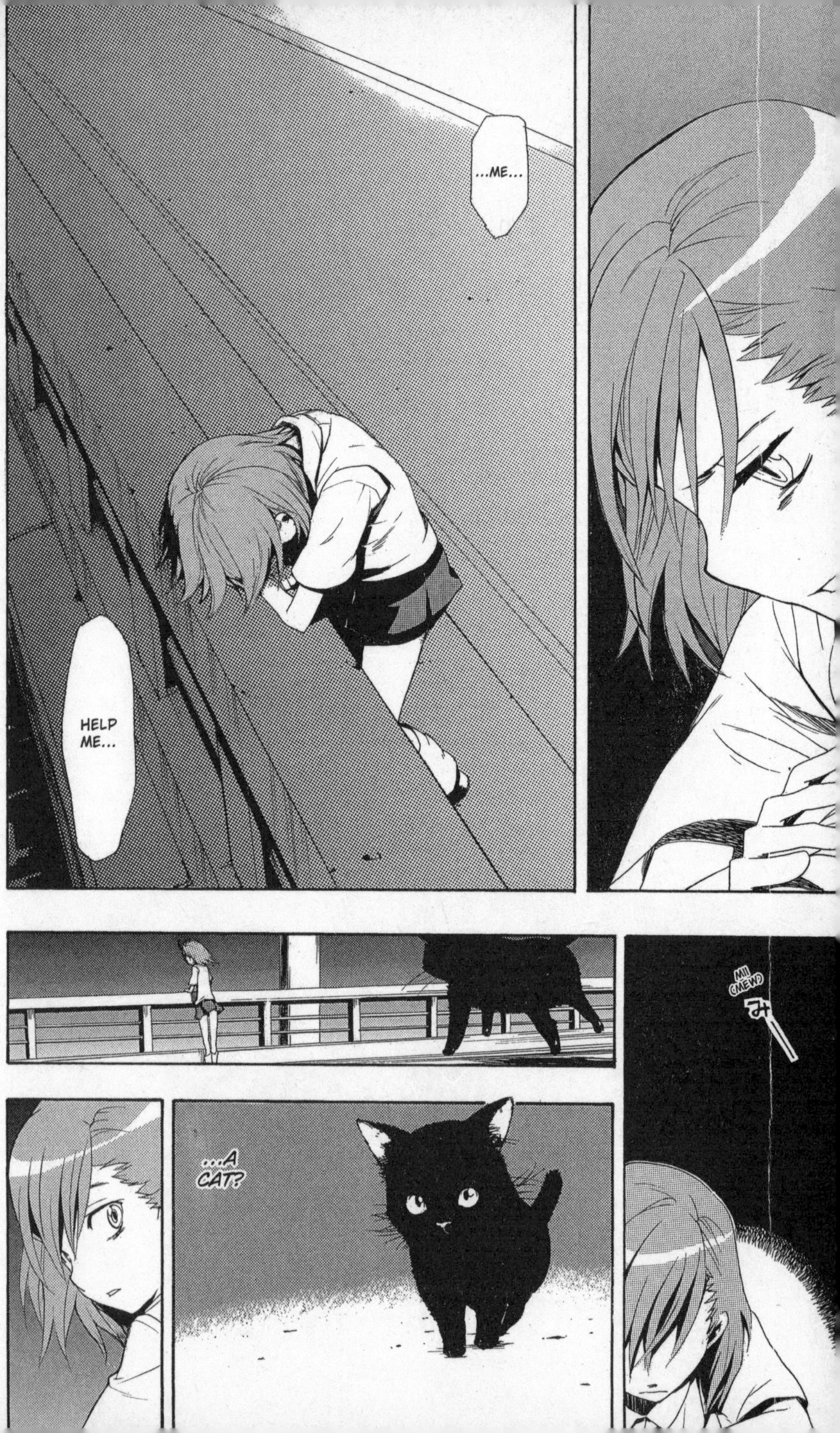
...ME...
HELP ME...
MII (MEW)
み
...A CAT?

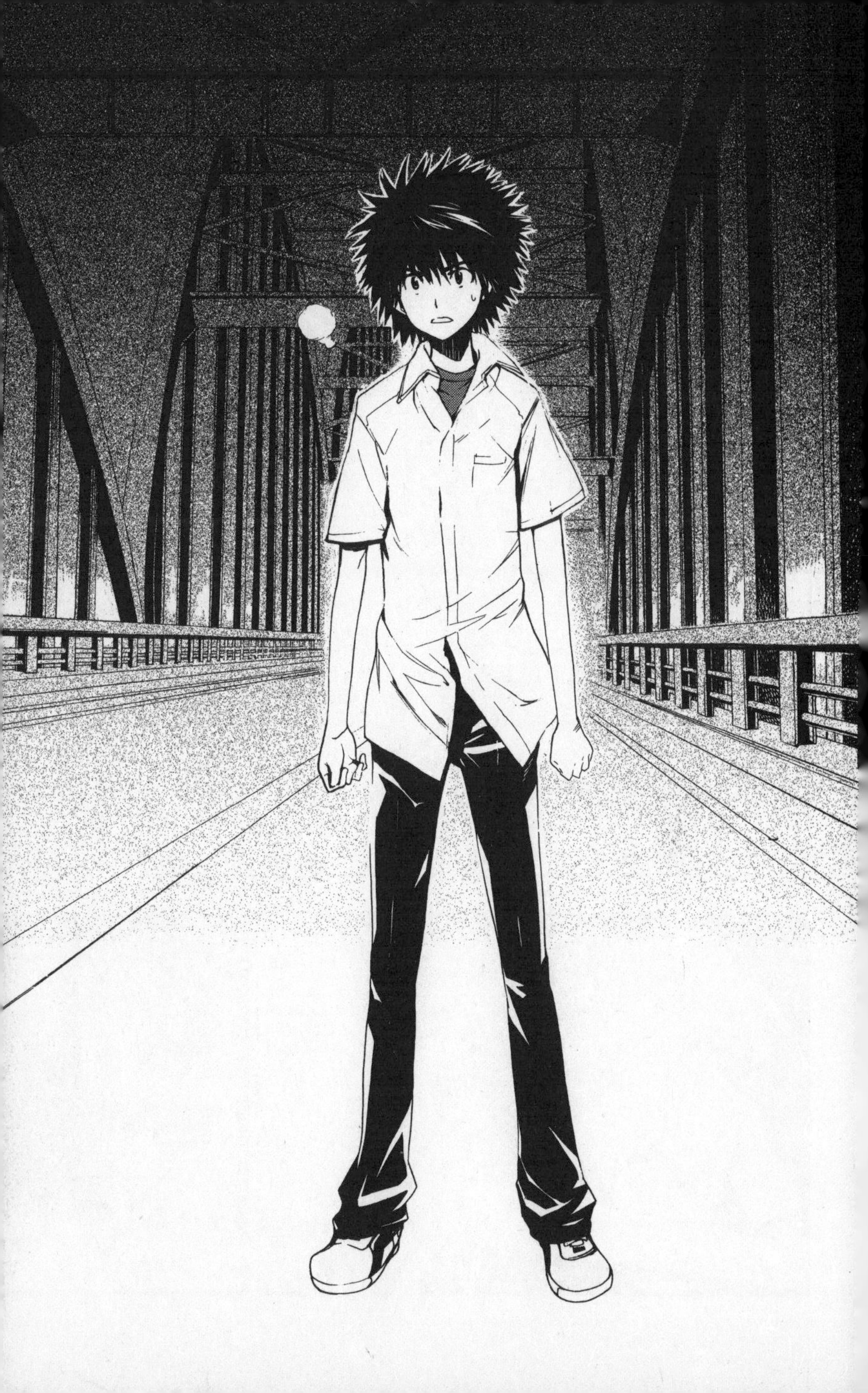

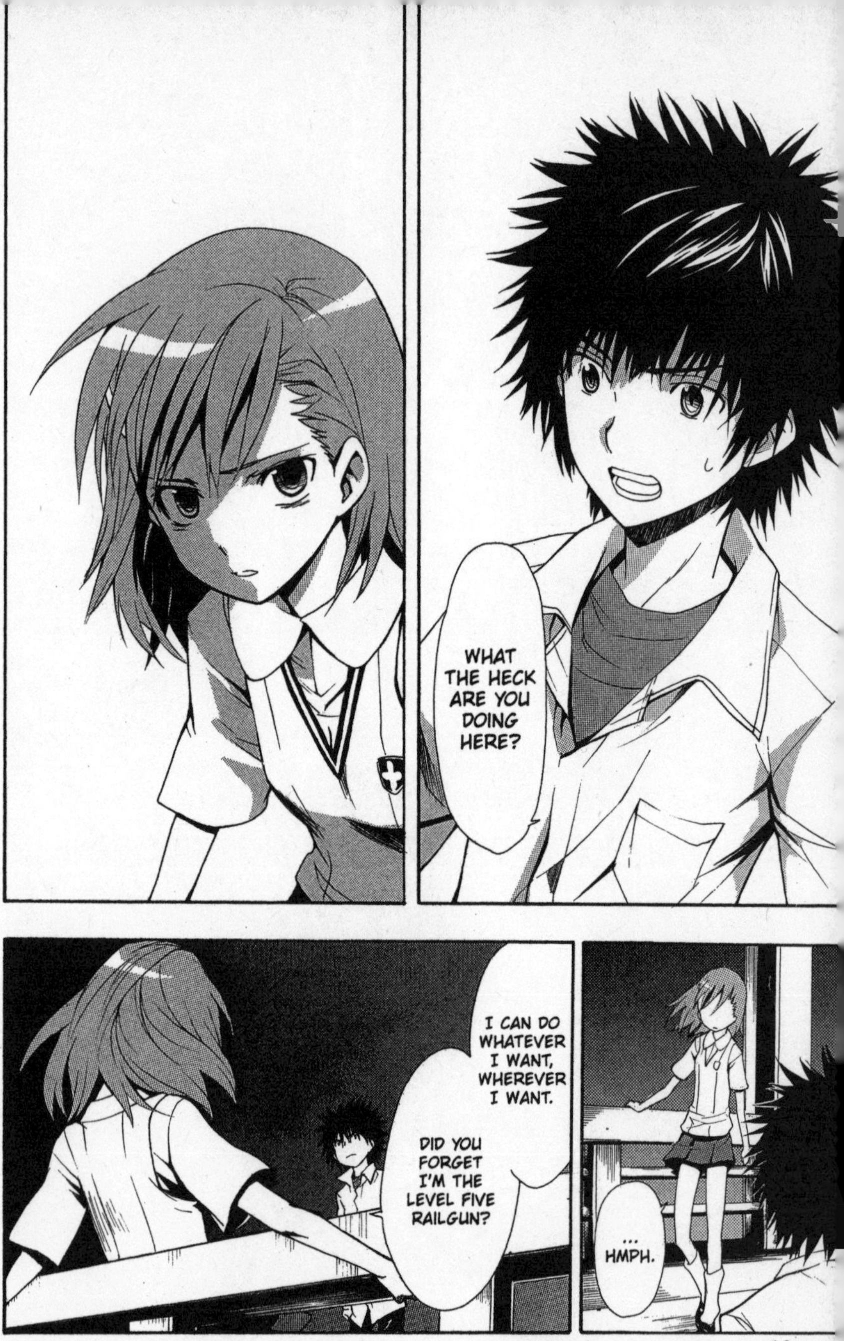
WHAT THE HECK ARE YOU DOING HERE?
... HMPH.
I CAN DO WHATEVER I WANT, WHEREVER I WANT.
DID YOU FORGET I'M THE LEVEL FIVE RAILGUN?

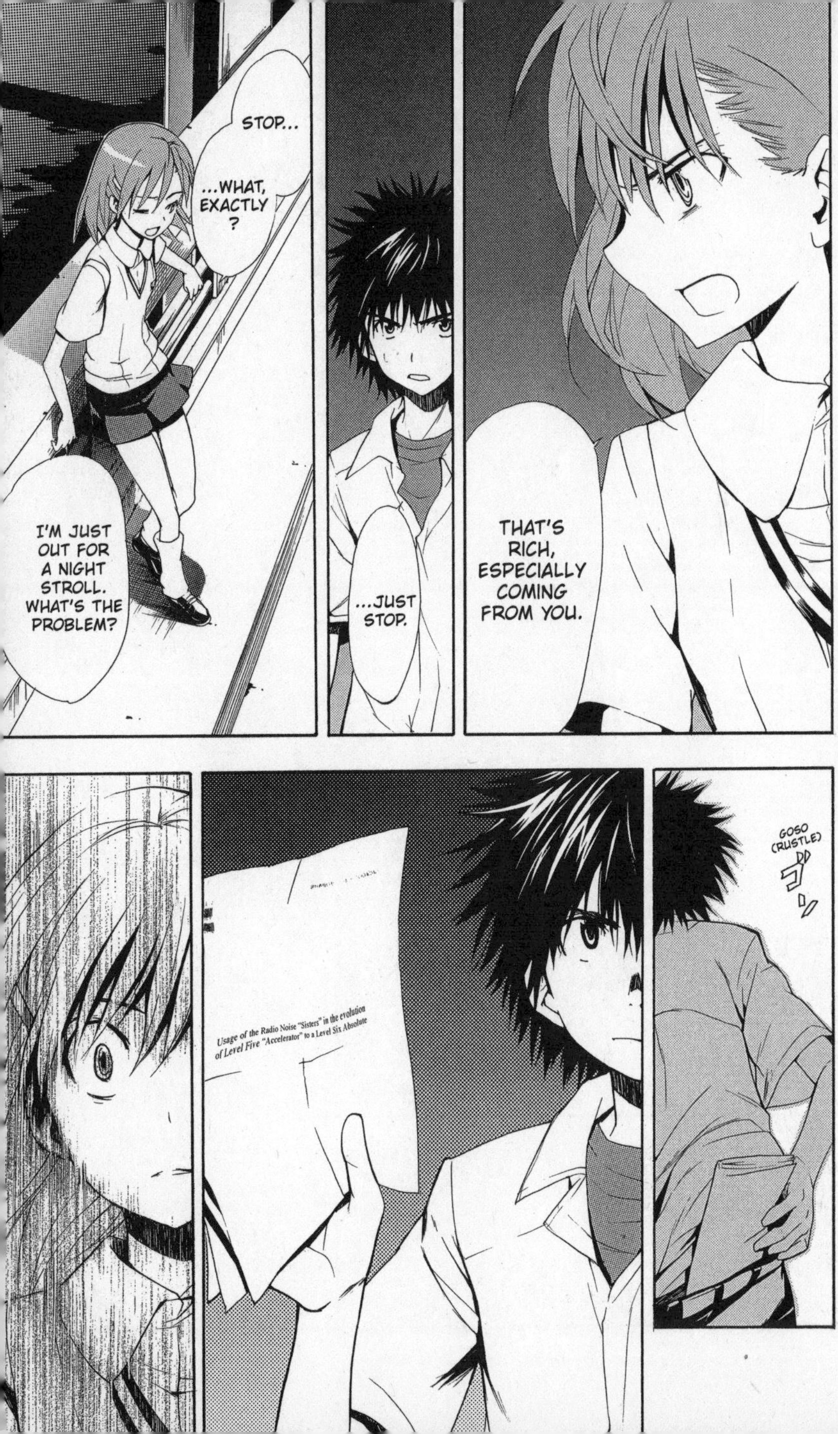
THAT'S RICH, ESPECIALLY COMING FROM YOU.
...JUST STOP.
STOP...
...WHAT, EXACTLY?
I'M JUST OUT FOR A NIGHT STROLL. WHAT'S THE PROBLEM?
GOSO (RUSTLE)
Usage of the Radio Noise "Sisters" in the evolution of Level Five "Accelerator" to a Level Six Absolute

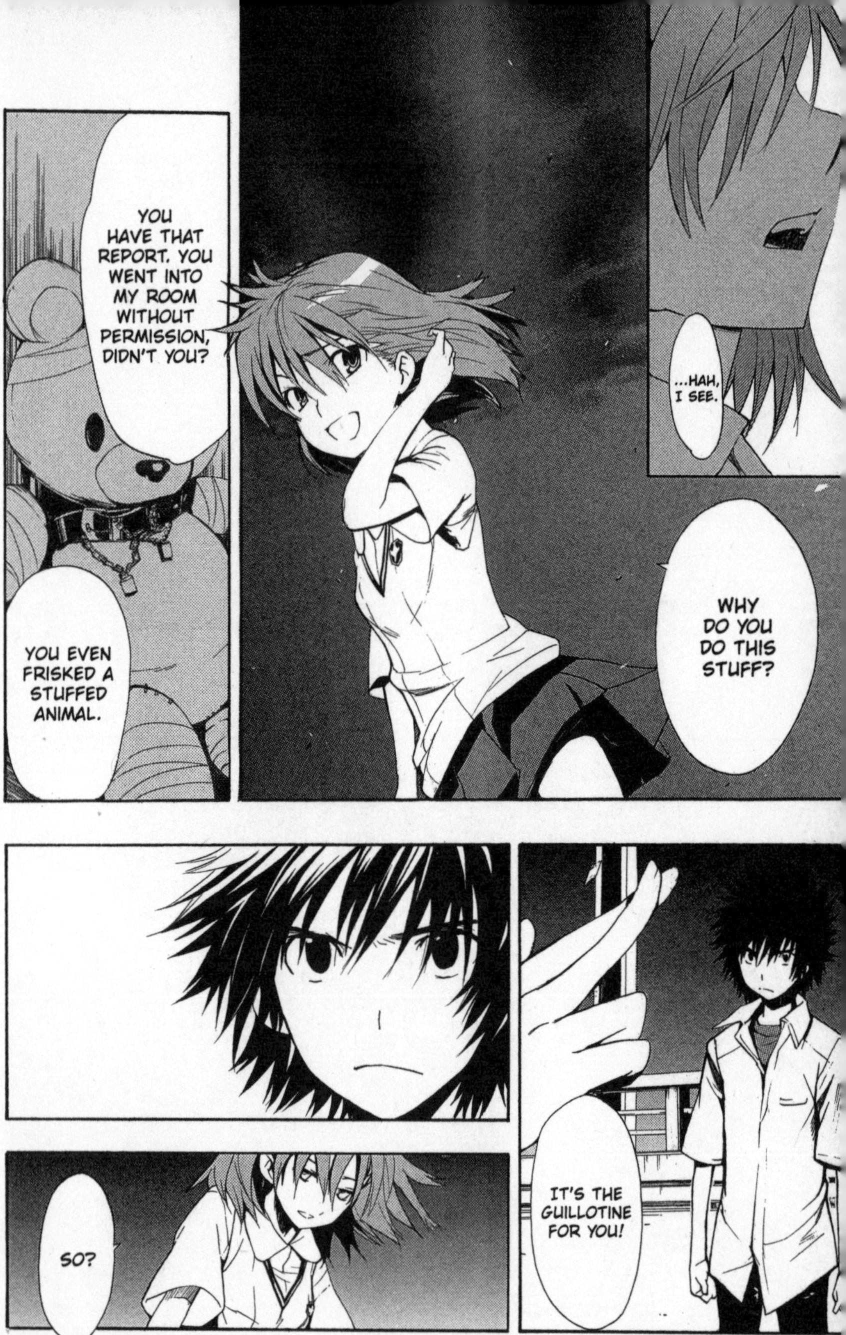
...HAH, I SEE.
WHY DO YOU DO THIS STUFF?
YOU HAVE THAT REPORT. YOU WENT INTO MY ROOM WITHOUT PERMISSION, DIDN'T YOU?
YOU EVEN FRISKED A STUFFED ANIMAL.
IT'S THE GUILLOTINE FOR YOU!
SO?

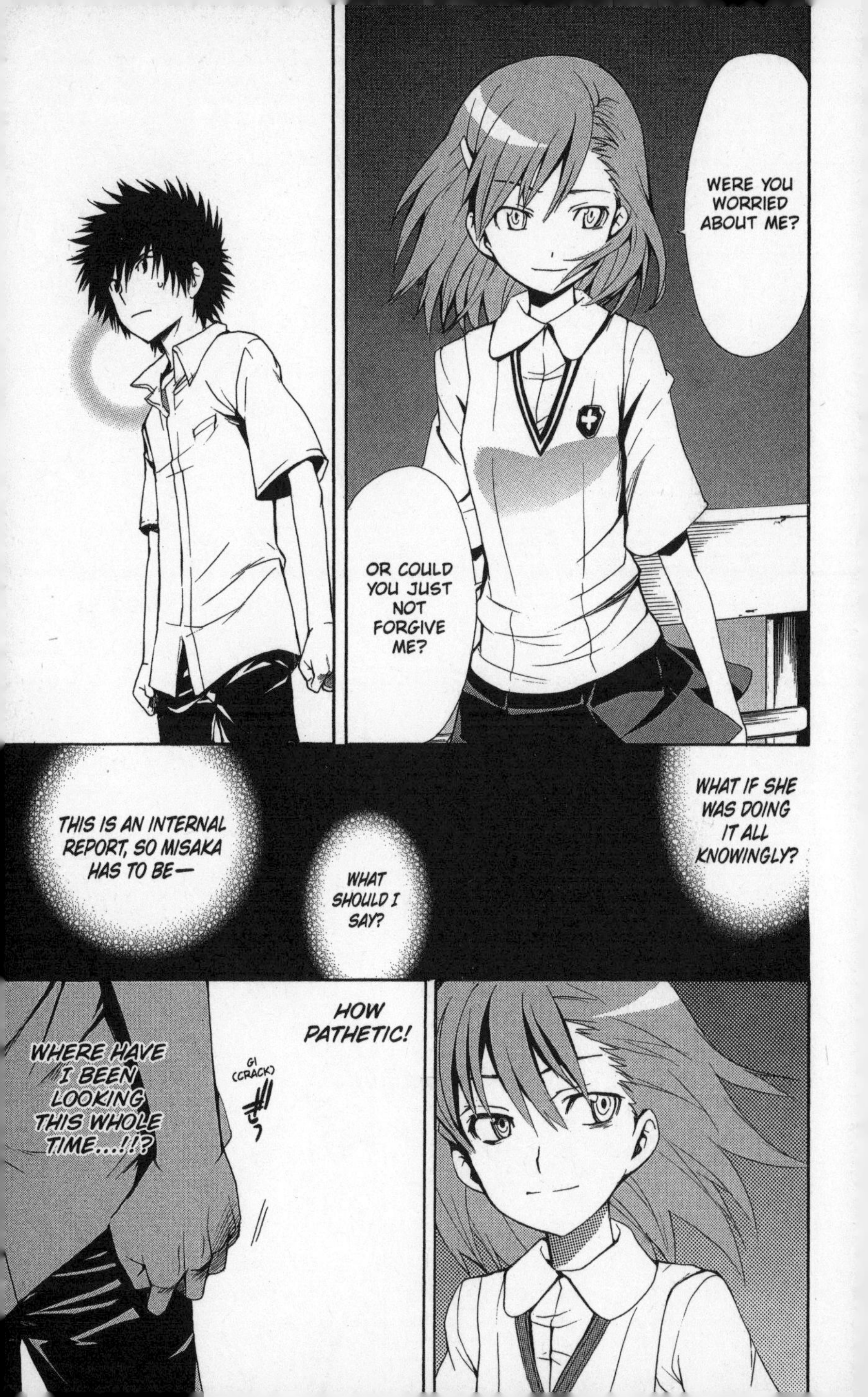
WERE YOU WORRIED ABOUT ME?
OR COULD YOU JUST NOT FORGIVE ME?
WHAT IF SHE WAS DOING IT ALL KNOWINGLY?
WHAT SHOULD I SAY?
THIS IS AN INTERNAL REPORT, SO MISAKA HAS TO BE—
HOW PATHETIC!
GI (CRACK)
WHERE HAVE I BEEN LOOKING THIS WHOLE TIME...!!?

I WAS WORRIED, OF COURSE!

I'M SORRY FOR GOING INTO YOUR ROOM LIKE THAT.

AND THIS MAP...

BUT I DON'T THINK YOU GOT AHOLD OF THIS REPORT IN AN...HONEST WAY.

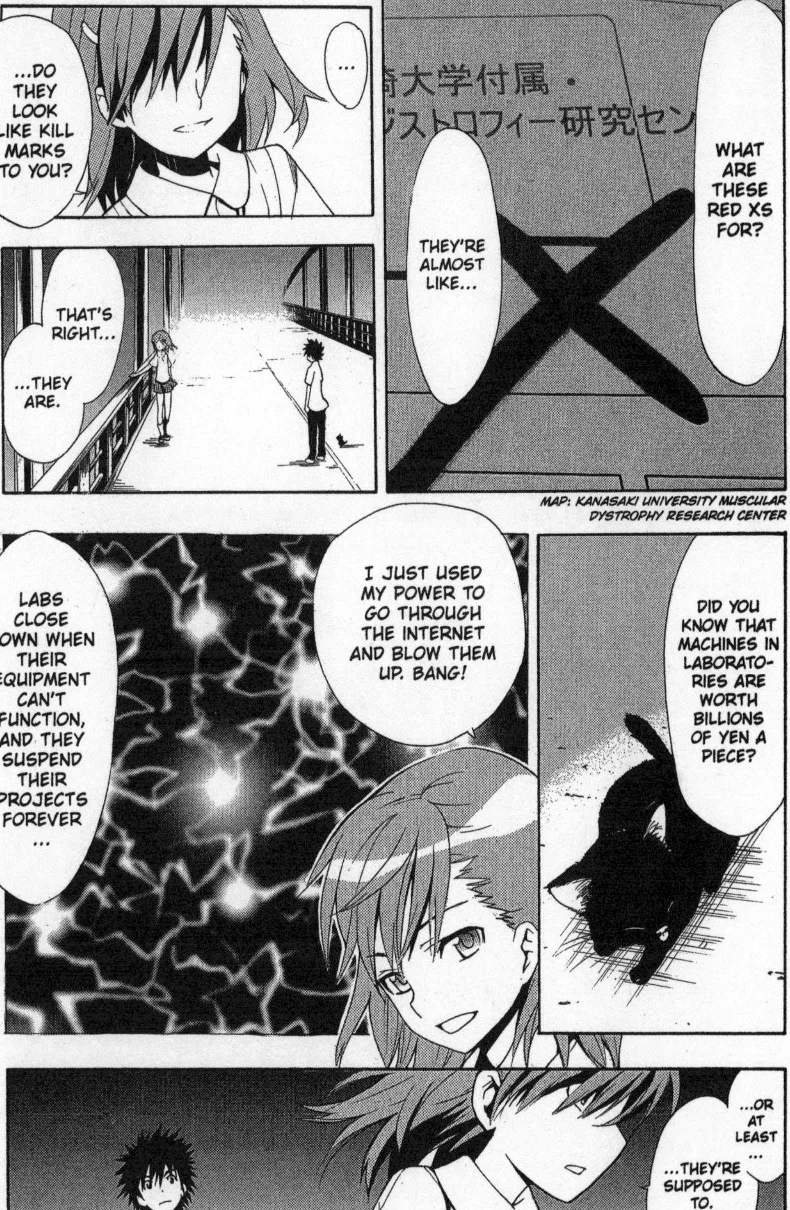

WHAT ARE THESE RED XS FOR?
崎大学付属・
ジストロフィー研究セン
THEY'RE ALMOST LIKE...
...
...DO THEY LOOK LIKE KILL MARKS TO YOU?
THAT'S RIGHT...
...THEY ARE.
MAP: KANASAKI UNIVERSITY MUSCULAR DYSTROPHY RESEARCH CENTER
DID YOU KNOW THAT MACHINES IN LABORATO-RIES ARE WORTH BILLIONS OF YEN A PIECE?
I JUST USED MY POWER TO GO THROUGH THE INTERNET AND BLOW THEM UP. BANG!
LABS CLOSE DOWN WHEN THEIR EQUIPMENT CAN'T FUNCTION, AND THEY SUSPEND THEIR PROJECTS FOREVER ...
...OR AT LEAST ...
...THEY'RE SUPPOSED TO.

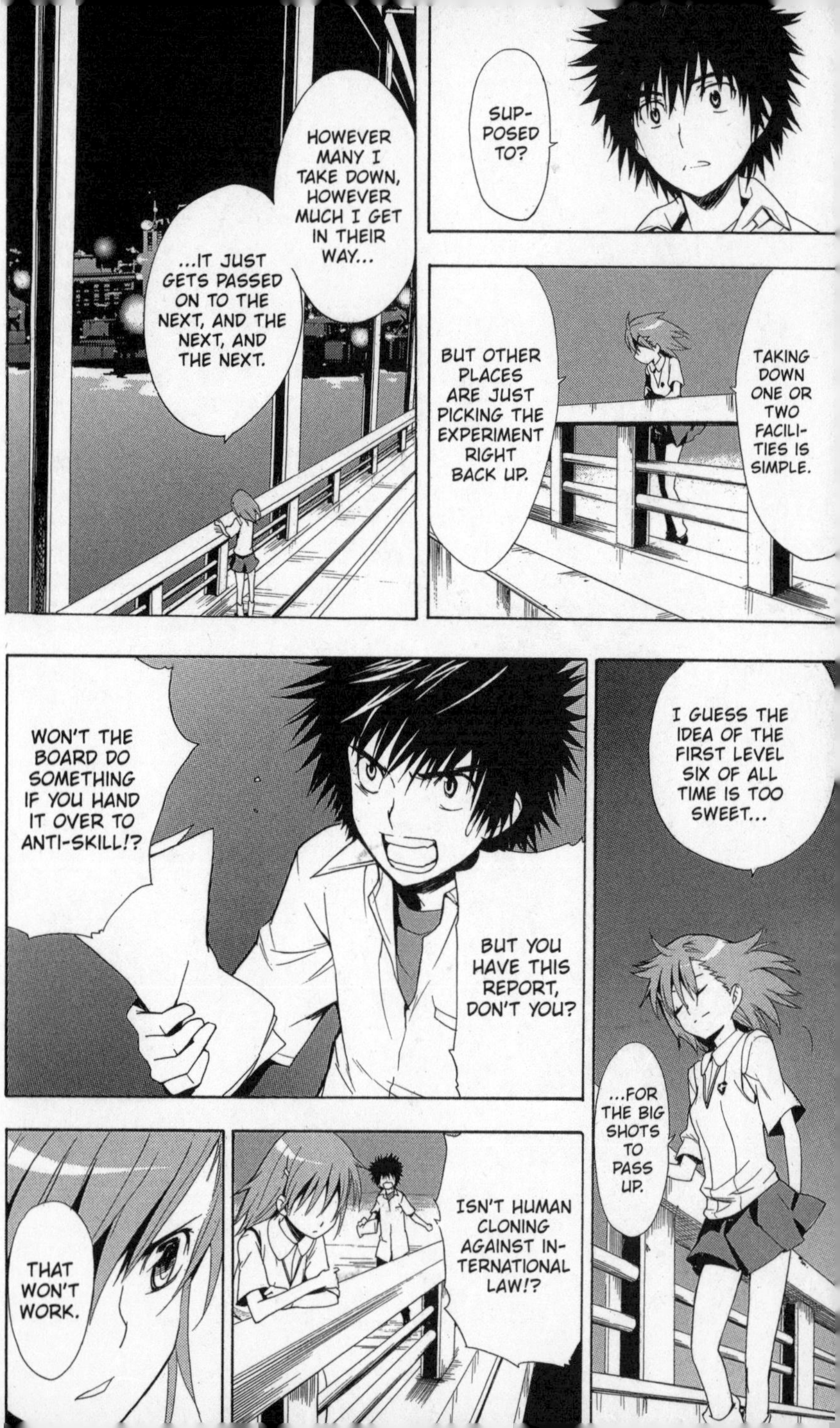
SUP-
POSED
TO?
TAKING DOWN ONE OR TWO FACILI-TIES IS SIMPLE.
BUT OTHER PLACES ARE JUST PICKING THE EXPERIMENT RIGHT BACK UP.
HOWEVER MANY I TAKE DOWN, HOWEVER MUCH I GET IN THEIR WAY...
...IT JUST GETS PASSED ON TO THE NEXT, AND THE NEXT, AND THE NEXT.
I GUESS THE IDEA OF THE FIRST LEVEL SIX OF ALL TIME IS TOO SWEET...
...FOR THE BIG SHOTS TO PASS UP.
BUT YOU HAVE THIS REPORT, DON'T YOU?
WON'T THE BOARD DO SOMETHING IF YOU HAND IT OVER TO ANTI-SKILL!?
ISN'T HUMAN CLONING AGAINST IN-TERNATIONAL LAW!?
THAT WON'T WORK.

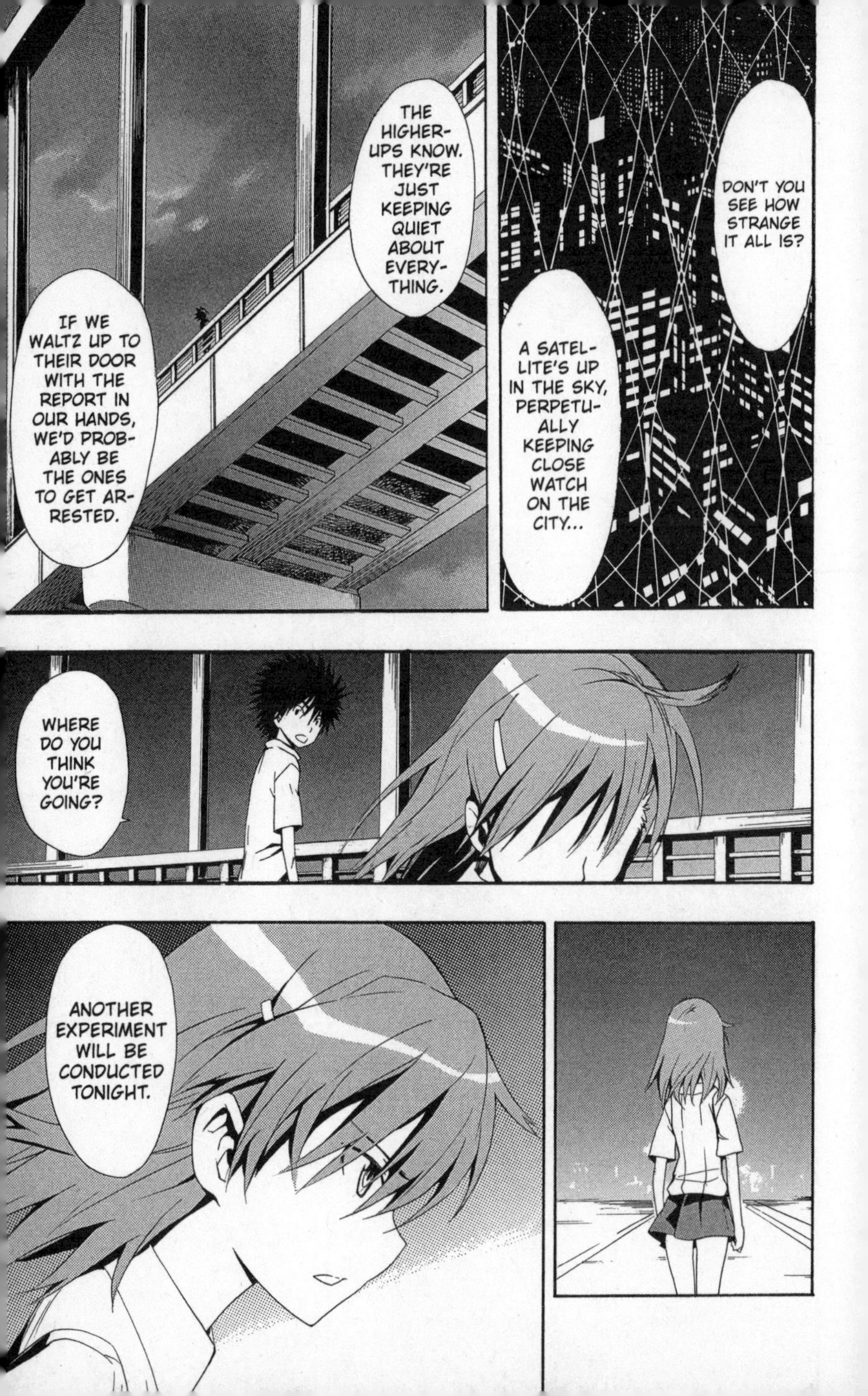
DON'T YOU SEE HOW STRANGE IT ALL IS?
A SATELLITE'S UP IN THE SKY, PERPETUALLY KEEPING CLOSE WATCH ON THE CITY...
THE HIGHER-UPS KNOW. THEY'RE JUST KEEPING QUIET ABOUT EVERYTHING.
IF WE WALTZ UP TO THEIR DOOR WITH THE REPORT IN OUR HANDS, WE'D PROBABLY BE THE ONES TO GET ARRESTED.
WHERE DO YOU THINK YOU'RE GOING?
ANOTHER EXPERIMENT WILL BE CONDUCTED TONIGHT.

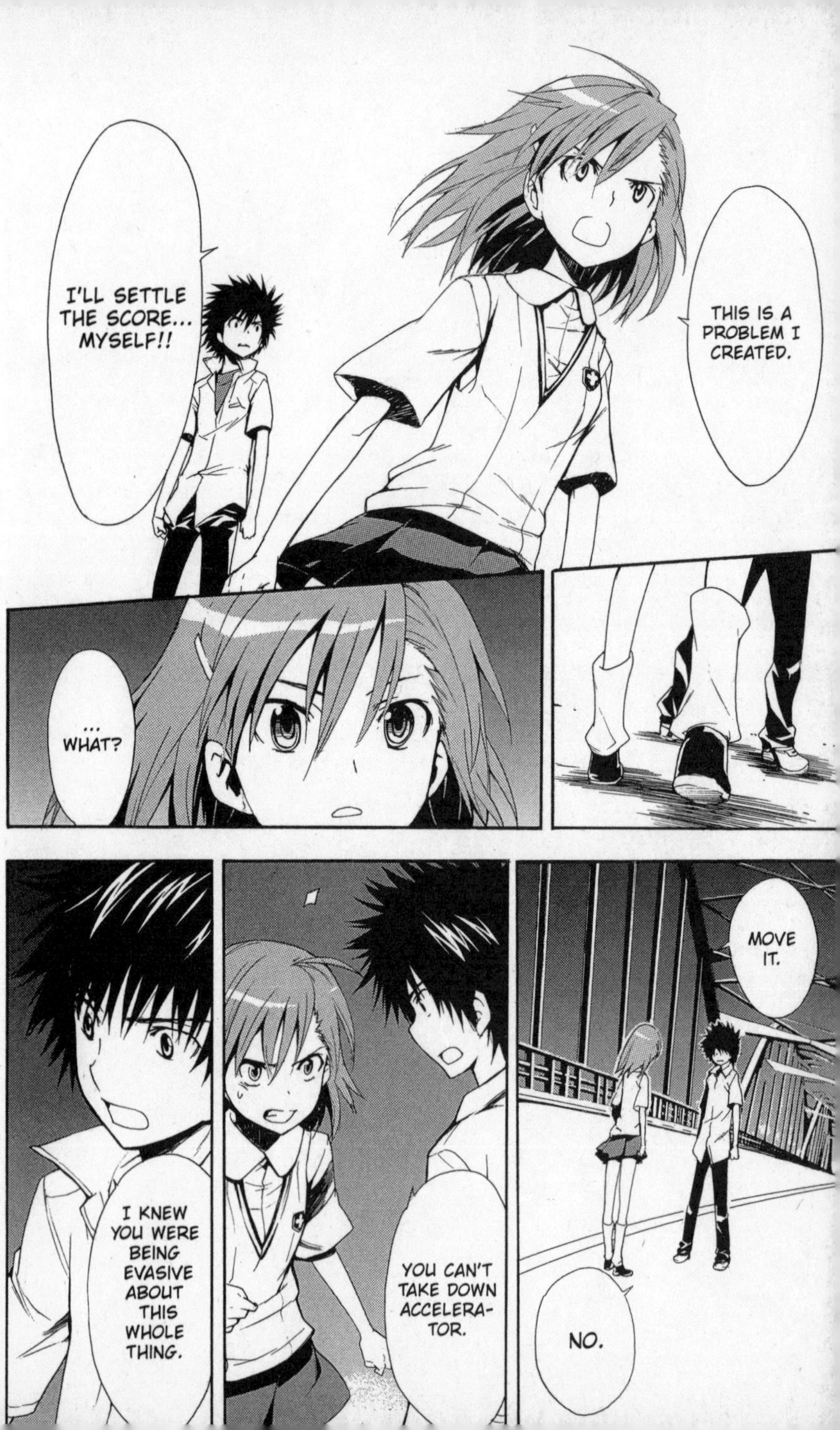
THIS IS A PROBLEM I CREATED.
I'LL SETTLE THE SCORE... MYSELF!!
... WHAT?
MOVE IT.
NO.
YOU CAN'T TAKE DOWN ACCELERA-TOR.
I KNEW YOU WERE BEING EVASIVE ABOUT THIS WHOLE THING.

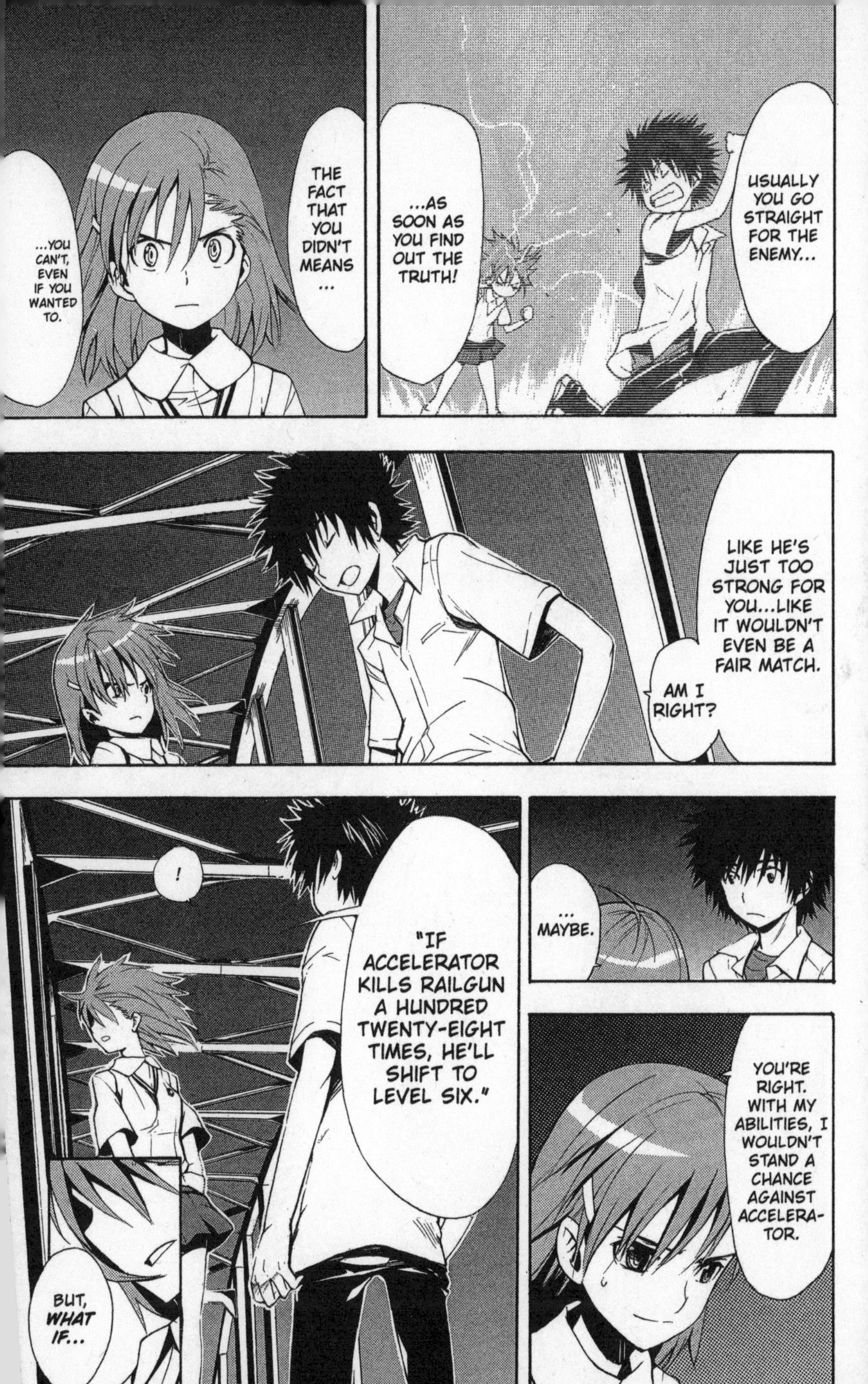
USUALLY YOU GO STRAIGHT FOR THE ENEMY...
...AS SOON AS YOU FIND OUT THE TRUTH!
THE FACT THAT YOU DIDN'T MEANS ...
...YOU CAN'T, EVEN IF YOU WANTED TO.
LIKE HE'S JUST TOO STRONG FOR YOU...LIKE IT WOULDN'T EVEN BE A FAIR MATCH.
AM I RIGHT?
... MAYBE.
YOU'RE RIGHT. WITH MY ABILITIES, I WOULDN'T STAND A CHANCE AGAINST ACCELERA-TOR.
"IF ACCELERATOR KILLS RAILGUN A HUNDRED TWENTY-EIGHT TIMES, HE'LL SHIFT TO LEVEL SIX."
!
BUT, *WHAT IF*...

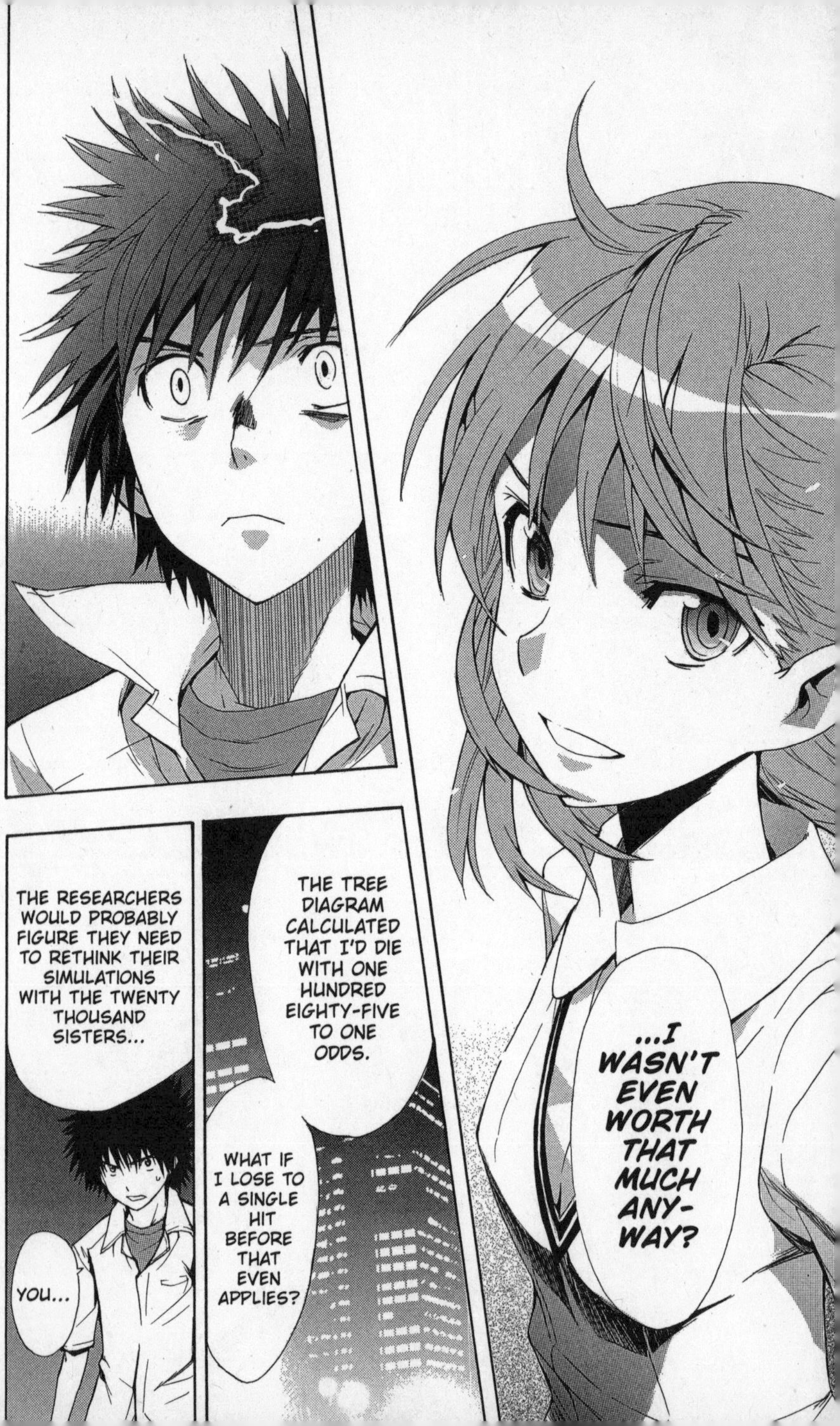
...I WASN'T EVEN WORTH THAT MUCH ANY-WAY?
THE TREE DIAGRAM CALCULATED THAT I'D DIE WITH ONE HUNDRED EIGHTY-FIVE TO ONE ODDS.
WHAT IF I LOSE TO A SINGLE HIT BEFORE THAT EVEN APPLIES?
THE RESEARCHERS WOULD PROBABLY FIGURE THEY NEED TO RETHINK THEIR SIMULATIONS WITH THE TWENTY THOUSAND SISTERS...
YOU...

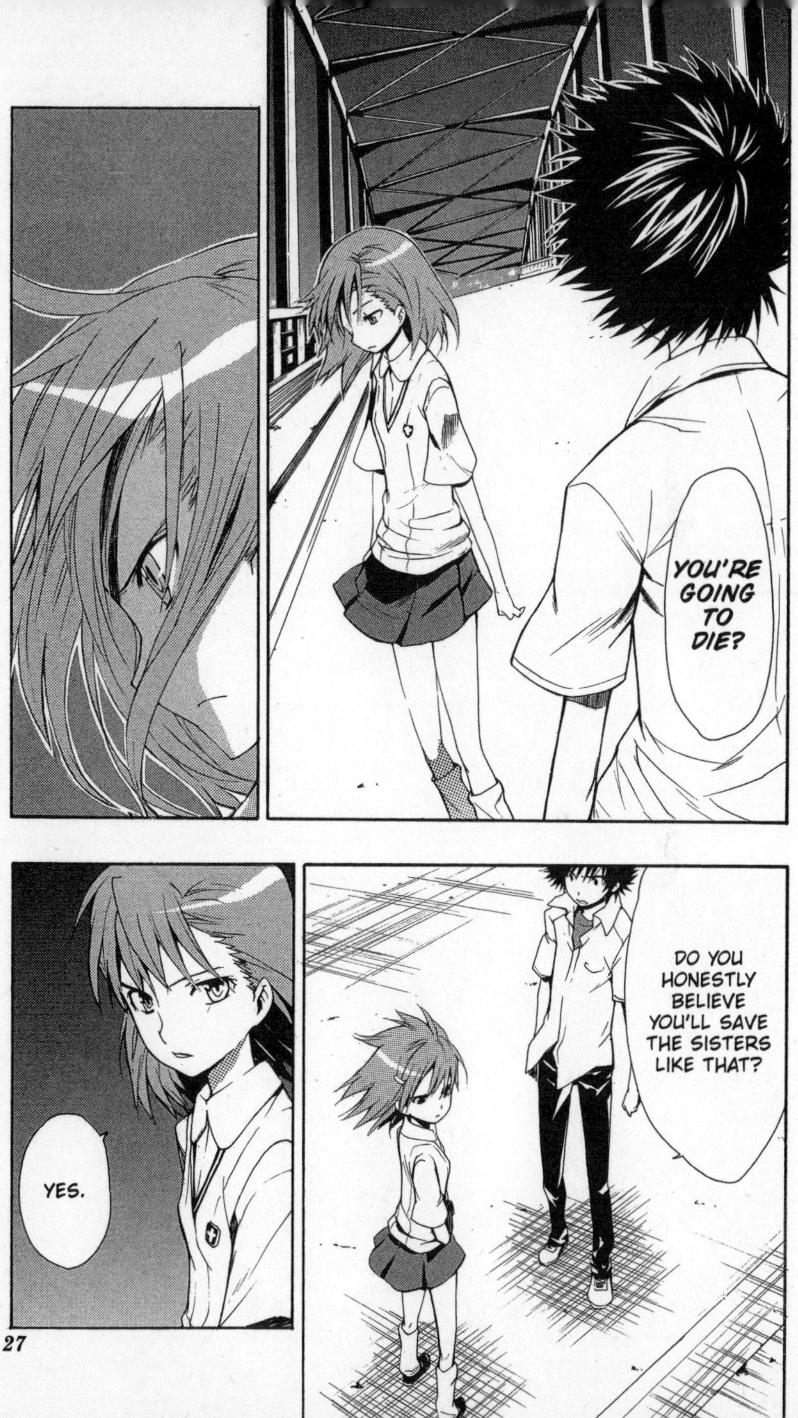
YOU'RE GOING TO DIE?
DO YOU HONESTLY BELIEVE YOU'LL SAVE THE SISTERS LIKE THAT?
YES.

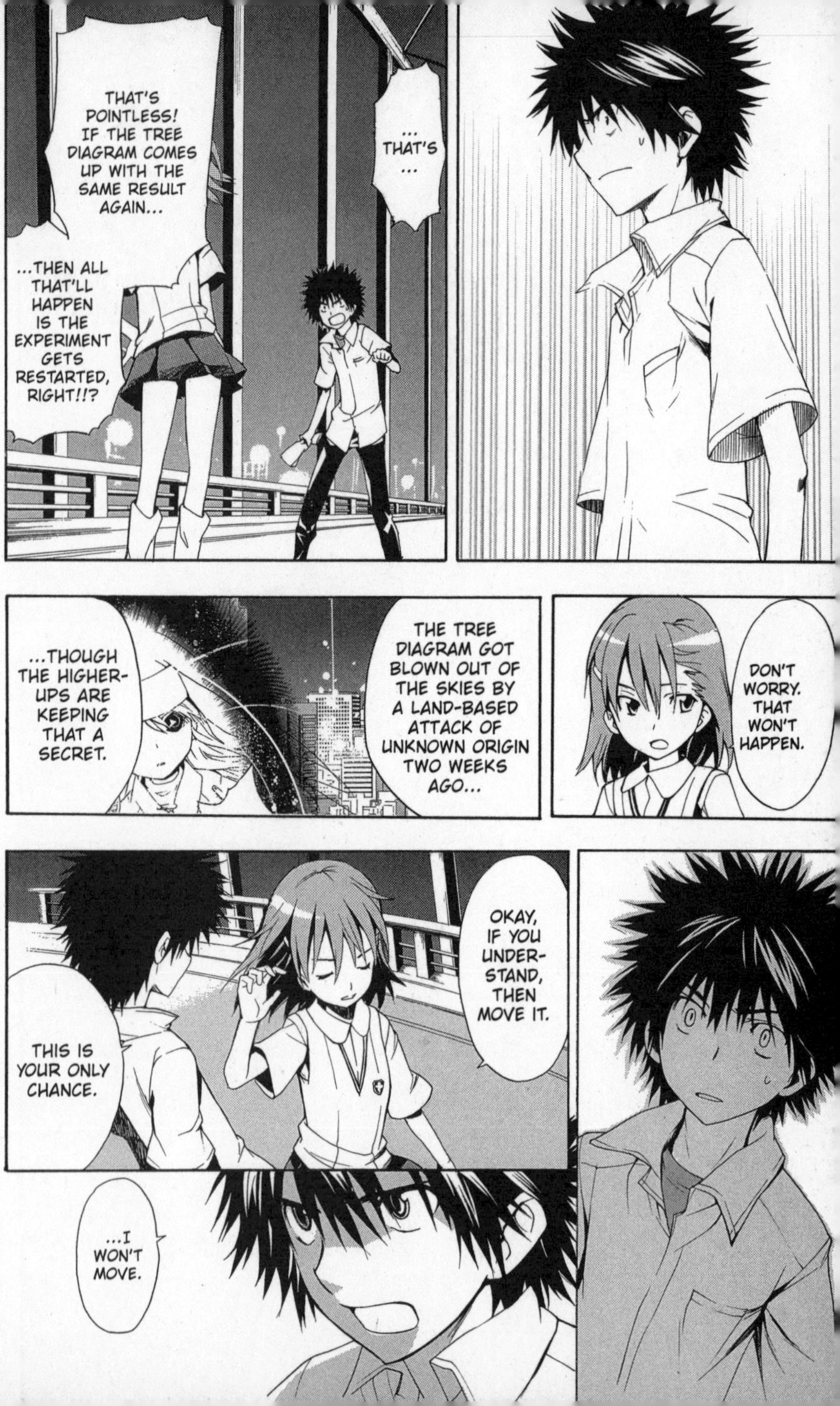
...THAT'S...
THAT'S POINTLESS! IF THE TREE DIAGRAM COMES UP WITH THE SAME RESULT AGAIN...
...THEN ALL THAT'LL HAPPEN IS THE EXPERIMENT GETS RESTARTED, RIGHT!!?
DON'T WORRY. THAT WON'T HAPPEN.
THE TREE DIAGRAM GOT BLOWN OUT OF THE SKIES BY A LAND-BASED ATTACK OF UNKNOWN ORIGIN TWO WEEKS AGO...
...THOUGH THE HIGHER-UPS ARE KEEPING THAT A SECRET.
OKAY, IF YOU UNDER-STAND, THEN MOVE IT.
THIS IS YOUR ONLY CHANCE.
...I WON'T MOVE.

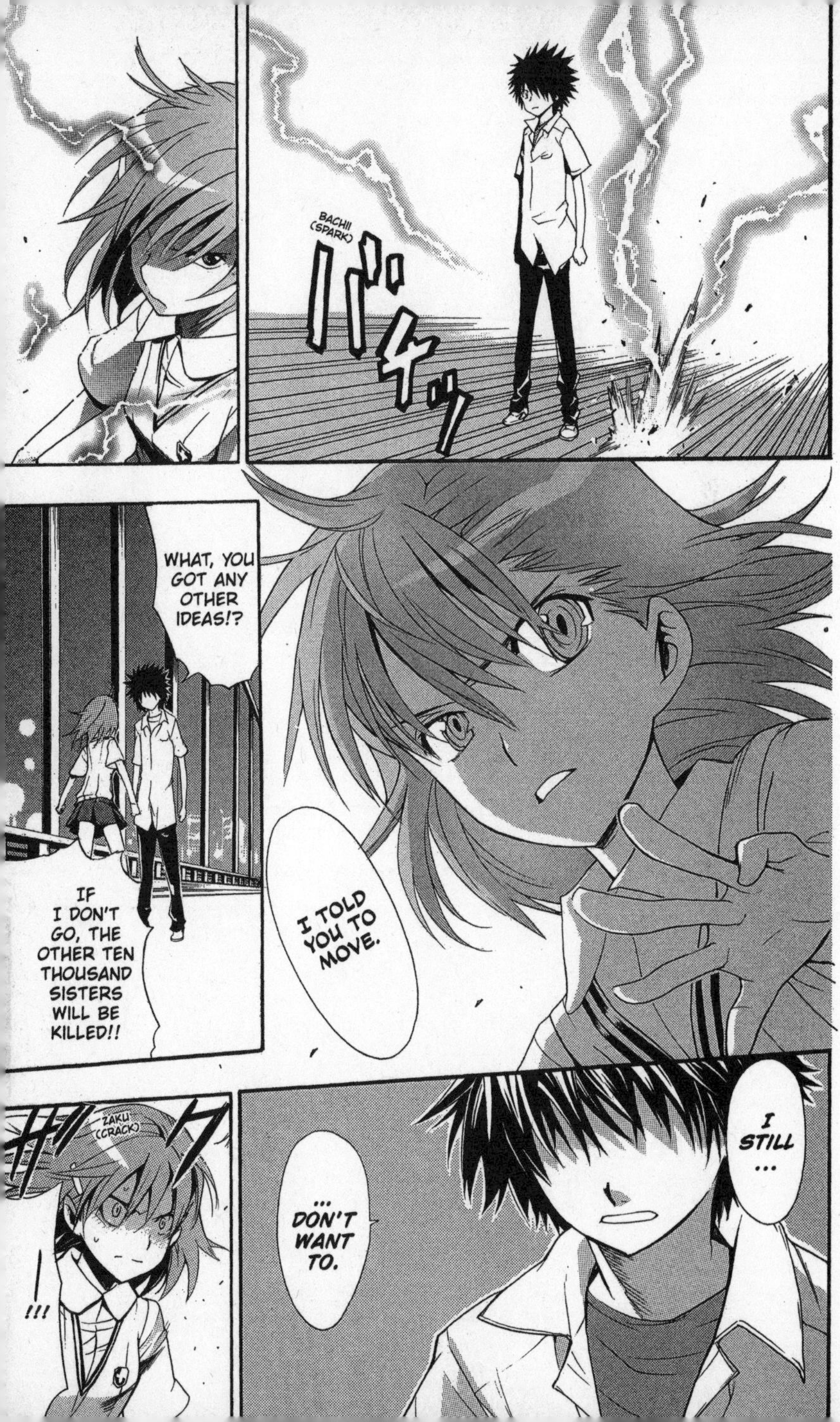
BACHII (SPARK)
I TOLD YOU TO MOVE.
WHAT, YOU GOT ANY OTHER IDEAS!?
IF I DON'T GO, THE OTHER TEN THOUSAND SISTERS WILL BE KILLED!!
I STILL ...
... DON'T WANT TO.
ZAKU (CRACK)
!!!

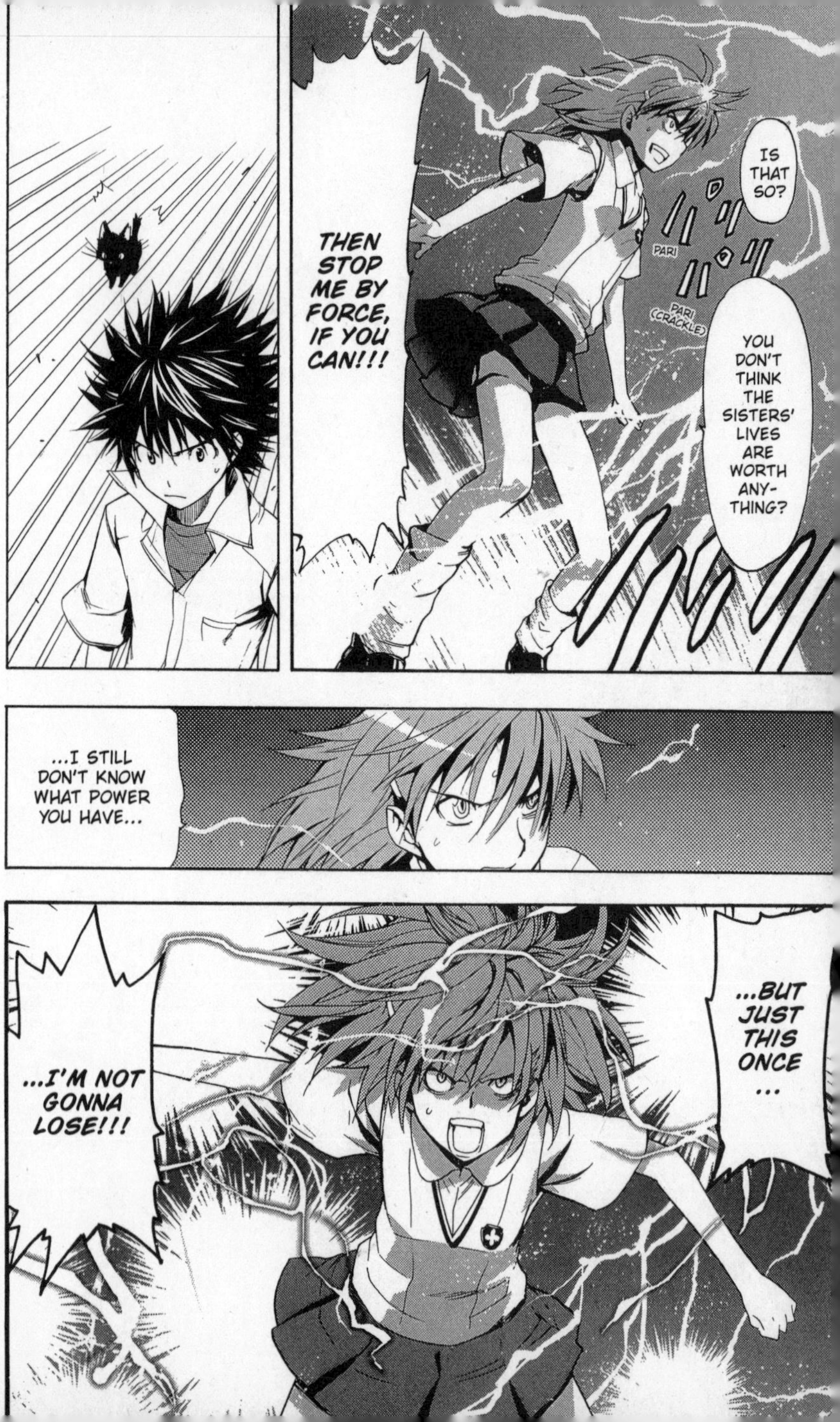
IS THAT SO?
PARI
PARI (CRACKLE)
YOU DON'T THINK THE SISTERS' LIVES ARE WORTH ANYTHING?
THEN STOP ME BY FORCE, IF YOU CAN!!!
...I STILL DON'T KNOW WHAT POWER YOU HAVE...
...BUT JUST THIS ONCE...
...I'M NOT GONNA LOSE!!!

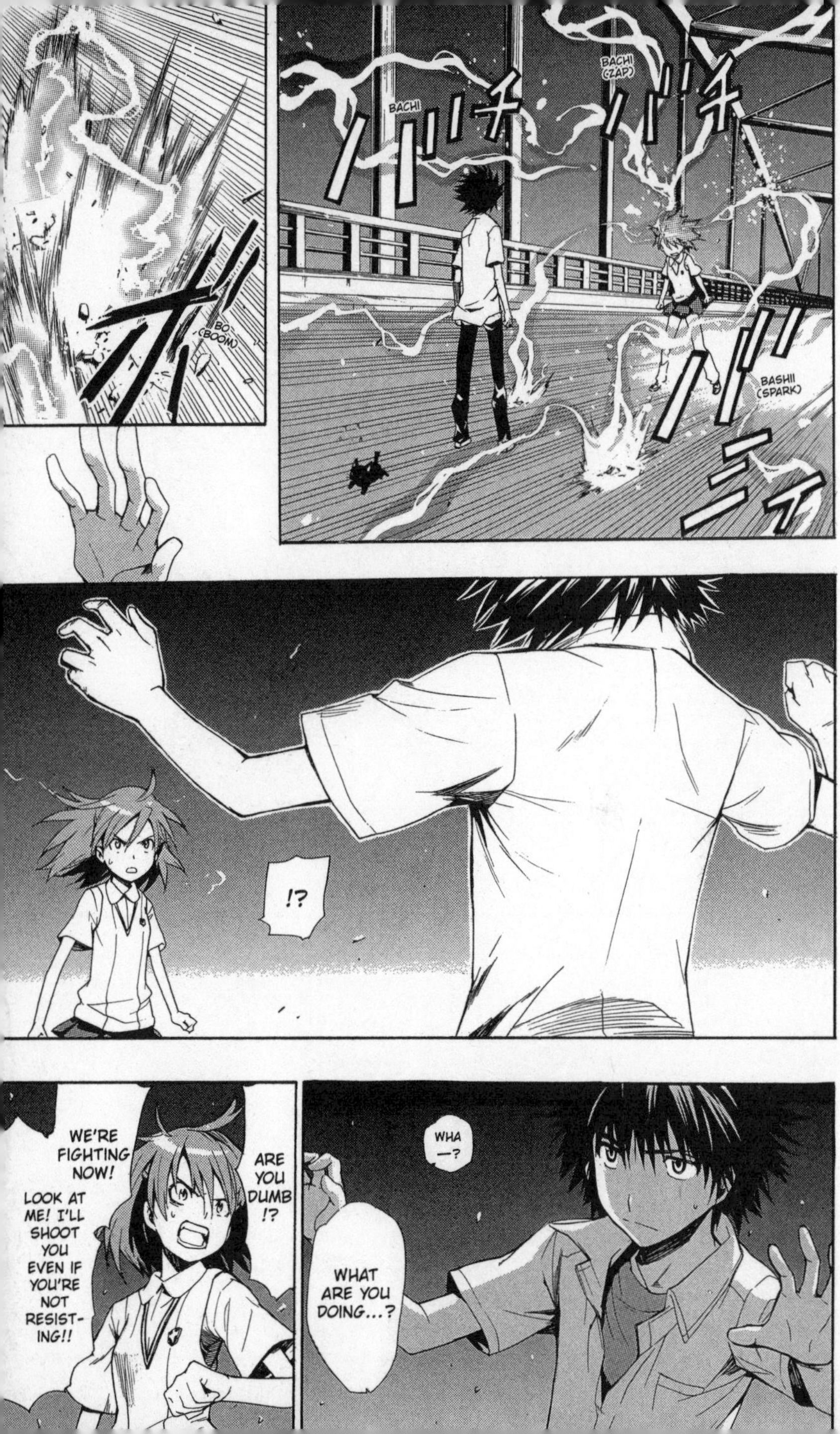
BACHI (ZAP)
BACHI
BASHII (SPARK)
BO (BOOM)
!?
WHA —?
WHAT ARE YOU DOING...?
ARE YOU DUMB !?
WE'RE FIGHTING NOW!
LOOK AT ME! I'LL SHOOT YOU EVEN IF YOU'RE NOT RESISTING!!

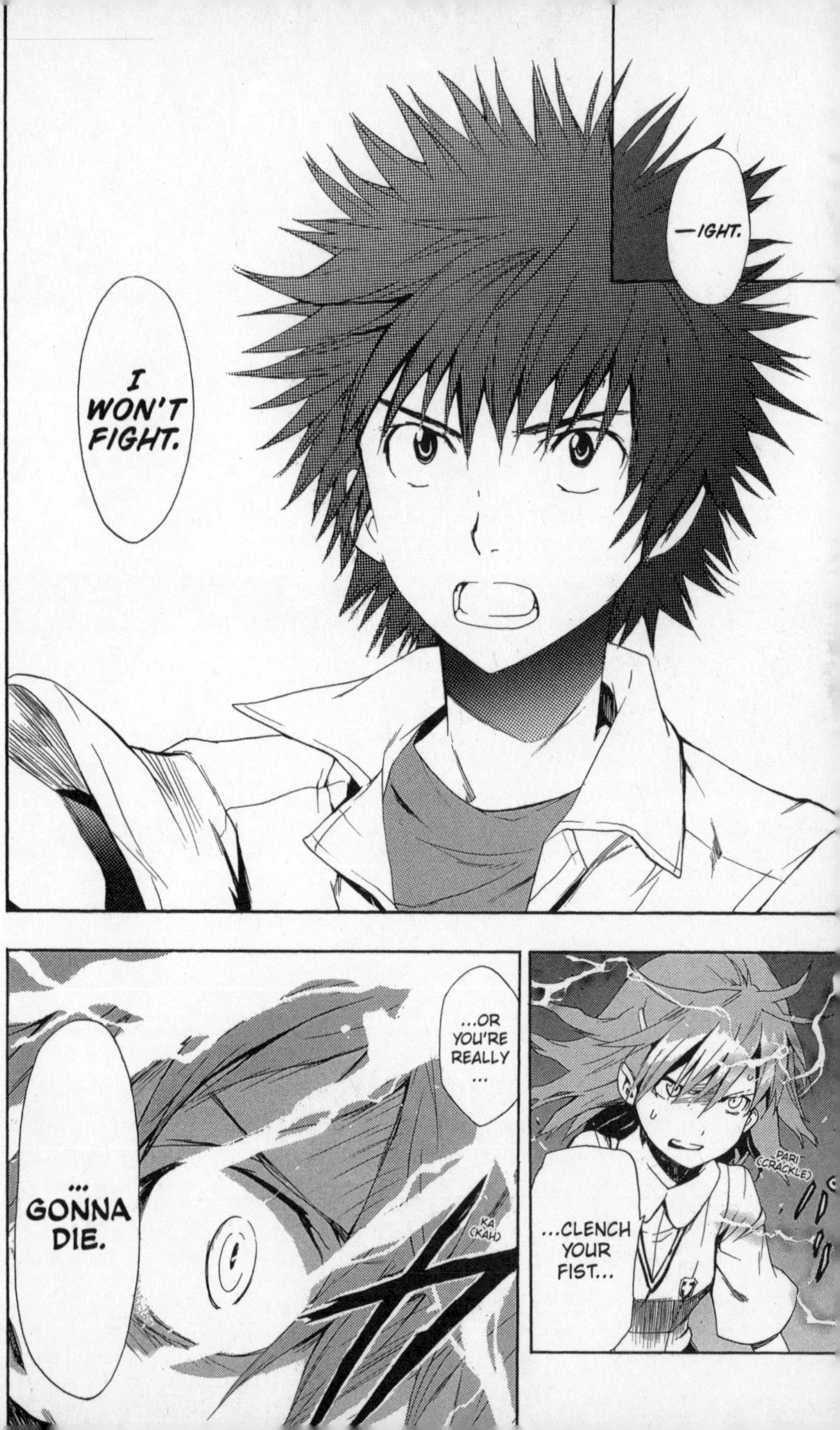
—IGHT.
I WON'T FIGHT.
PARI (CRACKLE)
...CLENCH YOUR FIST...
...OR YOU'RE REALLY ...
KA (KAH)
... GONNA DIE.

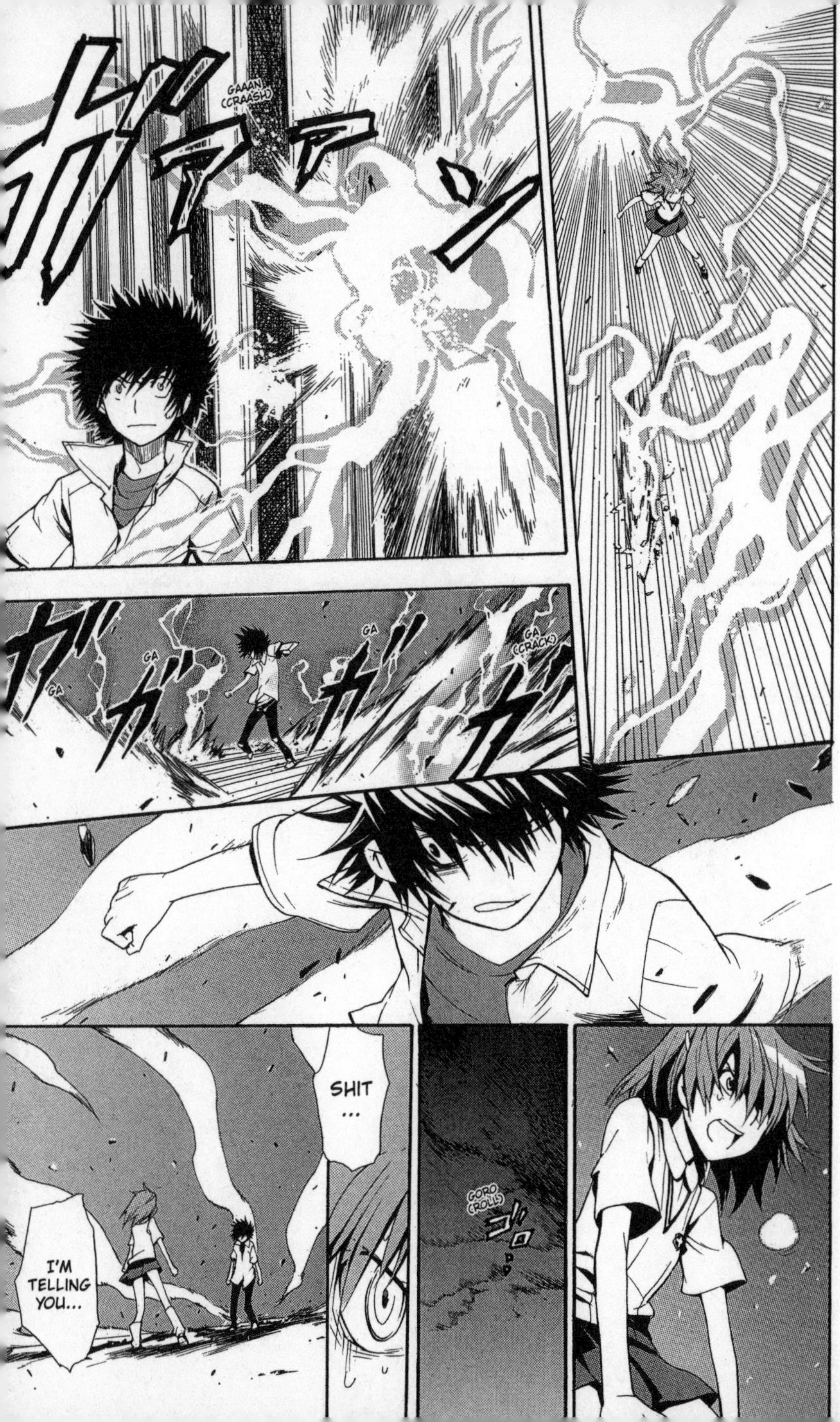
GAAAN (CRAASH)
GA (CRACK)
GA
GA
GA
GORO (ROLL)
SHIT ...
I'M TELLING YOU...

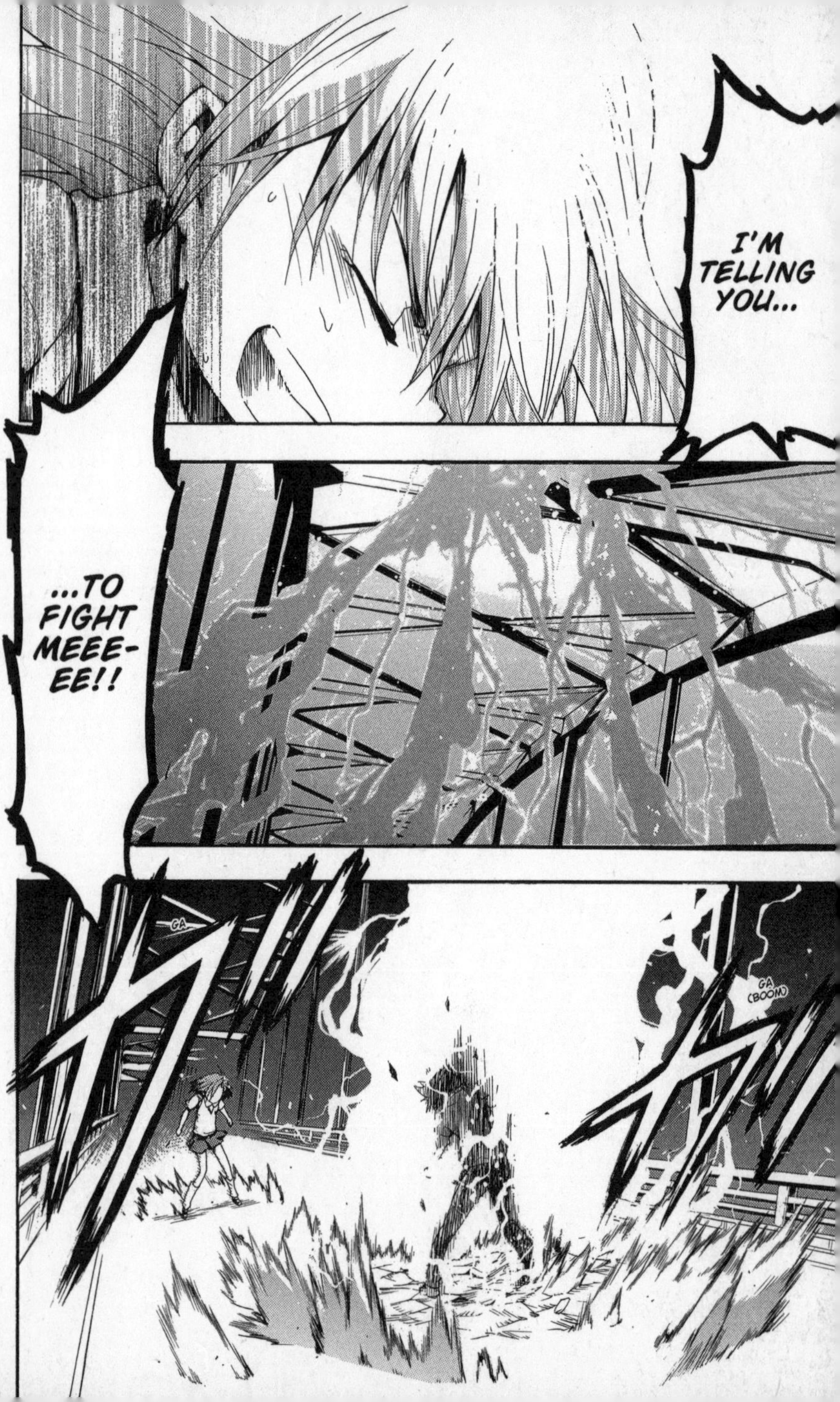
I'M TELLING YOU...
...TO FIGHT MEEEE-EE!!
GA
GA (BOOM)

GO
(BUM)

A Certain Magical Index

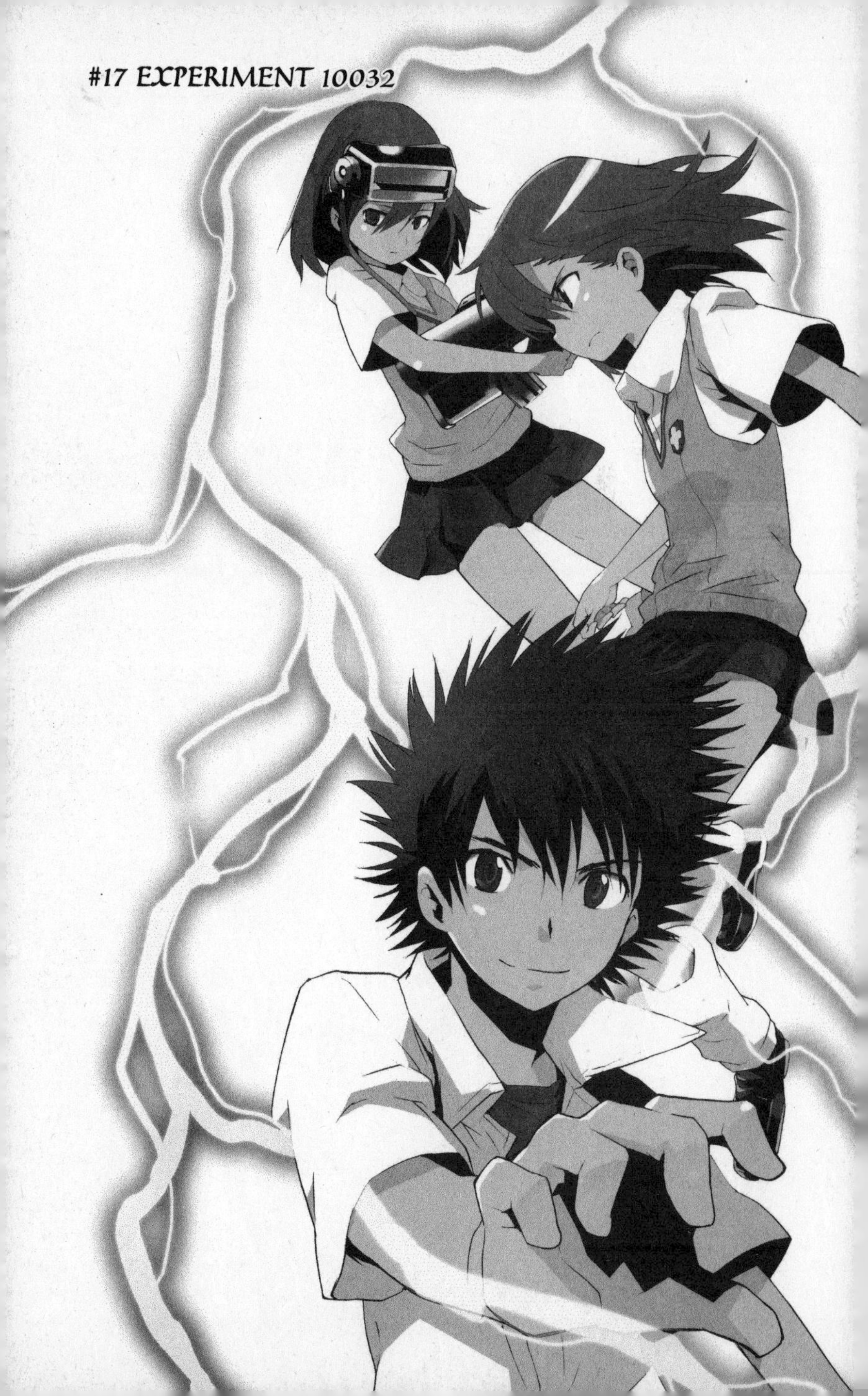
#17 EXPERIMENT 10032

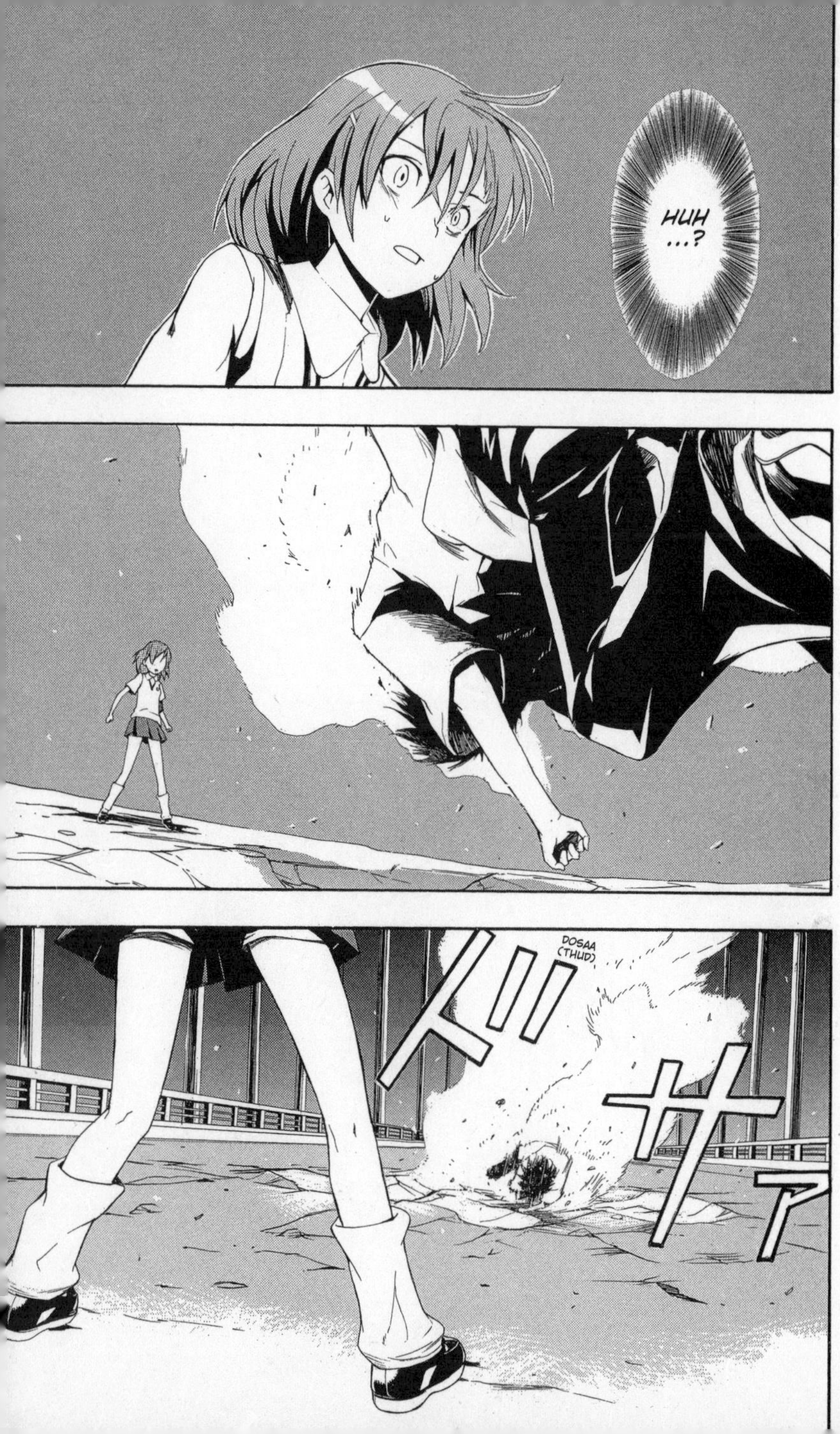
HUH ...?
DOSAA (THUD)

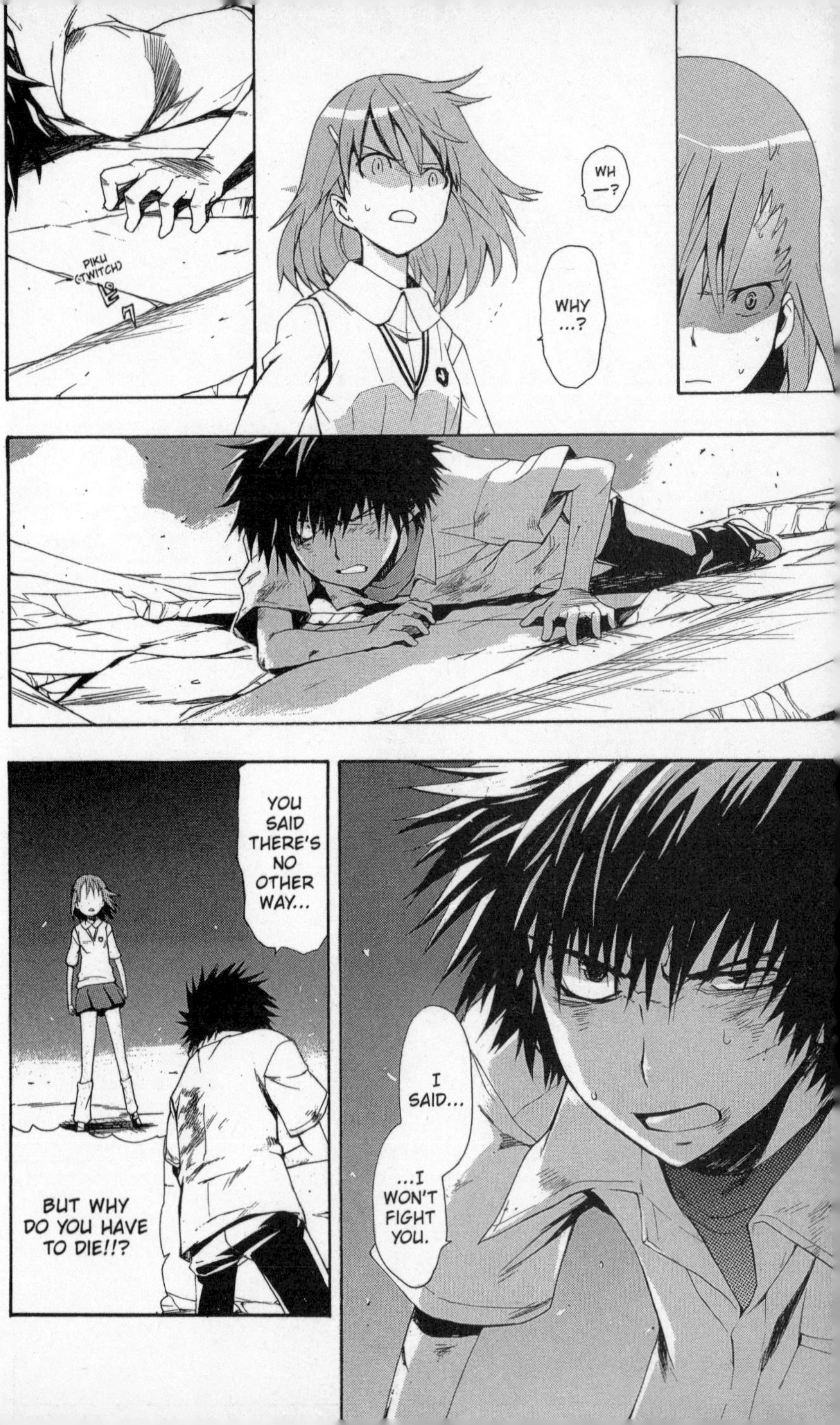
WH—?
WHY ...?
PIKU (TWITCH)
I SAID...
...I WON'T FIGHT YOU.
YOU SAID THERE'S NO OTHER WAY...
BUT WHY DO YOU HAVE TO DIE!!?

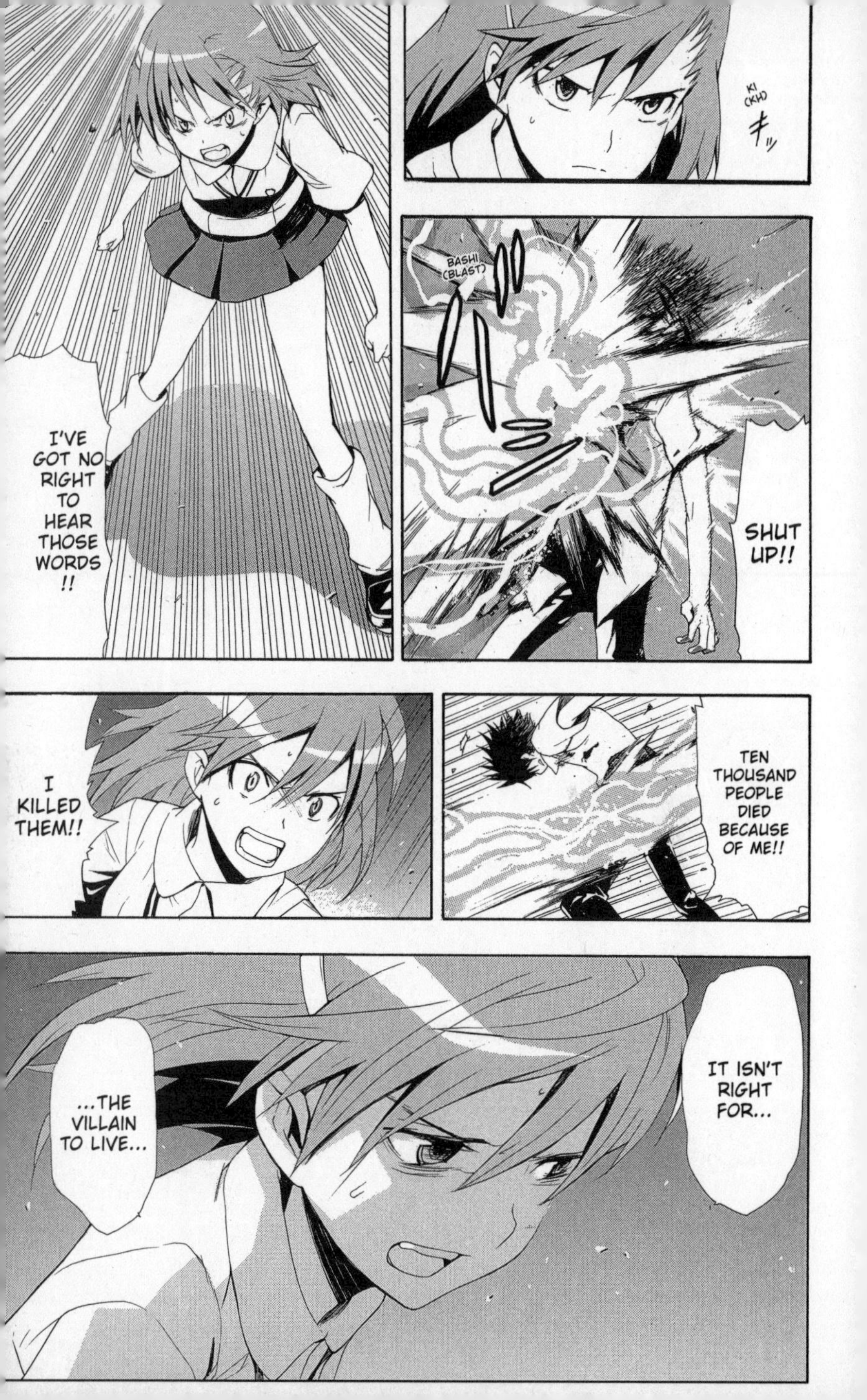
KI (KH)
ギッ
BASHI (BLAST)
SHUT UP!!
I'VE GOT NO RIGHT TO HEAR THOSE WORDS!!
TEN THOUSAND PEOPLE DIED BECAUSE OF ME!!
I KILLED THEM!!
IT ISN'T RIGHT FOR...
...THE VILLAIN TO LIVE...

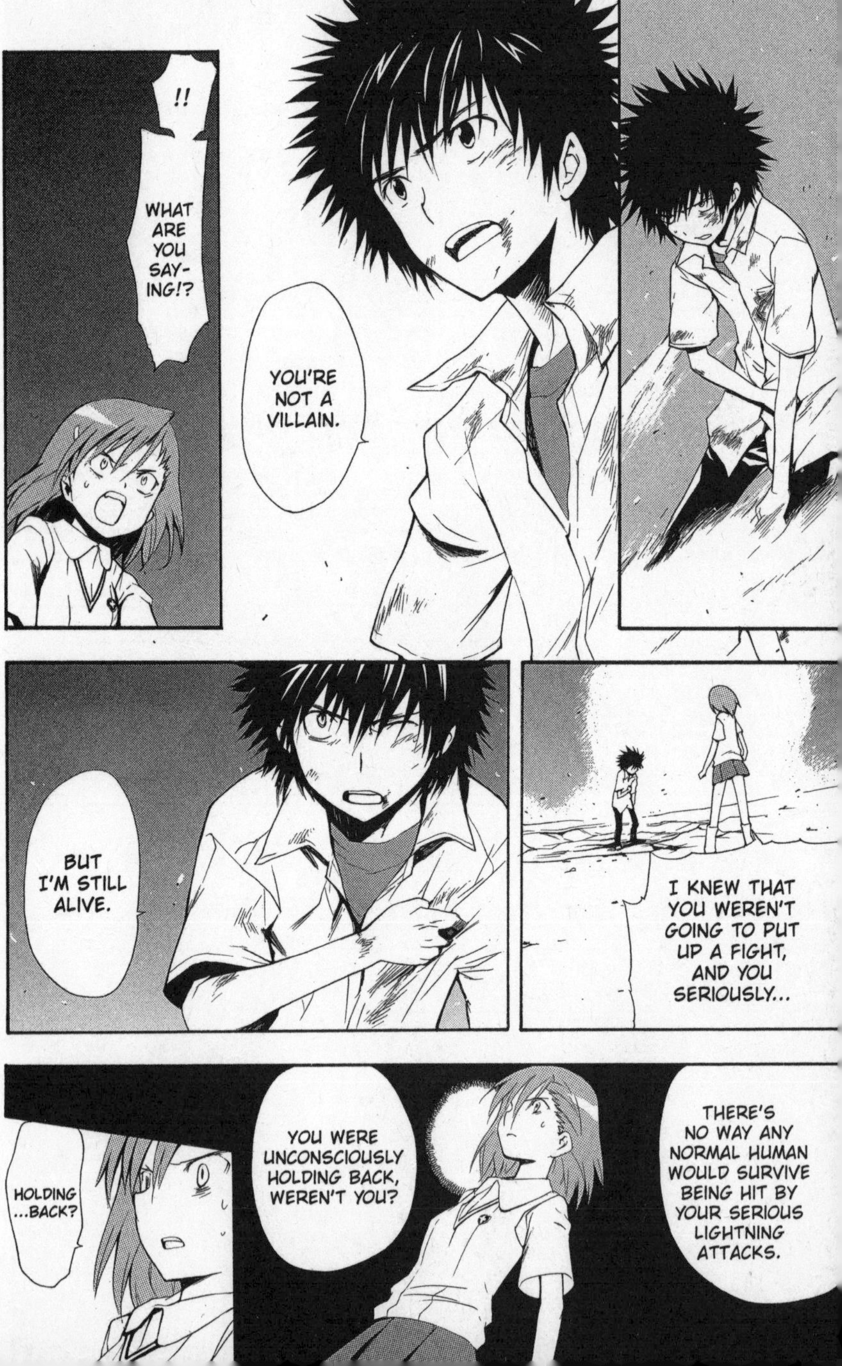
YOU'RE NOT A VILLAIN.
!!
WHAT ARE YOU SAYING!?
I KNEW THAT YOU WEREN'T GOING TO PUT UP A FIGHT, AND YOU SERIOUSLY...
BUT I'M STILL ALIVE.
THERE'S NO WAY ANY NORMAL HUMAN WOULD SURVIVE BEING HIT BY YOUR SERIOUS LIGHTNING ATTACKS.
YOU WERE UNCONSCIOUSLY HOLDING BACK, WEREN'T YOU?
HOLDING ...BACK?

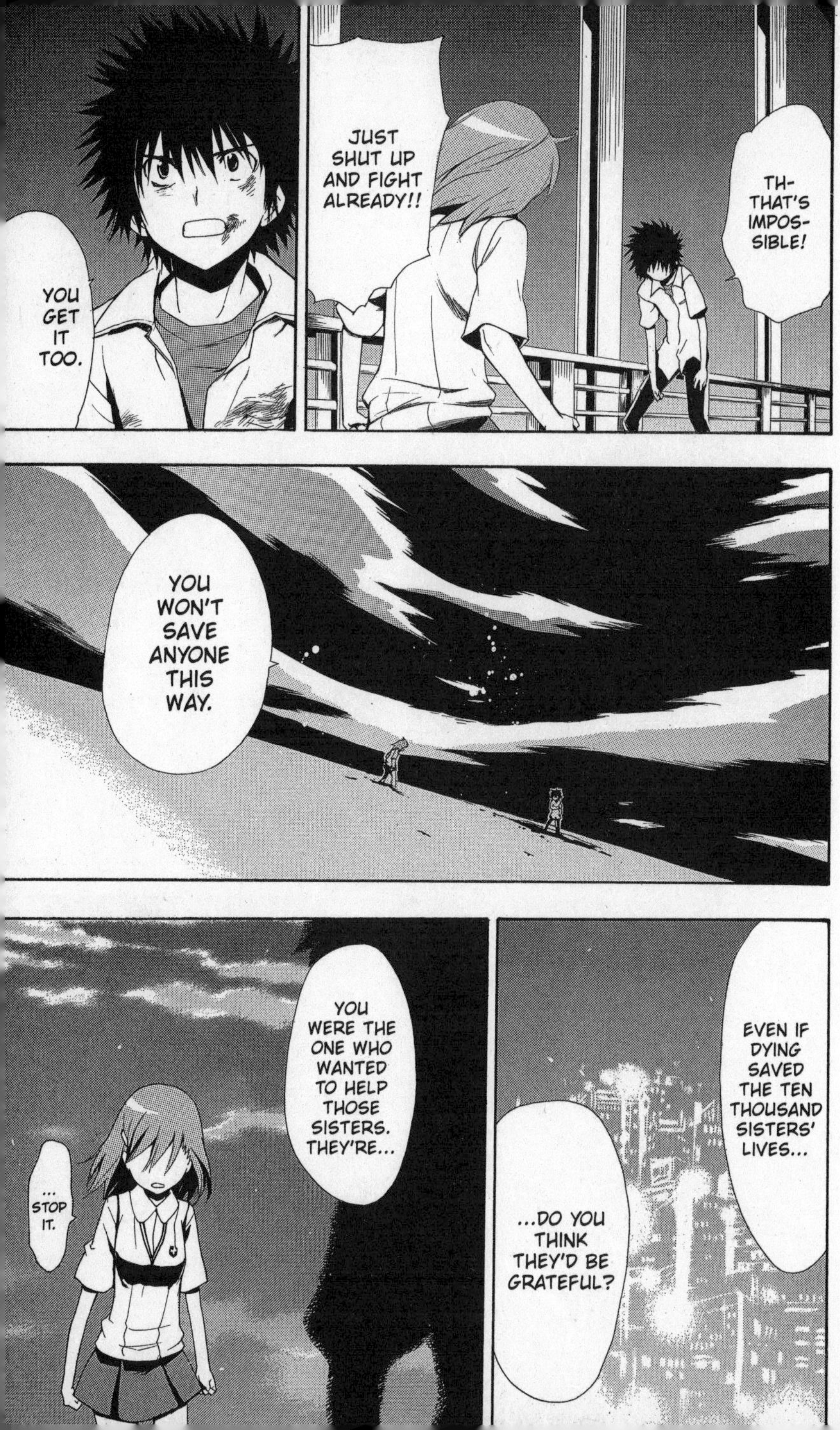
TH- THAT'S IMPOSSIBLE!
JUST SHUT UP AND FIGHT ALREADY!!
YOU GET IT TOO.
YOU WON'T SAVE ANYONE THIS WAY.
EVEN IF DYING SAVED THE TEN THOUSAND SISTERS' LIVES...
...DO YOU THINK THEY'D BE GRATEFUL?
YOU WERE THE ONE WHO WANTED TO HELP THOSE SISTERS. THEY'RE...
...STOP IT.

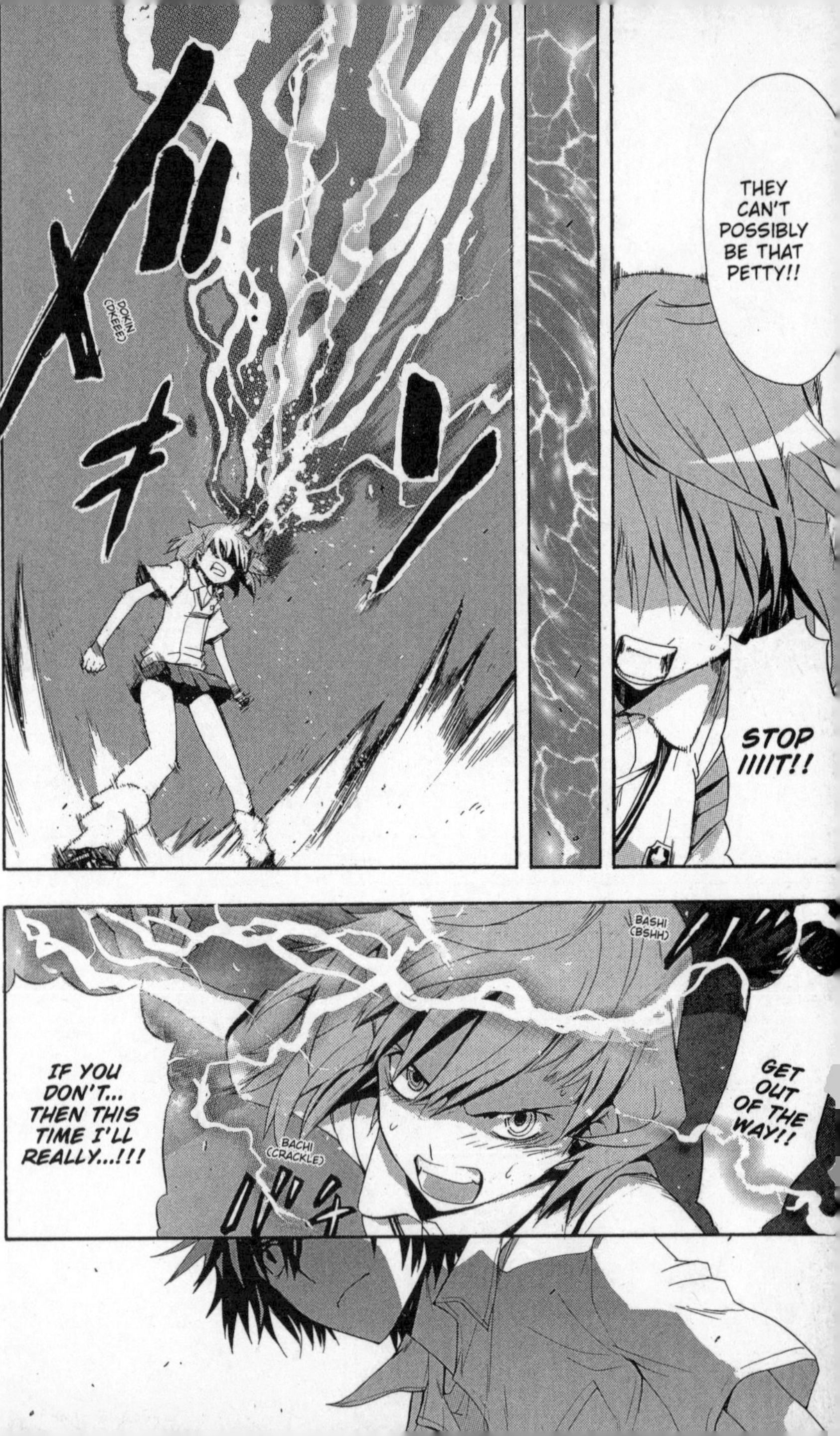
THEY CAN'T POSSIBLY BE THAT PETTY!!
STOP IIIIT!!
DOKIN (DKEEE)
BASHI (BSHH)
GET OUT OF THE WAY!!
IF YOU DON'T... THEN THIS TIME I'LL REALLY...!!!
BACHI (CRACKLE)

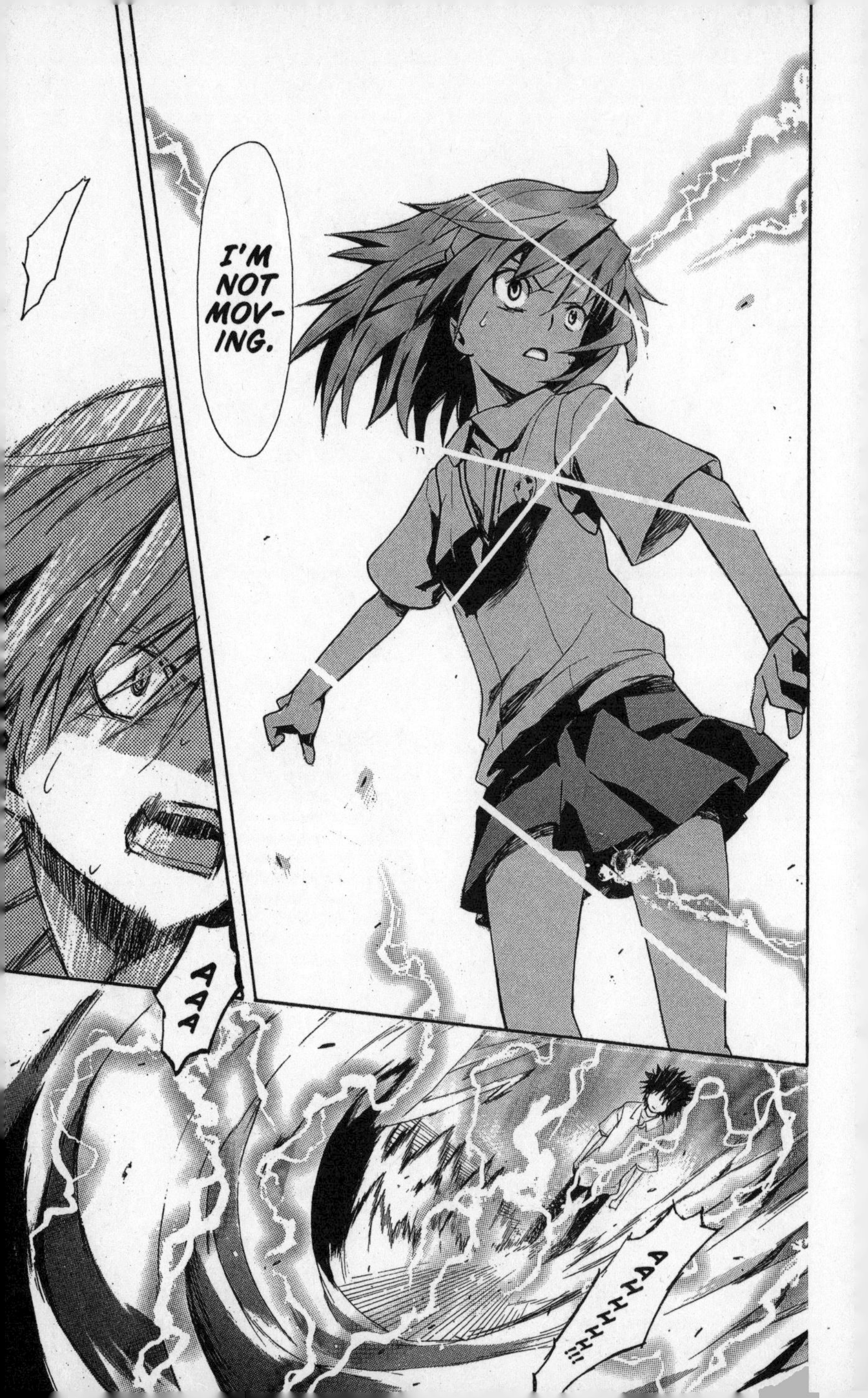
I'M NOT MOVING.
AAA
AAHHHHH!!!

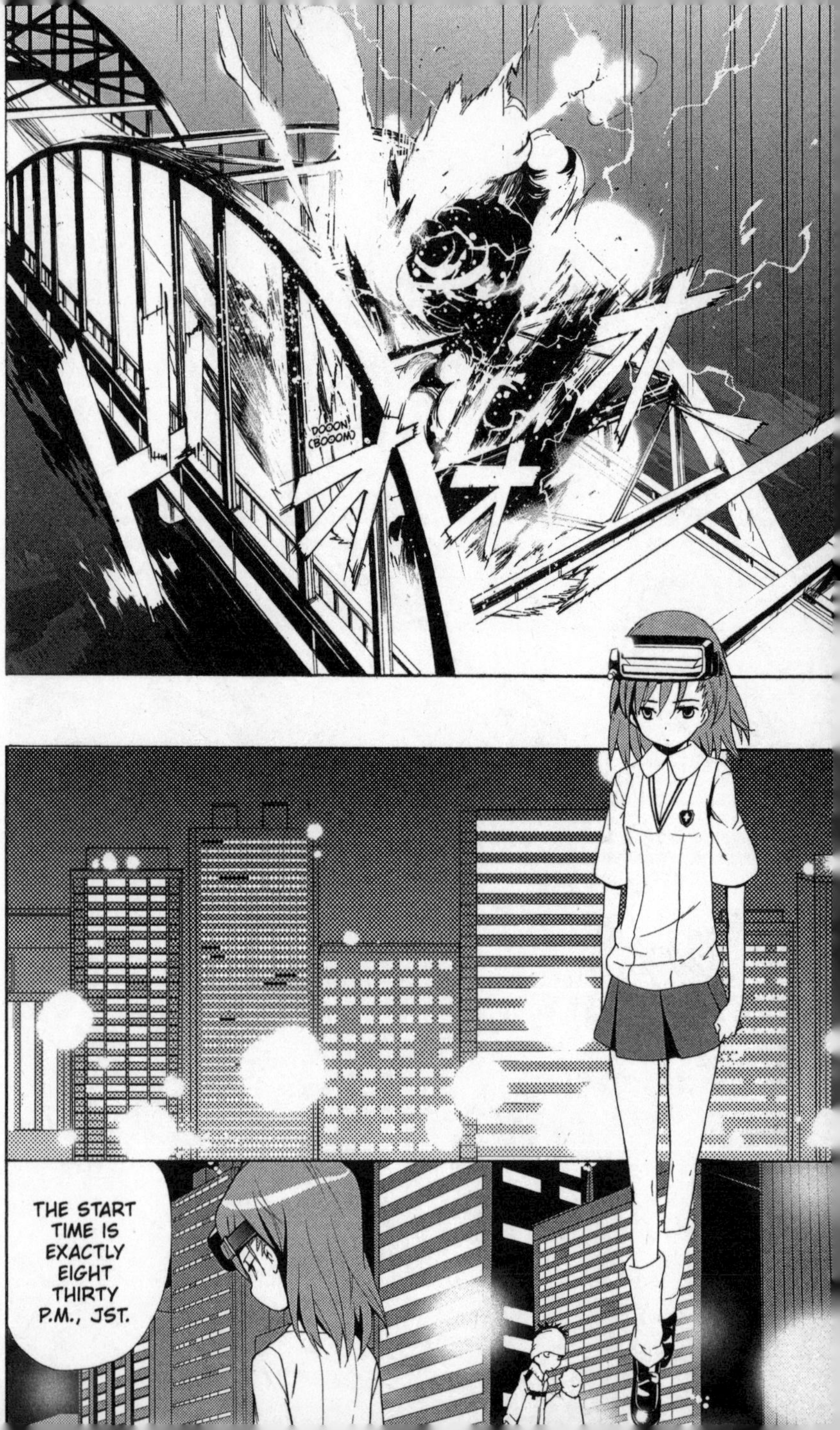
DOOON!
(BOOOM)
THE START TIME IS EXACTLY EIGHT THIRTY P.M., JST.

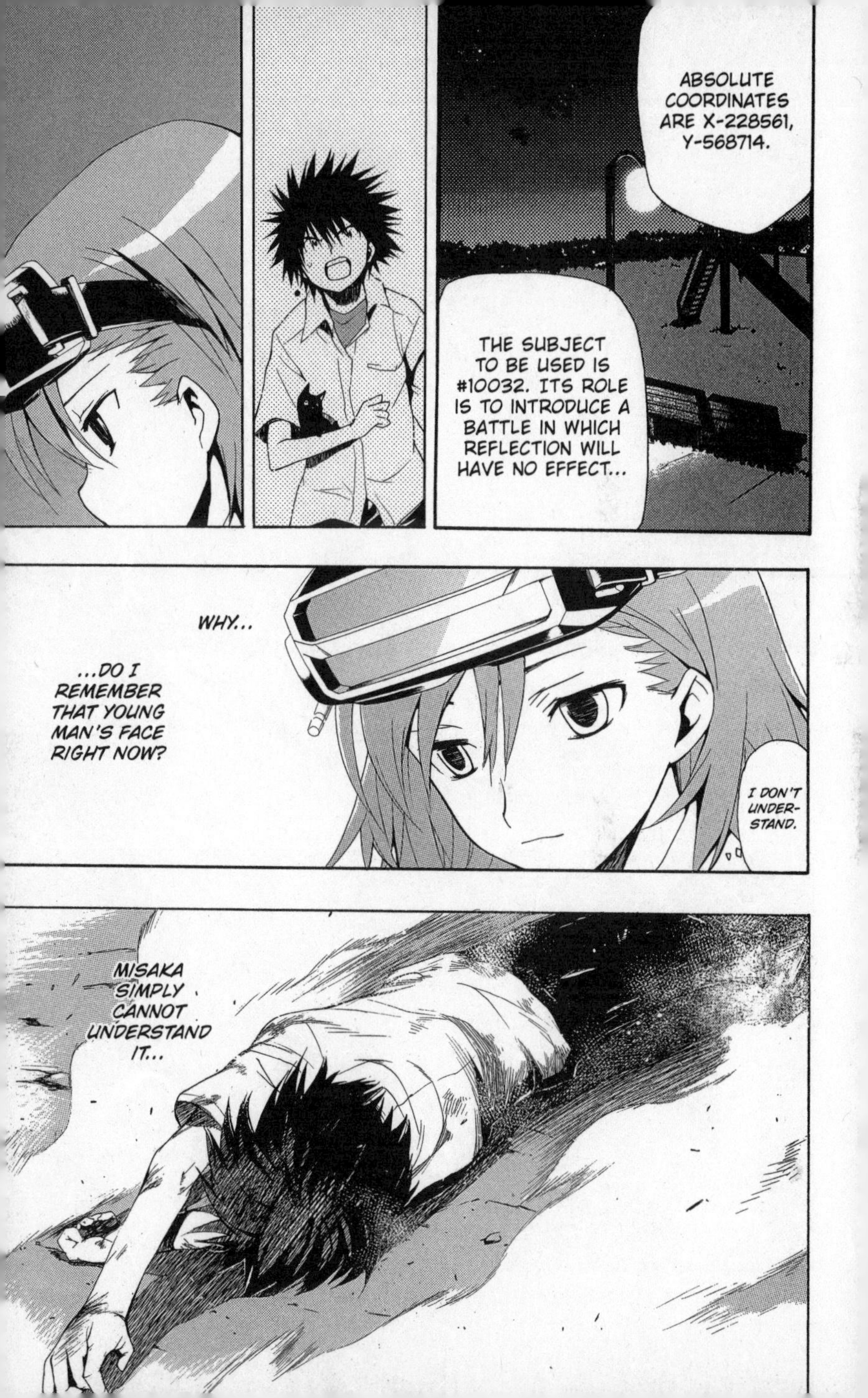
ABSOLUTE COORDINATES ARE X-228561, Y-568714.
THE SUBJECT TO BE USED IS #10032. ITS ROLE IS TO INTRODUCE A BATTLE IN WHICH REFLECTION WILL HAVE NO EFFECT...
I DON'T UNDER-STAND.
WHY...
...DO I REMEMBER THAT YOUNG MAN'S FACE RIGHT NOW?
MISAKA SIMPLY CANNOT UNDERSTAND IT...

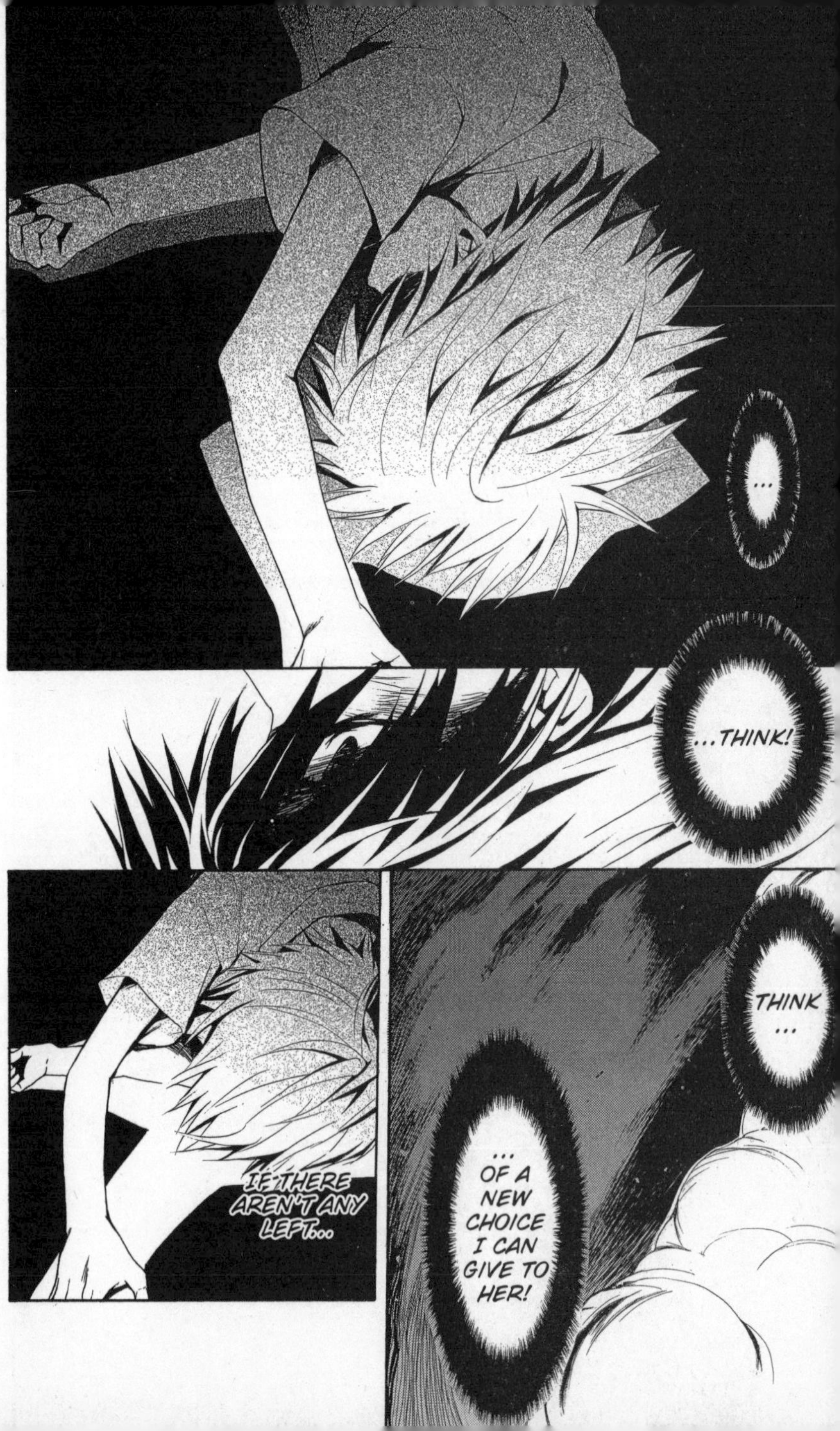
...
...THINK!
THINK ...
... OF A NEW CHOICE I CAN GIVE TO HER!
IF THERE AREN'T ANY LEFT...

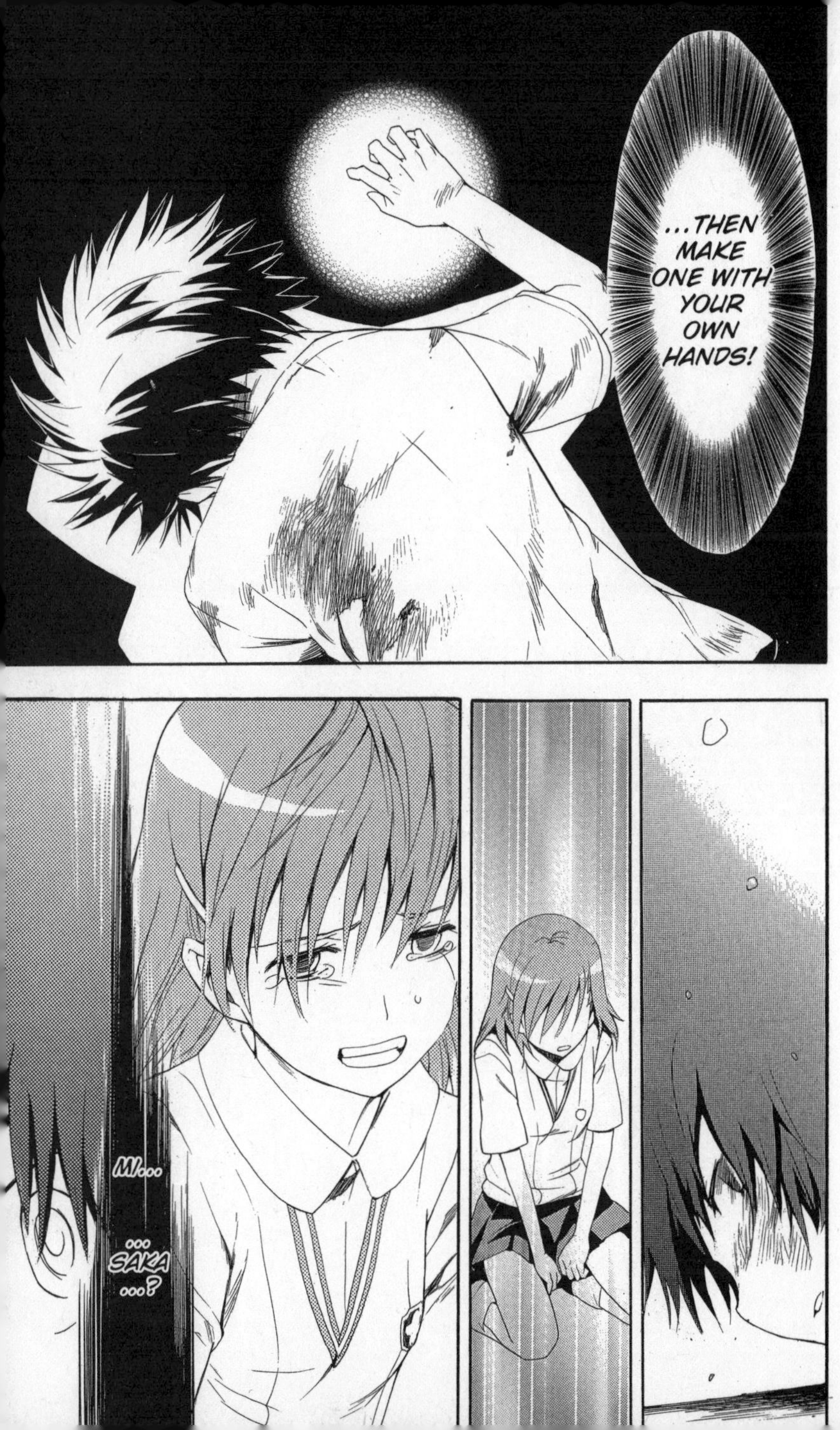
...THEN MAKE ONE WITH YOUR OWN HANDS!
MI...
...SAKA...?

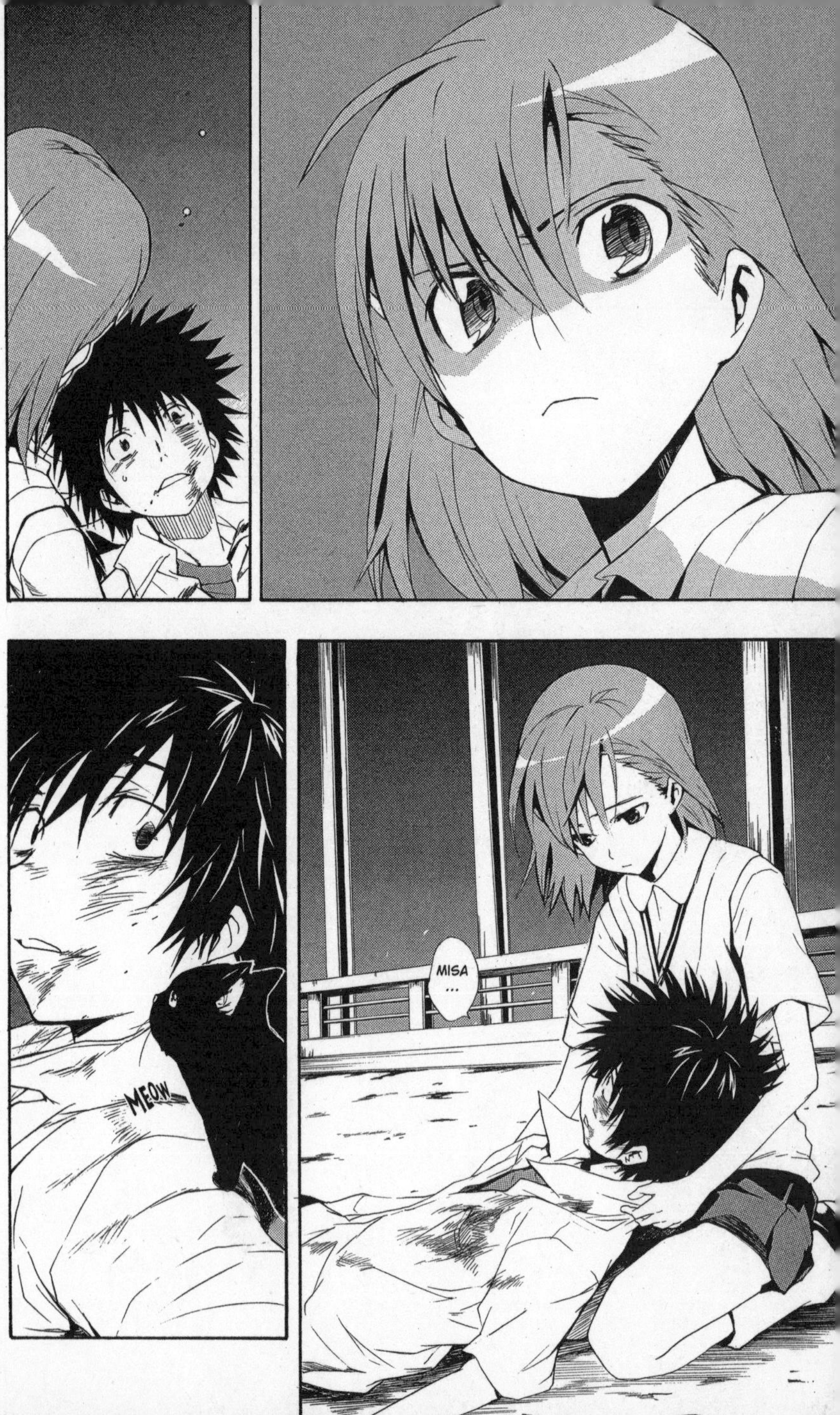
MISA
...
MEOW

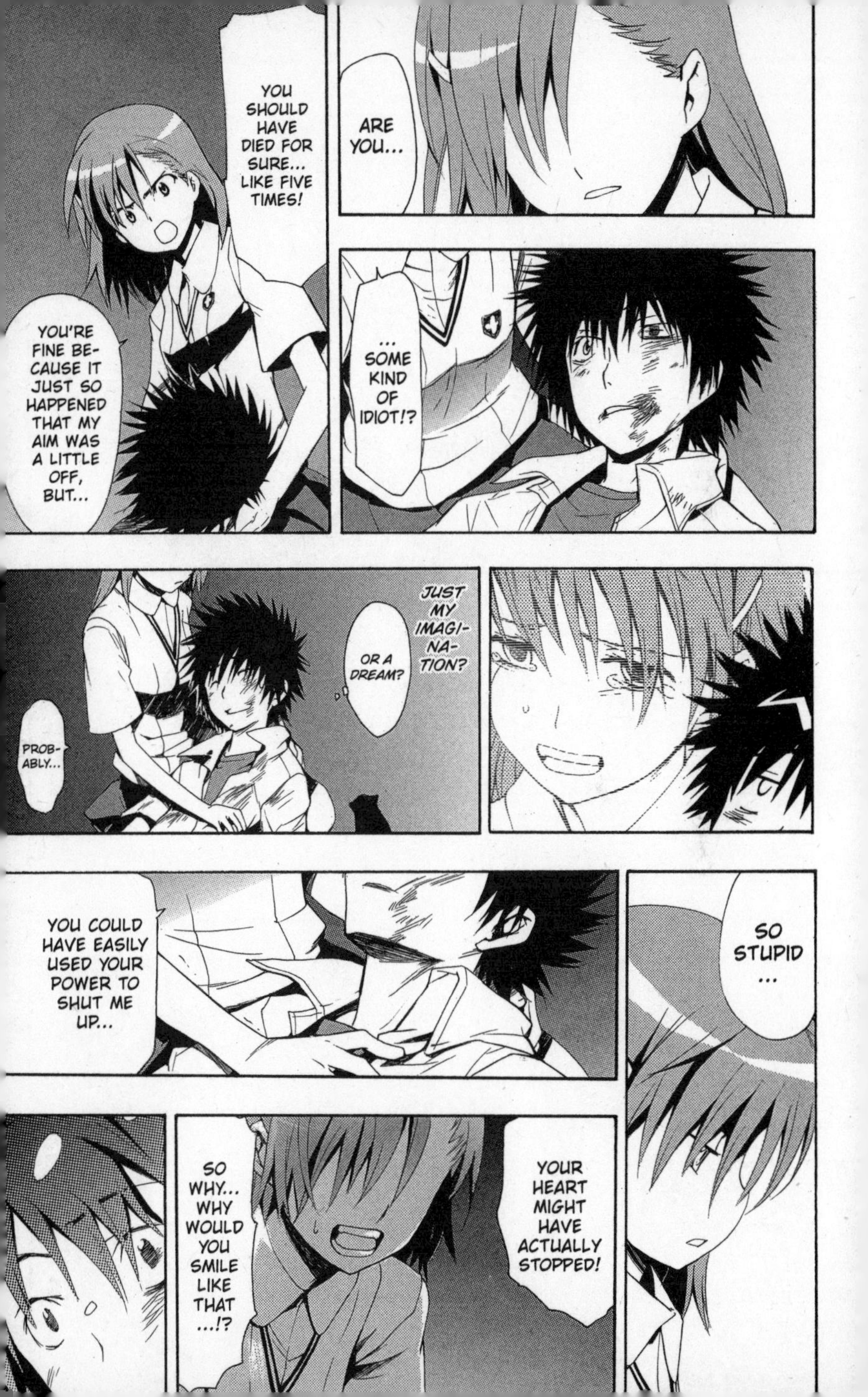
ARE YOU...
...SOME KIND OF IDIOT!?
YOU SHOULD HAVE DIED FOR SURE... LIKE FIVE TIMES!
YOU'RE FINE BE-CAUSE IT JUST SO HAPPENED THAT MY AIM WAS A LITTLE OFF, BUT...
JUST MY IMAGI-NA-TION?
OR A DREAM?
PROB-ABLY...
SO STUPID ...
YOU COULD HAVE EASILY USED YOUR POWER TO SHUT ME UP...
YOUR HEART MIGHT HAVE ACTUALLY STOPPED!
SO WHY... WHY WOULD YOU SMILE LIKE THAT ...!?

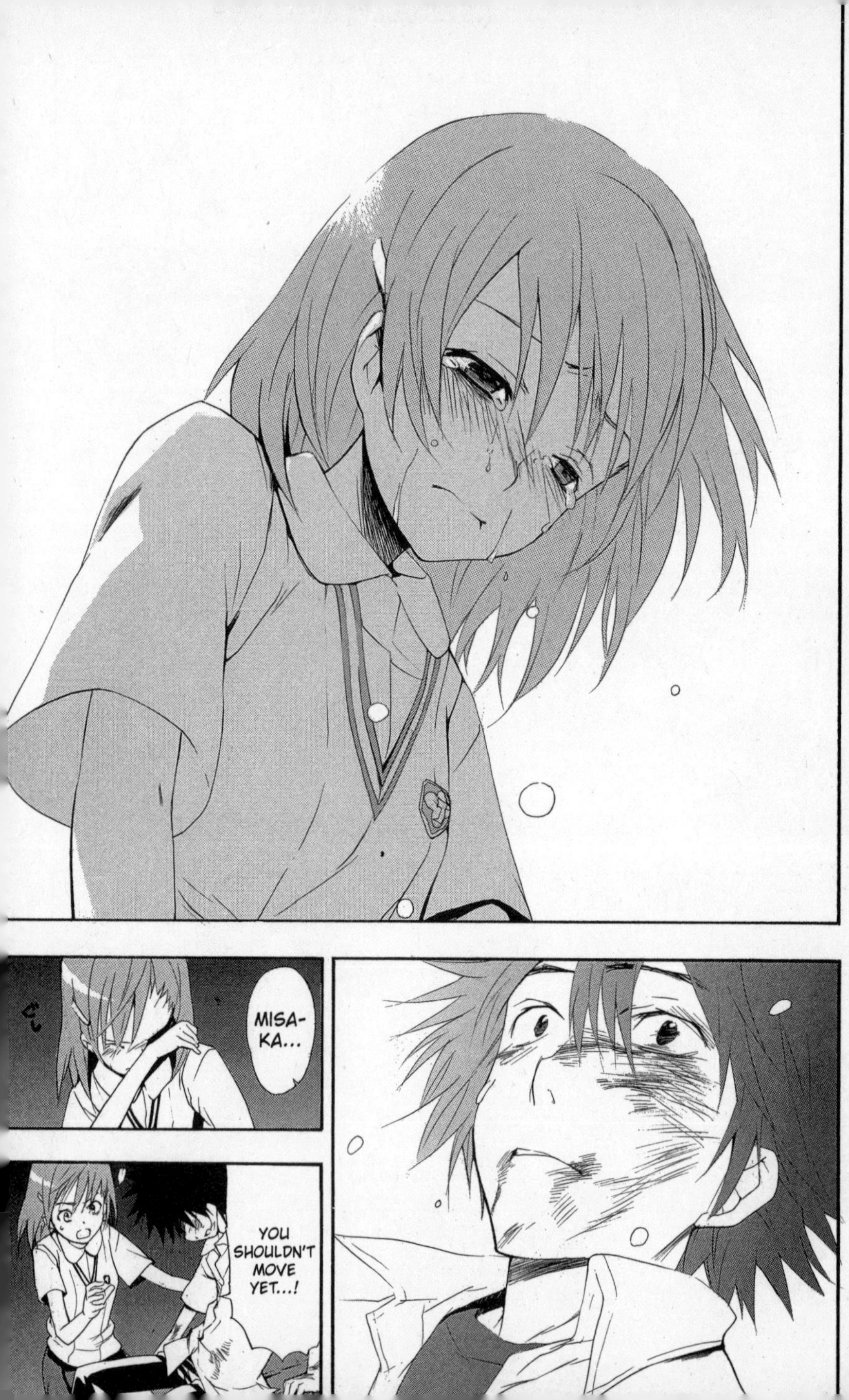
MISA-KA...
YOU SHOULDN'T MOVE YET...!

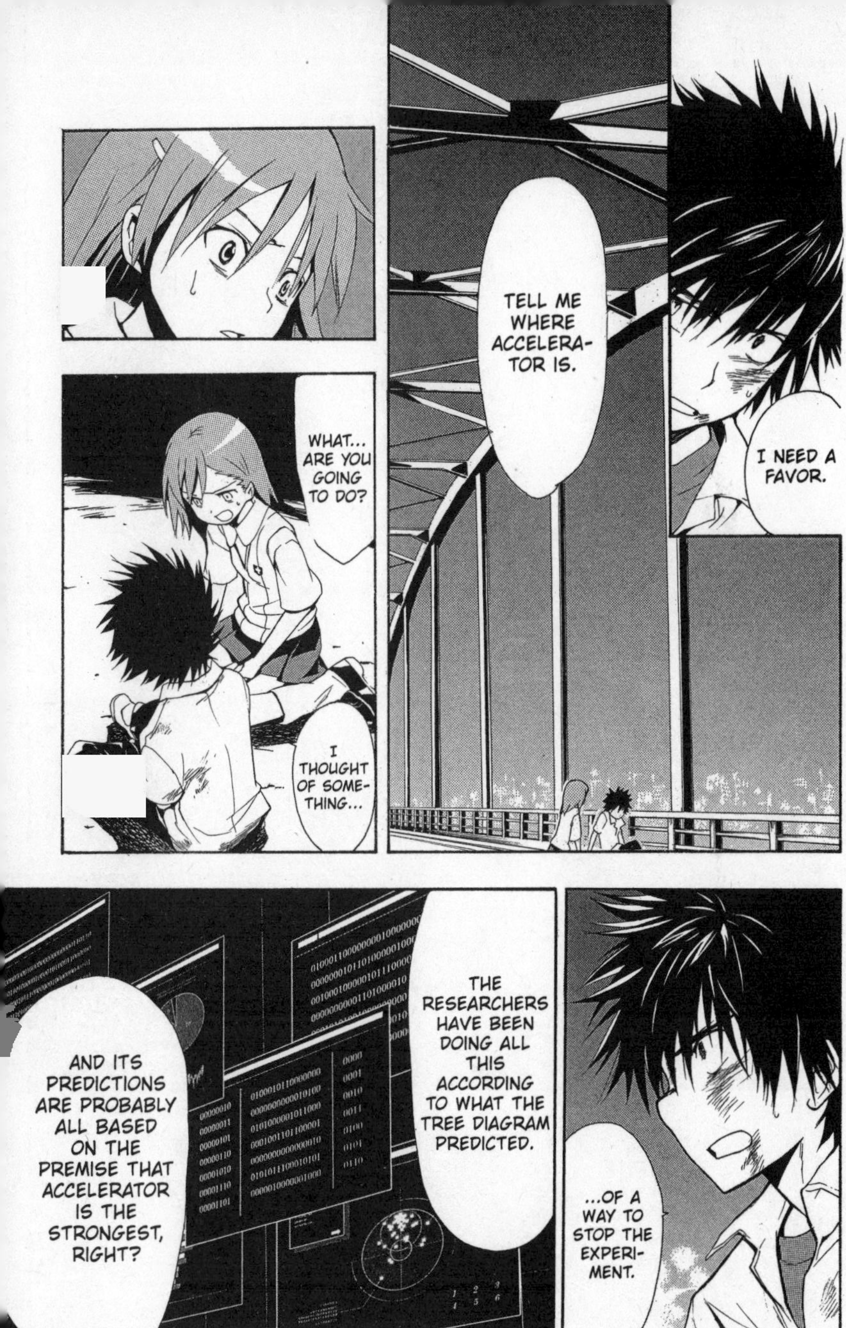
I NEED A FAVOR.
TELL ME WHERE ACCELERATOR IS.
WHAT... ARE YOU GOING TO DO?
I THOUGHT OF SOMETHING...
...OF A WAY TO STOP THE EXPERIMENT.
THE RESEARCHERS HAVE BEEN DOING ALL THIS ACCORDING TO WHAT THE TREE DIAGRAM PREDICTED.
AND ITS PREDICTIONS ARE PROBABLY ALL BASED ON THE PREMISE THAT ACCELERATOR IS THE STRONGEST, RIGHT?

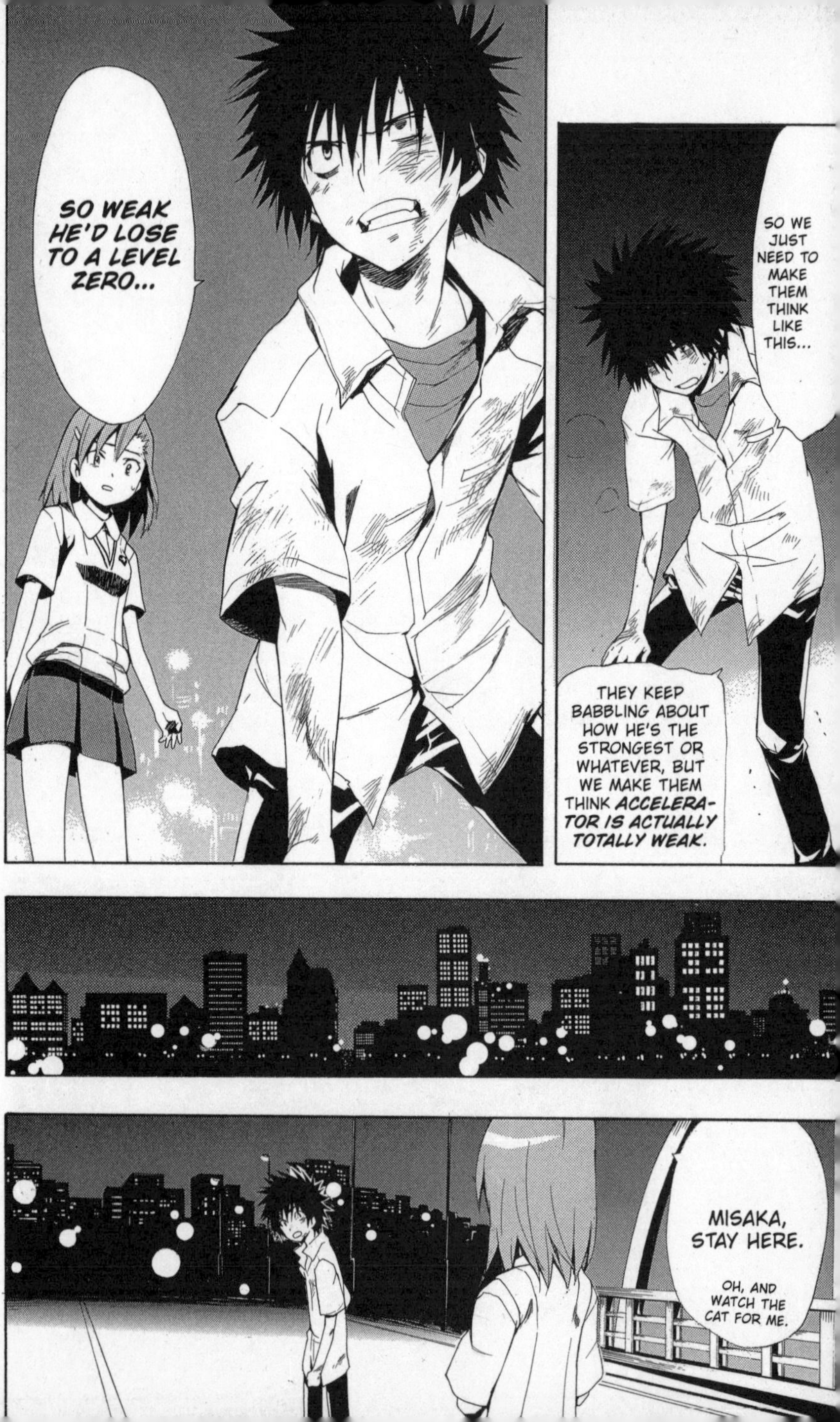
SO WE JUST NEED TO MAKE THEM THINK LIKE THIS...
THEY KEEP BABBLING ABOUT HOW HE'S THE STRONGEST OR WHATEVER, BUT WE MAKE THEM THINK ACCELERATOR IS ACTUALLY TOTALLY WEAK.
SO WEAK HE'D LOSE TO A LEVEL ZERO...
MISAKA, STAY HERE.
OH, AND WATCH THE CAT FOR ME.

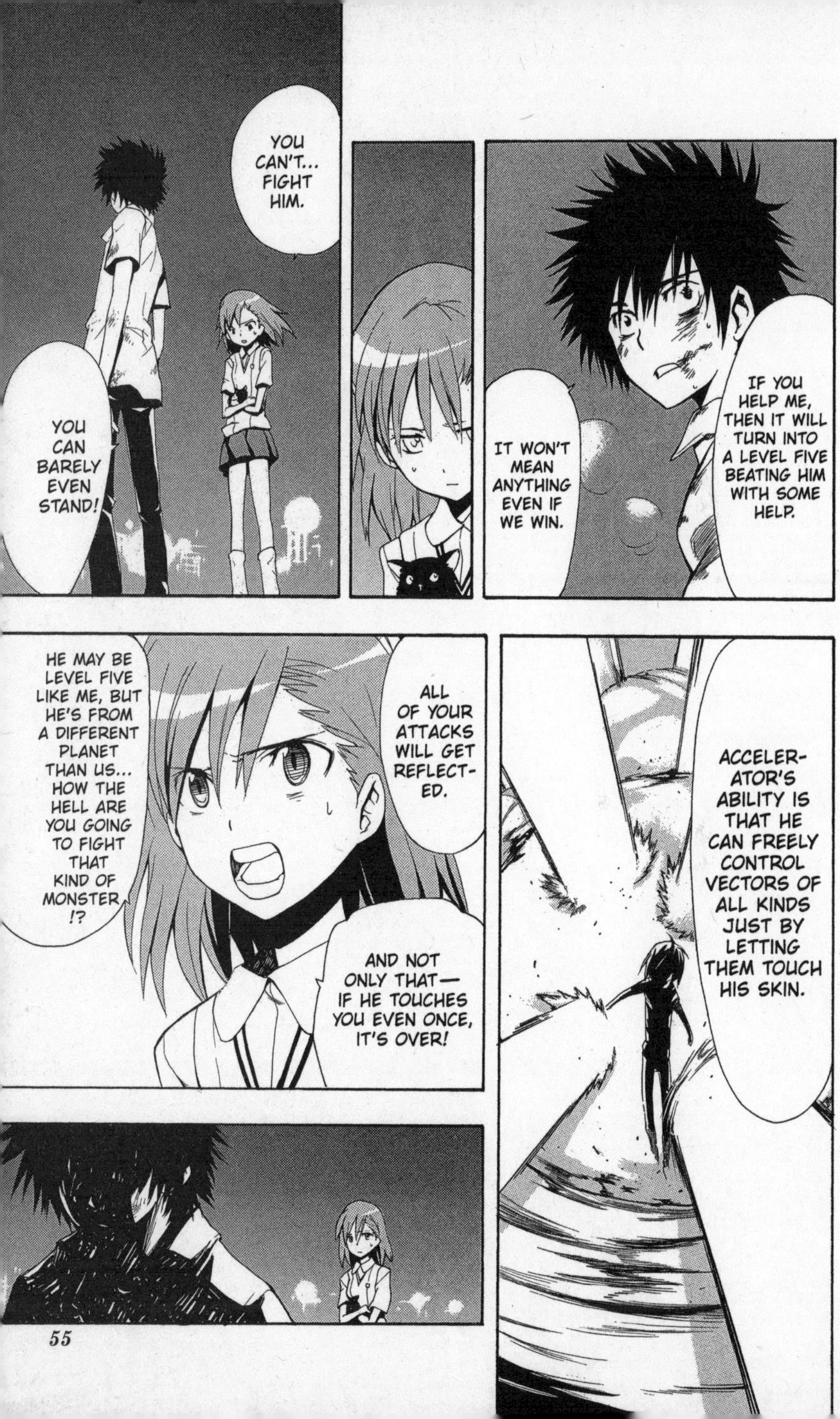
IF YOU HELP ME, THEN IT WILL TURN INTO A LEVEL FIVE BEATING HIM WITH SOME HELP.
IT WON'T MEAN ANYTHING EVEN IF WE WIN.
YOU CAN'T... FIGHT HIM.
YOU CAN BARELY EVEN STAND!
ACCELER-ATOR'S ABILITY IS THAT HE CAN FREELY CONTROL VECTORS OF ALL KINDS JUST BY LETTING THEM TOUCH HIS SKIN.
ALL OF YOUR ATTACKS WILL GET REFLECT-ED.
AND NOT ONLY THAT— IF HE TOUCHES YOU EVEN ONCE, IT'S OVER!
HE MAY BE LEVEL FIVE LIKE ME, BUT HE'S FROM A DIFFERENT PLANET THAN US... HOW THE HELL ARE YOU GOING TO FIGHT THAT KIND OF MONSTER !?

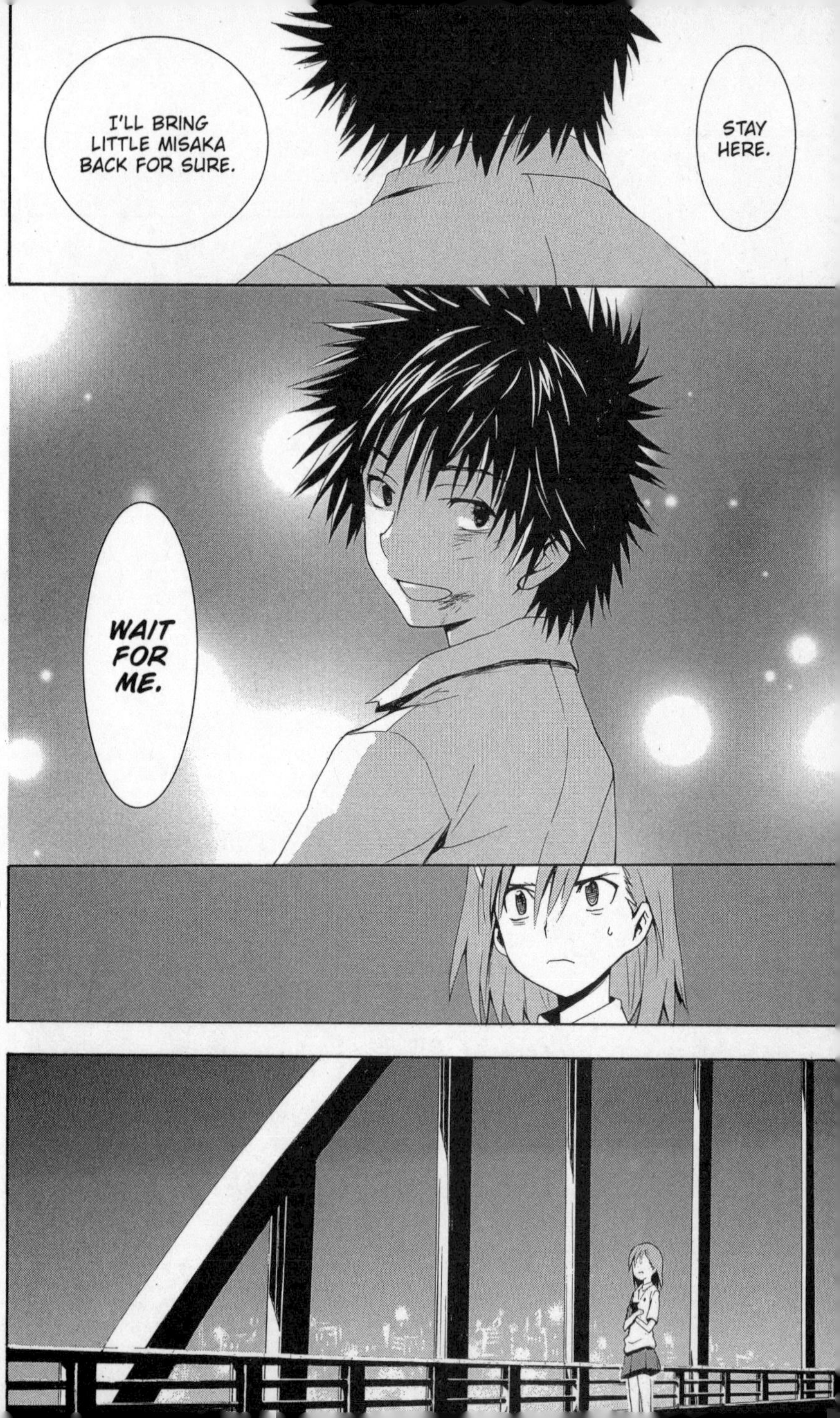
STAY HERE.
I'LL BRING LITTLE MISAKA BACK FOR SURE.
WAIT FOR ME.

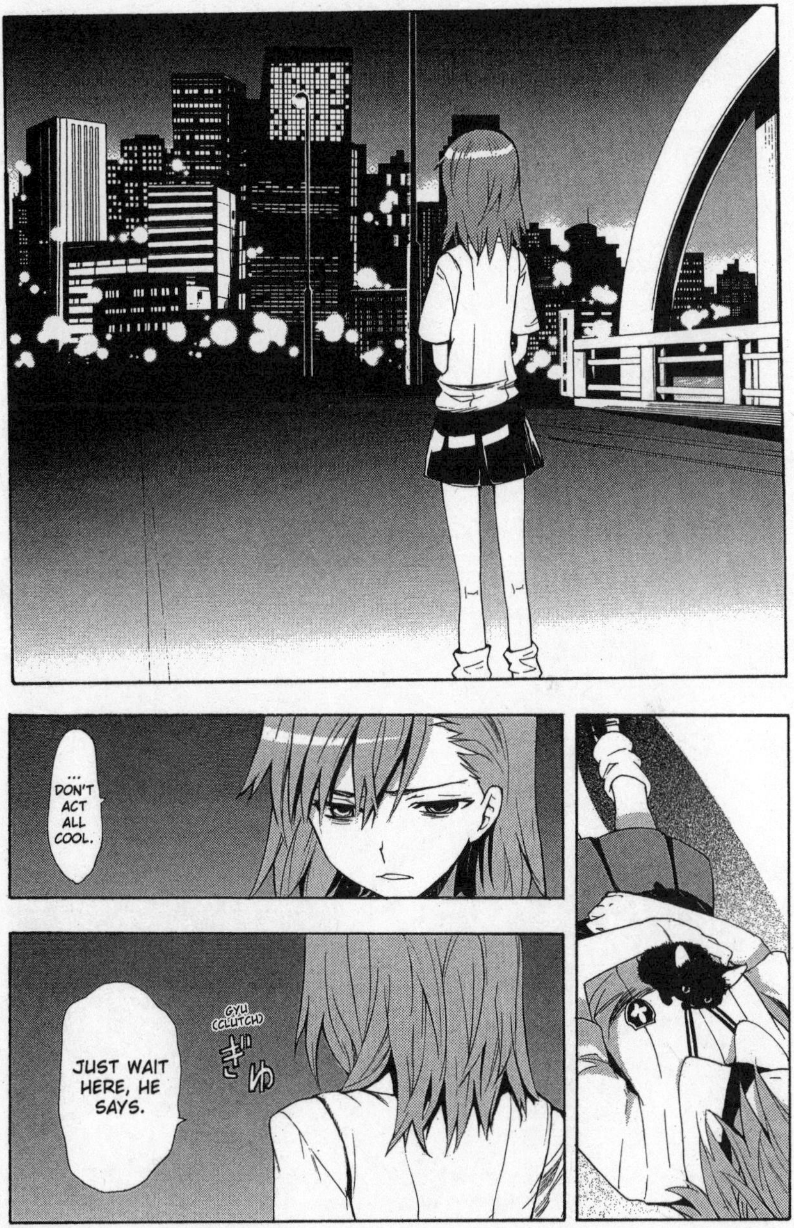
...DON'T ACT ALL COOL.
JUST WAIT HERE, HE SAYS.
GYU (CLUTCH)
ぎゅ

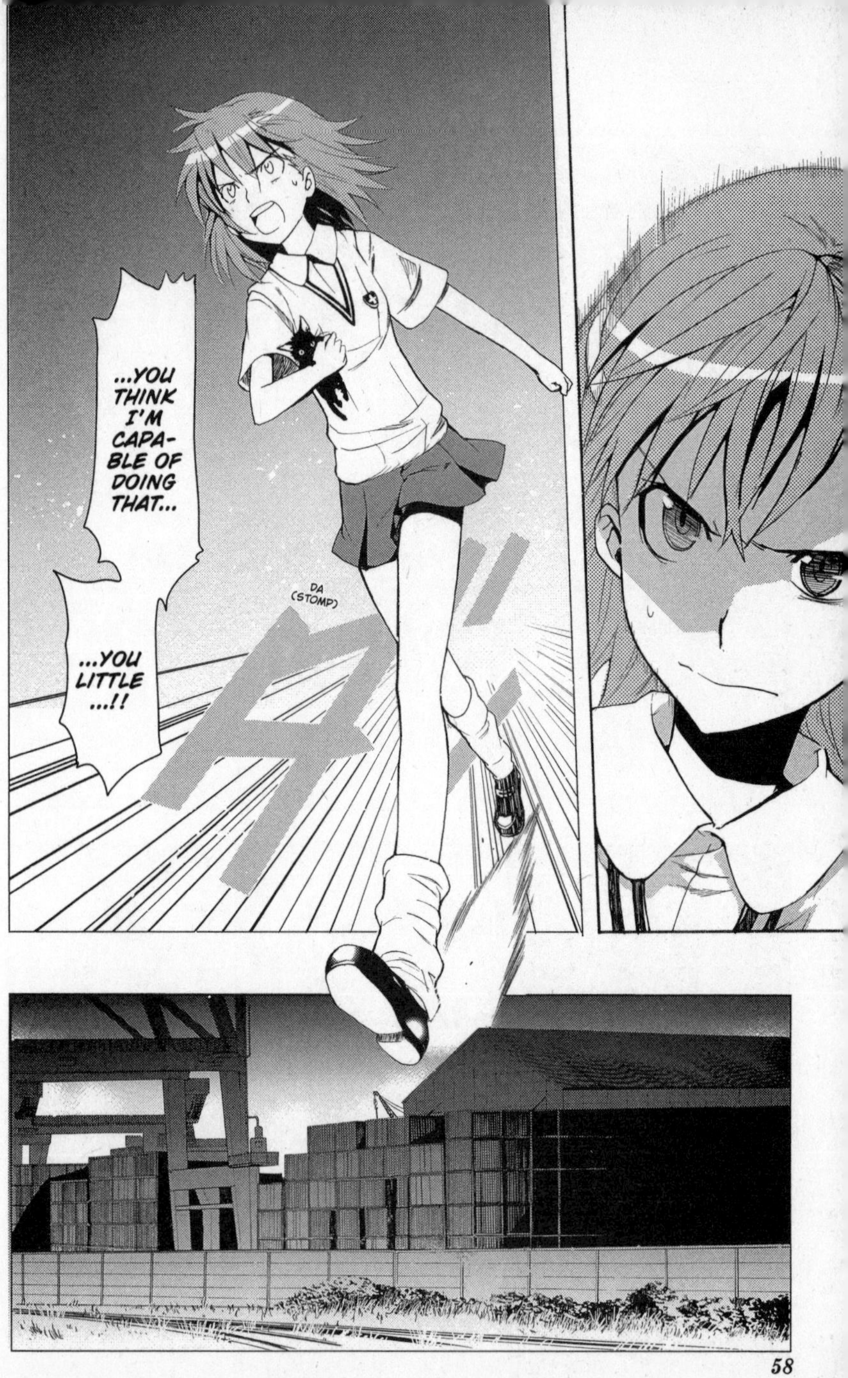
...YOU THINK I'M CAPABLE OF DOING THAT...
...YOU LITTLE ...!!
DA (STOMP)

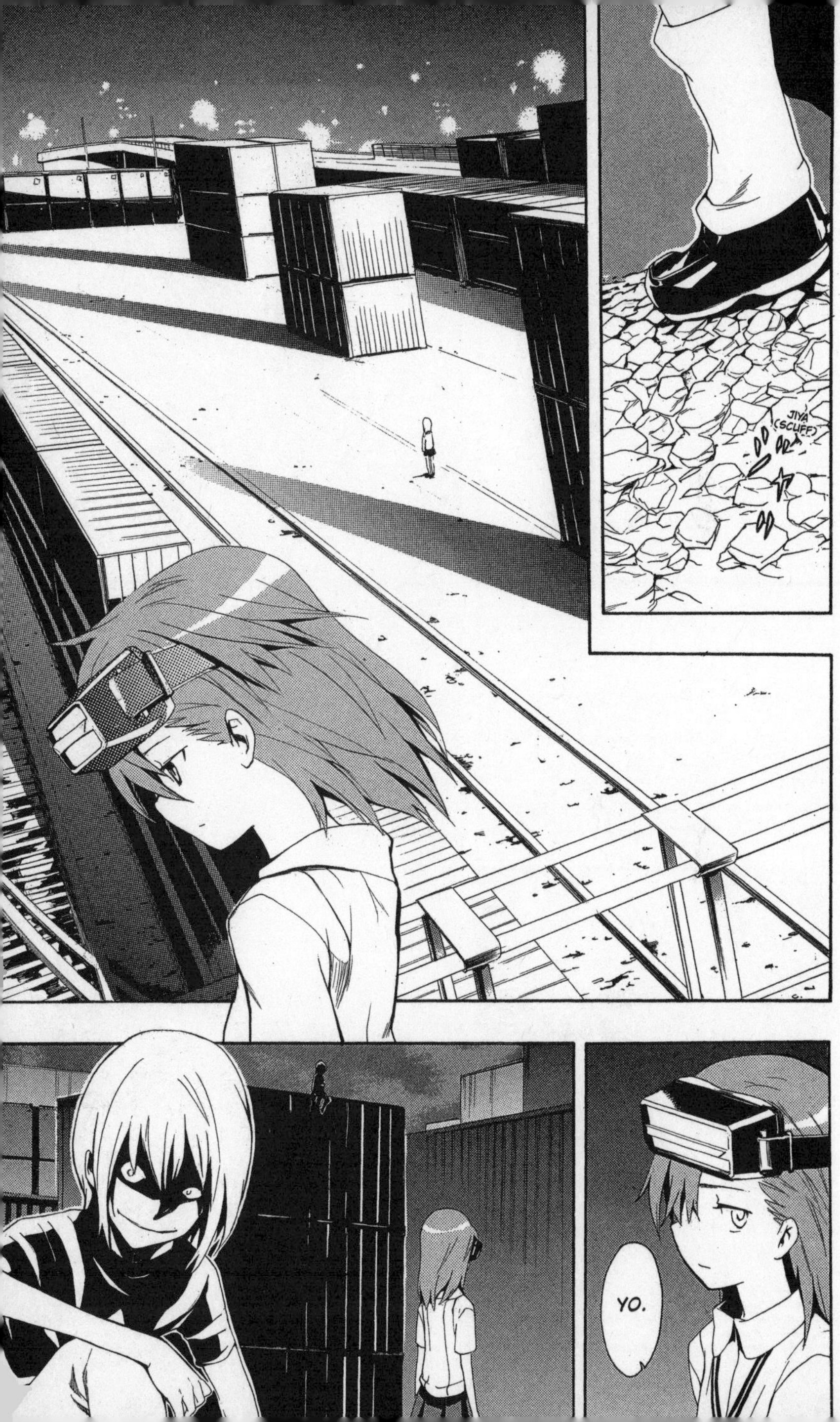
JIYA (SCUFF)
YO.

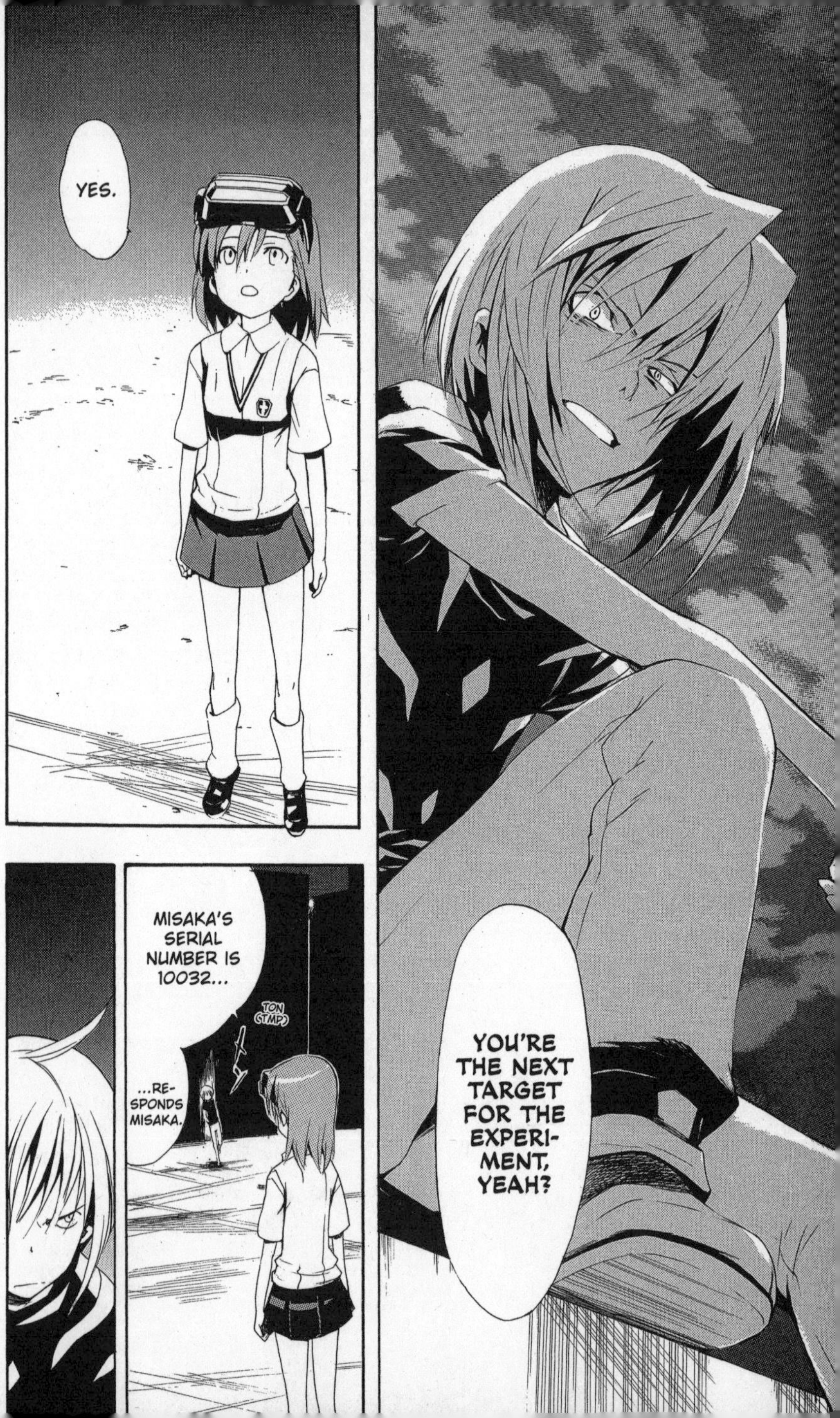
YOU'RE THE NEXT TARGET FOR THE EXPERIMENT, YEAH?
YES.
MISAKA'S SERIAL NUMBER IS 10032...
TON (TMP)
...RESPONDS MISAKA.

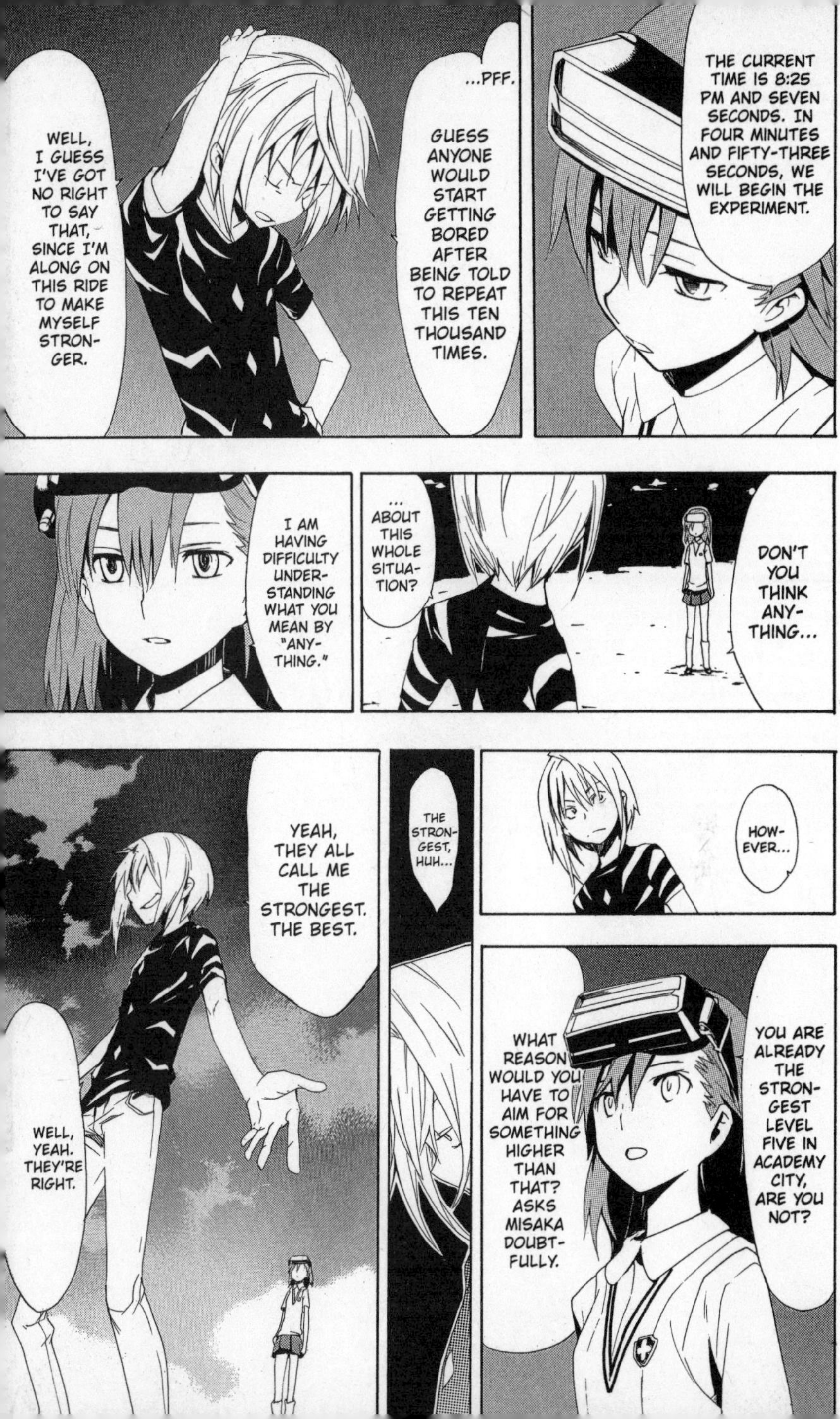
THE CURRENT TIME IS 8:25 PM AND SEVEN SECONDS. IN FOUR MINUTES AND FIFTY-THREE SECONDS, WE WILL BEGIN THE EXPERIMENT.
...PFF.
GUESS ANYONE WOULD START GETTING BORED AFTER BEING TOLD TO REPEAT THIS TEN THOUSAND TIMES.
WELL, I GUESS I'VE GOT NO RIGHT TO SAY THAT, SINCE I'M ALONG ON THIS RIDE TO MAKE MYSELF STRON-GER.
DON'T YOU THINK ANY-THING...
... ABOUT THIS WHOLE SITUA-TION?
I AM HAVING DIFFICULTY UNDER-STANDING WHAT YOU MEAN BY "ANY-THING."
HOW-EVER...
YOU ARE ALREADY THE STRON-GEST LEVEL FIVE IN ACADEMY CITY, ARE YOU NOT?
WHAT REASON WOULD YOU HAVE TO AIM FOR SOMETHING HIGHER THAN THAT? ASKS MISAKA DOUBT-FULLY.
THE STRON-GEST, HUH...
YEAH, THEY ALL CALL ME THE STRONGEST. THE BEST.
WELL, YEAH. THEY'RE RIGHT.

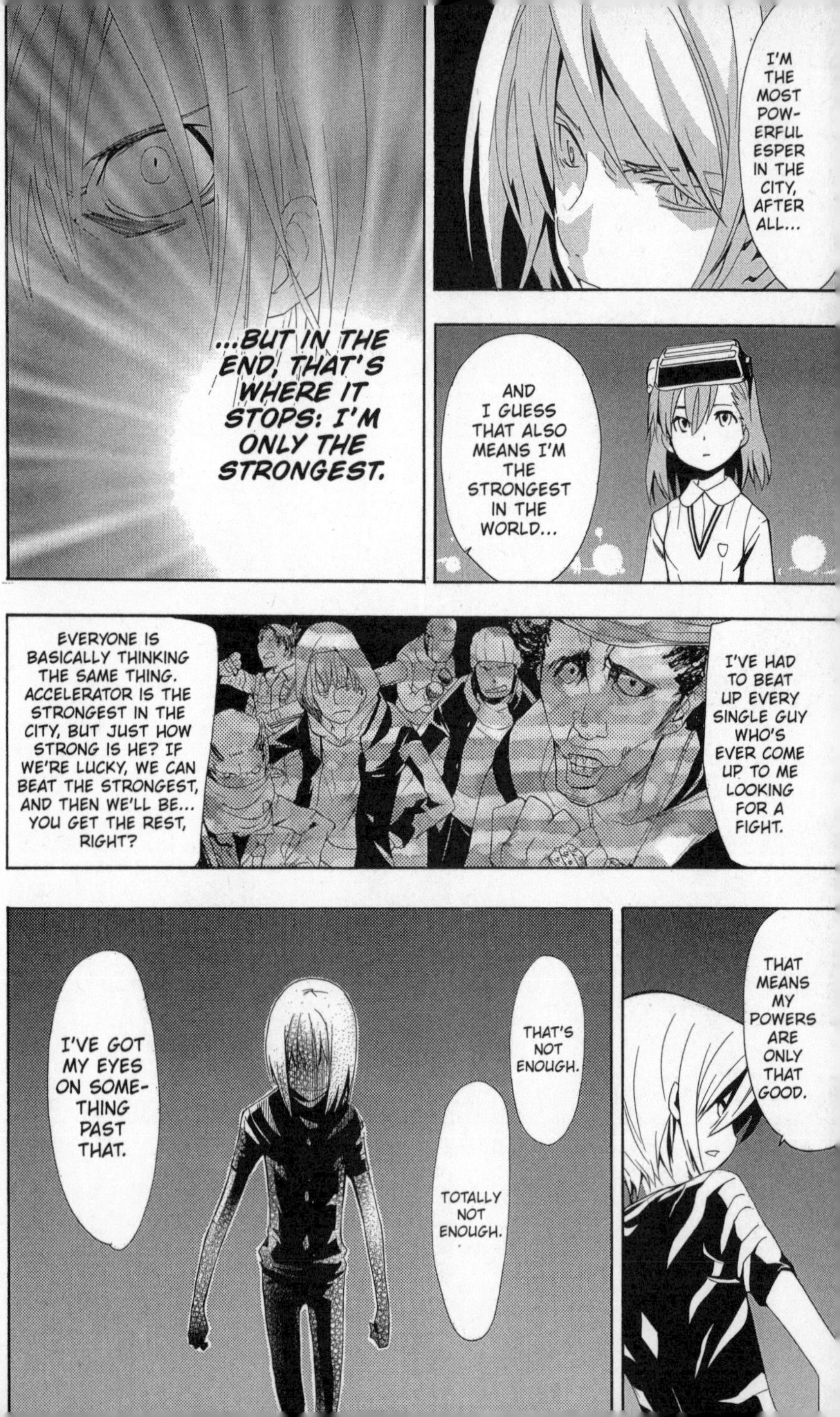
I'M THE MOST POWERFUL ESPER IN THE CITY, AFTER ALL...
AND I GUESS THAT ALSO MEANS I'M THE STRONGEST IN THE WORLD...
...BUT IN THE END, THAT'S WHERE IT STOPS: I'M ONLY THE STRONGEST.
I'VE HAD TO BEAT UP EVERY SINGLE GUY WHO'S EVER COME UP TO ME LOOKING FOR A FIGHT.
EVERYONE IS BASICALLY THINKING THE SAME THING. ACCELERATOR IS THE STRONGEST IN THE CITY, BUT JUST HOW STRONG IS HE? IF WE'RE LUCKY, WE CAN BEAT THE STRONGEST, AND THEN WE'LL BE... YOU GET THE REST, RIGHT?
THAT MEANS MY POWERS ARE ONLY THAT GOOD.
THAT'S NOT ENOUGH.
TOTALLY NOT ENOUGH.
I'VE GOT MY EYES ON SOMETHING PAST THAT.

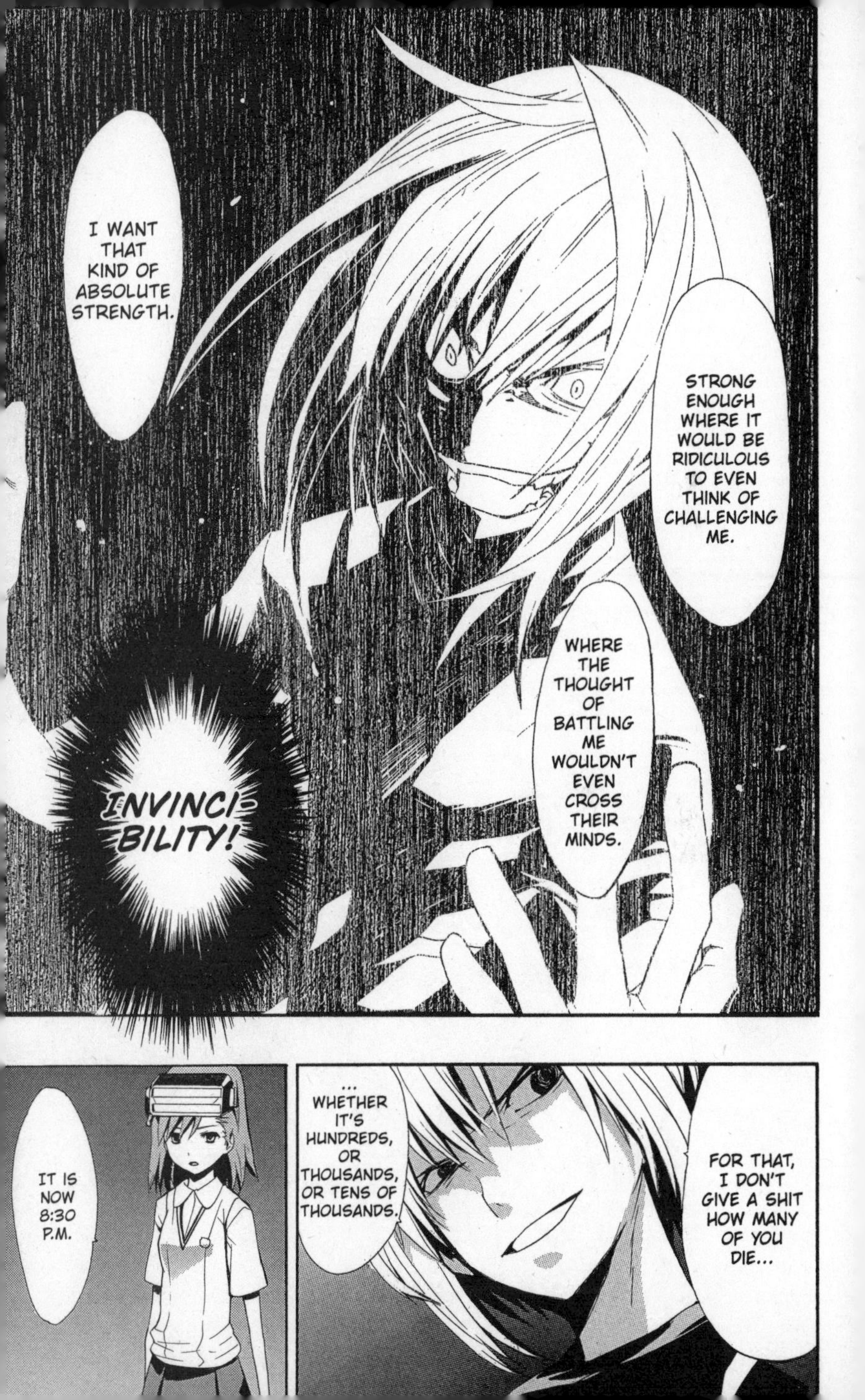
I WANT THAT KIND OF ABSOLUTE STRENGTH.
STRONG ENOUGH WHERE IT WOULD BE RIDICULOUS TO EVEN THINK OF CHALLENGING ME.
WHERE THE THOUGHT OF BATTLING ME WOULDN'T EVEN CROSS THEIR MINDS.
INVINCI-BILITY!
FOR THAT, I DON'T GIVE A SHIT HOW MANY OF YOU DIE...
... WHETHER IT'S HUNDREDS, OR THOUSANDS, OR TENS OF THOUSANDS.
IT IS NOW 8:30 P.M.

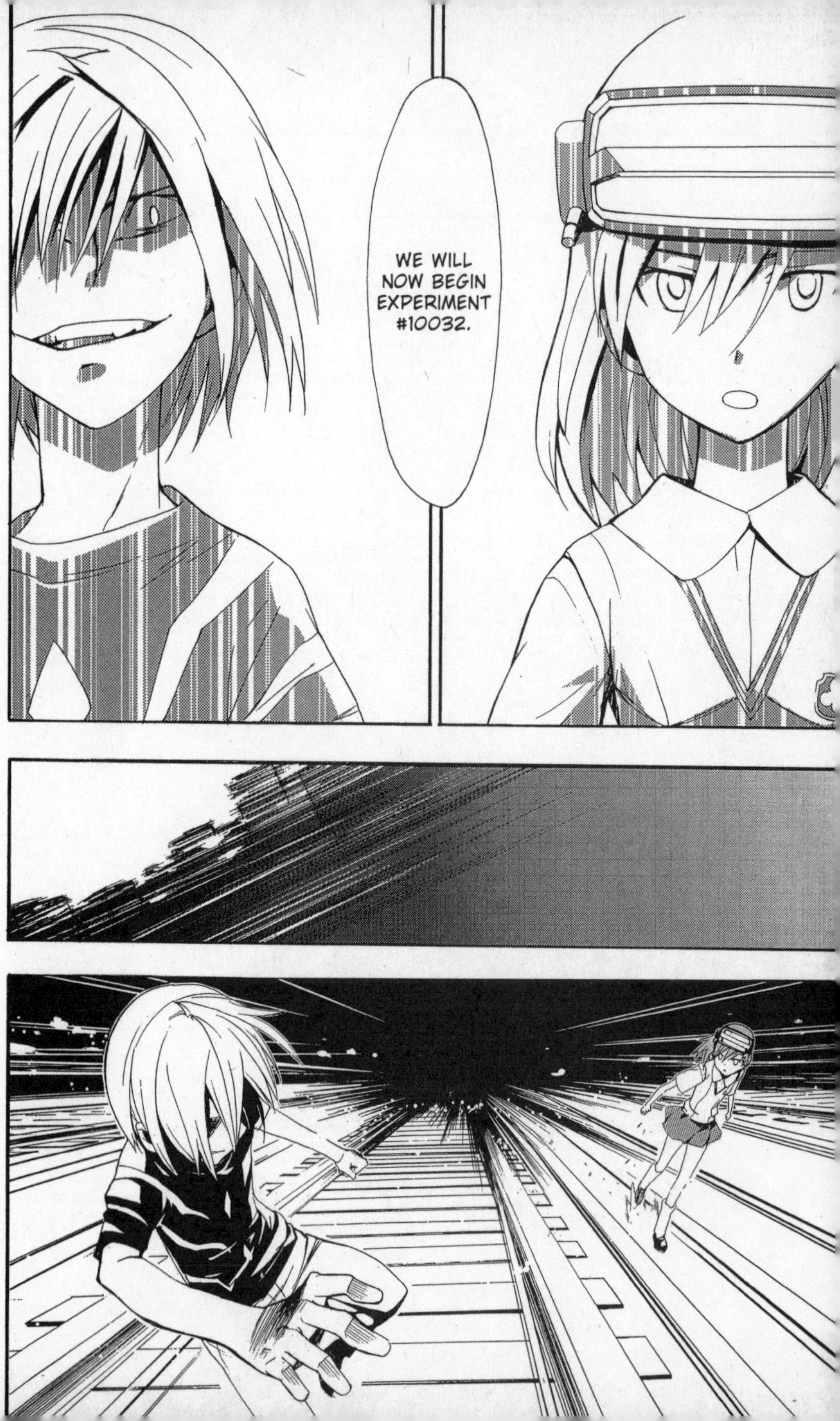
WE WILL NOW BEGIN EXPERIMENT #10032.

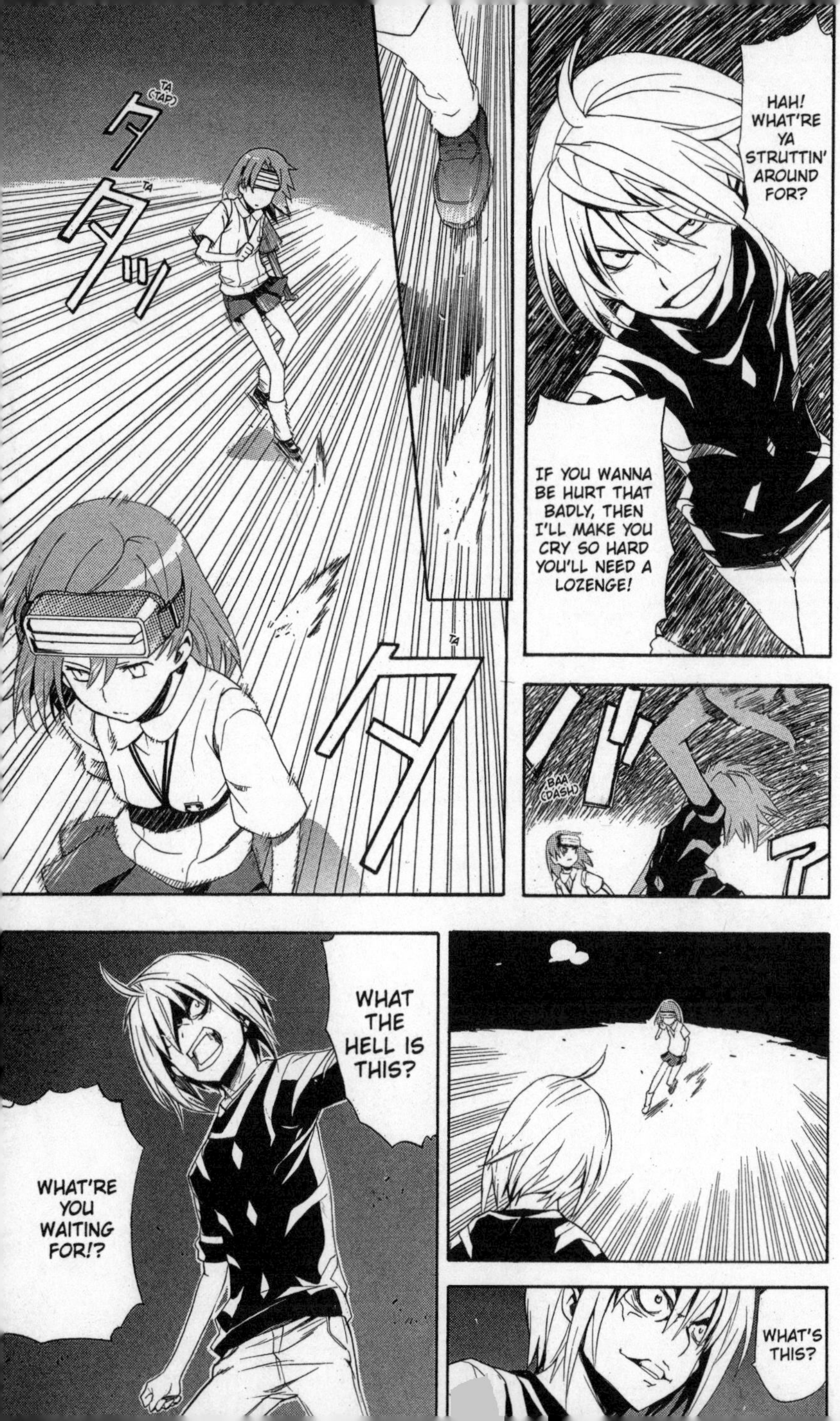
HAH! WHAT'RE YA STRUTTIN' AROUND FOR?
IF YOU WANNA BE HURT THAT BADLY, THEN I'LL MAKE YOU CRY SO HARD YOU'LL NEED A LOZENGE!
BAA (DASH)
TA (TAP)
TA
TA
WHAT'S THIS?
WHAT THE HELL IS THIS?
WHAT'RE YOU WAITING FOR!?

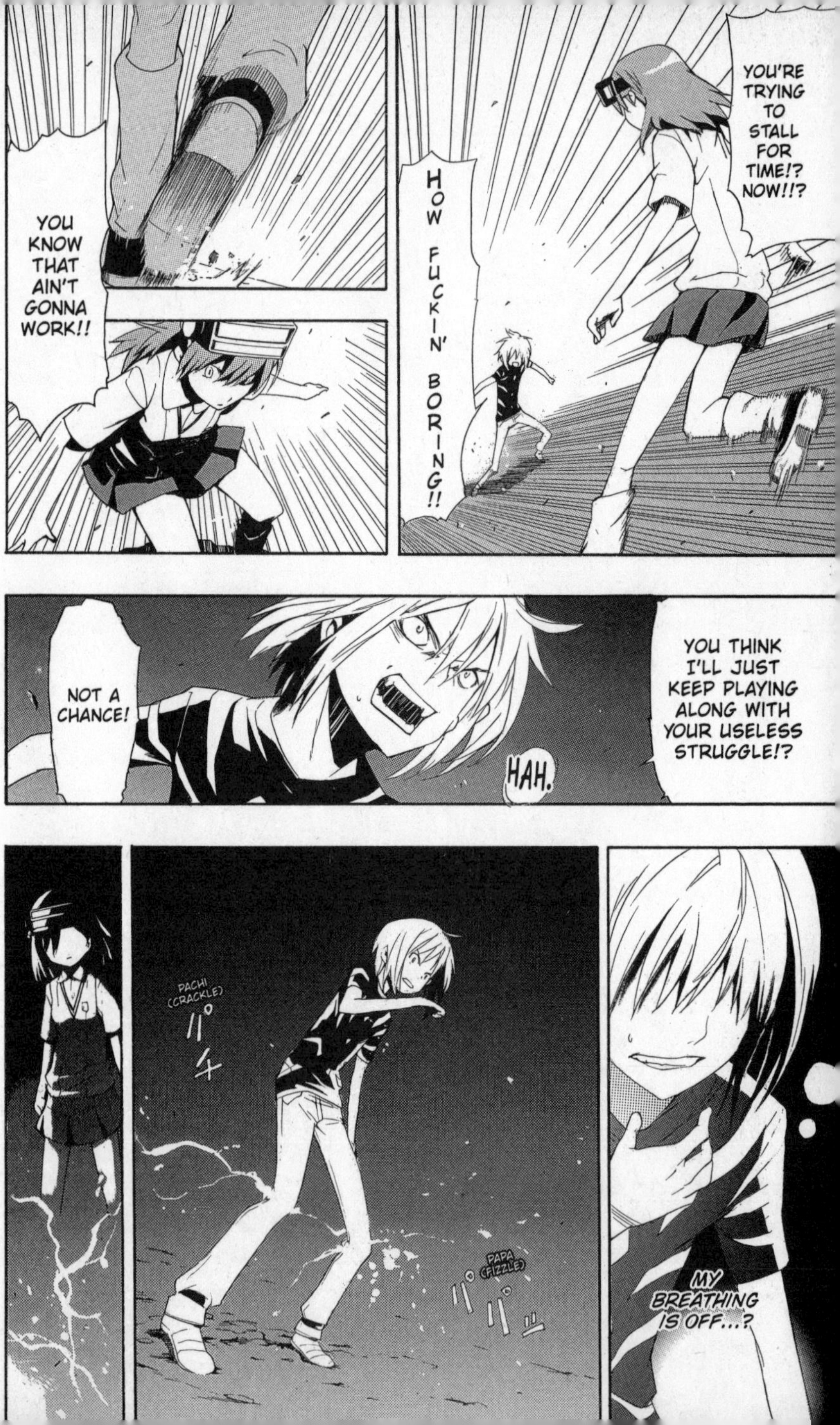
YOU'RE TRYING TO STALL FOR TIME!? NOW!!?
HOW FUCKIN' BORING!!
YOU KNOW THAT AIN'T GONNA WORK!!
YOU THINK I'LL JUST KEEP PLAYING ALONG WITH YOUR USELESS STRUGGLE!?
HAH.
NOT A CHANCE!
MY BREATHING IS OFF...?
PAPA (FIZZLE)
PACHI (CRACKLE)

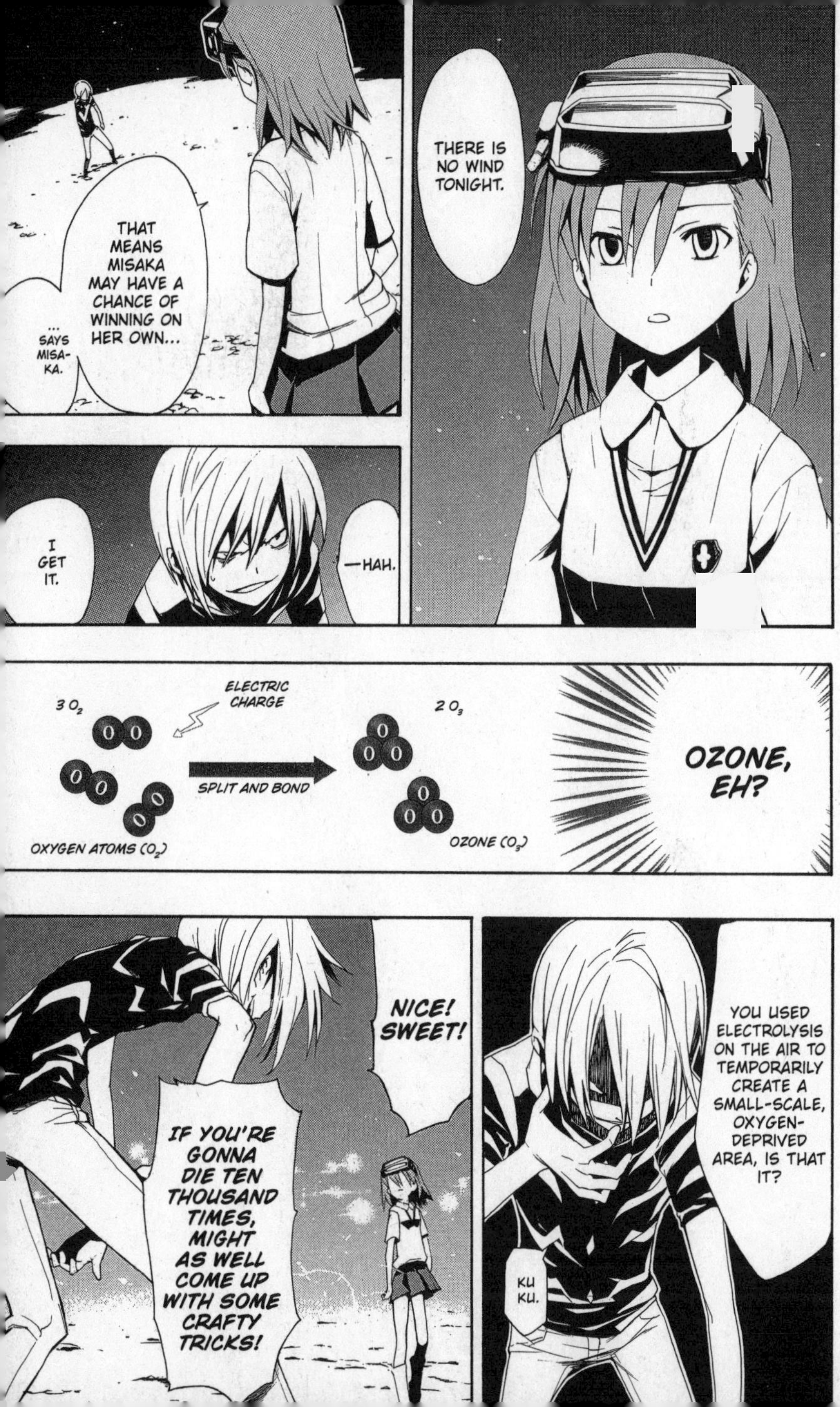
THERE IS NO WIND TONIGHT.
THAT MEANS MISAKA MAY HAVE A CHANCE OF WINNING ON HER OWN...
...SAYS MISAKA.
—HAH.
I GET IT.
OZONE, EH?
$2 O_3$
ELECTRIC CHARGE
$3 O_2$
SPLIT AND BOND
OZONE (O_3)
OXYGEN ATOMS (O_2)
YOU USED ELECTROLYSIS ON THE AIR TO TEMPORARILY CREATE A SMALL-SCALE, OXYGEN-DEPRIVED AREA, IS THAT IT?
KU KU.
NICE! SWEET!
IF YOU'RE GONNA DIE TEN THOUSAND TIMES, MIGHT AS WELL COME UP WITH SOME CRAFTY TRICKS!

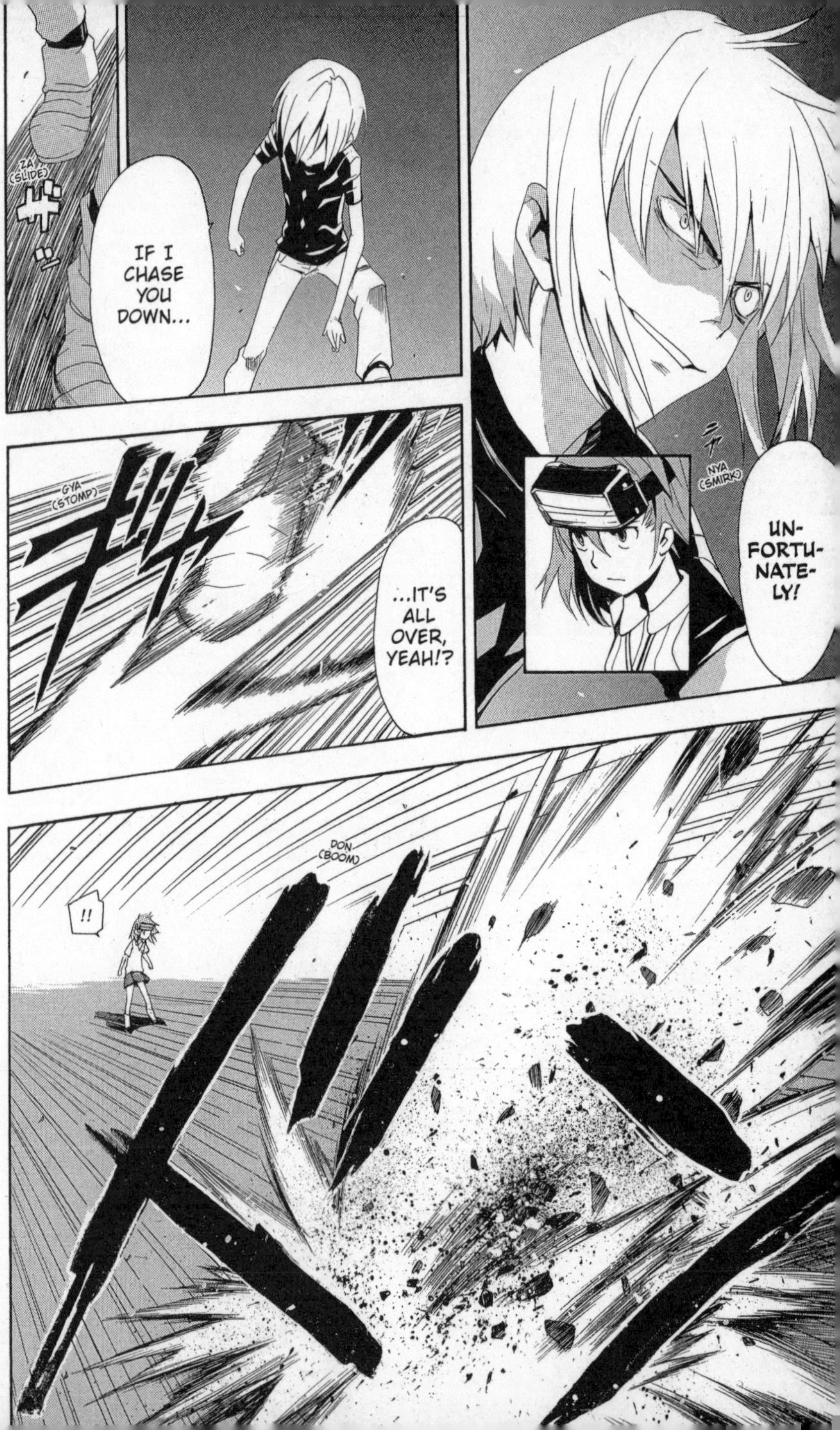
NYA (SMIRK)
UN-FORTU-NATE-LY!
ZA (SLIDE)
IF I CHASE YOU DOWN...
GYA (STOMP)
...IT'S ALL OVER, YEAH!?
DON (BOOM)
!!

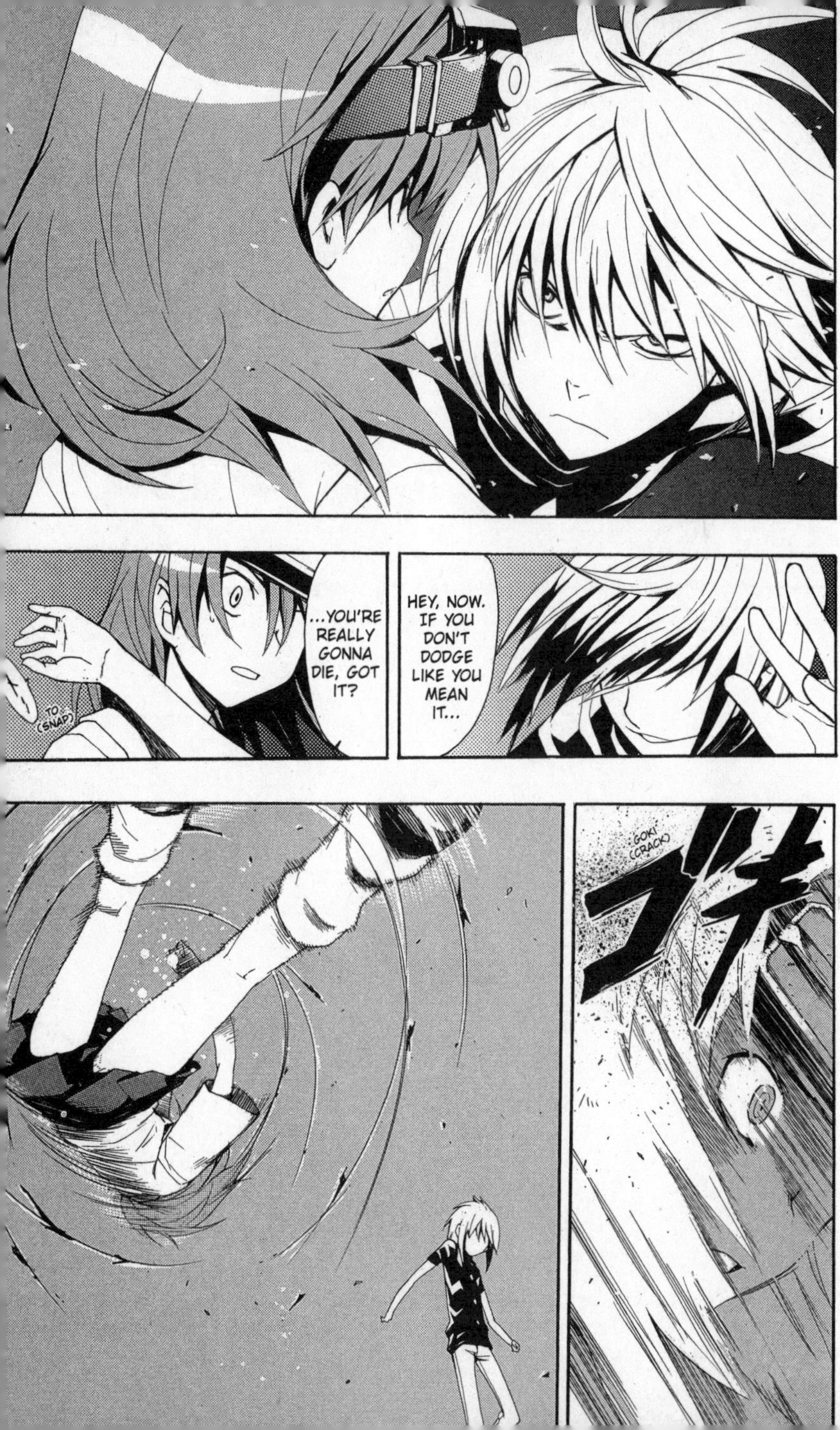
HEY, NOW. IF YOU DON'T DODGE LIKE YOU MEAN IT...
...YOU'RE REALLY GONNA DIE, GOT IT?
TO (SNAP)
GOKI (CRACK)

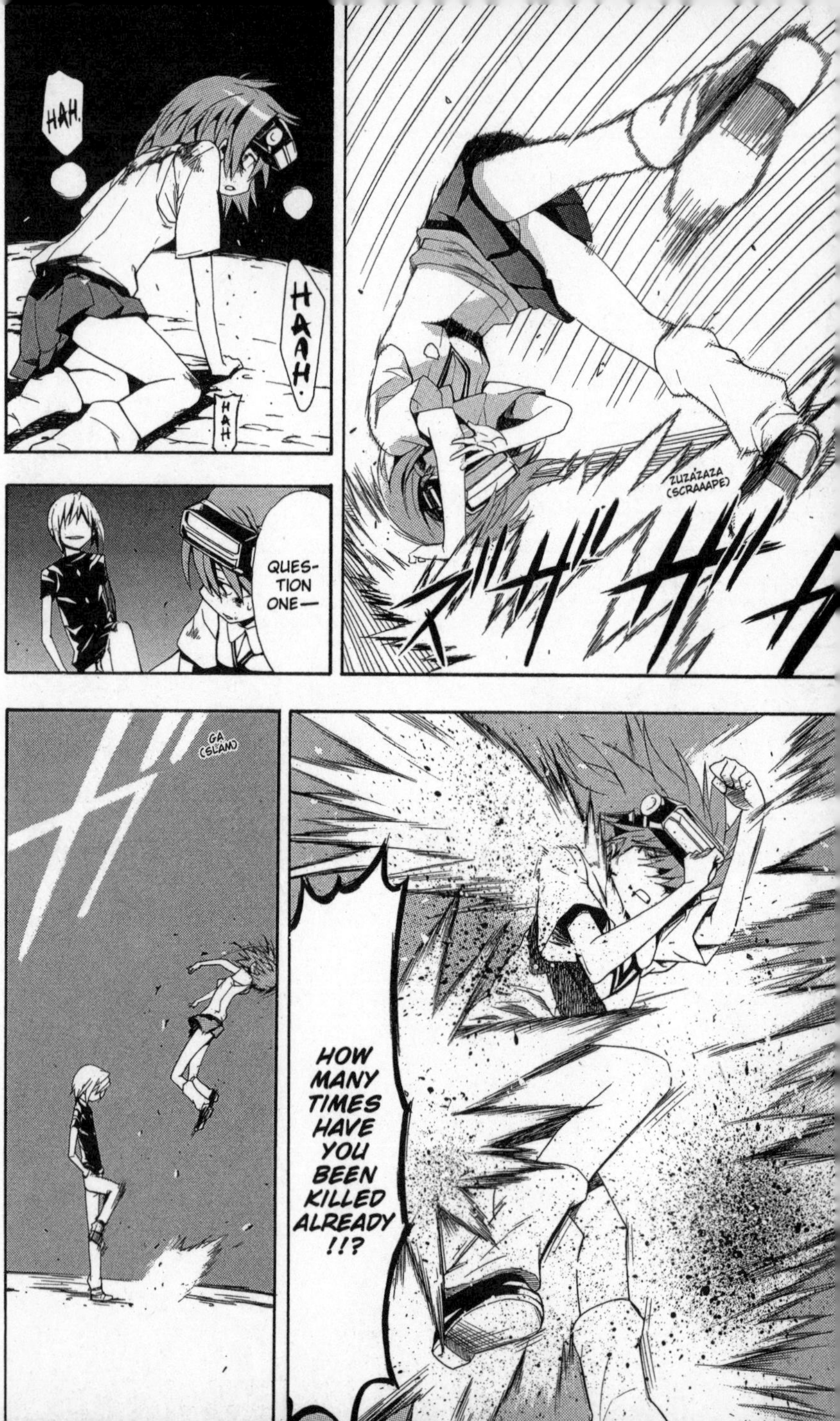
ZUZAZAZA (SCRAAAPE)
HAH.
HAAAH.
HAH.
QUESTION ONE—
HOW MANY TIMES HAVE YOU BEEN KILLED ALREADY!!?
GA (SLAM)

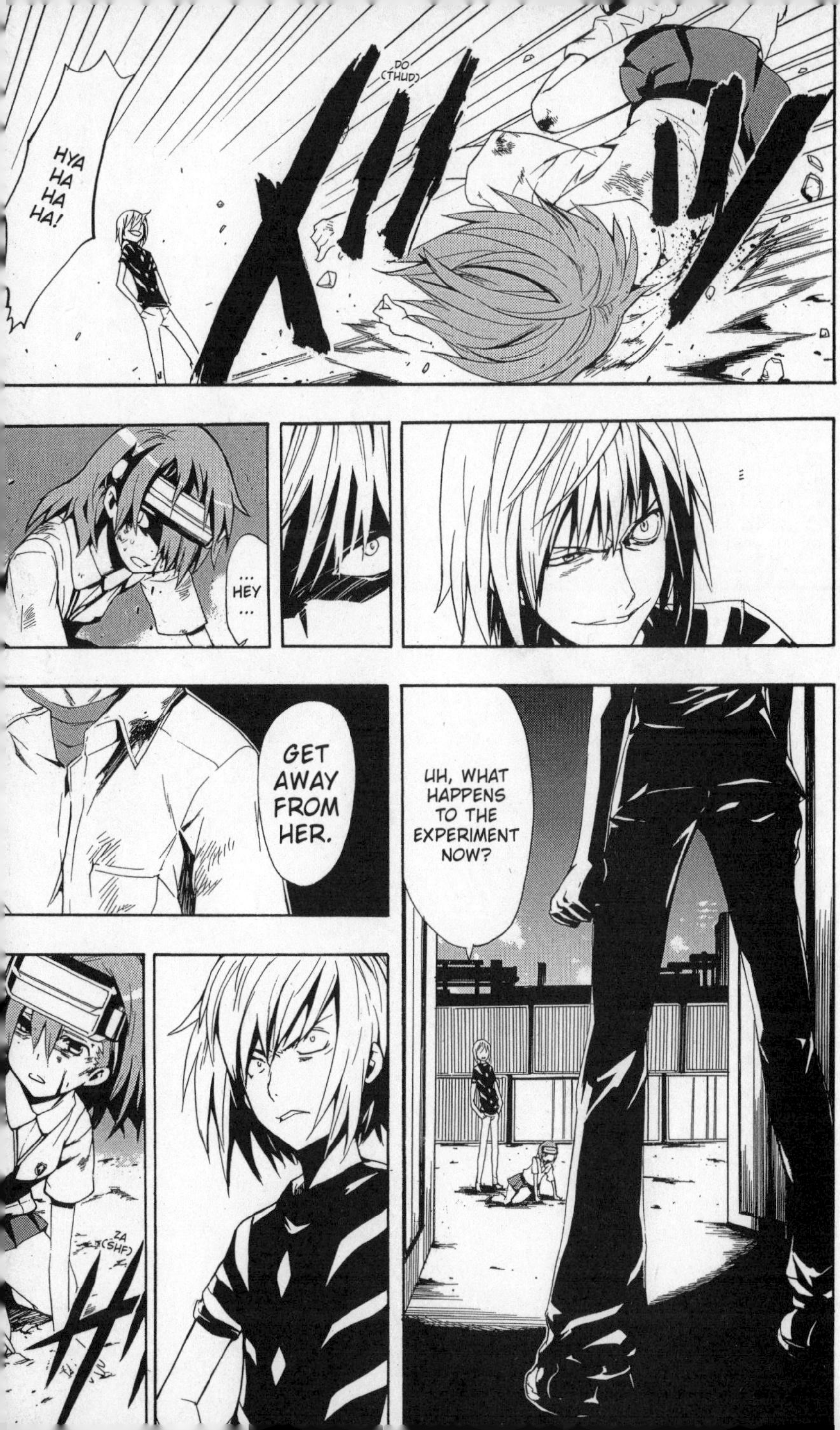
DO (THUD)
HYA HA HA HA!
... HEY ...
UH, WHAT HAPPENS TO THE EXPERIMENT NOW?
GET AWAY FROM HER.
ZA (SHF)

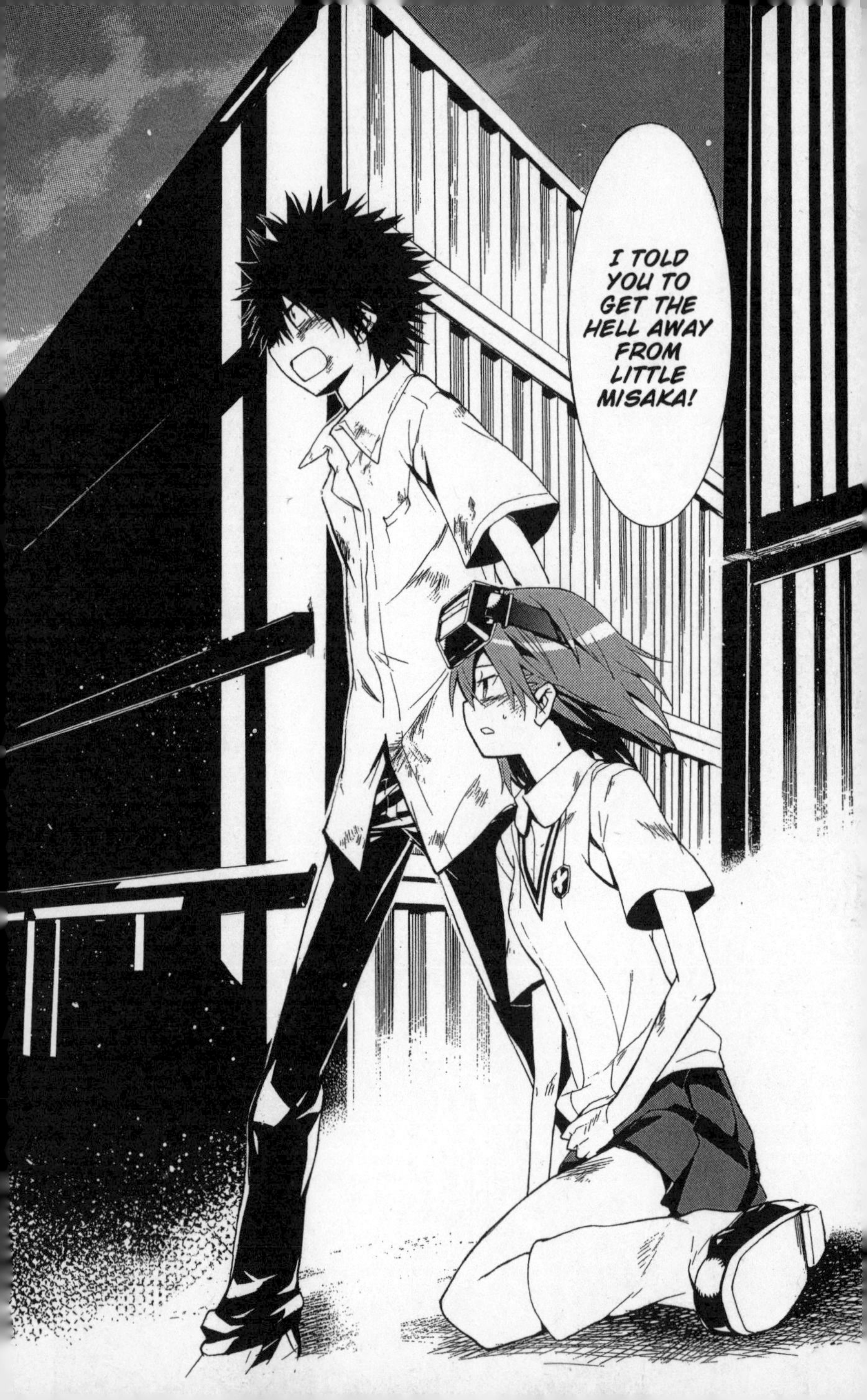
I TOLD YOU TO GET THE HELL AWAY FROM LITTLE MISAKA!

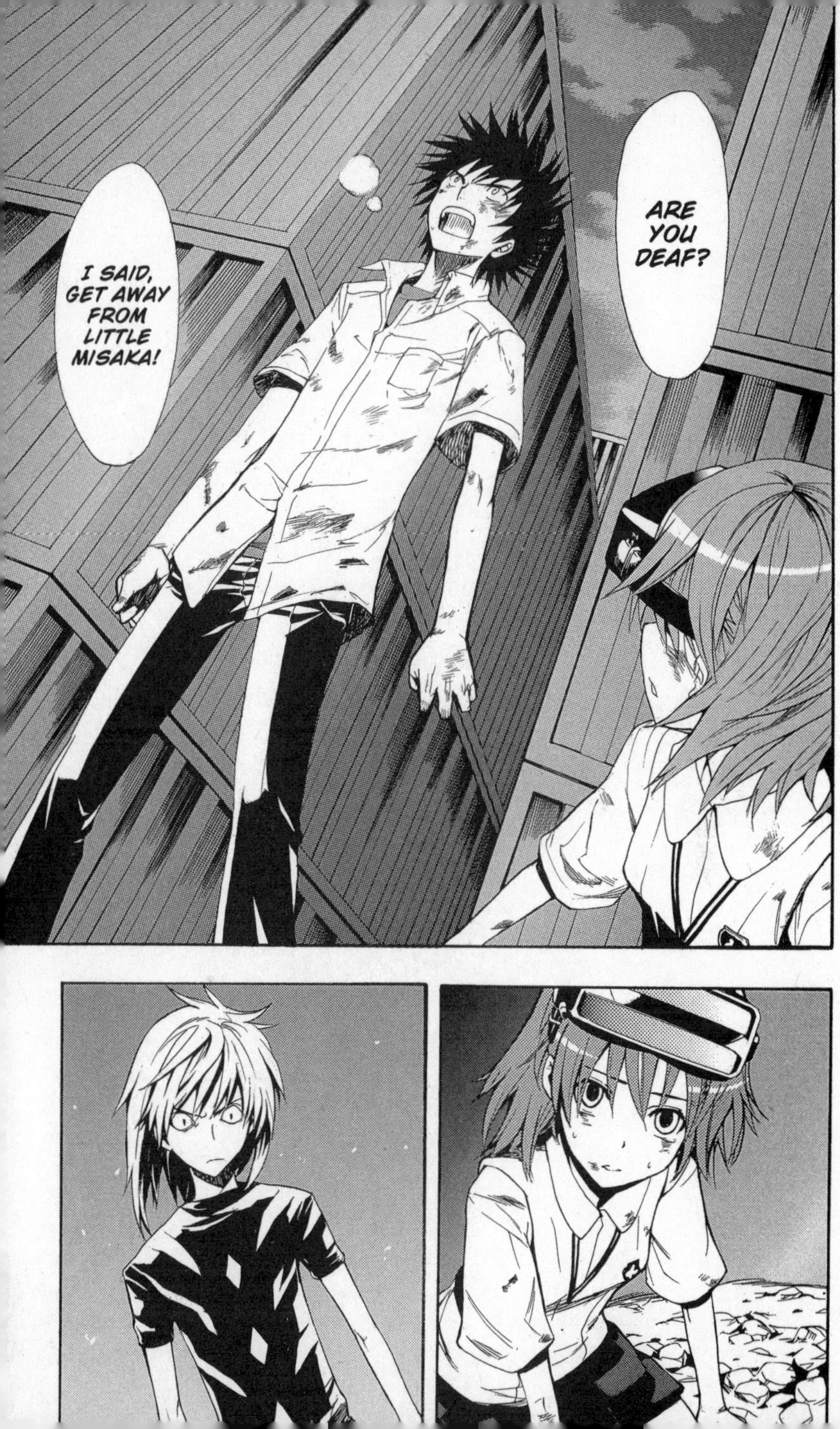
ARE YOU DEAF?
I SAID, GET AWAY FROM LITTLE MISAKA!

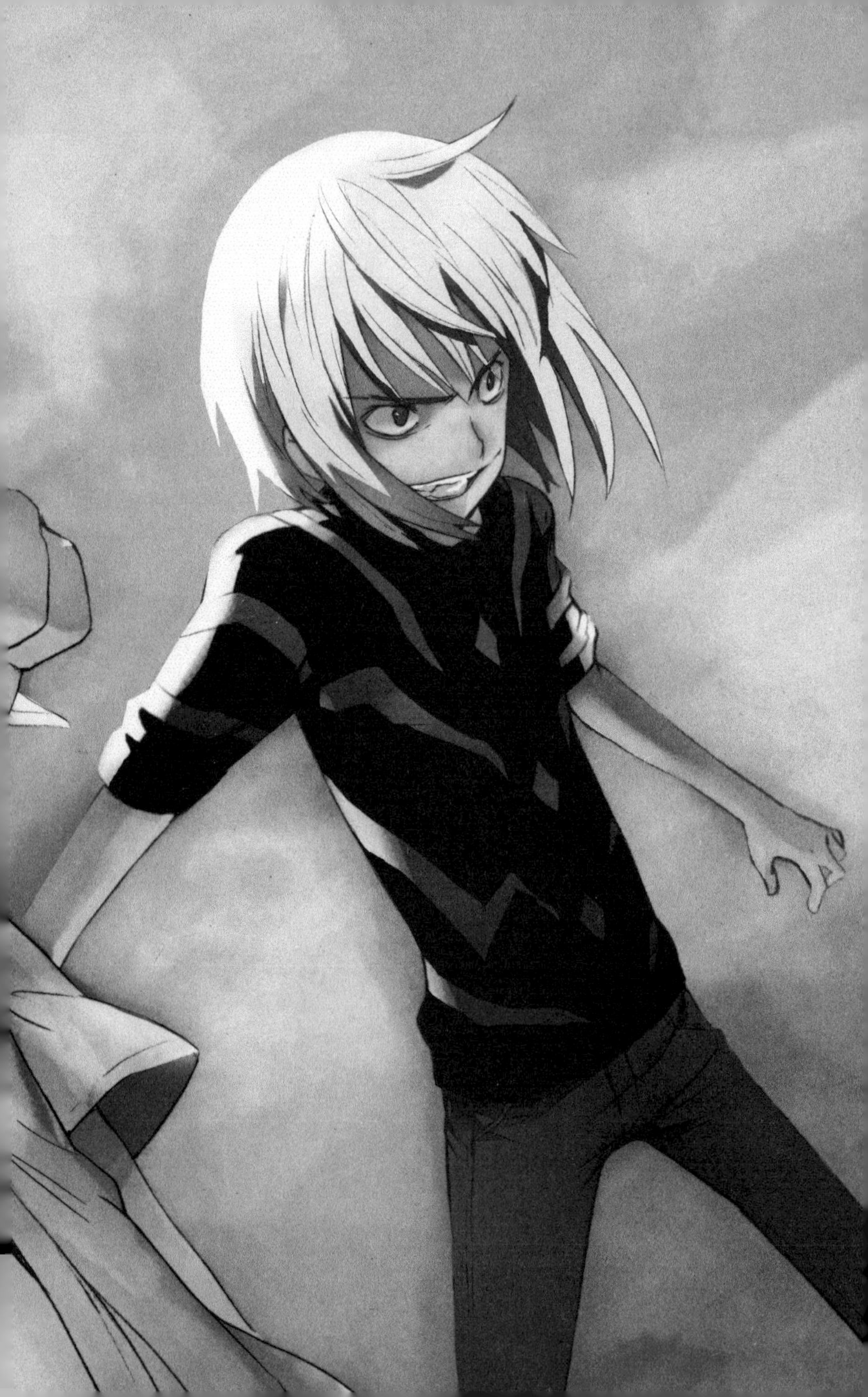

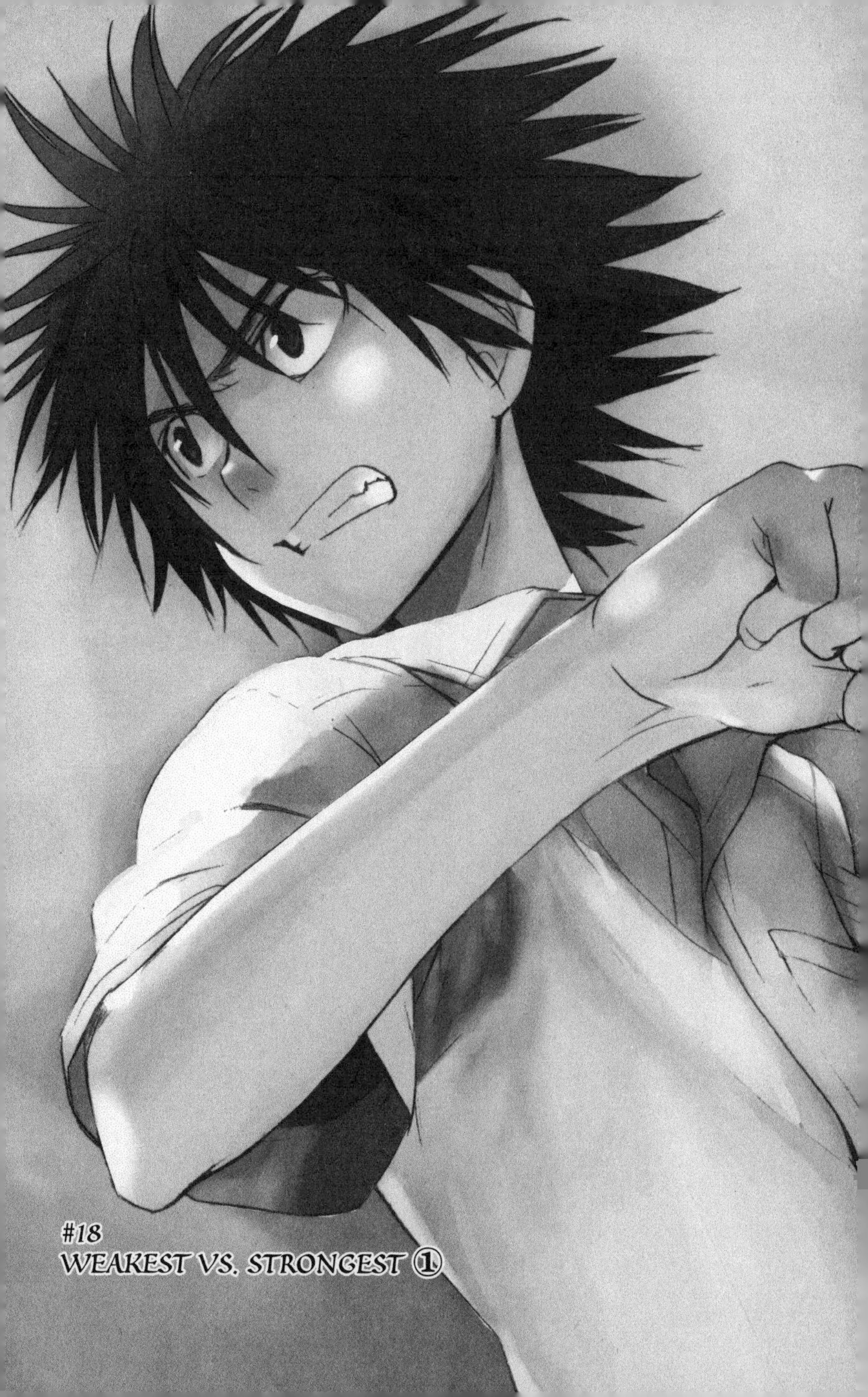
#18
WEAKEST VS. STRONGEST ①

A Certain Magical Index

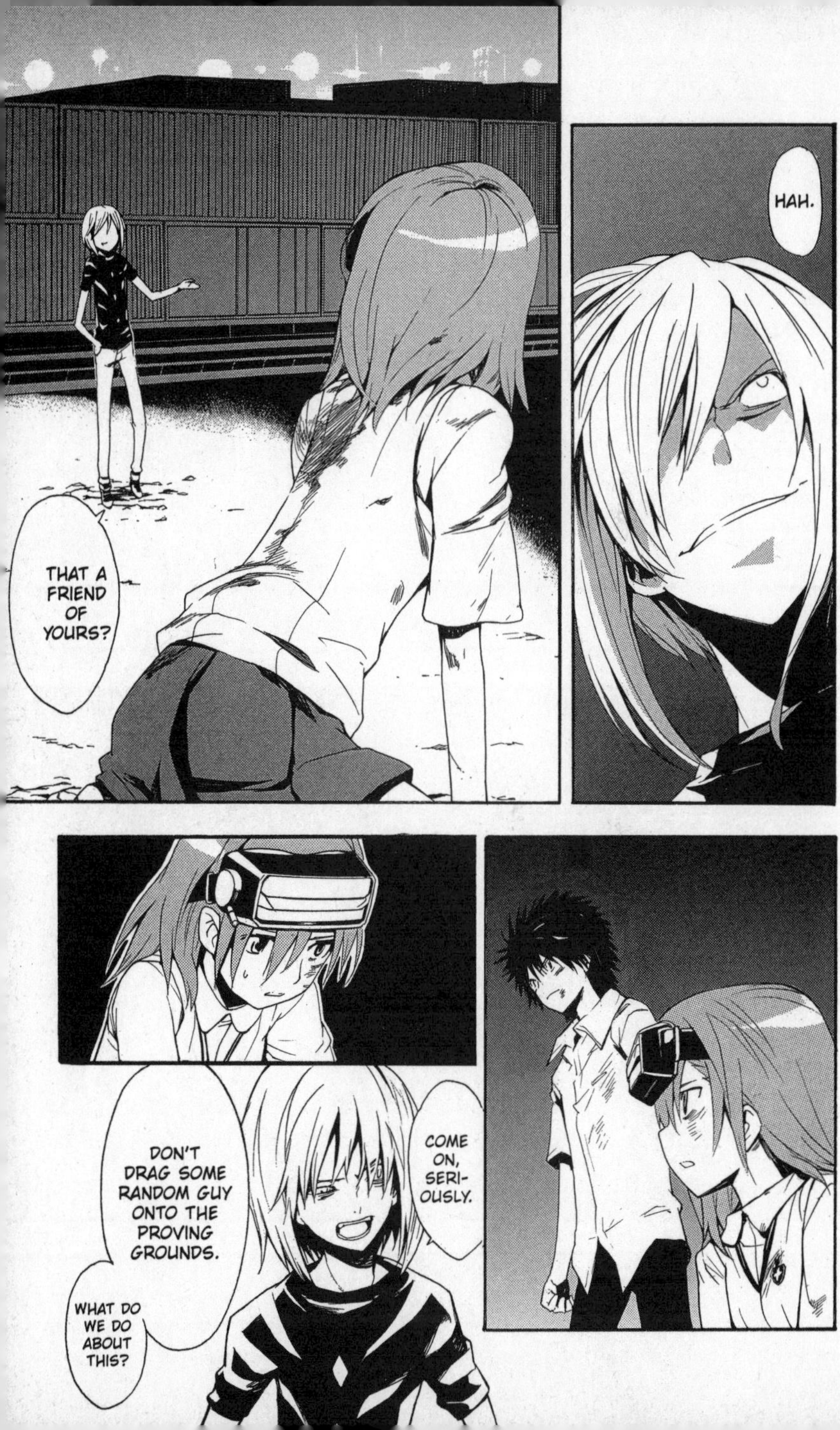
HAH.
THAT A FRIEND OF YOURS?
COME ON, SERI-OUSLY.
DON'T DRAG SOME RANDOM GUY ONTO THE PROVING GROUNDS.
WHAT DO WE DO ABOUT THIS?

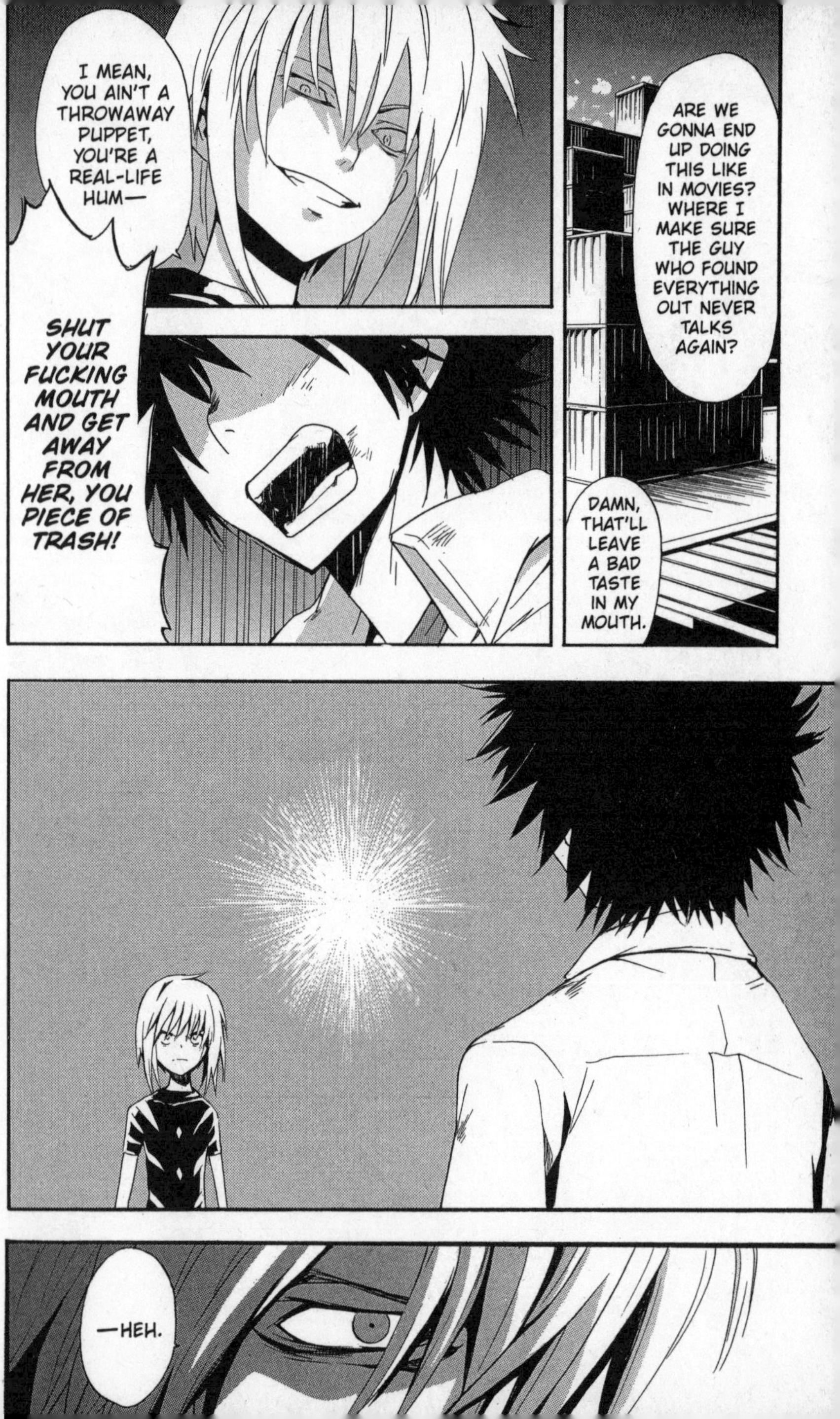
ARE WE GONNA END UP DOING THIS LIKE IN MOVIES? WHERE I MAKE SURE THE GUY WHO FOUND EVERYTHING OUT NEVER TALKS AGAIN?
DAMN, THAT'LL LEAVE A BAD TASTE IN MY MOUTH.
I MEAN, YOU AIN'T A THROWAWAY PUPPET, YOU'RE A REAL-LIFE HUM—
SHUT YOUR FUCKING MOUTH AND GET AWAY FROM HER, YOU PIECE OF TRASH!
—HEH.

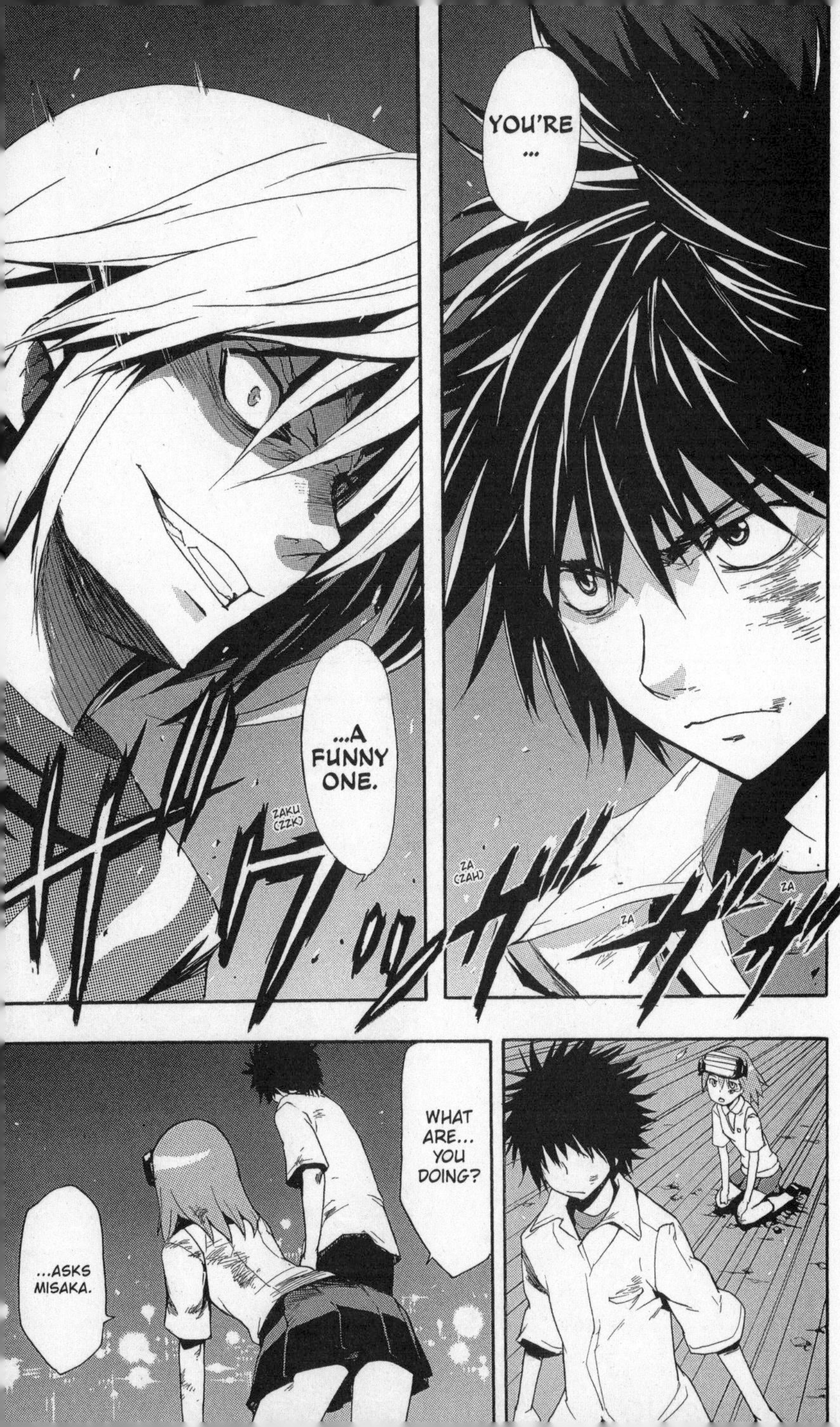

YOU'RE ...
ZA (ZAH)
ZA
ZA
...A FUNNY ONE.
ZAKU (ZZK)
WHAT ARE... YOU DOING?
...ASKS MISAKA.

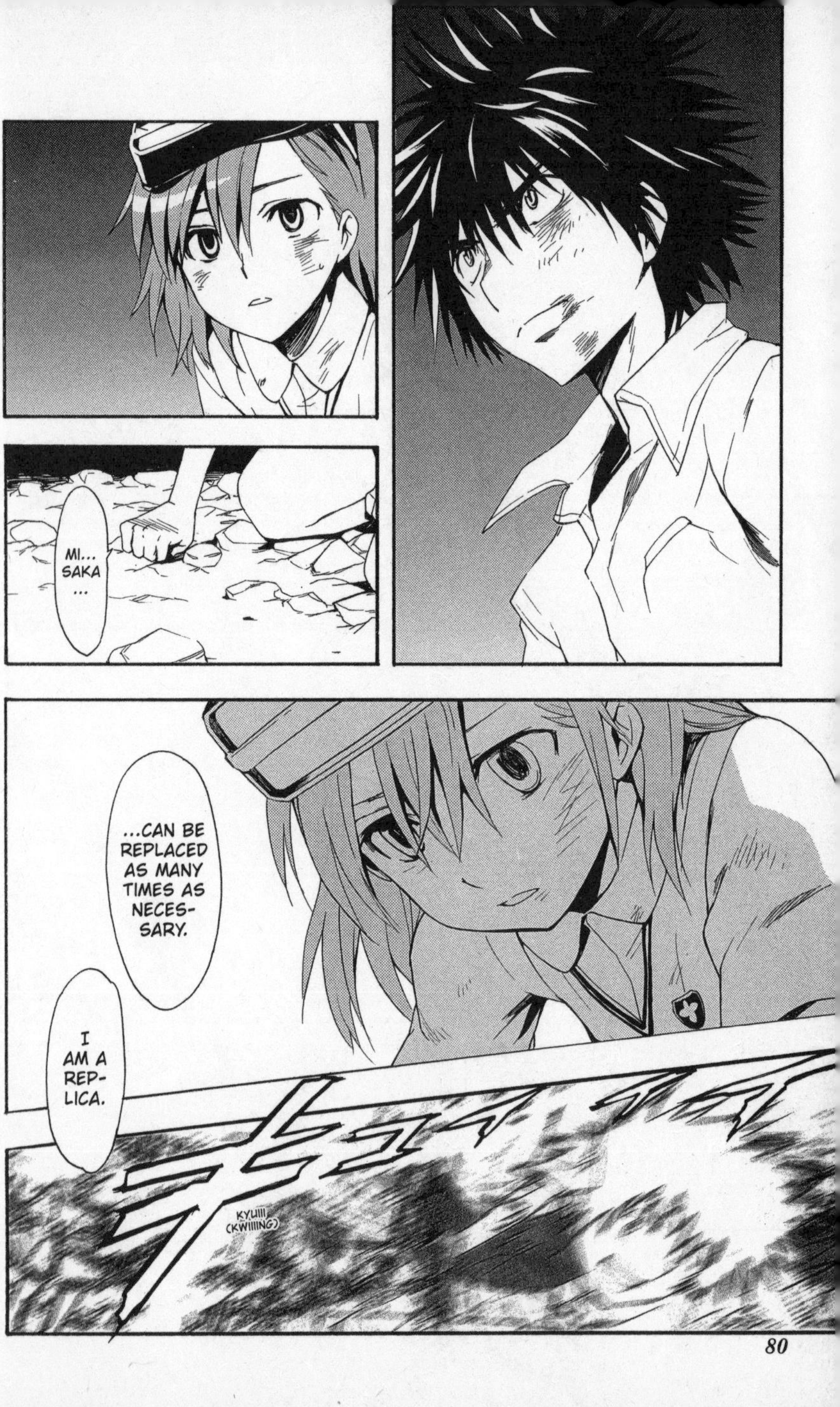
MI... SAKA ...
...CAN BE REPLACED AS MANY TIMES AS NECES-SARY.
I AM A REP-LICA.
KYUIII (KWIIIING)

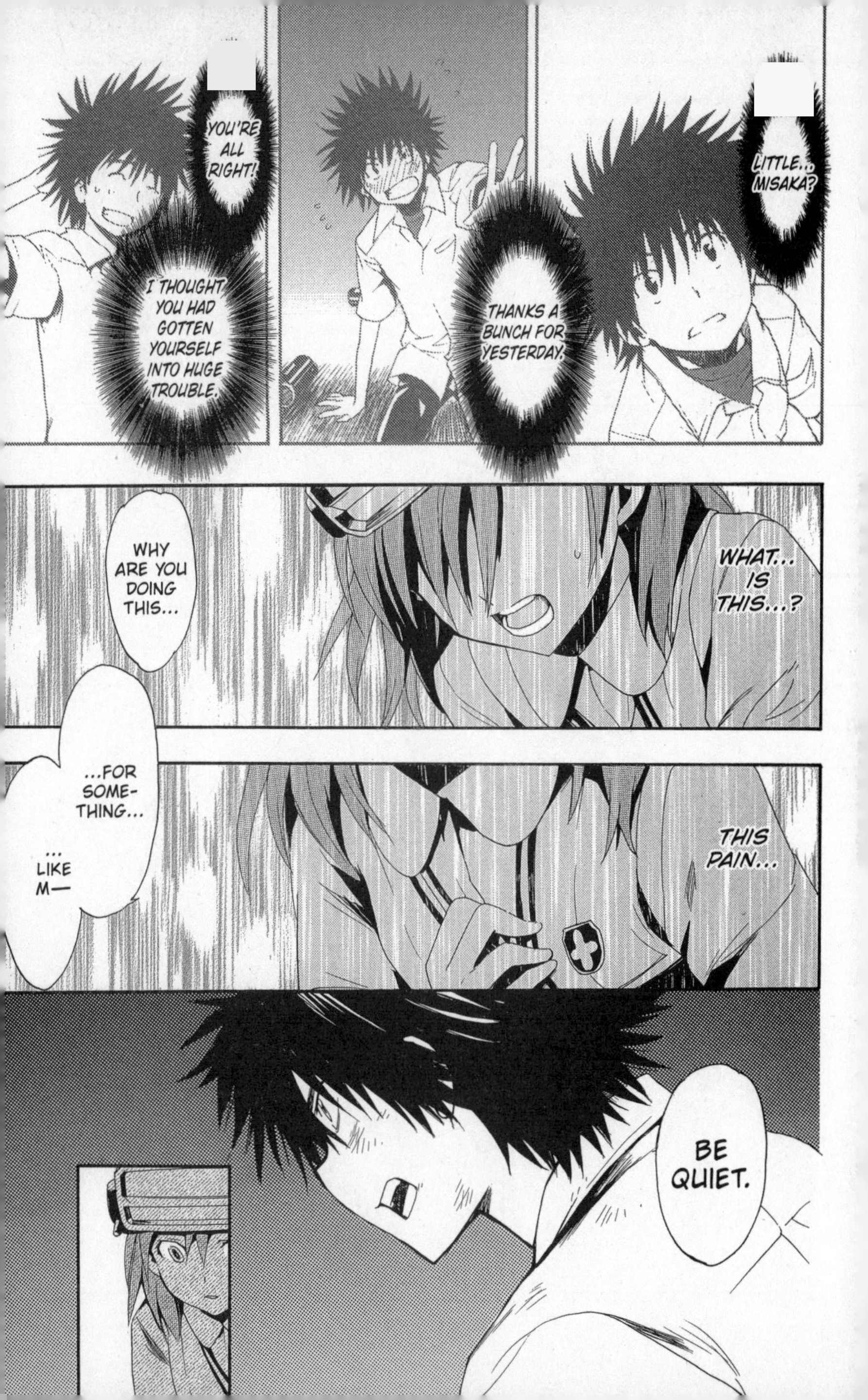
LITTLE... MISAKA?
THANKS A BUNCH FOR YESTERDAY.
YOU'RE ALL RIGHT!
I THOUGHT YOU HAD GOTTEN YOURSELF INTO HUGE TROUBLE.
WHAT... IS THIS...?
WHY ARE YOU DOING THIS...
THIS PAIN...
...FOR SOMETHING... ...LIKE M—
BE QUIET.

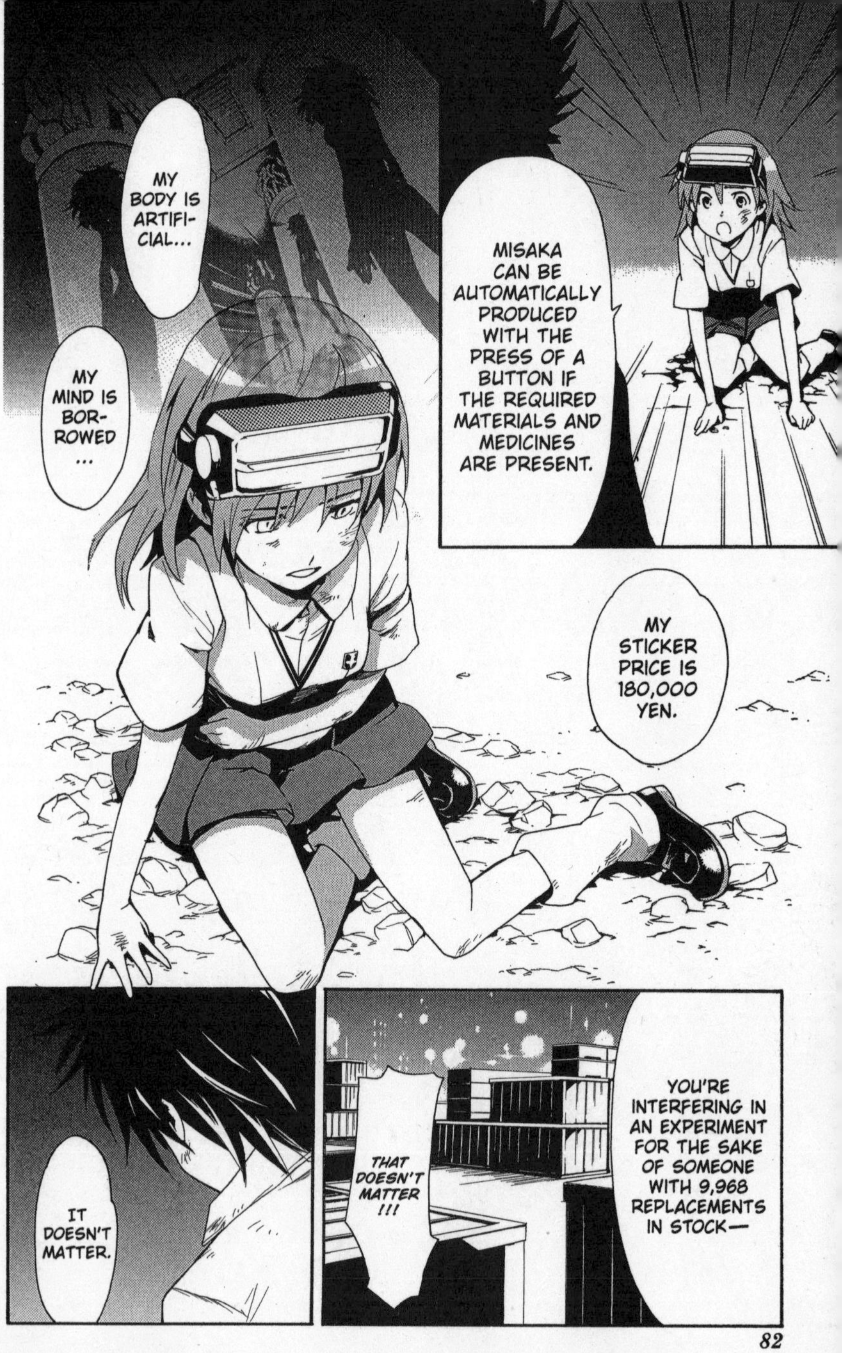
MISAKA CAN BE AUTOMATICALLY PRODUCED WITH THE PRESS OF A BUTTON IF THE REQUIRED MATERIALS AND MEDICINES ARE PRESENT.
MY BODY IS ARTIFICIAL...
MY MIND IS BORROWED...
MY STICKER PRICE IS 180,000 YEN.
YOU'RE INTERFERING IN AN EXPERIMENT FOR THE SAKE OF SOMEONE WITH 9,968 REPLACEMENTS IN STOCK—
THAT DOESN'T MATTER!!!
IT DOESN'T MATTER.

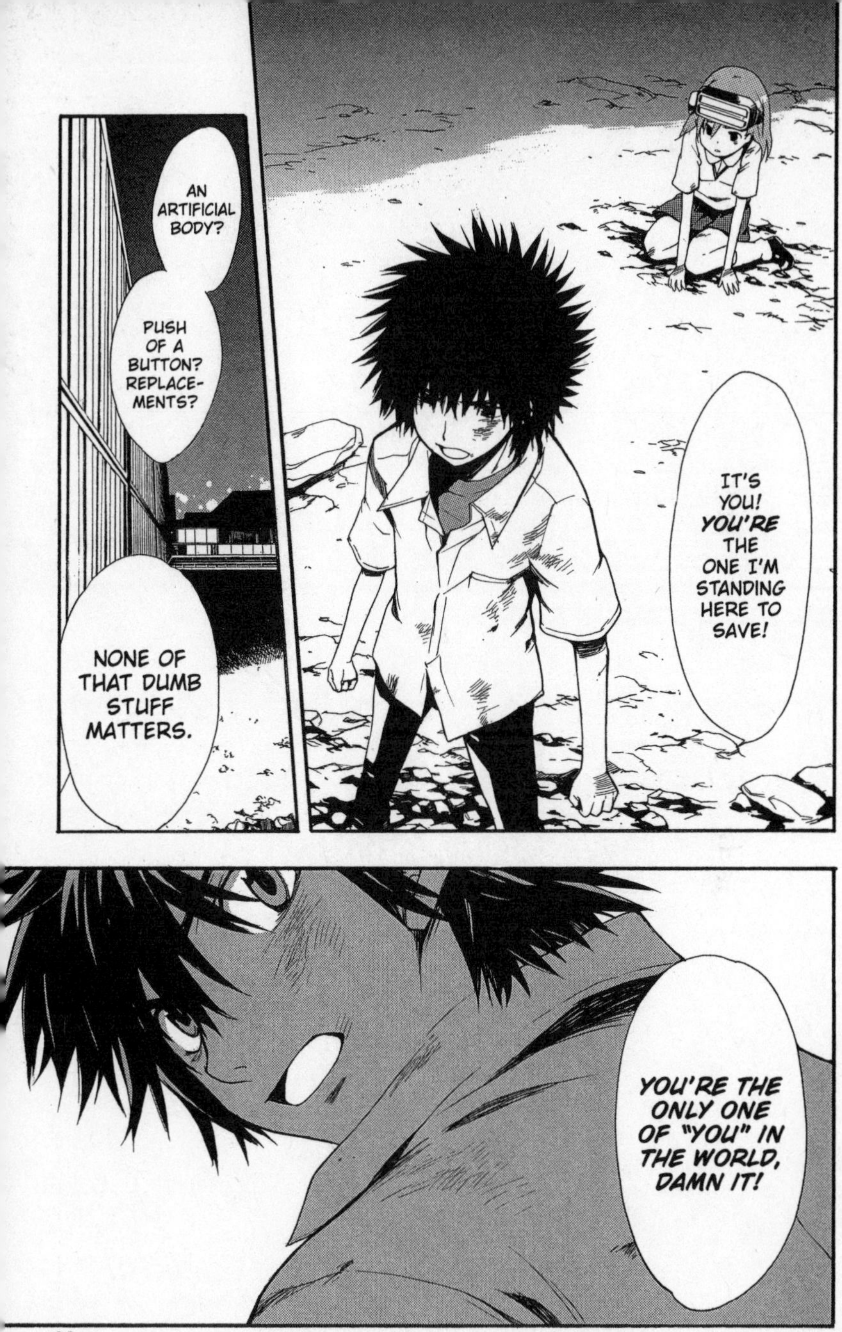
IT'S YOU! YOU'RE THE ONE I'M STANDING HERE TO SAVE!
AN ARTIFICIAL BODY?
PUSH OF A BUTTON? REPLACEMENTS?
NONE OF THAT DUMB STUFF MATTERS.
YOU'RE THE ONLY ONE OF "YOU" IN THE WORLD, DAMN IT!

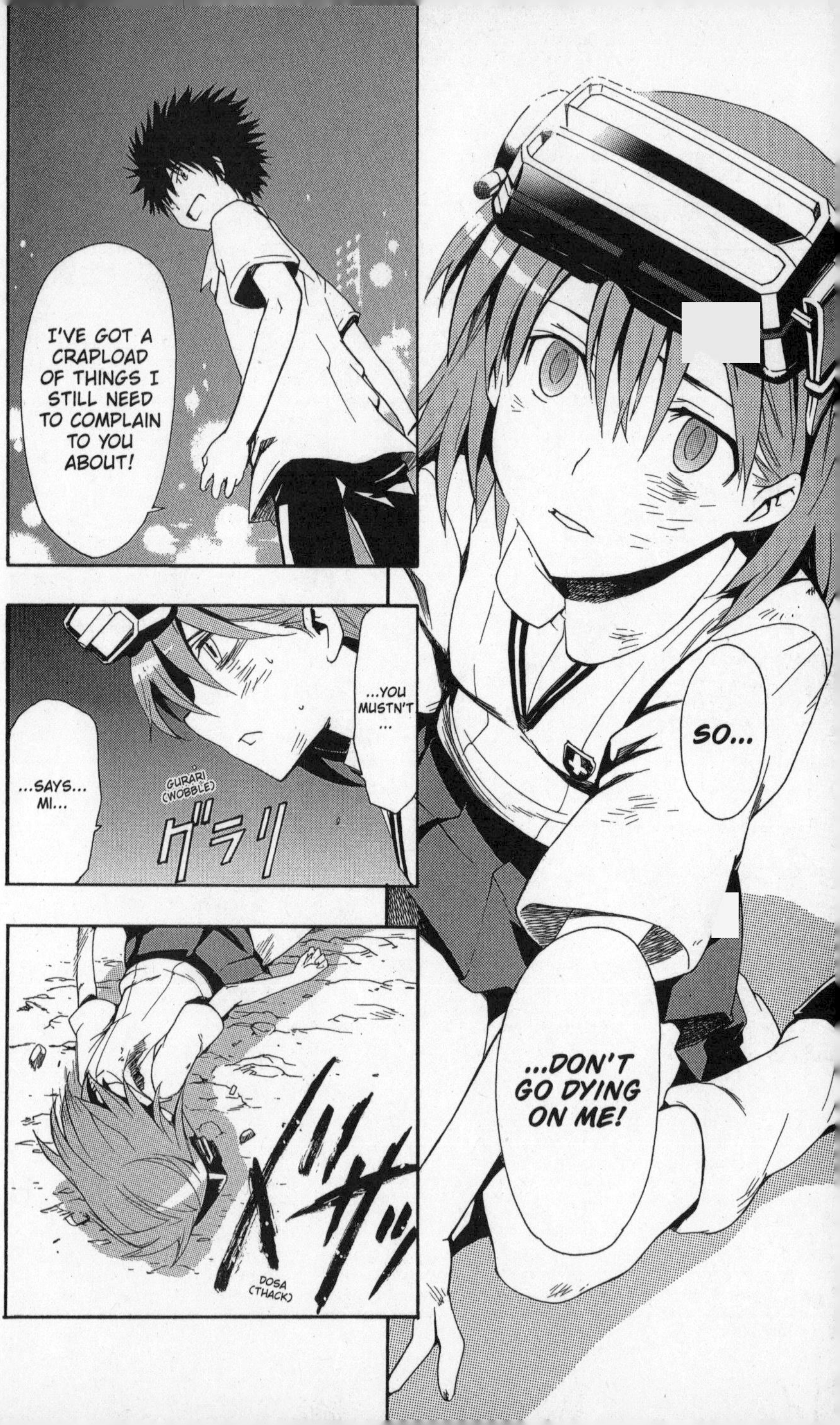
SO...
...DON'T GO DYING ON ME!
I'VE GOT A CRAPLOAD OF THINGS I STILL NEED TO COMPLAIN TO YOU ABOUT!
...YOU MUSTN'T ...
...SAYS... MI...
GURARI (WOBBLE)
グラリ
DOSA (THACK)

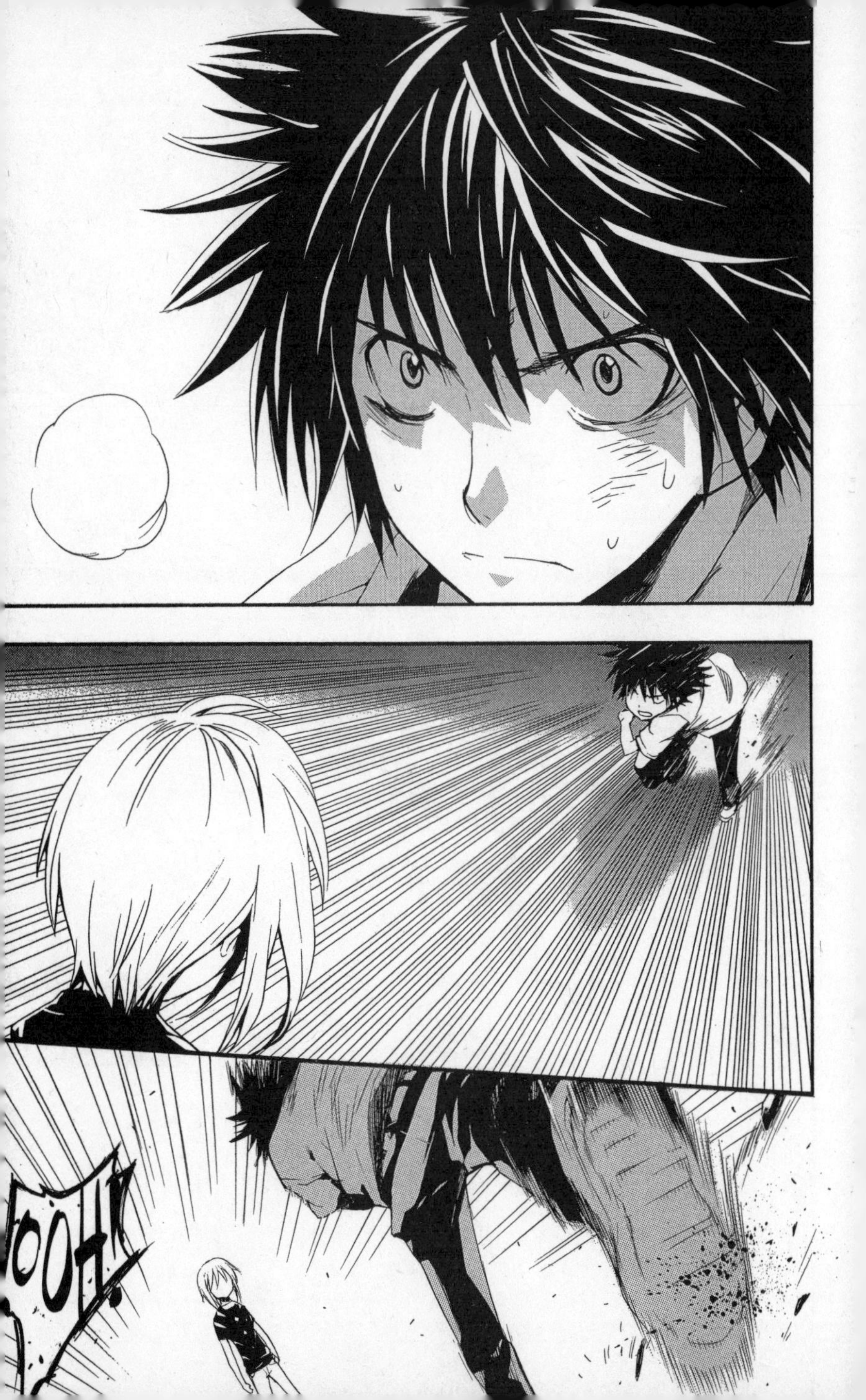
OOH!

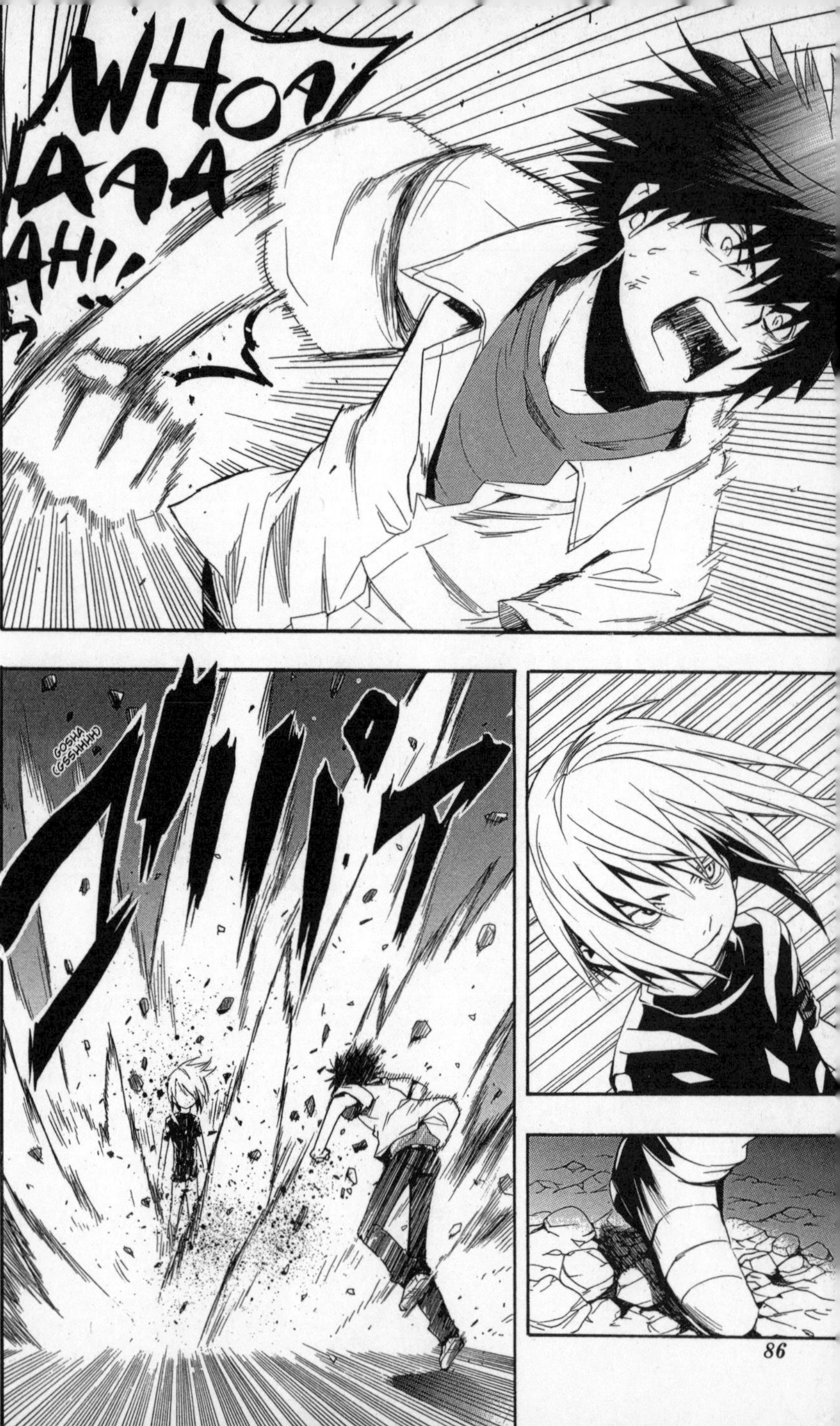
WHOA AAAA AH!!
GOSHA (GSSHHHH)

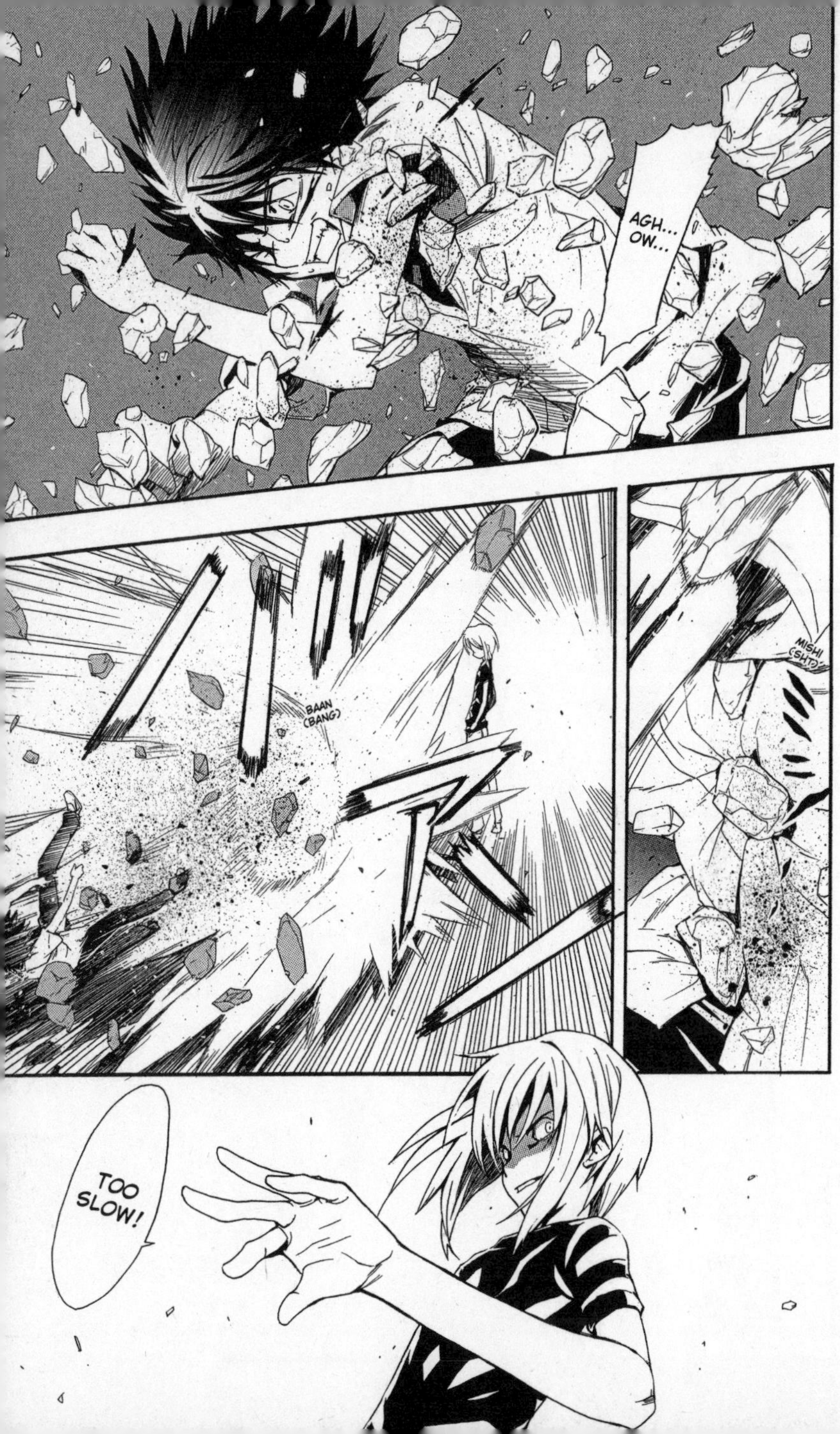
AGH... OW...
MISHI (SHT)
BAAN (BANG)
TOO SLOW!

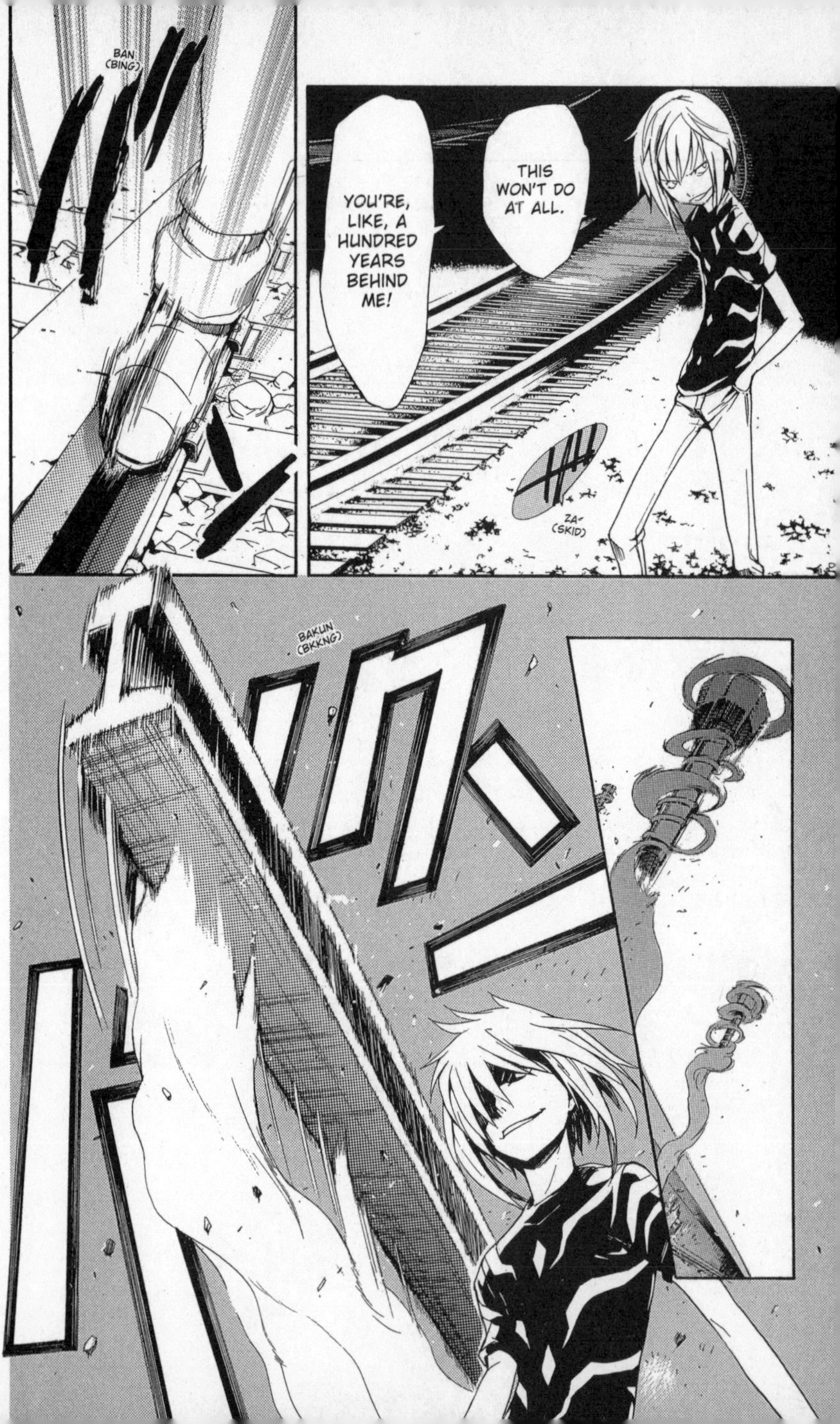
THIS WON'T DO AT ALL.
YOU'RE, LIKE, A HUNDRED YEARS BEHIND ME!
ZA (SKID)
BAN (BING)
BAKUN (BKKNG)

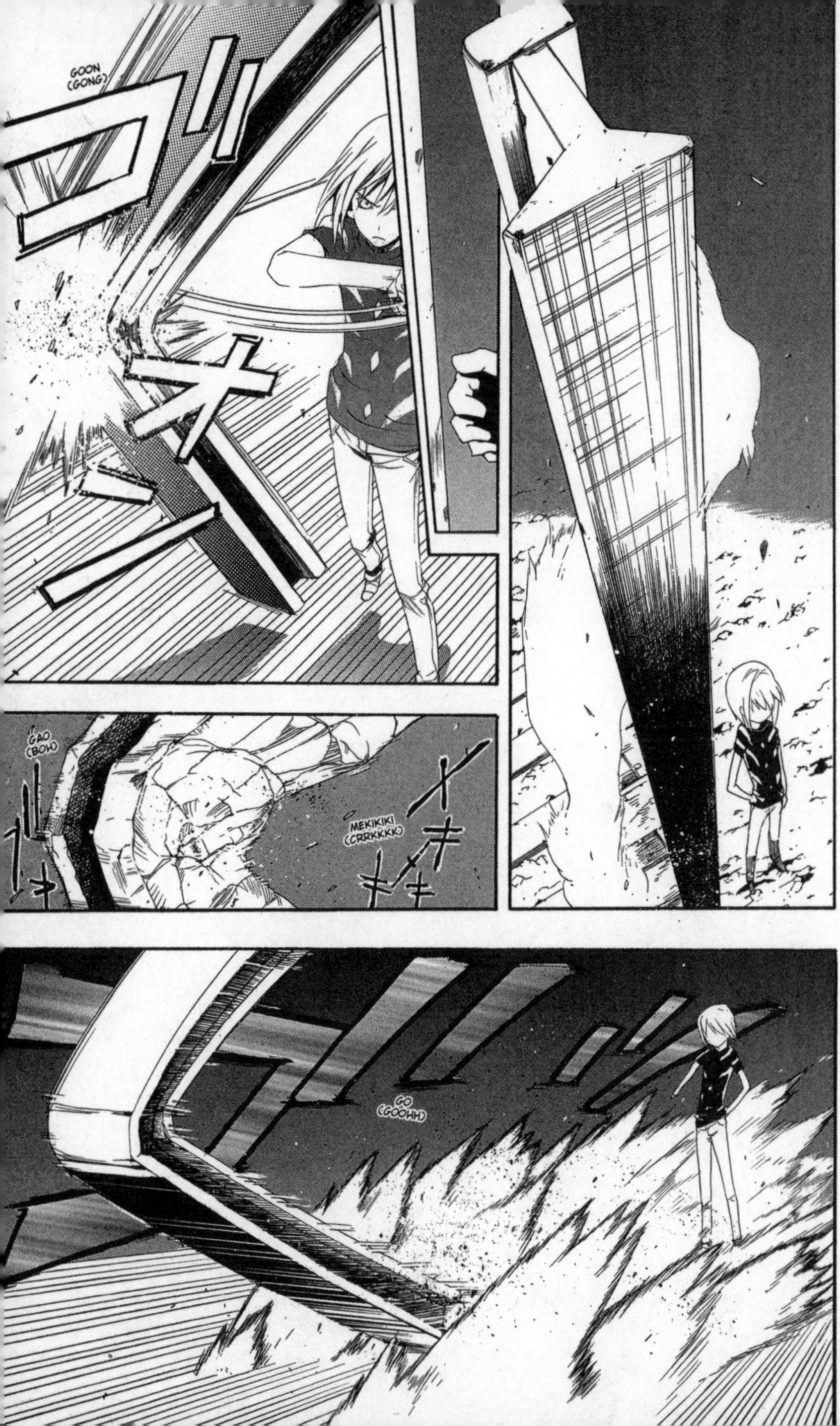
GOON (GONG)
GAO (BOH)
MEKIKIKI (CRRKKKK)
GO (GOOHH)

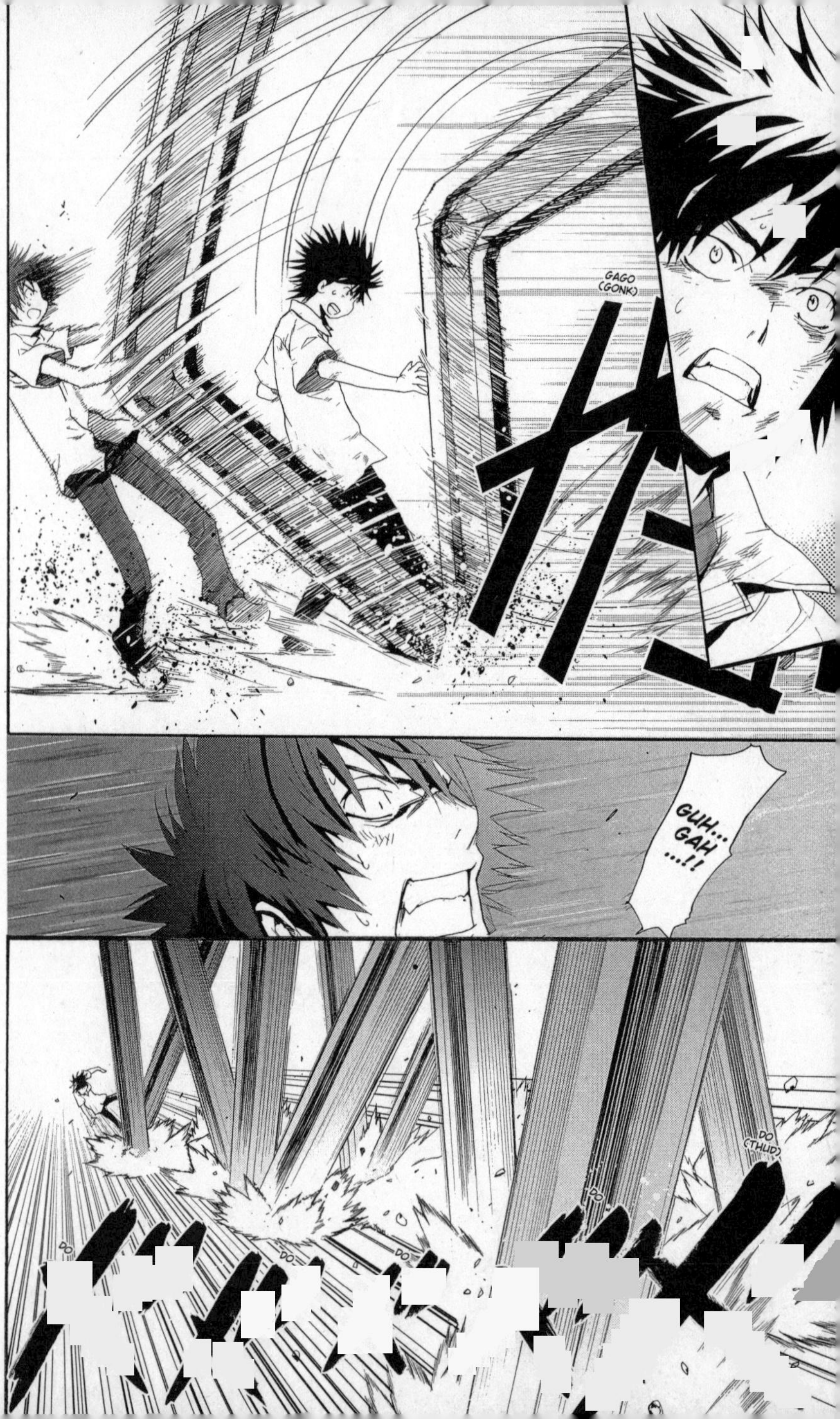
GAGO
(GONK)
GUH... GAH ...!!
DO
(THUD)
DO

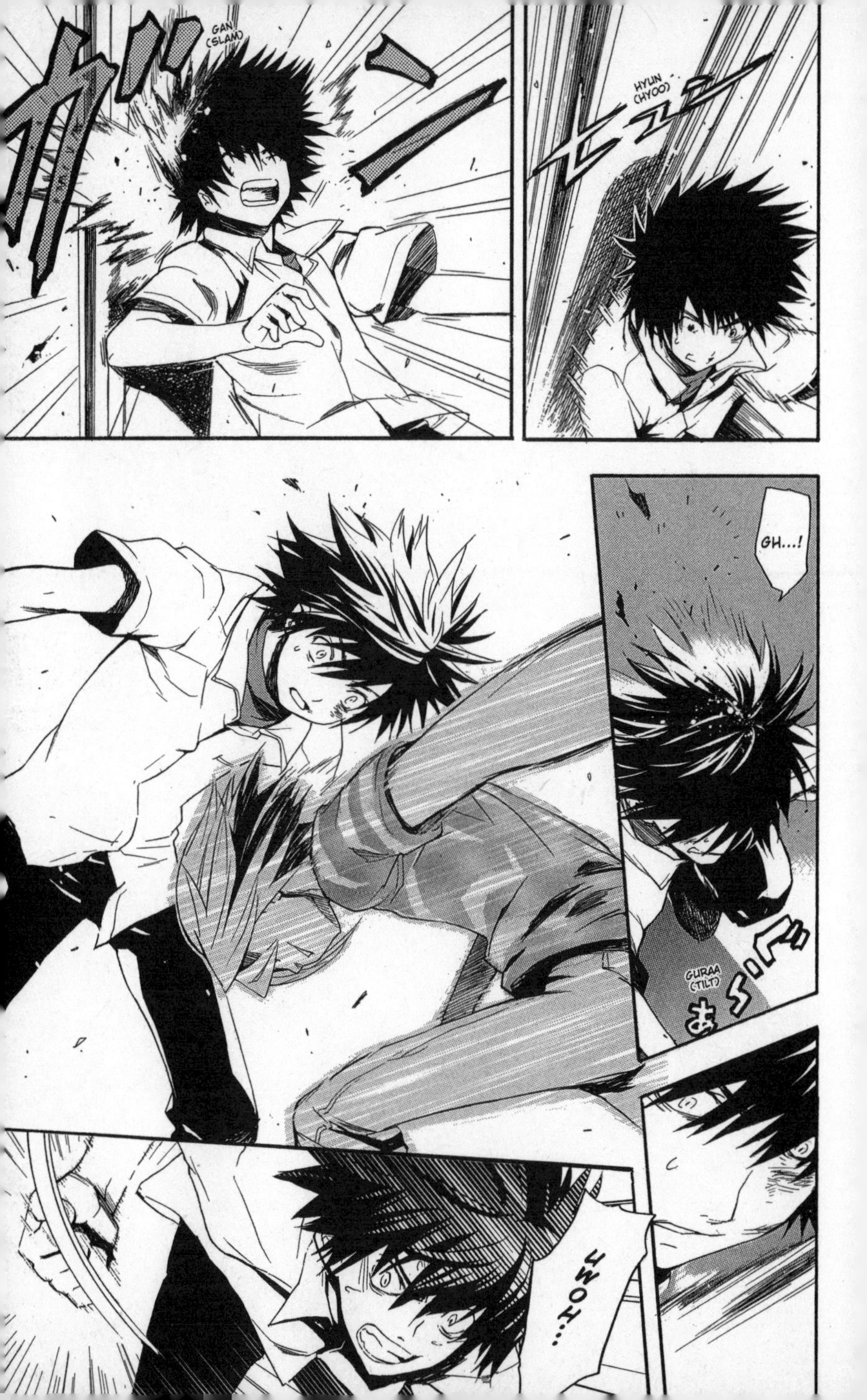
HYUN (HYOO)
GAN (SLAM)
GH...!
GURAA (TILT)
WHOA...

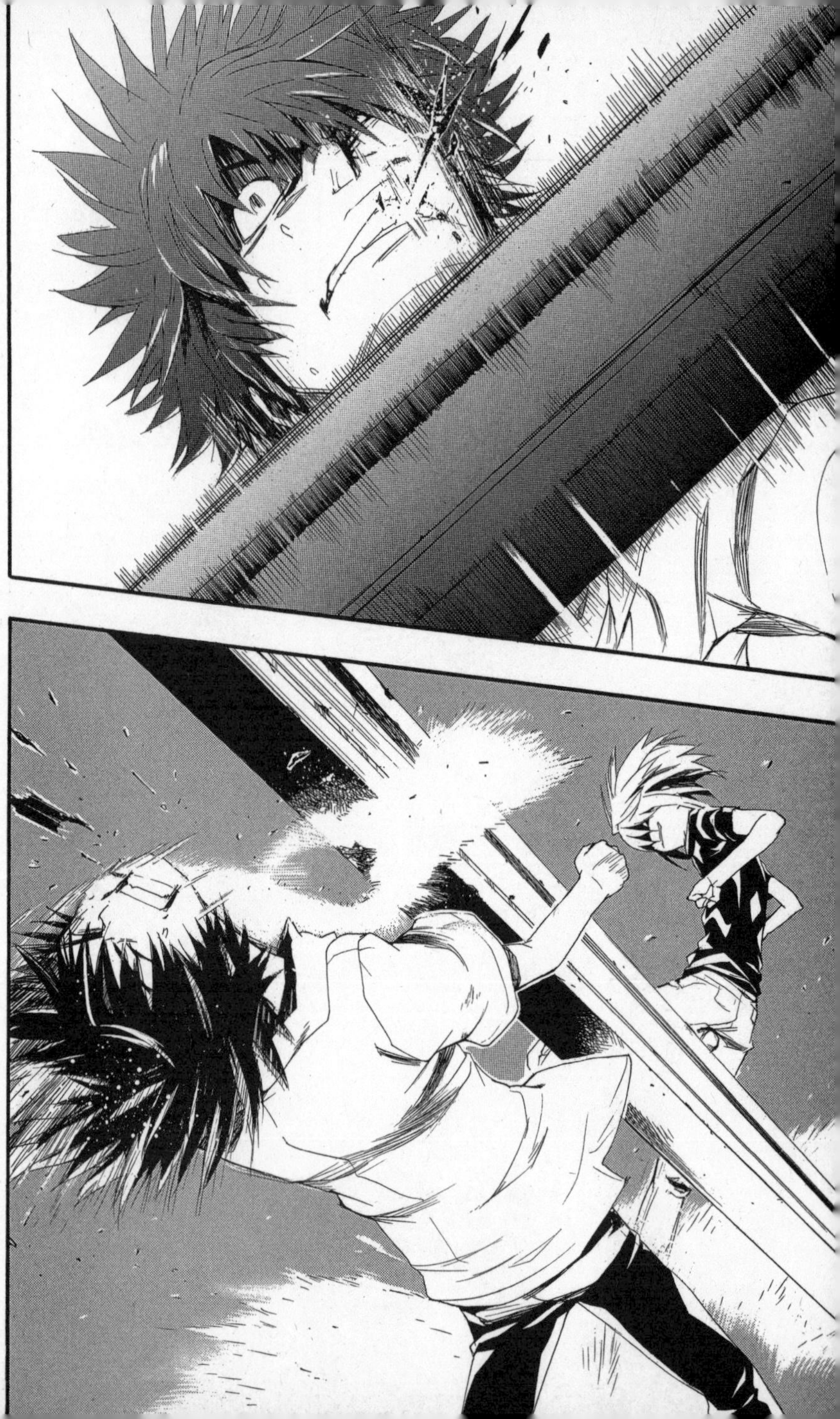

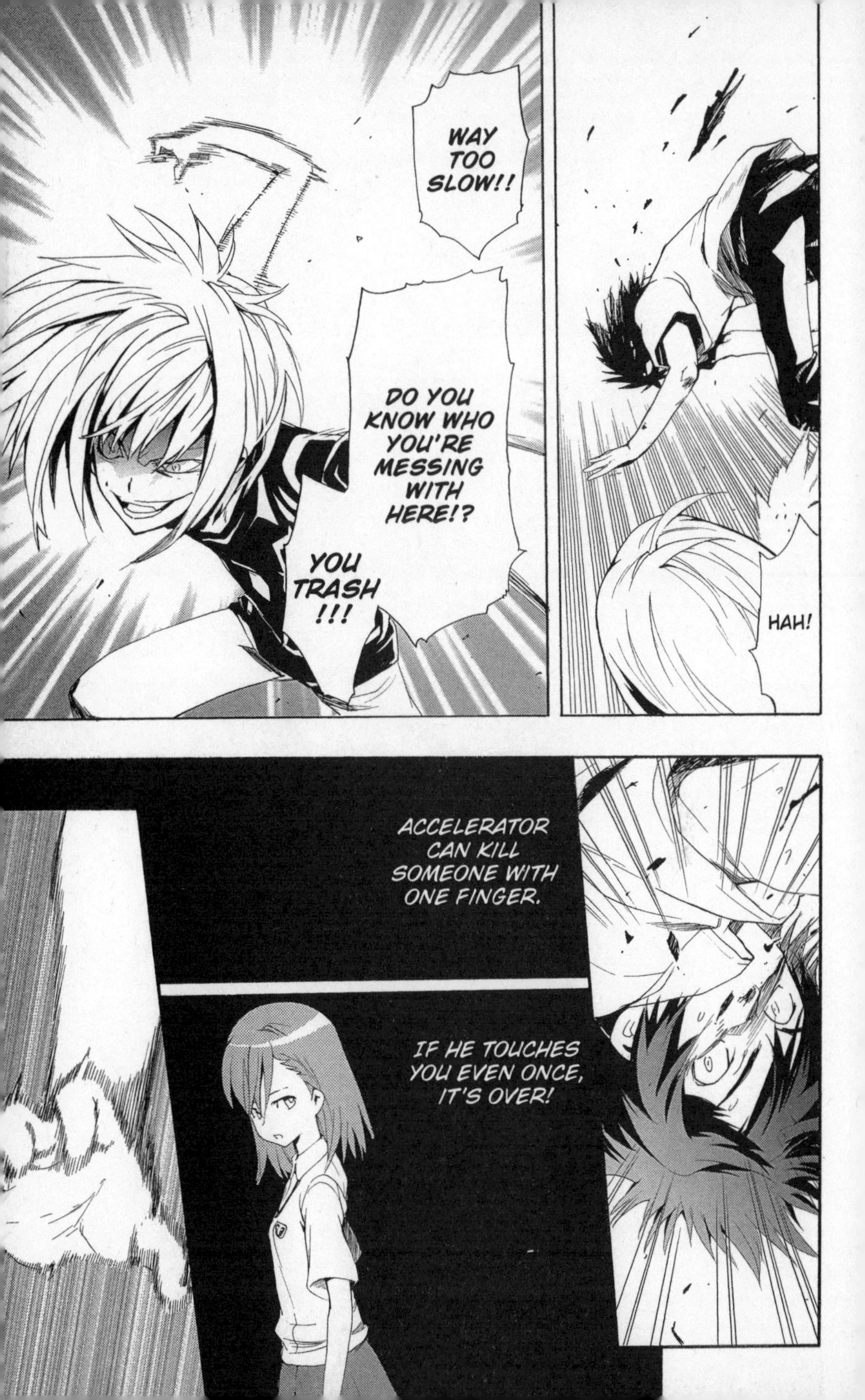
HAH!
WAY TOO SLOW!!
DO YOU KNOW WHO YOU'RE MESSING WITH HERE!?
YOU TRASH!!!
ACCELERATOR CAN KILL SOMEONE WITH ONE FINGER.
IF HE TOUCHES YOU EVEN ONCE, IT'S OVER!

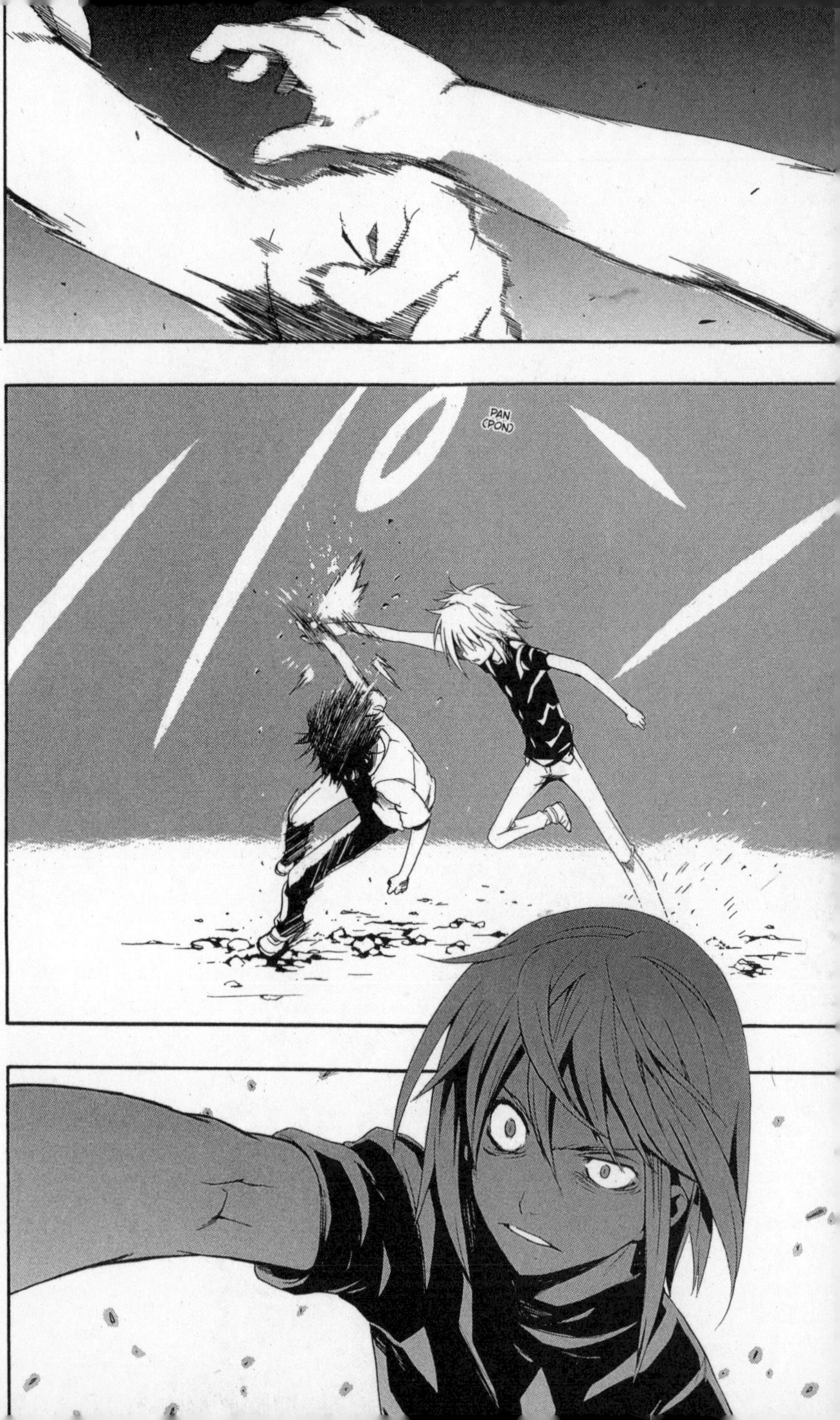
PAN
(PON)

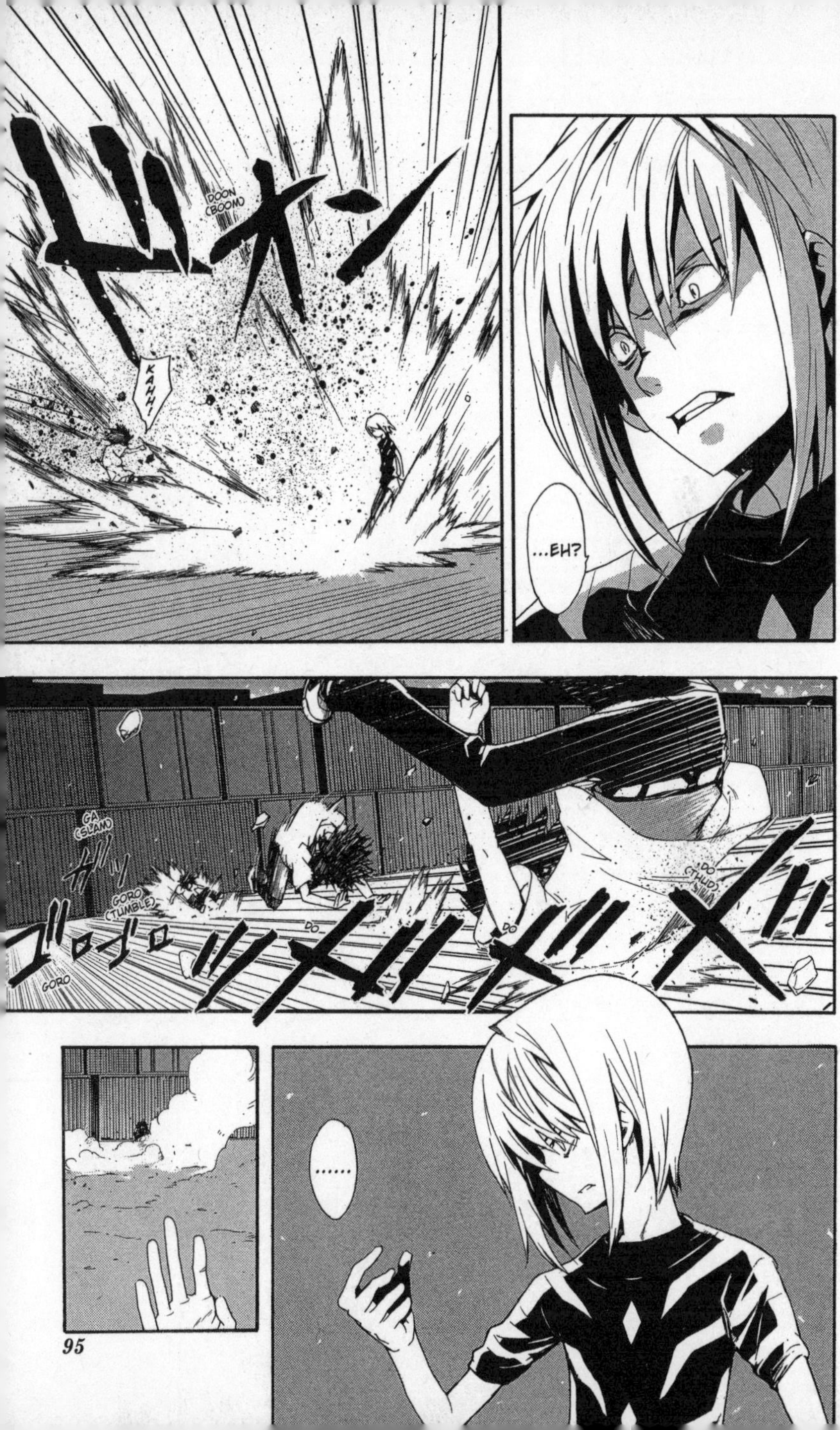
...EH?
DOON (BOOM)
KAHH!
DO (THUD)
DO
DO
GA (SLAM)
GORO (TUMBLE)
GORO
......

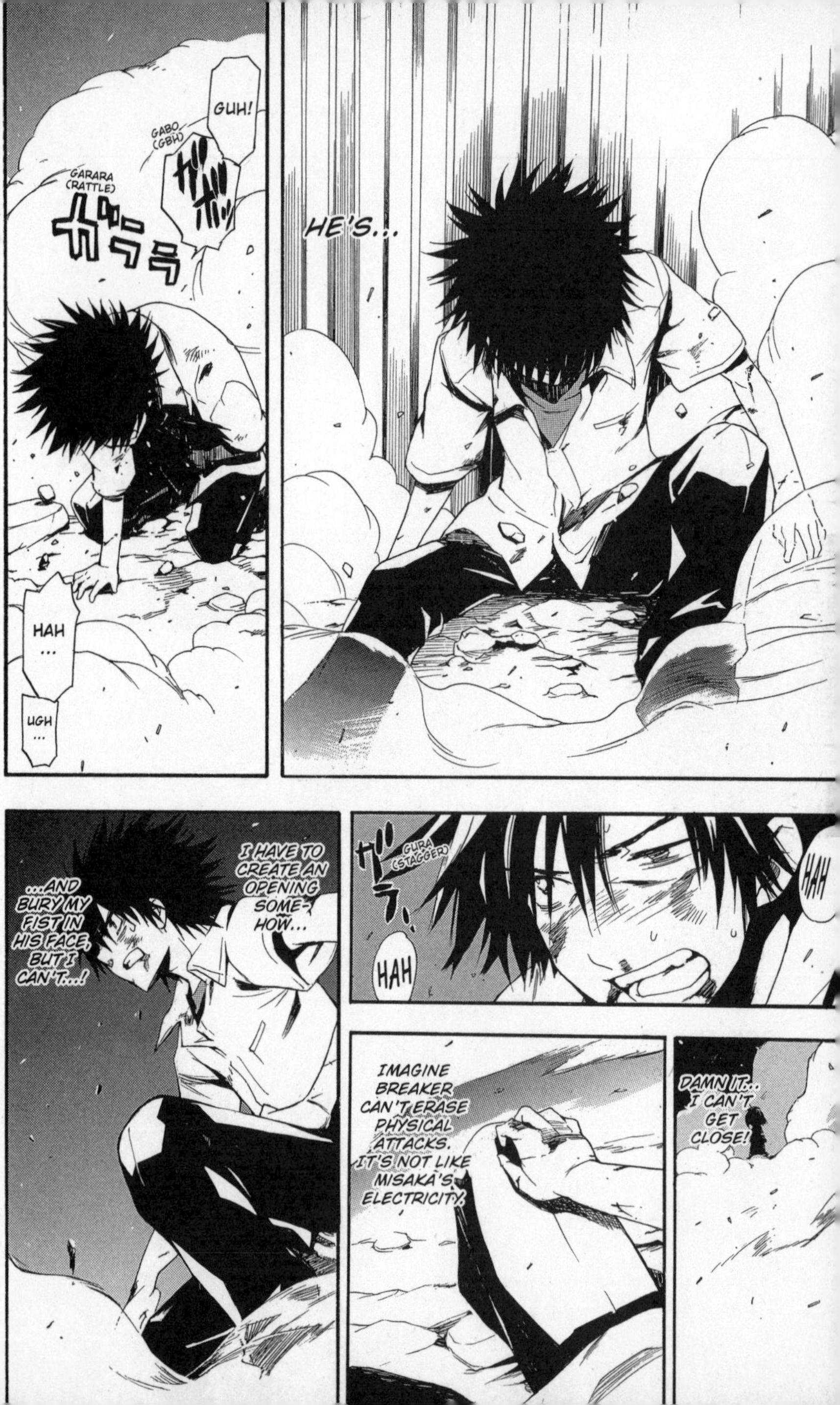
HE'S...
GUH!
GABO (GBH)
GARARA (RATTLE)
HAH ...
UGH ...
GURA (STAGGER)
HAH
HAH
DAMN IT... I CAN'T GET CLOSE!
IMAGINE BREAKER CAN'T ERASE PHYSICAL ATTACKS. IT'S NOT LIKE MISAKA'S ELECTRICITY.
I HAVE TO CREATE AN OPENING SOME-HOW...
...AND BURY MY FIST IN HIS FACE, BUT I CAN'T...!

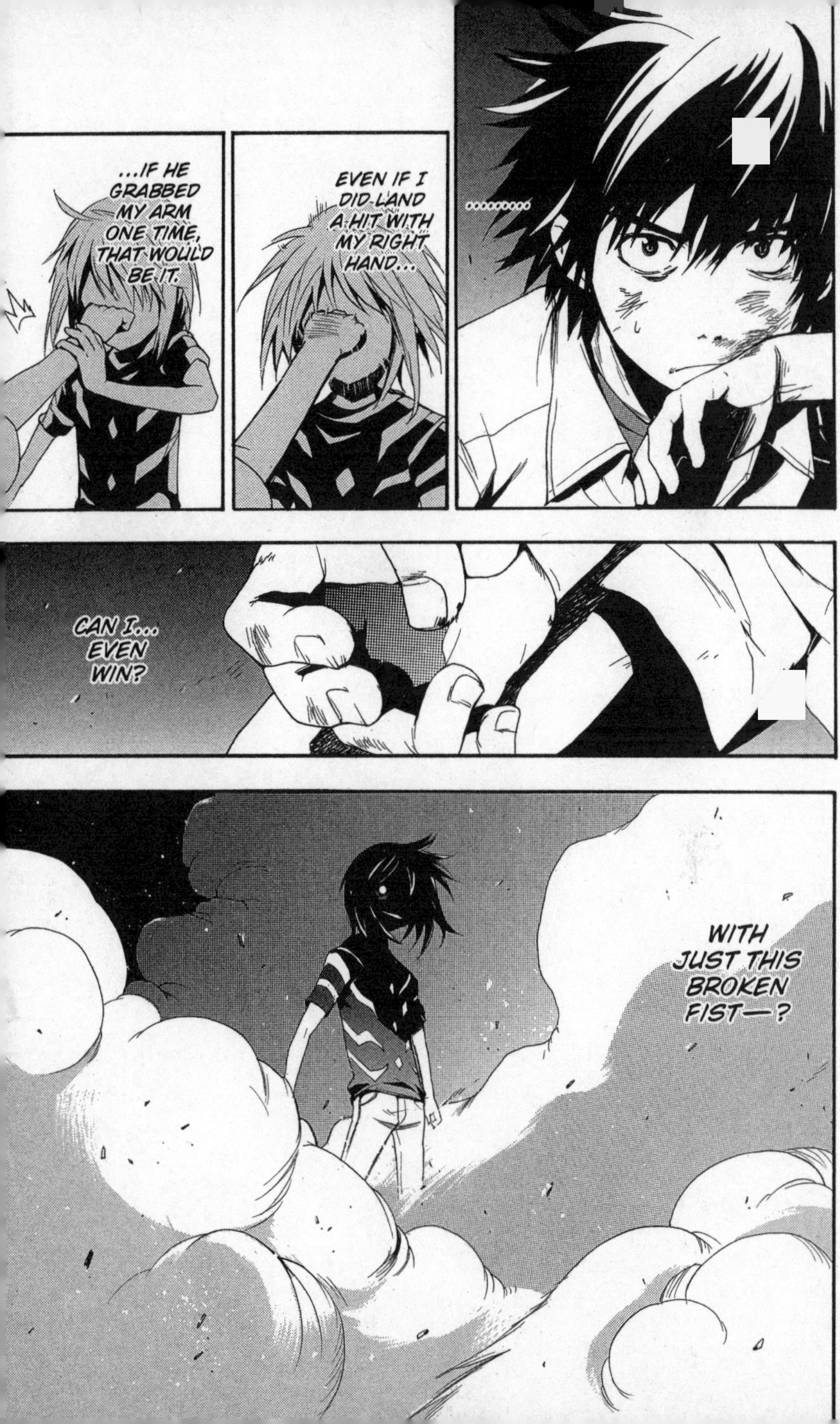
....
EVEN IF I DID LAND A HIT WITH MY RIGHT HAND...
...IF HE GRABBED MY ARM ONE TIME, THAT WOULD BE IT.
CAN I... EVEN WIN?
WITH JUST THIS BROKEN FIST—?

A Certain Magical Index

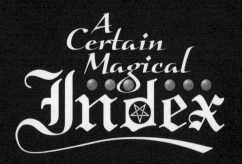

#19 WEAKEST VS. STRONGEST ②

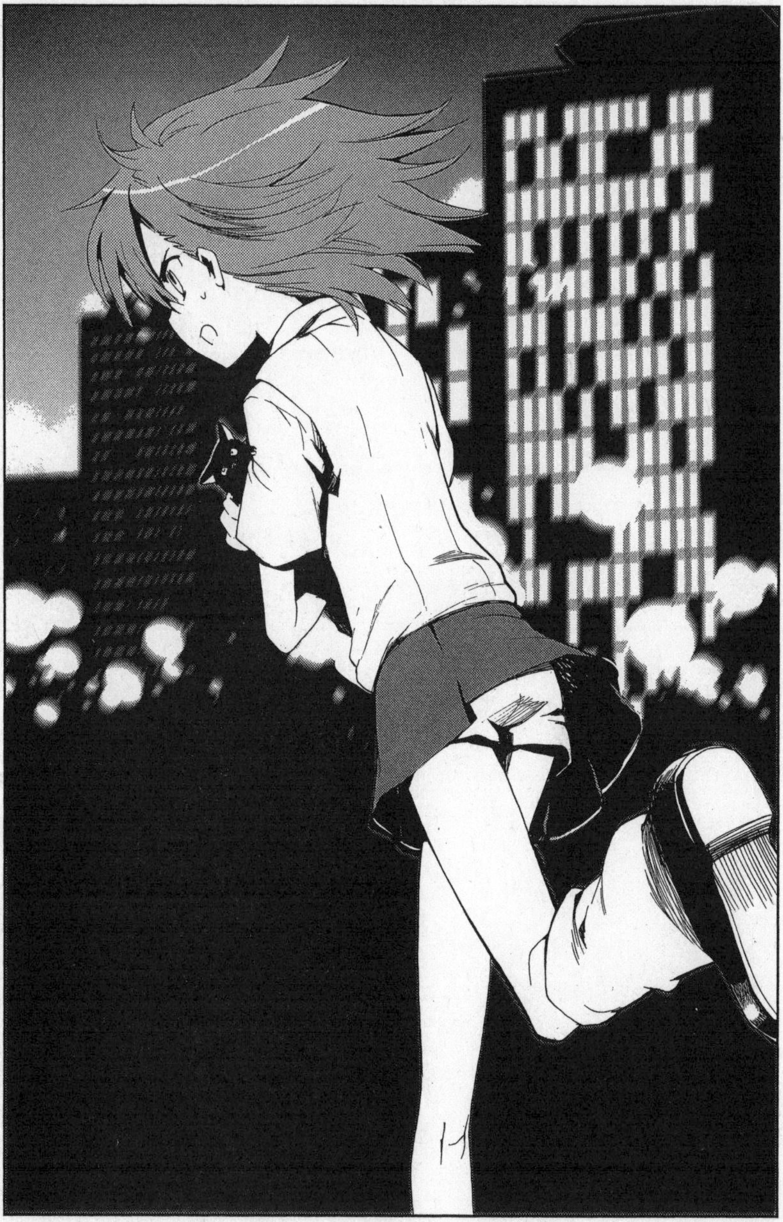

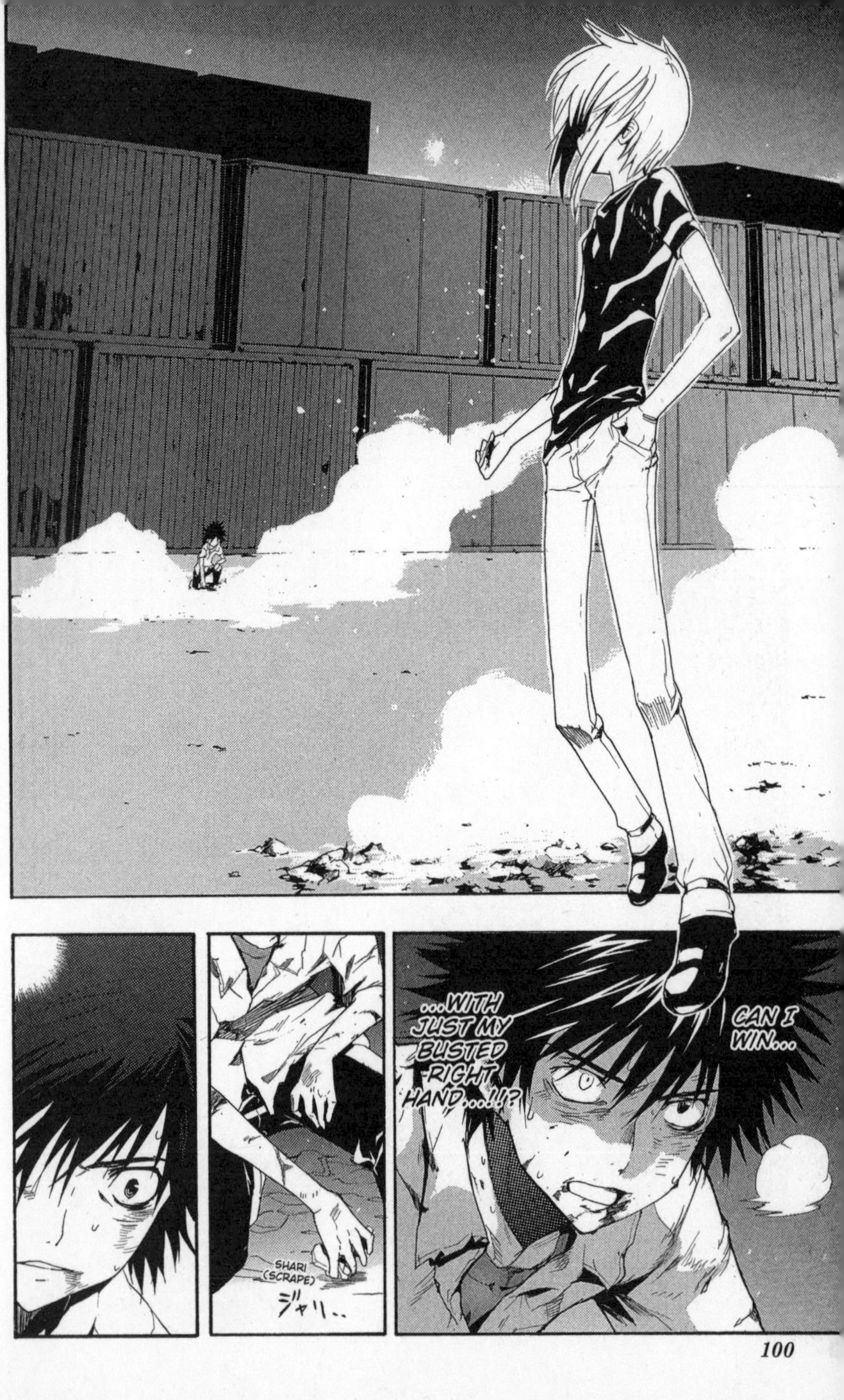
CAN I WIN...
...WITH JUST MY BUSTED RIGHT HAND...!!?
SHARI (SCRAPE)
ジャリ..

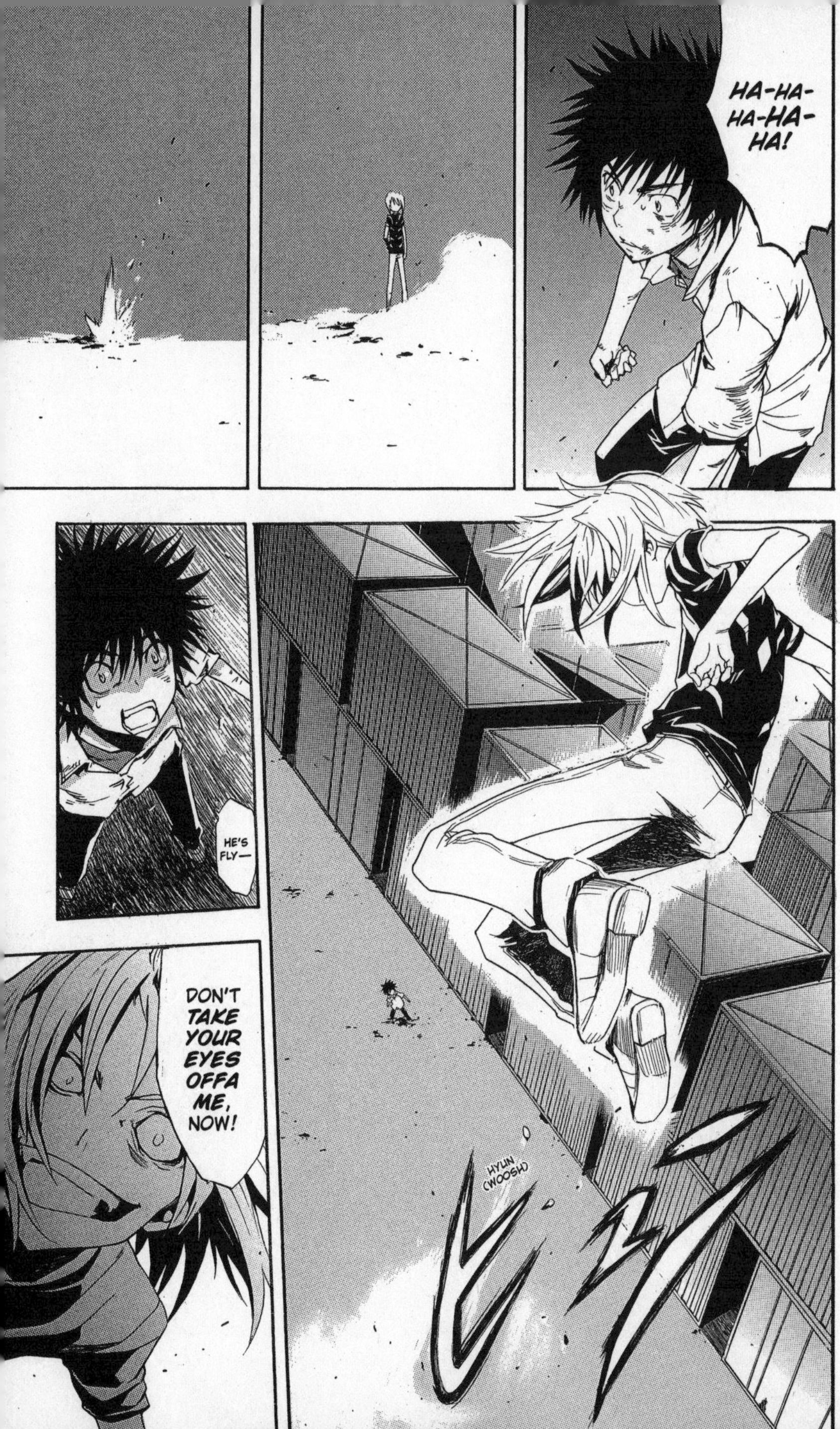
HA-HA-HA-HA-HA!
HYUN (WOOSH)
HE'S FLY—
DON'T TAKE YOUR EYES OFFA ME, NOW!

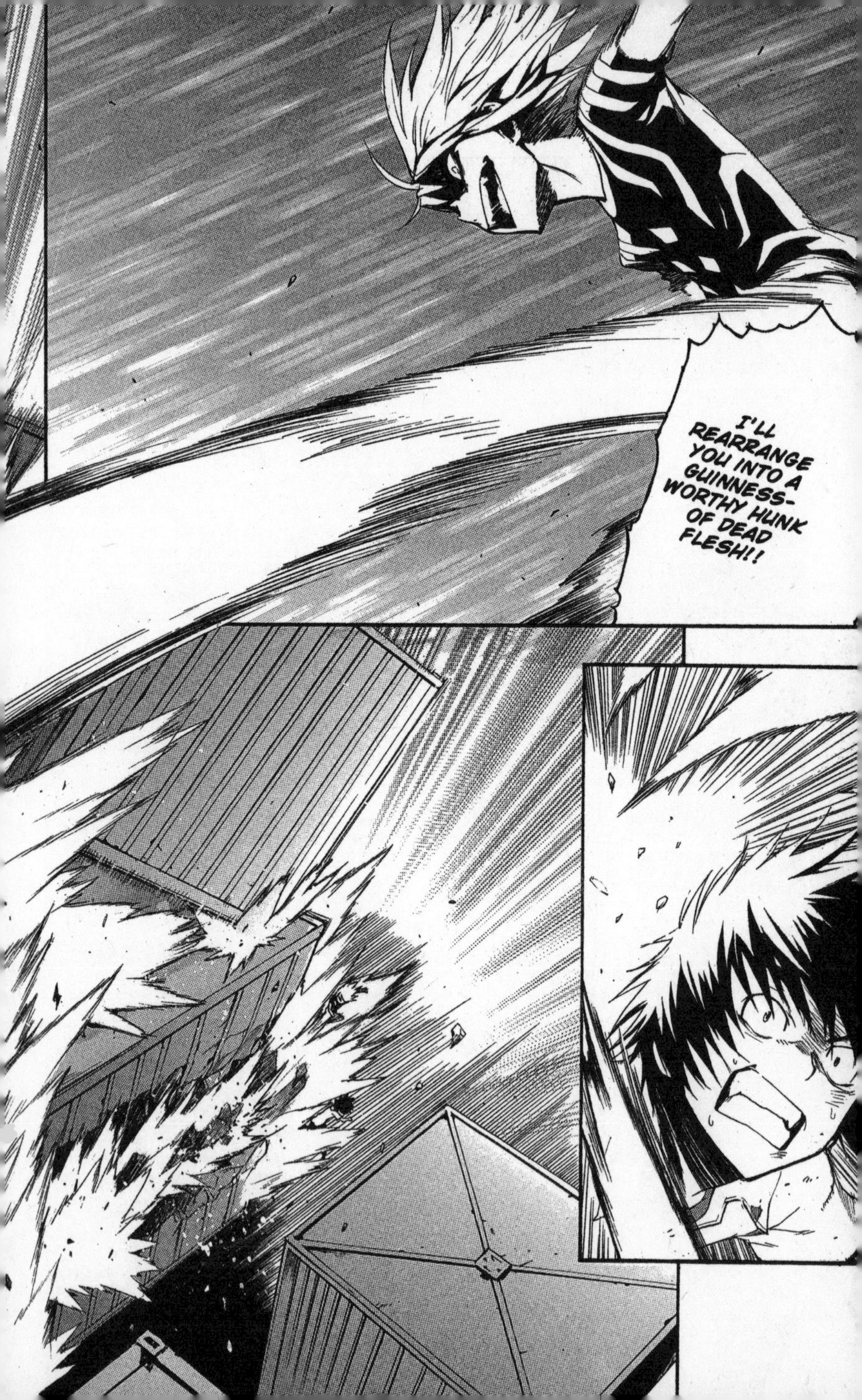
I'LL REARRANGE YOU INTO A GUINNESS-WORTHY HUNK OF DEAD FLESH!!

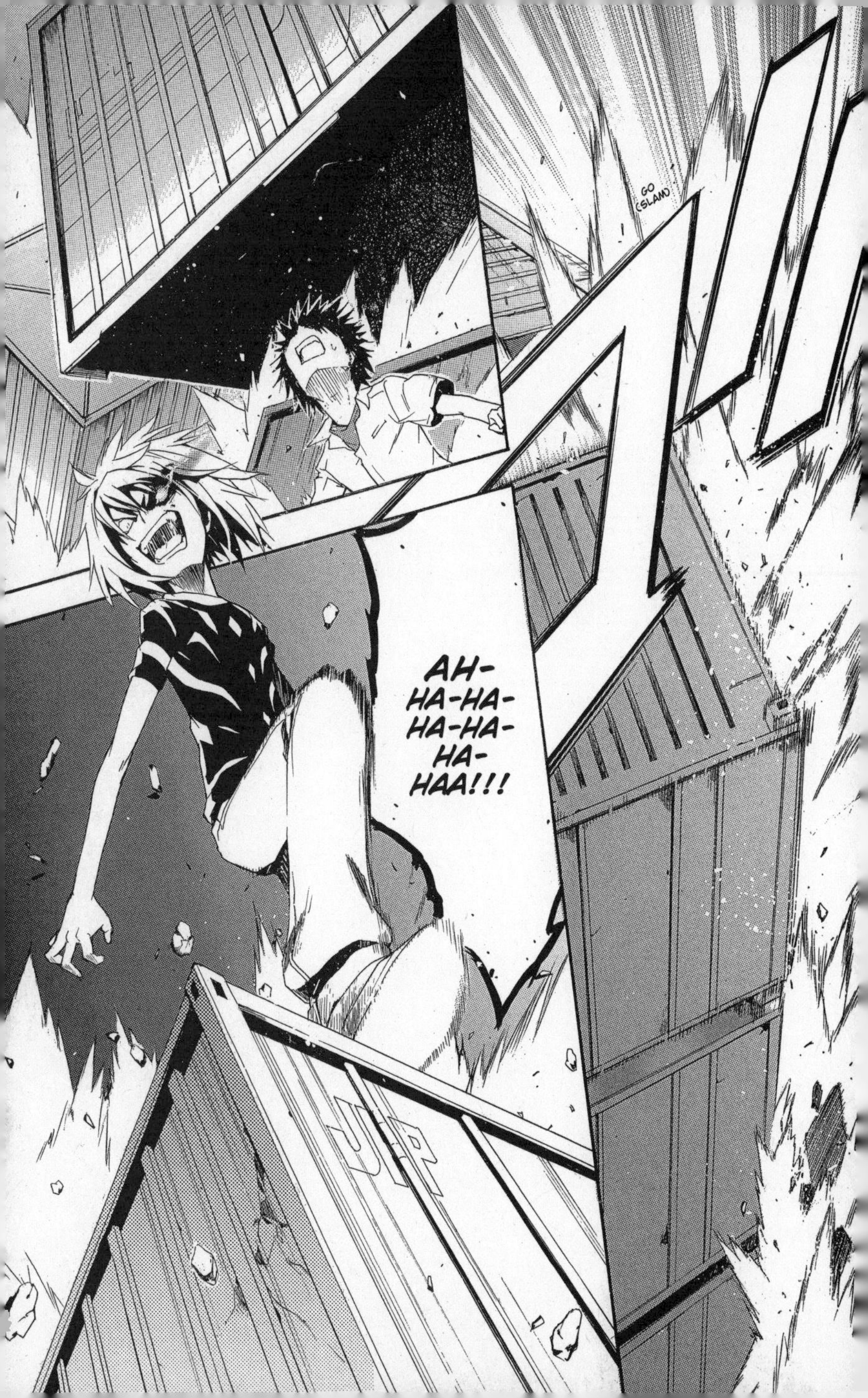
GO (SLAM)
AH-HA-HA-HA-HA-HA-HAA!!!

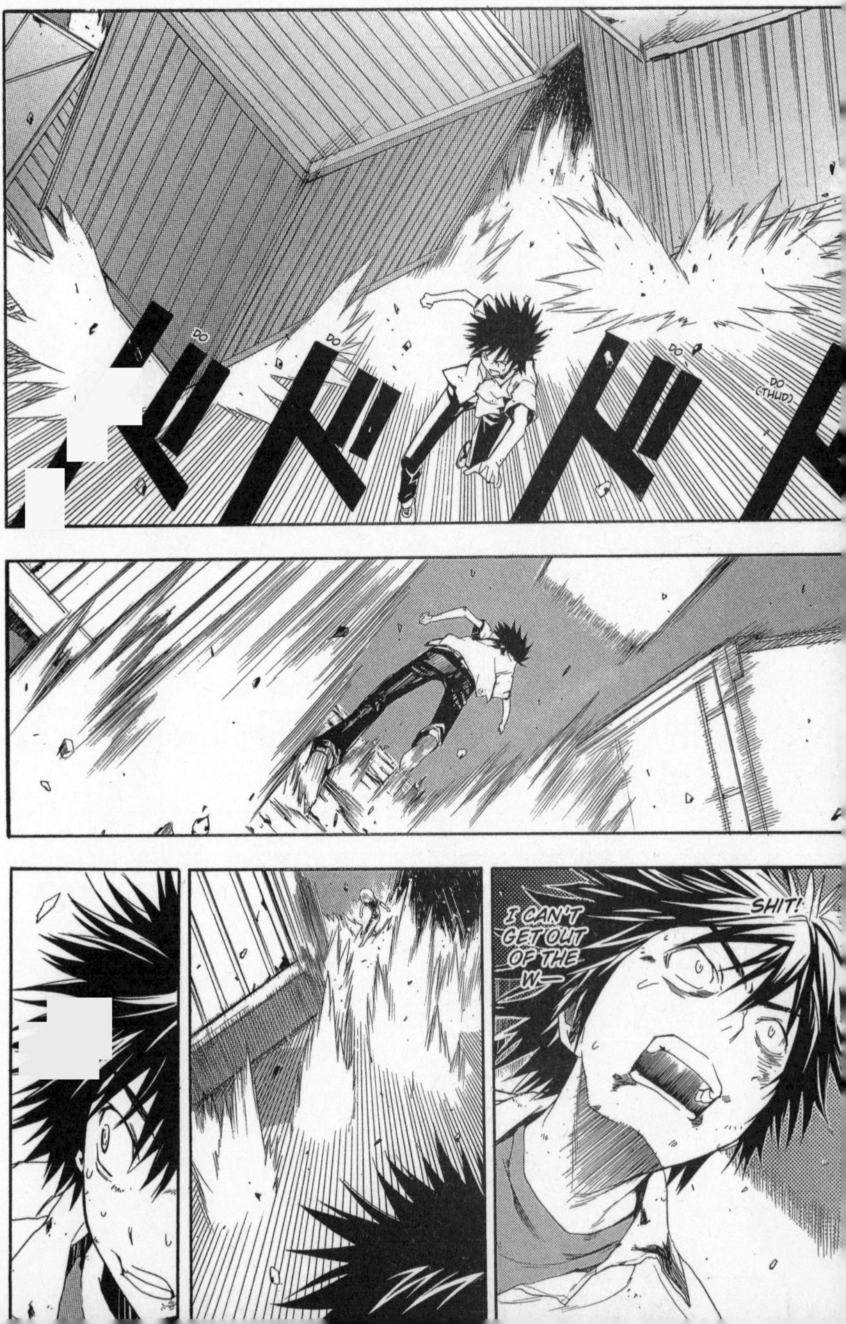
DO (THUD)
DO
DO
DO
SHIT!
I CAN'T GET OUT OF THE W—

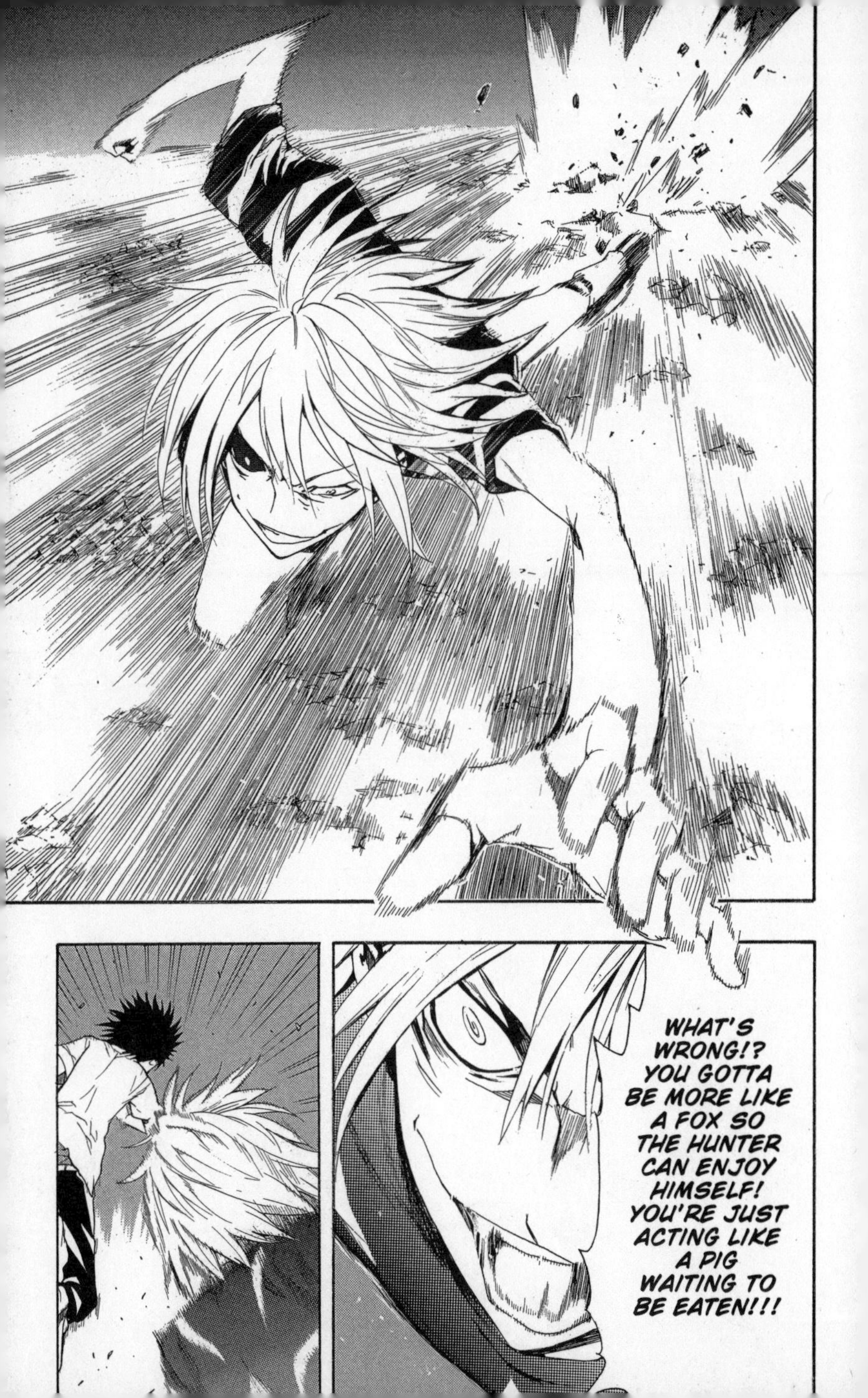
WHAT'S WRONG!? YOU GOTTA BE MORE LIKE A FOX SO THE HUNTER CAN ENJOY HIMSELF! YOU'RE JUST ACTING LIKE A PIG WAITING TO BE EATEN!!!

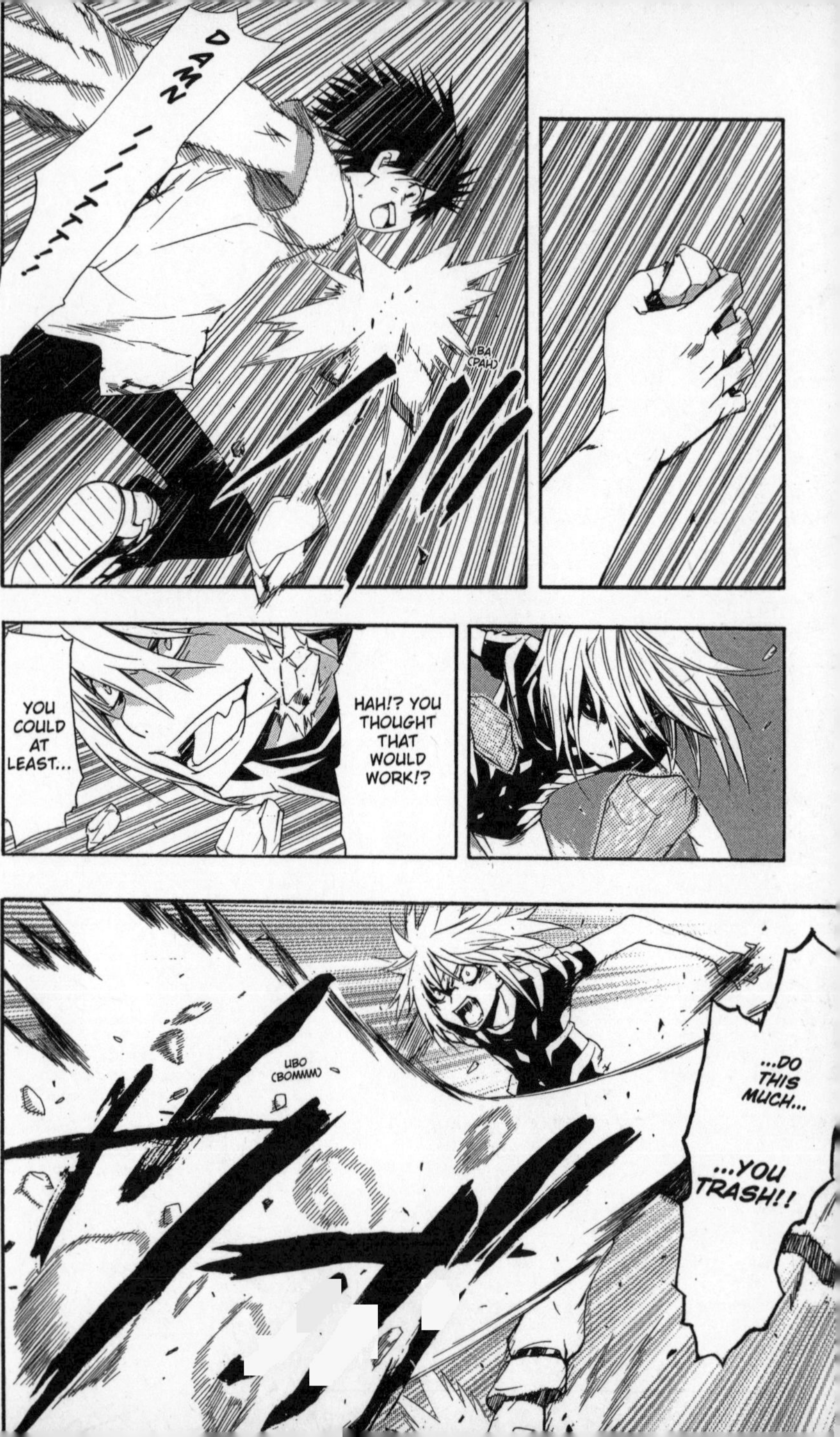
DAMN IIIITTT!!!
BA (PAH)
HAH!? YOU THOUGHT THAT WOULD WORK!?
YOU COULD AT LEAST...
...DO THIS MUCH...
...YOU TRASH!!
UBO (BOMMM)

GAKON
(CRASH)

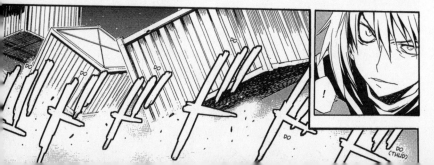

DO

DO

DO

DO
(THUD)

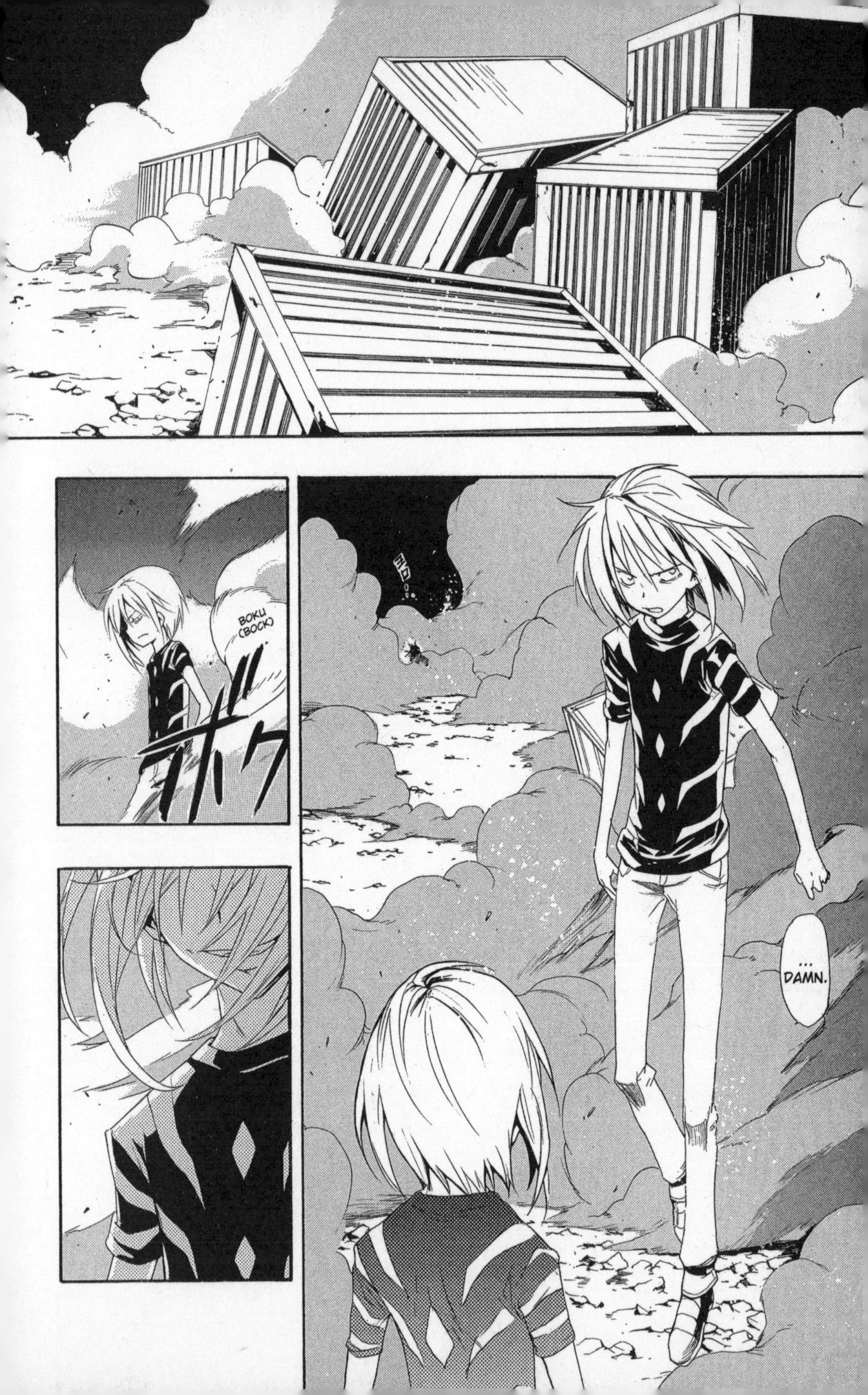
... DAMN.
BOKU (BOCK)

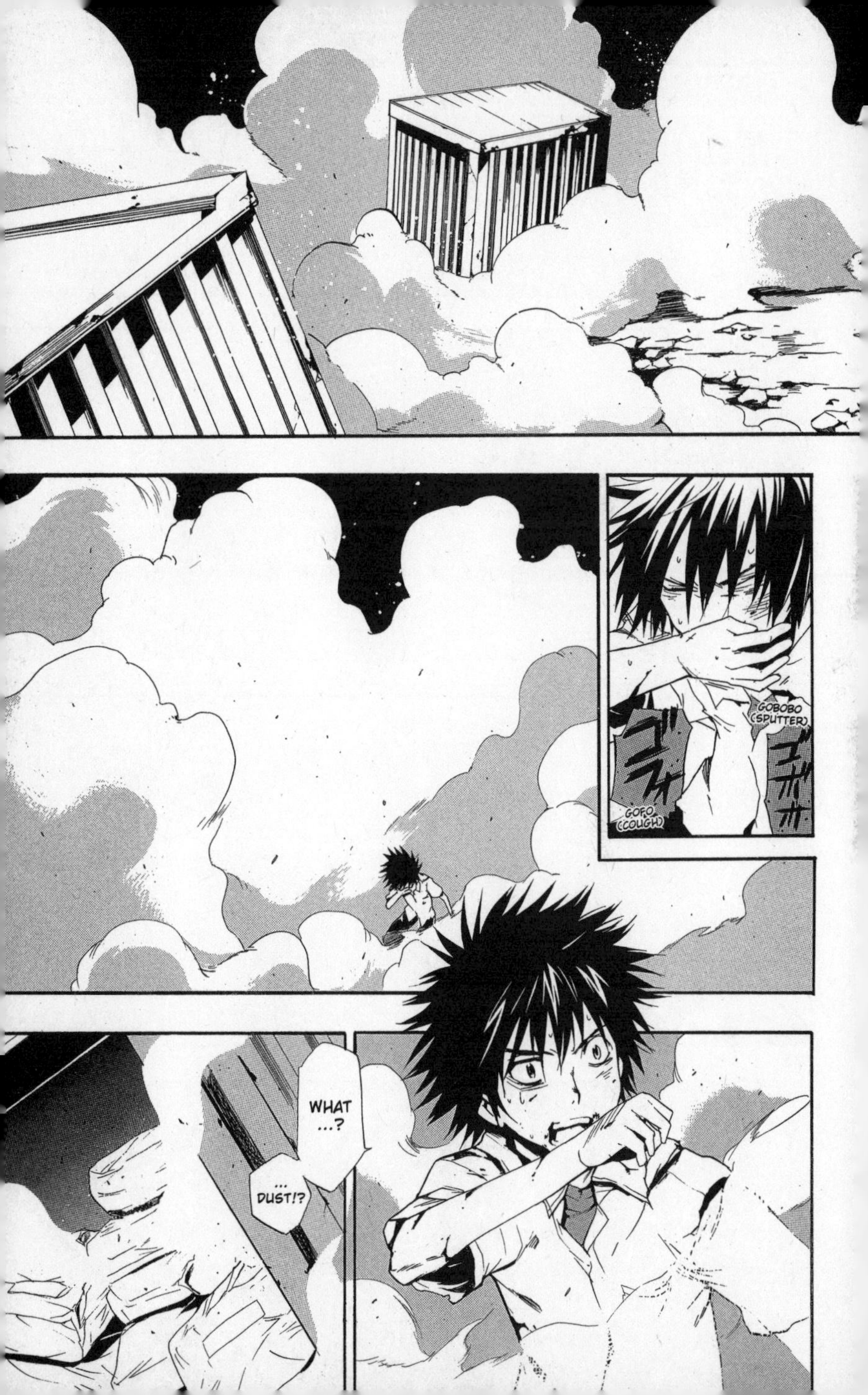
GOBOBO (SPUTTER)
GOFO (COUGH)
WHAT ...?
... DUST!?

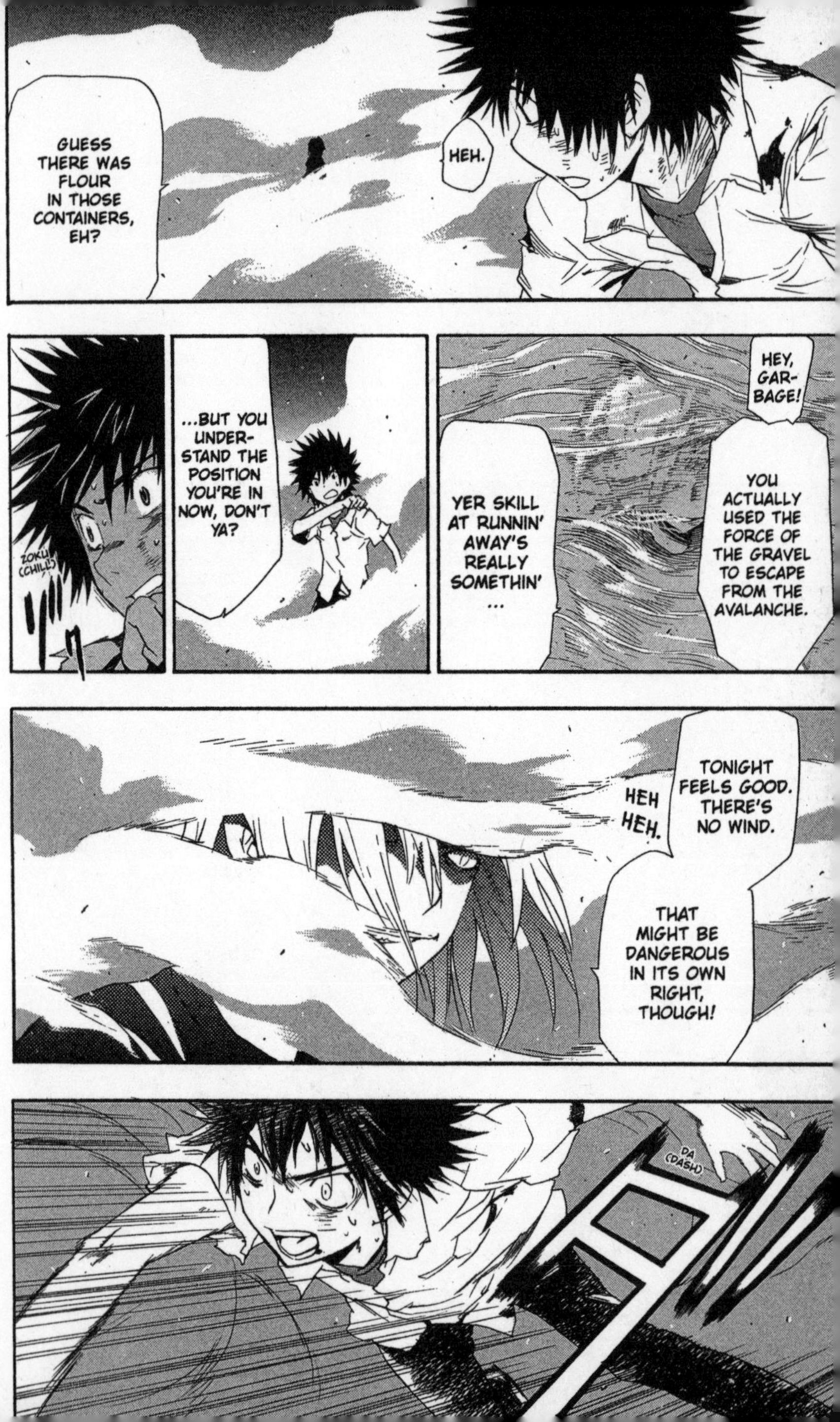
HEH.
GUESS THERE WAS FLOUR IN THOSE CONTAINERS, EH?
HEY, GARBAGE!
YOU ACTUALLY USED THE FORCE OF THE GRAVEL TO ESCAPE FROM THE AVALANCHE.
YER SKILL AT RUNNIN' AWAY'S REALLY SOMETHIN' ...
...BUT YOU UNDERSTAND THE POSITION YOU'RE IN NOW, DON'T YA?
ZOKU (CHILL)
TONIGHT FEELS GOOD. THERE'S NO WIND.
HEH HEH.
THAT MIGHT BE DANGEROUS IN ITS OWN RIGHT, THOUGH!
DA (DASH)

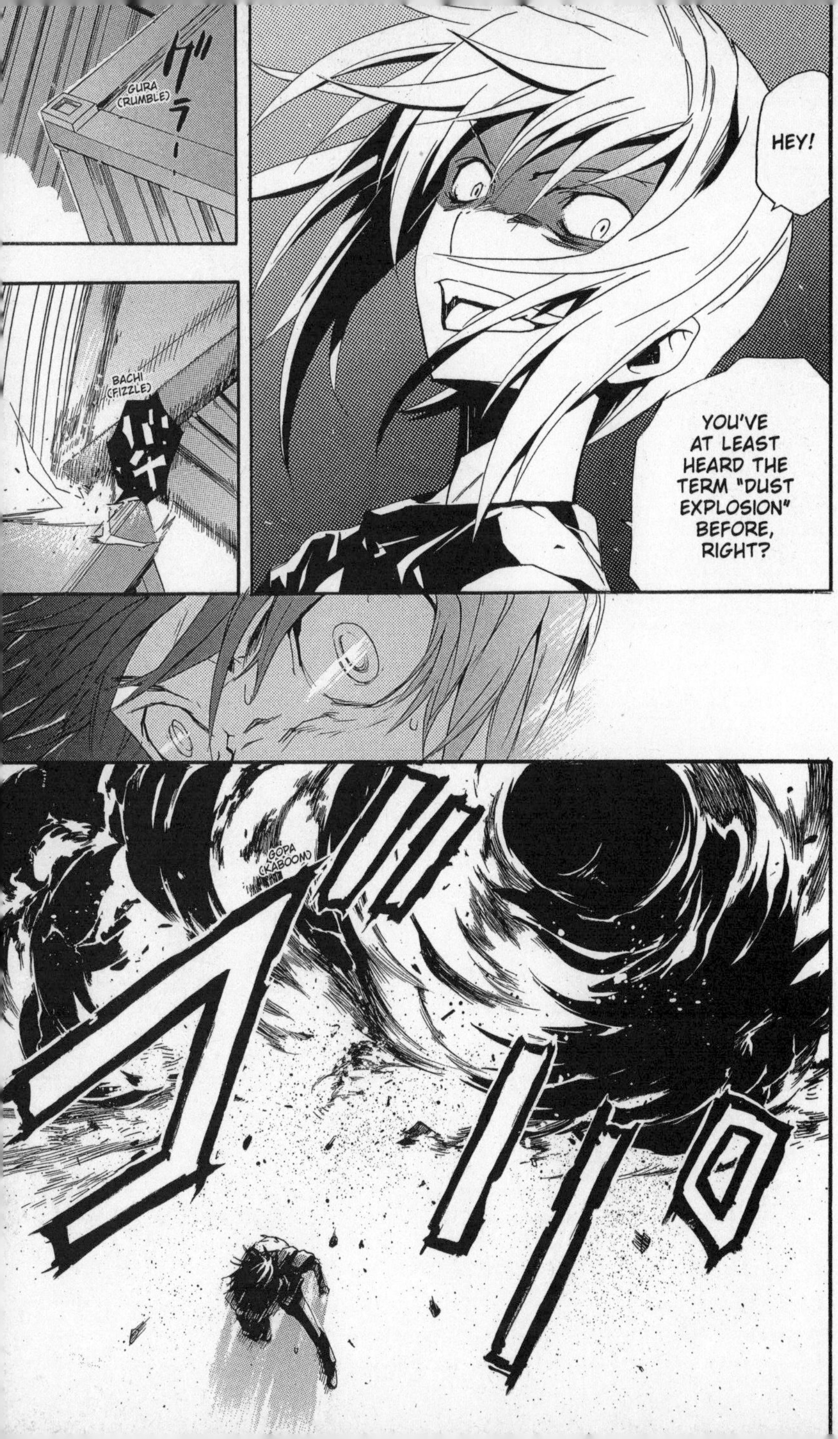
HEY!
YOU'VE AT LEAST HEARD THE TERM "DUST EXPLOSION" BEFORE, RIGHT?
GURA (RUMBLE)
BACHI (FIZZLE)
GOPA (KABOOM)

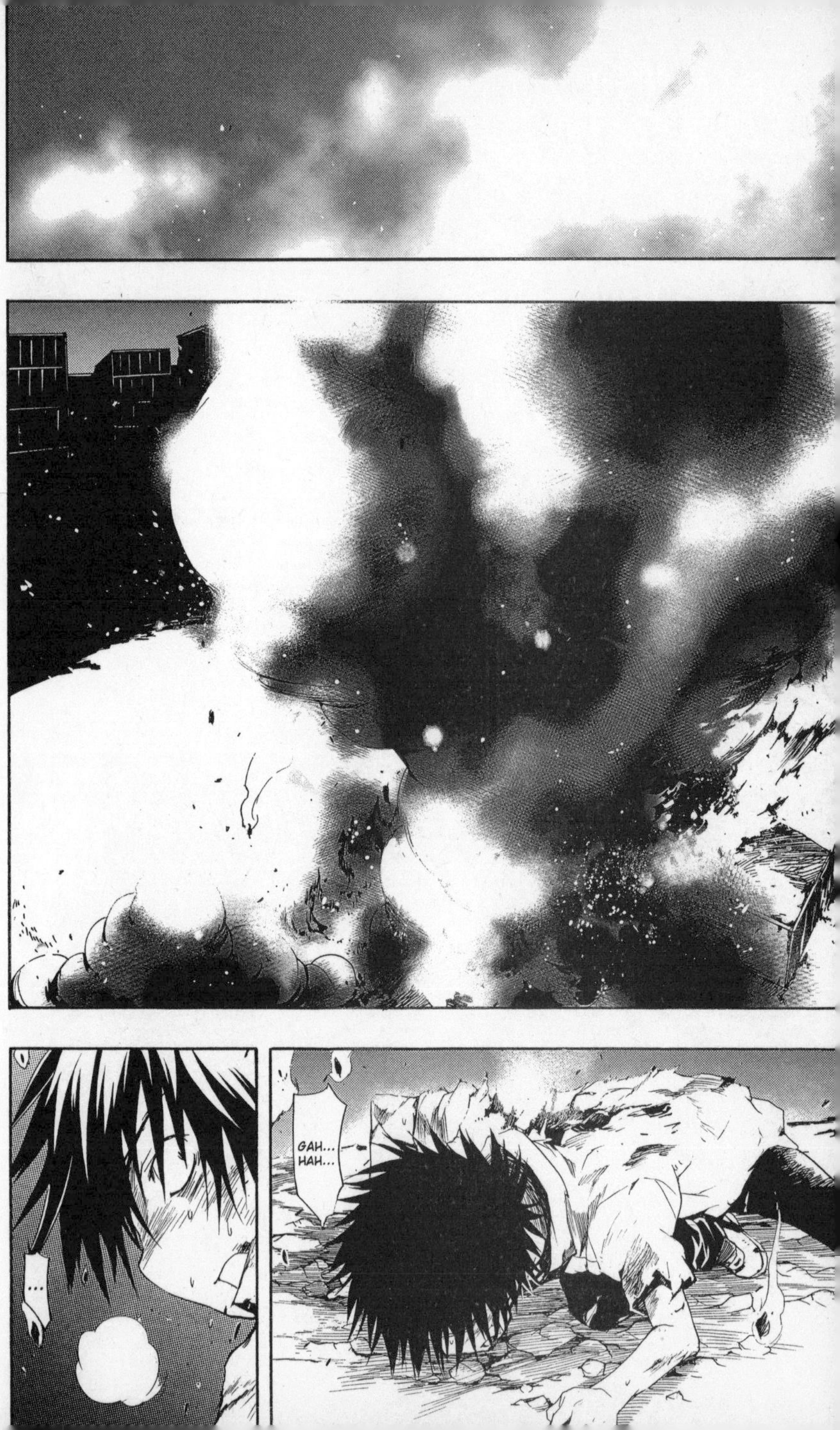
GAH... HAH...
...

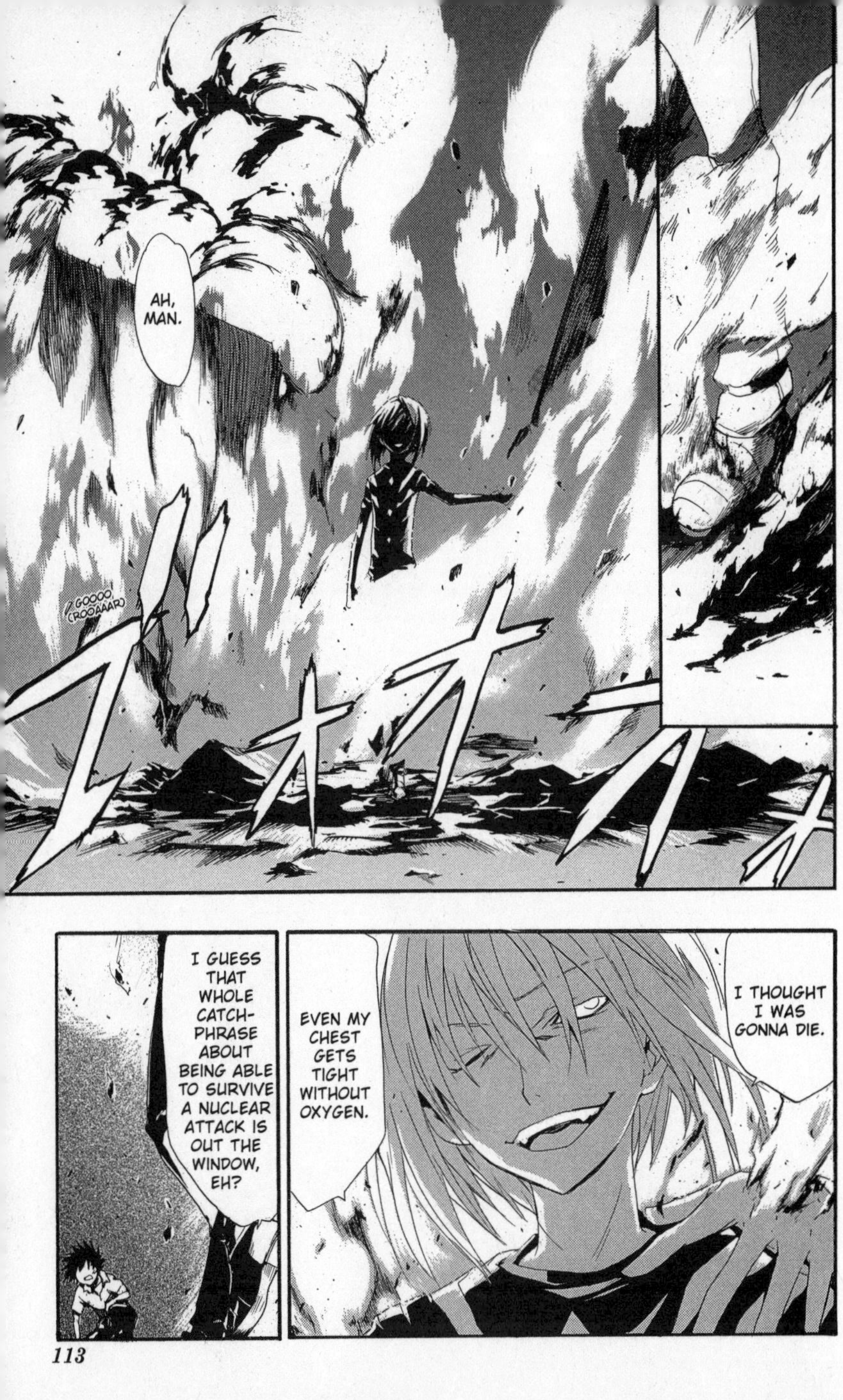
AH, MAN.
GOOOO (ROOAAAR)
I THOUGHT I WAS GONNA DIE.
EVEN MY CHEST GETS TIGHT WITHOUT OXYGEN.
I GUESS THAT WHOLE CATCH-PHRASE ABOUT BEING ABLE TO SURVIVE A NUCLEAR ATTACK IS OUT THE WINDOW, EH?

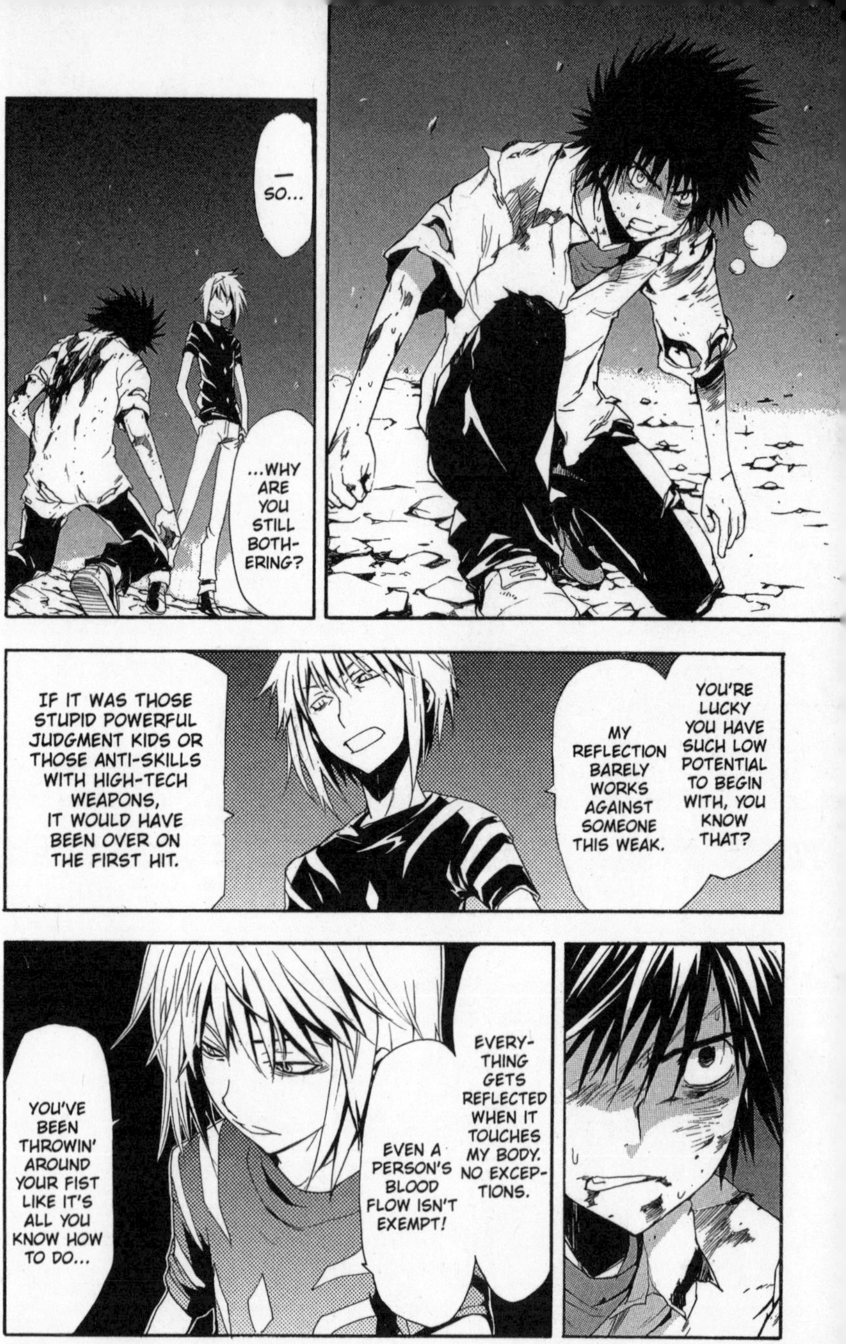
—SO...
...WHY ARE YOU STILL BOTHERING?
YOU'RE LUCKY YOU HAVE SUCH LOW POTENTIAL TO BEGIN WITH, YOU KNOW THAT?
MY REFLECTION BARELY WORKS AGAINST SOMEONE THIS WEAK.
IF IT WAS THOSE STUPID POWERFUL JUDGMENT KIDS OR THOSE ANTI-SKILLS WITH HIGH-TECH WEAPONS, IT WOULD HAVE BEEN OVER ON THE FIRST HIT.
EVERYTHING GETS REFLECTED WHEN IT TOUCHES MY BODY. NO EXCEPTIONS.
EVEN A PERSON'S BLOOD FLOW ISN'T EXEMPT!
YOU'VE BEEN THROWIN' AROUND YOUR FIST LIKE IT'S ALL YOU KNOW HOW TO DO...

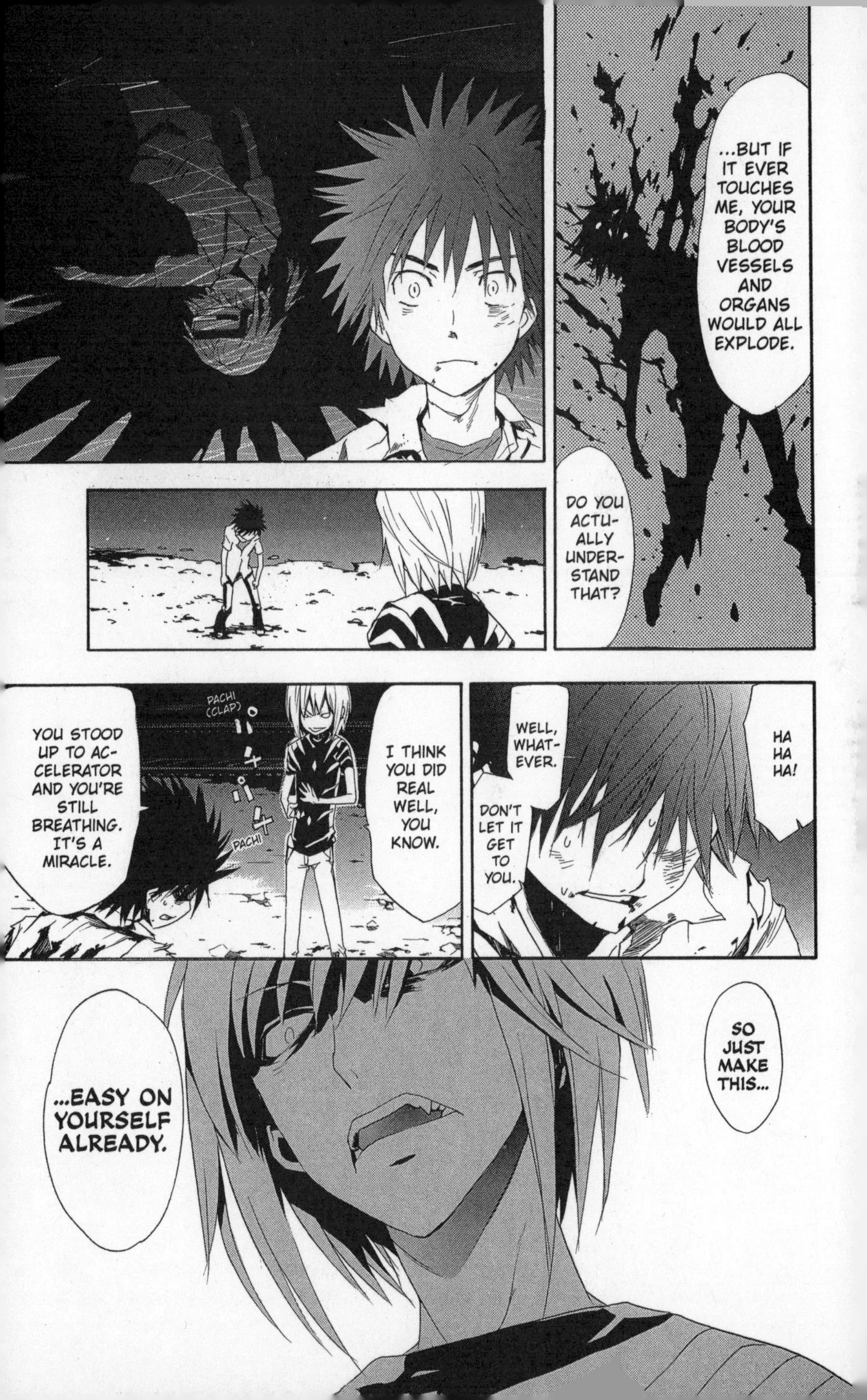
...BUT IF IT EVER TOUCHES ME, YOUR BODY'S BLOOD VESSELS AND ORGANS WOULD ALL EXPLODE.
DO YOU ACTUALLY UNDERSTAND THAT?
HA HA HA!
WELL, WHATEVER.
DON'T LET IT GET TO YOU.
I THINK YOU DID REAL WELL, YOU KNOW.
PACHI (CLAP)
PACHI
YOU STOOD UP TO ACCELERATOR AND YOU'RE STILL BREATHING. IT'S A MIRACLE.
SO JUST MAKE THIS...
...EASY ON YOURSELF ALREADY.

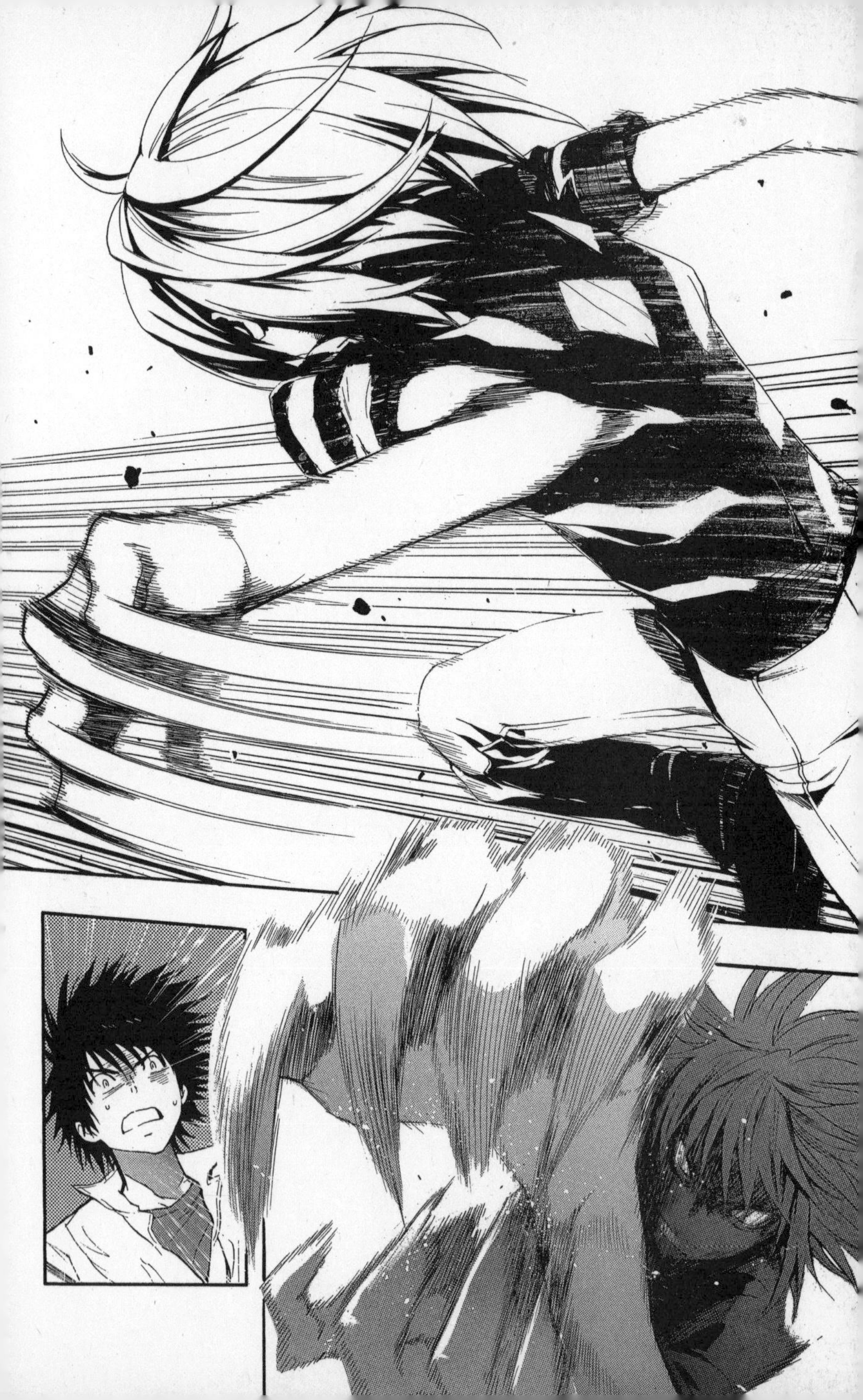

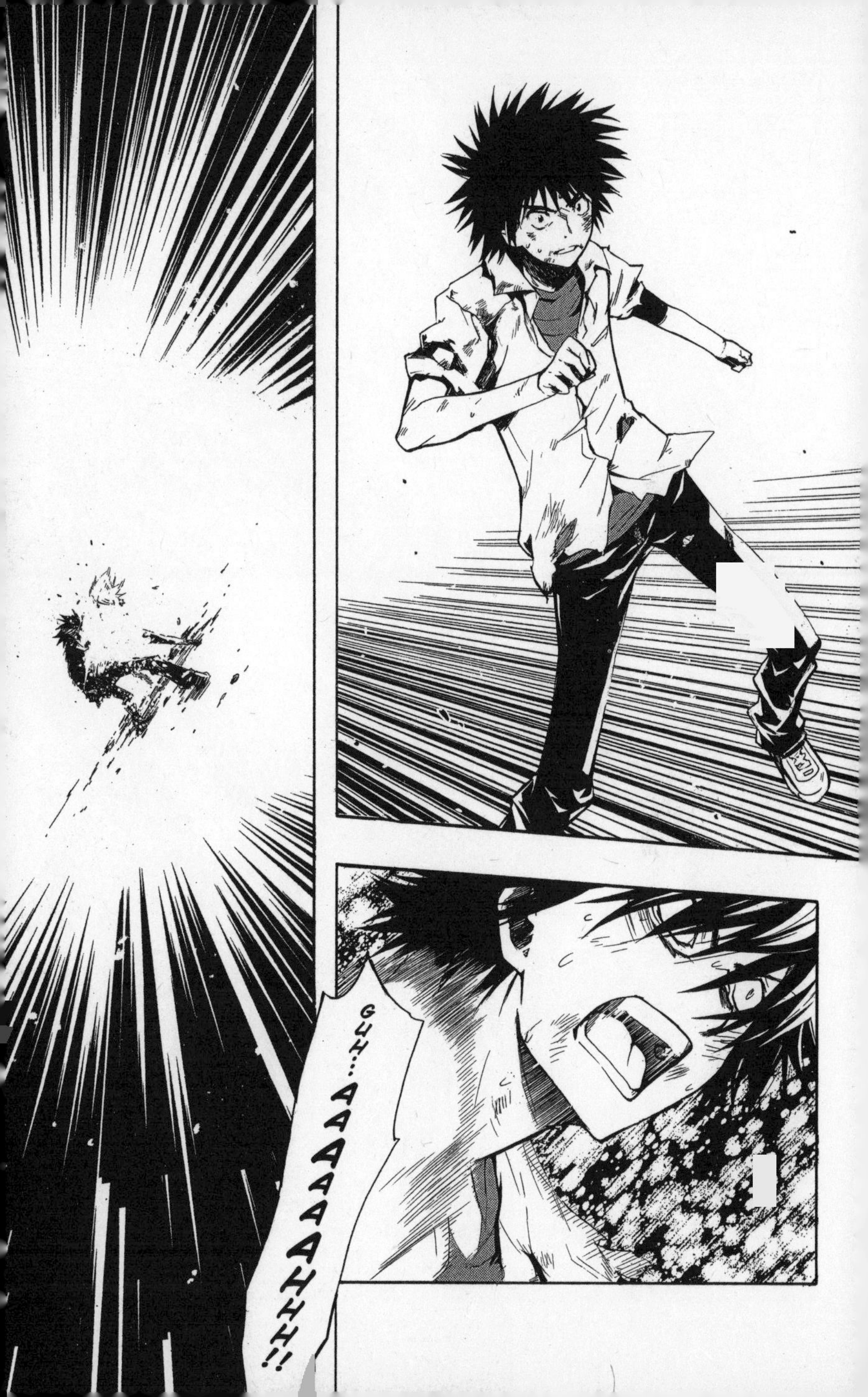
GUH... AAAAAAHHH!!

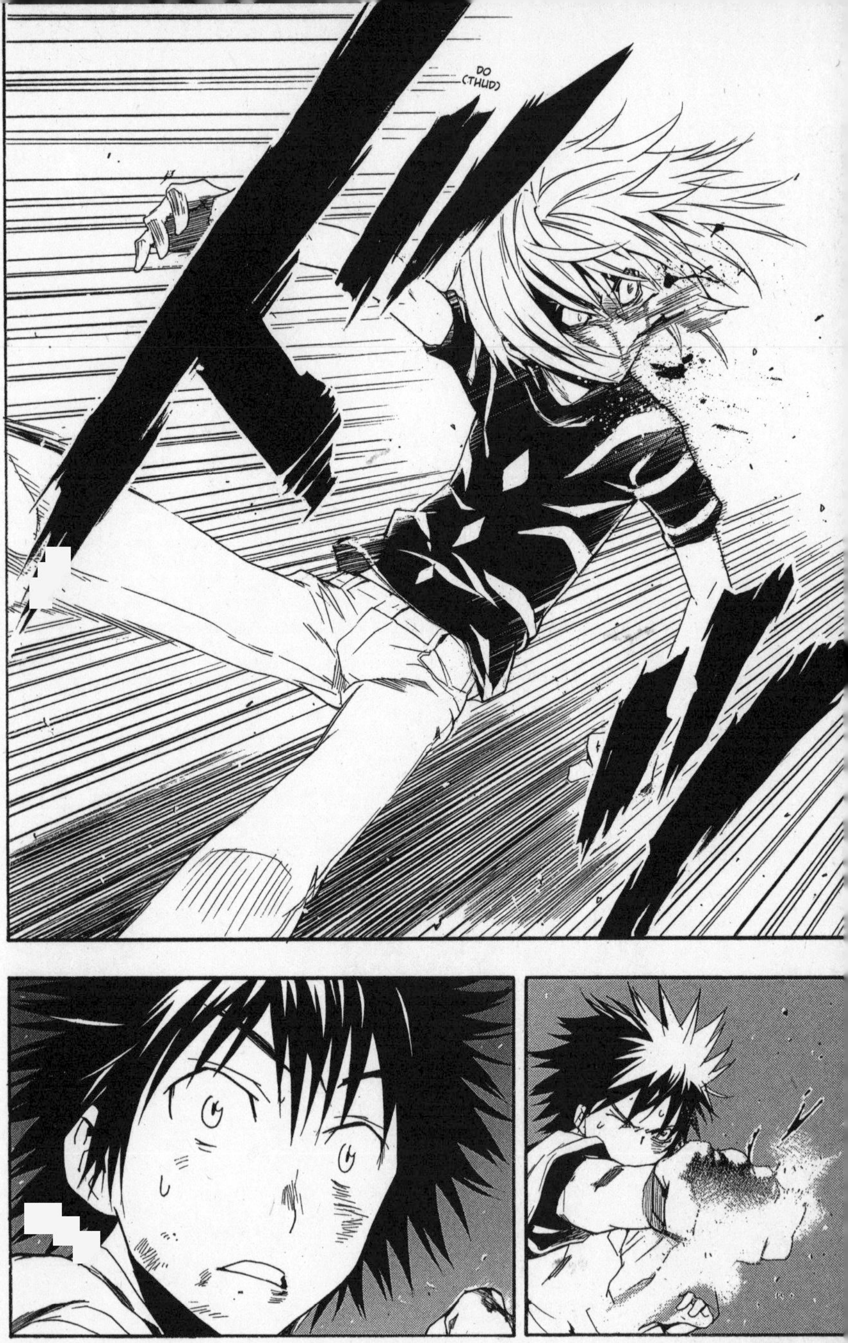
DO
(THUD)

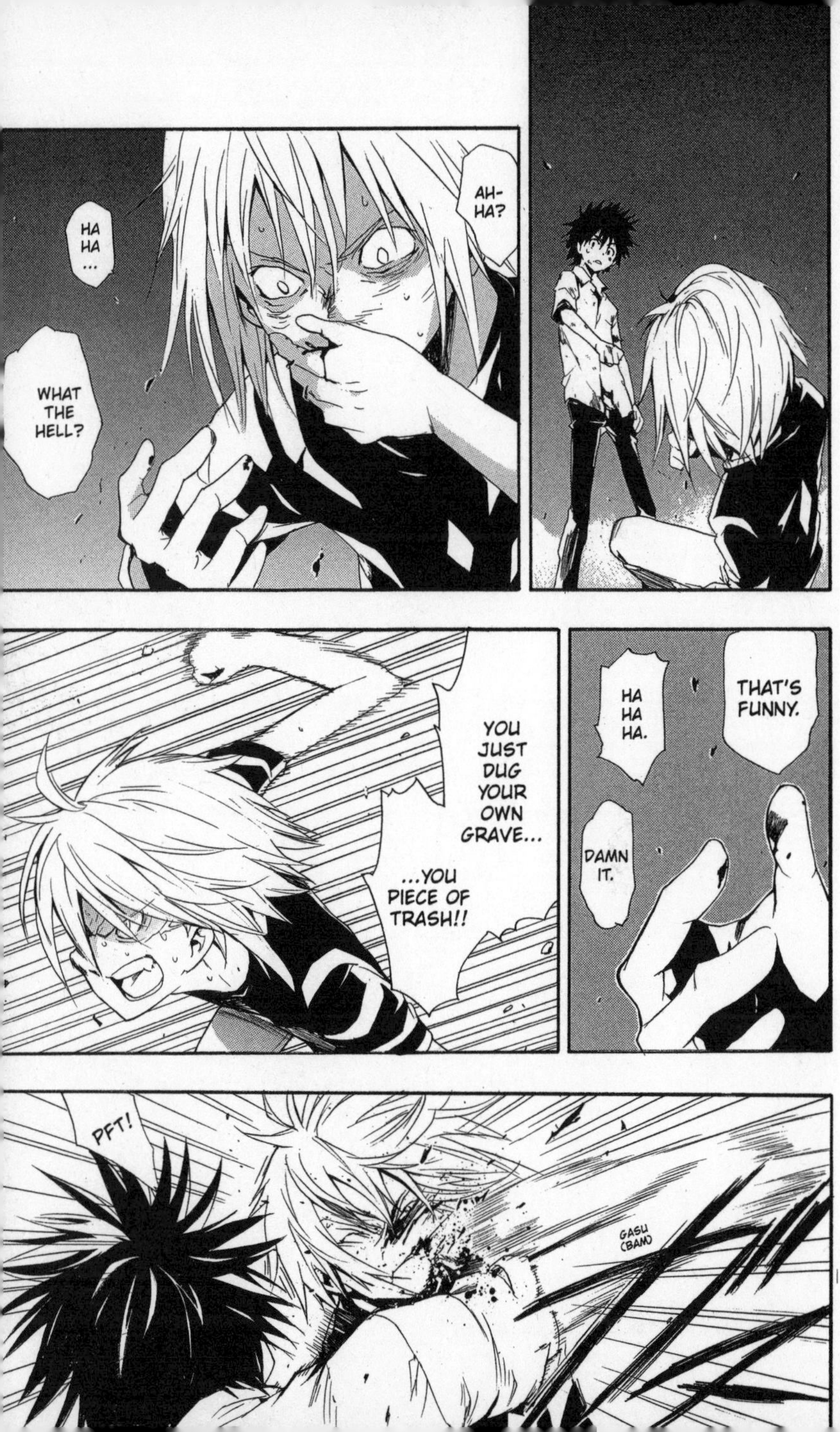
AH-HA?
HA HA ...
WHAT THE HELL?
THAT'S FUNNY.
HA HA HA.
DAMN IT.
YOU JUST DUG YOUR OWN GRAVE...
...YOU PIECE OF TRASH!!
PFT!
GASU (BAM)

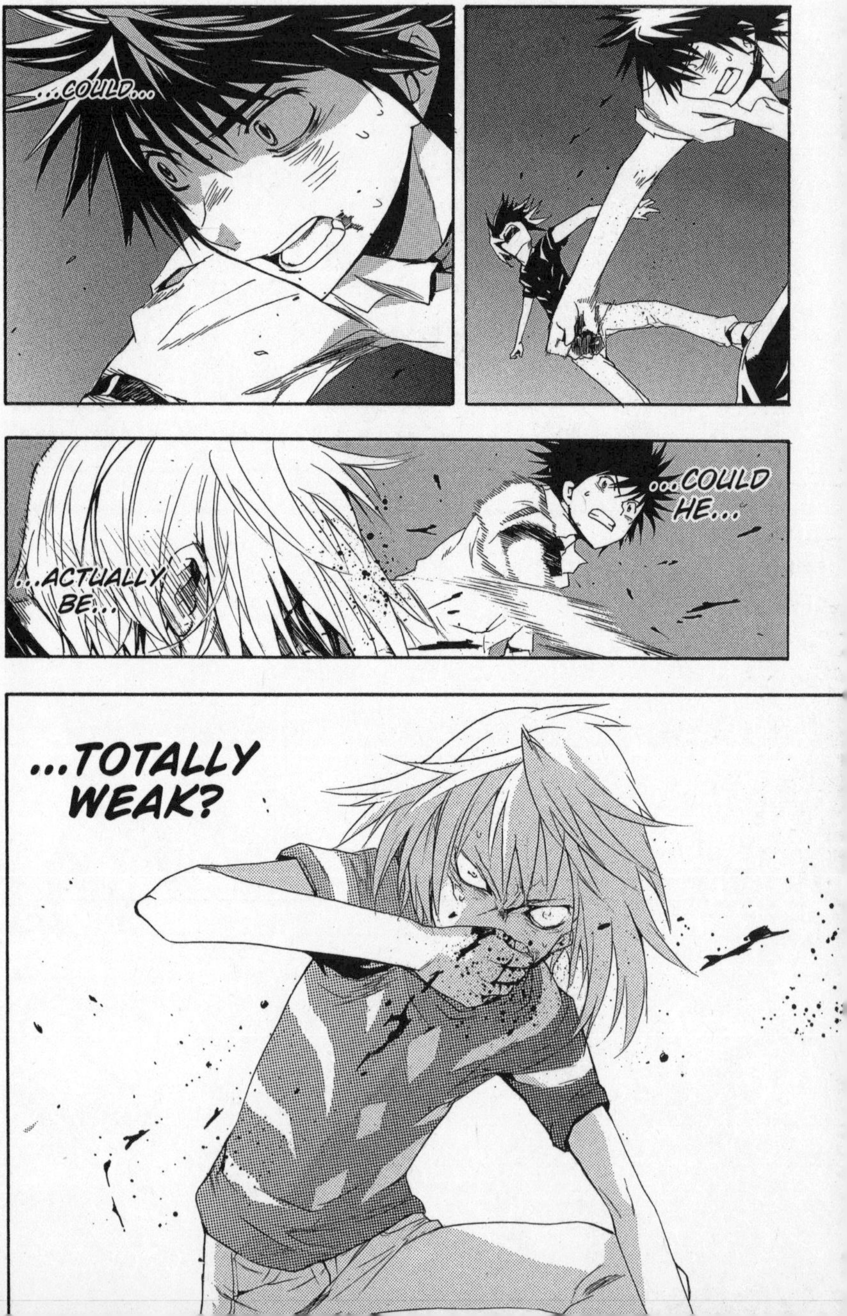
...COULD...
...COULD HE...
...ACTUALLY BE...
...TOTALLY WEAK?

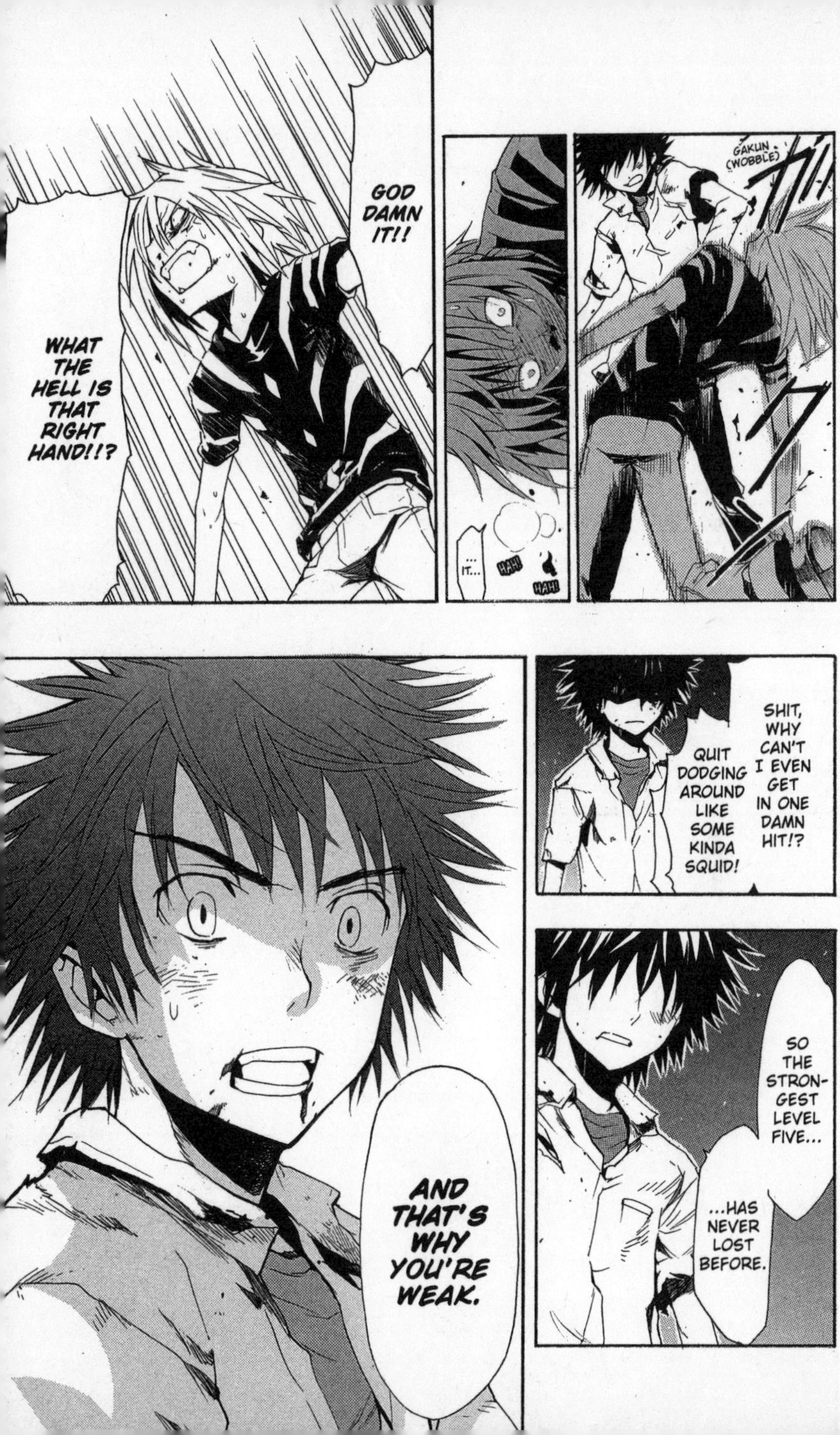
GAKUN (WOBBLE)
... IT...
HAH!
HAH!
GOD DAMN IT!!
WHAT THE HELL IS THAT RIGHT HAND!!?
SHIT, WHY CAN'T I EVEN GET IN ONE DAMN HIT!?
QUIT DODGING AROUND LIKE SOME KINDA SQUID!
SO THE STRONGEST LEVEL FIVE...
...HAS NEVER LOST BEFORE.
AND THAT'S WHY YOU'RE WEAK.

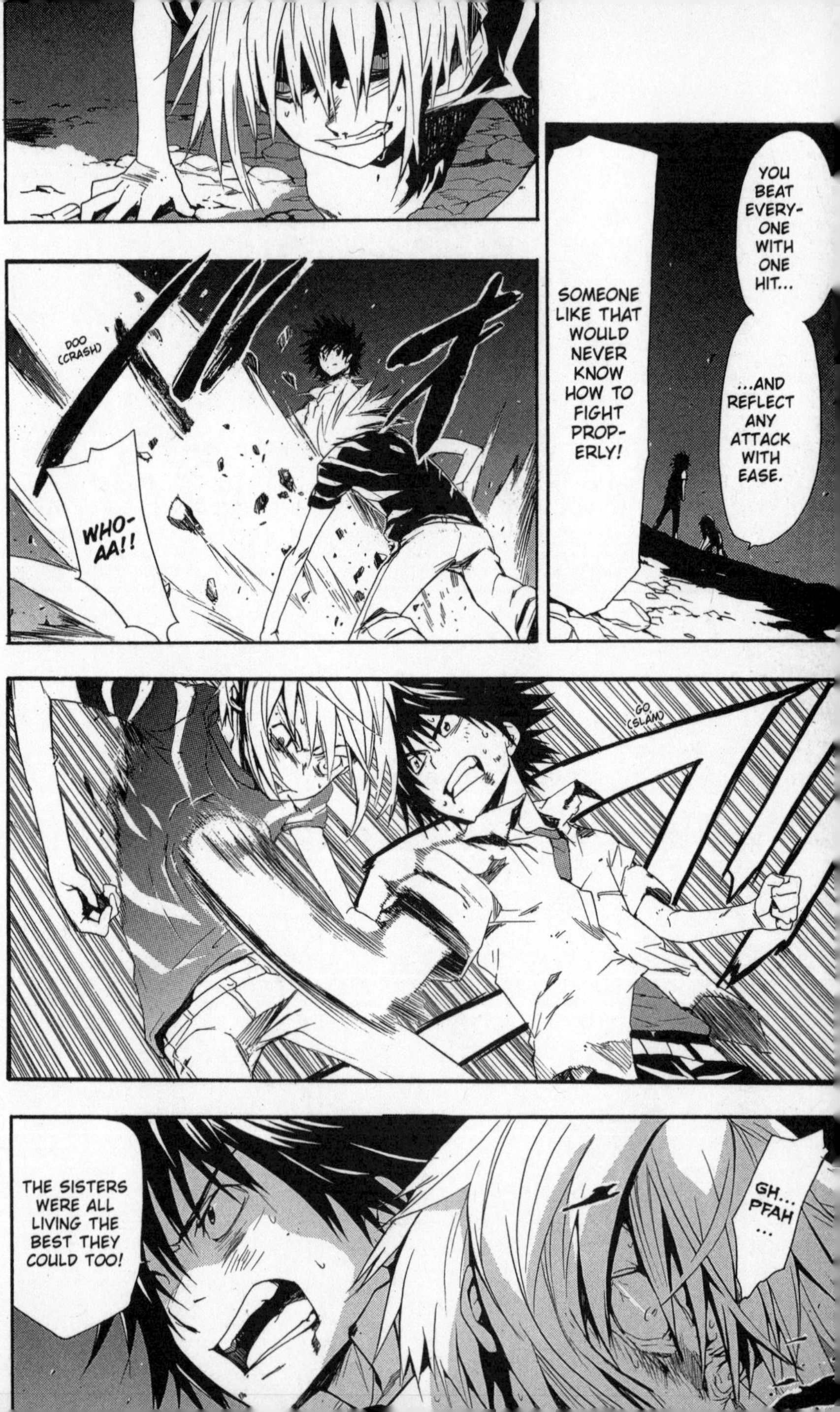
YOU BEAT EVERY-ONE WITH ONE HIT...
...AND REFLECT ANY ATTACK WITH EASE.
SOMEONE LIKE THAT WOULD NEVER KNOW HOW TO FIGHT PROP-ERLY!
DOO (CRASH)
WHO-AA!!
GO (SLAM)
GH... PFAH...
THE SISTERS WERE ALL LIVING THE BEST THEY COULD TOO!

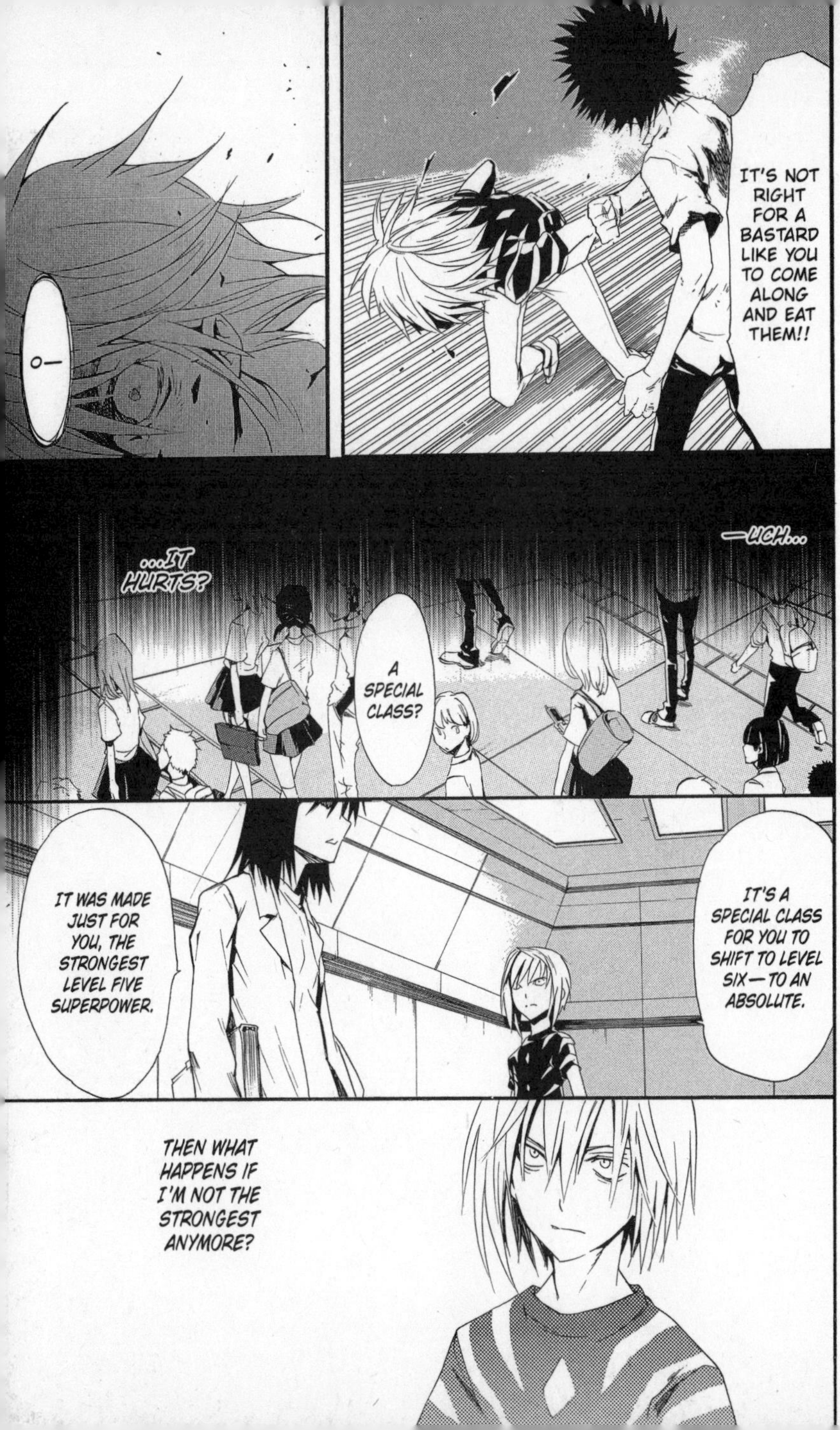
IT'S NOT RIGHT FOR A BASTARD LIKE YOU TO COME ALONG AND EAT THEM!!
O—
—UCH...
...IT HURTS?
A SPECIAL CLASS?
IT'S A SPECIAL CLASS FOR YOU TO SHIFT TO LEVEL SIX—TO AN ABSOLUTE.
IT WAS MADE JUST FOR YOU, THE STRONGEST LEVEL FIVE SUPERPOWER.
THEN WHAT HAPPENS IF I'M NOT THE STRONGEST ANYMORE?

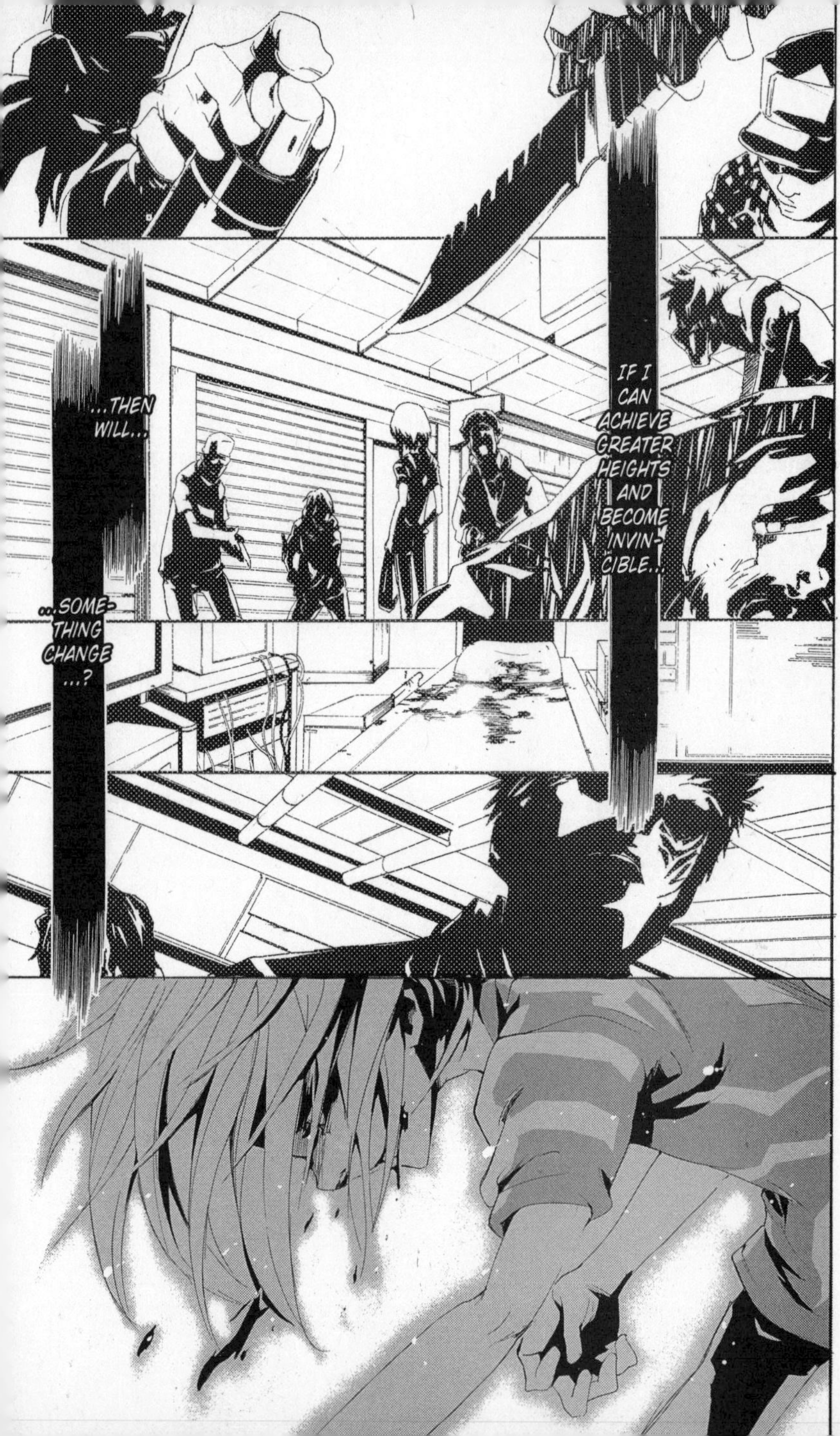
IF I CAN ACHIEVE GREATER HEIGHTS AND BECOME INVIN-CIBLE...
...THEN WILL...
...SOME-THING CHANGE ...?

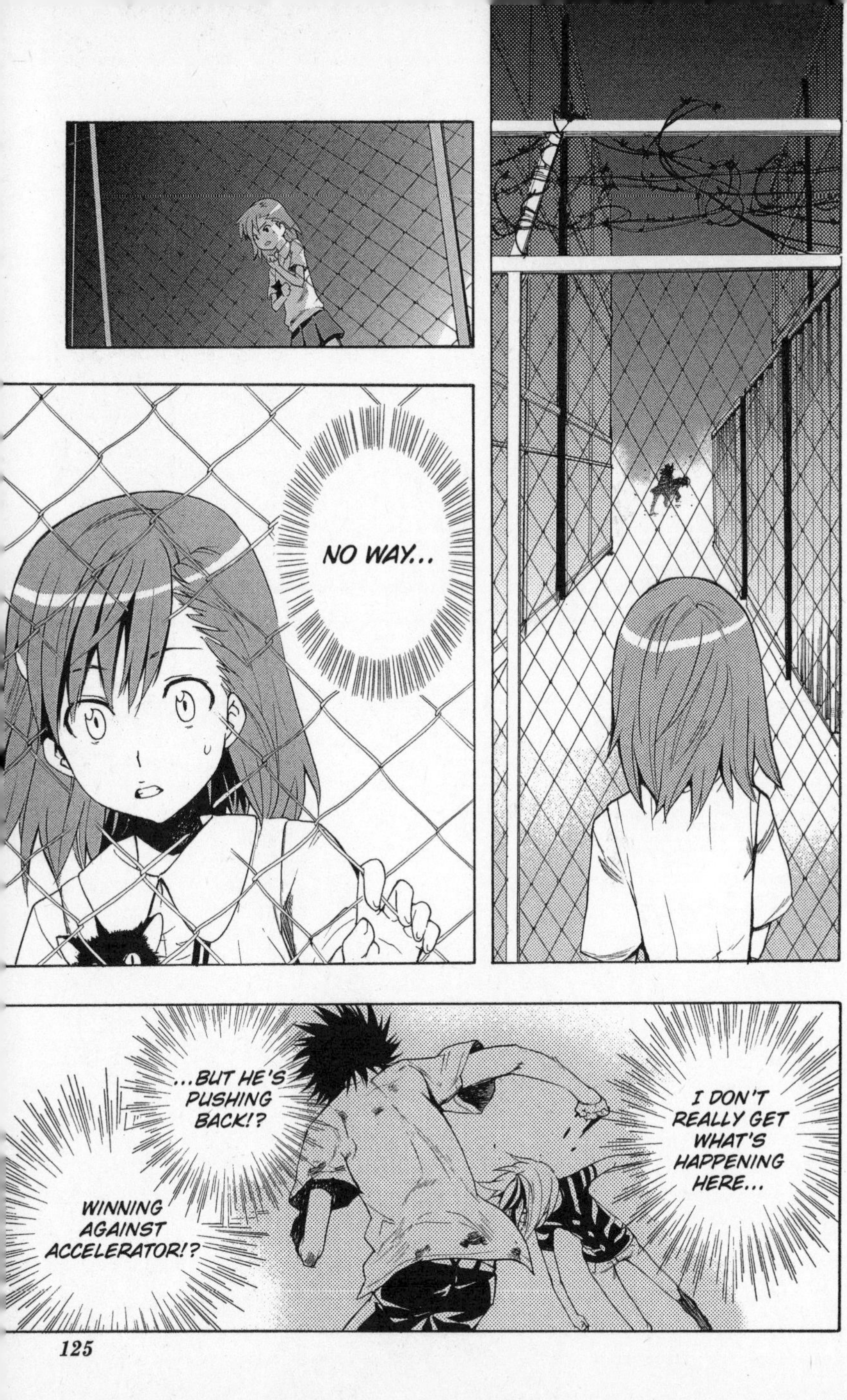
NO WAY...
I DON'T REALLY GET WHAT'S HAPPENING HERE...
...BUT HE'S PUSHING BACK!?
WINNING AGAINST ACCELERATOR!?

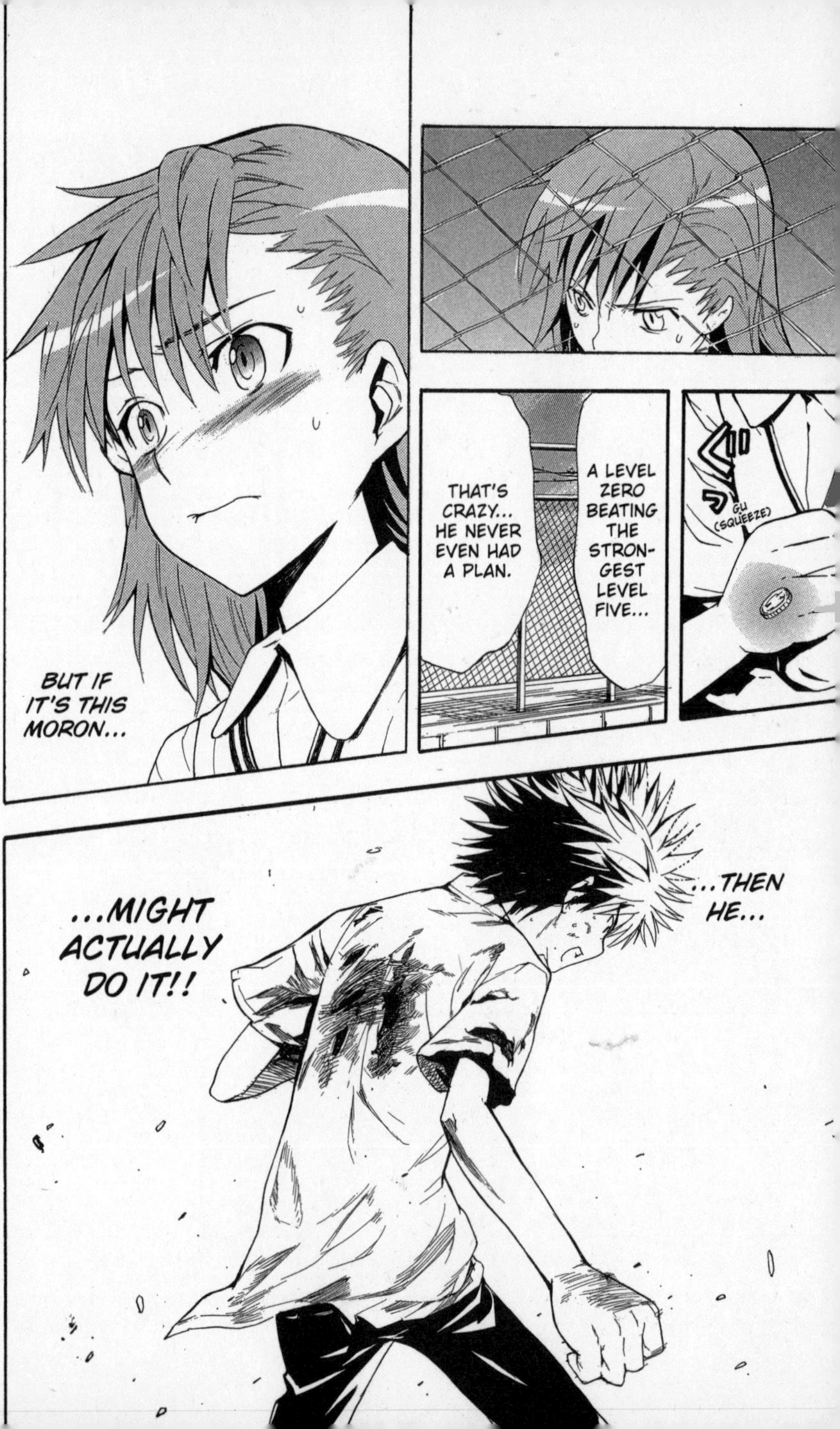
GU (SQUEEZE)
A LEVEL ZERO BEATING THE STRONGEST LEVEL FIVE...
THAT'S CRAZY... HE NEVER EVEN HAD A PLAN.
BUT IF IT'S THIS MORON...
...THEN HE...
...MIGHT ACTUALLY DO IT!!

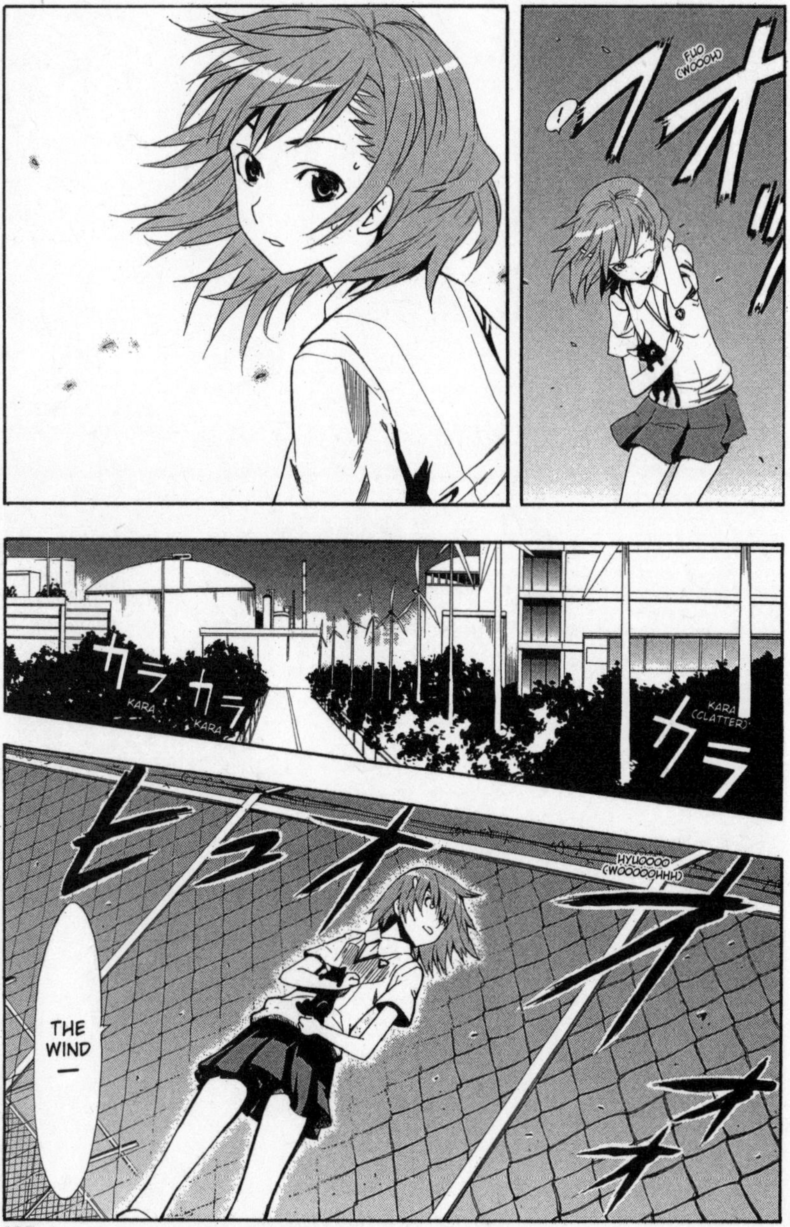
FUO
(WOOOH)
!
KARA
(CLATTER)
KARA
KARA
HYUOOOO
(WOOOOHHH)
THE WIND —

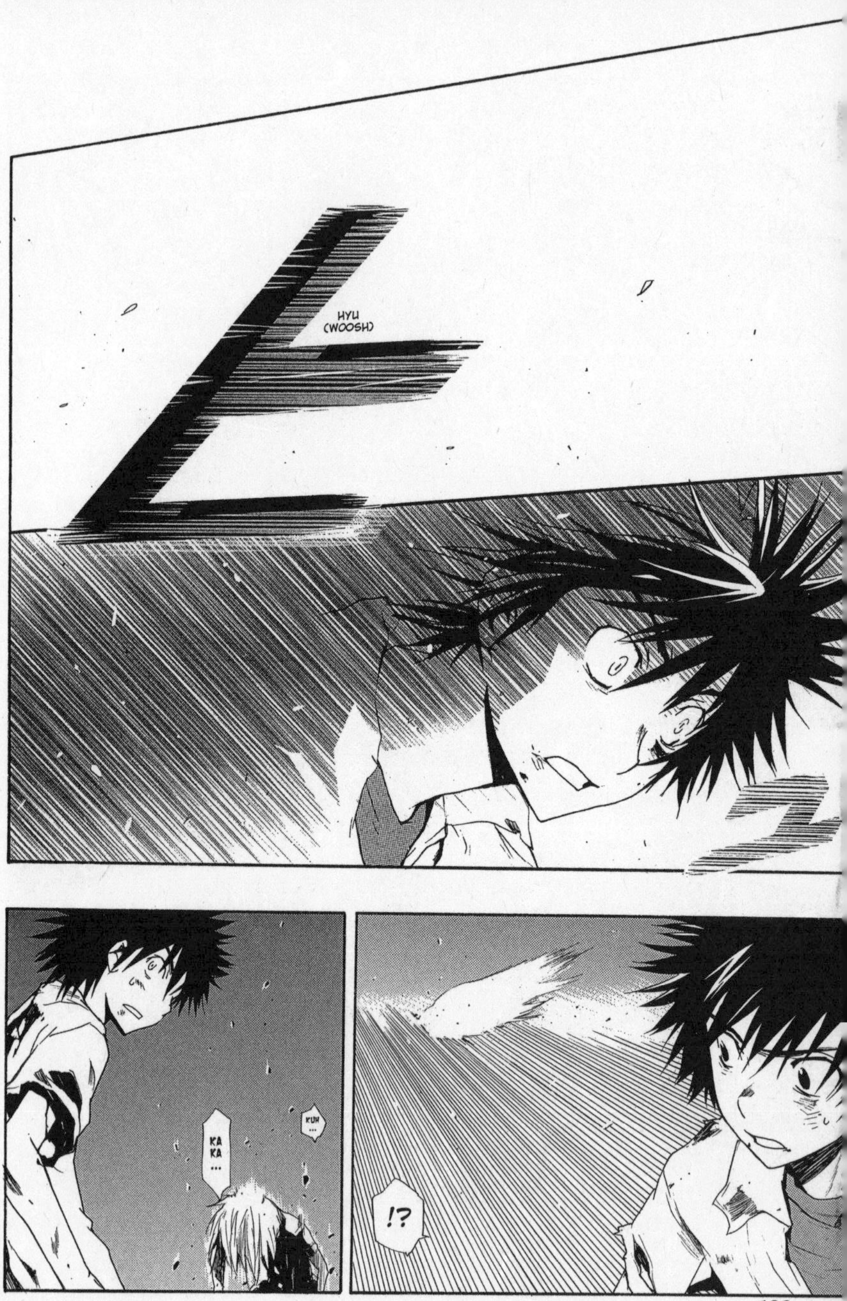
HYU
(WOOSH)
!?
KUH ...
KA KA ...

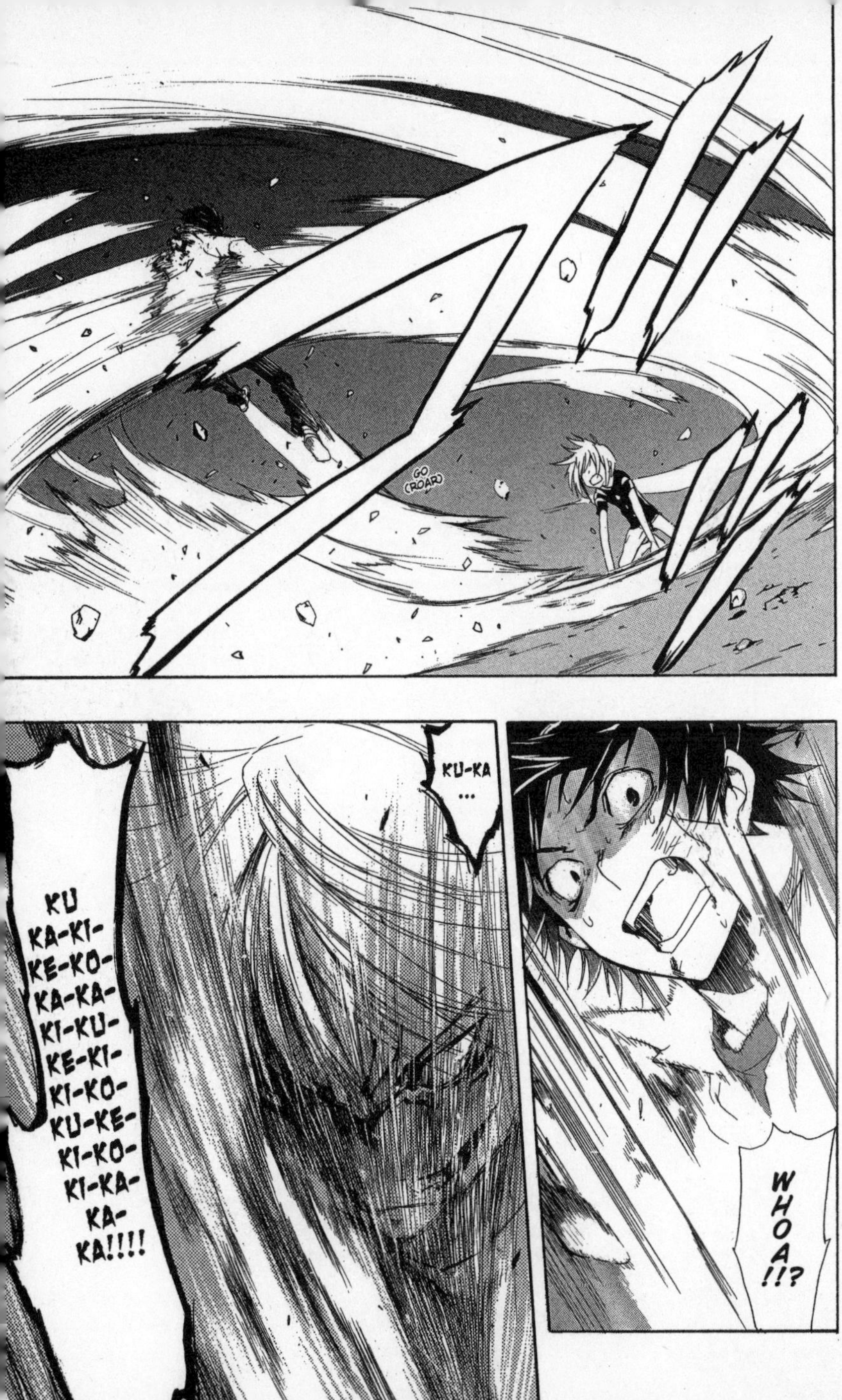
GO (ROAR)
WHOA!!?
KU-KA ...
KU KA-KI-KE-KO-KA-KA-KI-KU-KE-KI-KI-KO-KU-KE-KI-KO-KI-KA-KA-KA!!!!

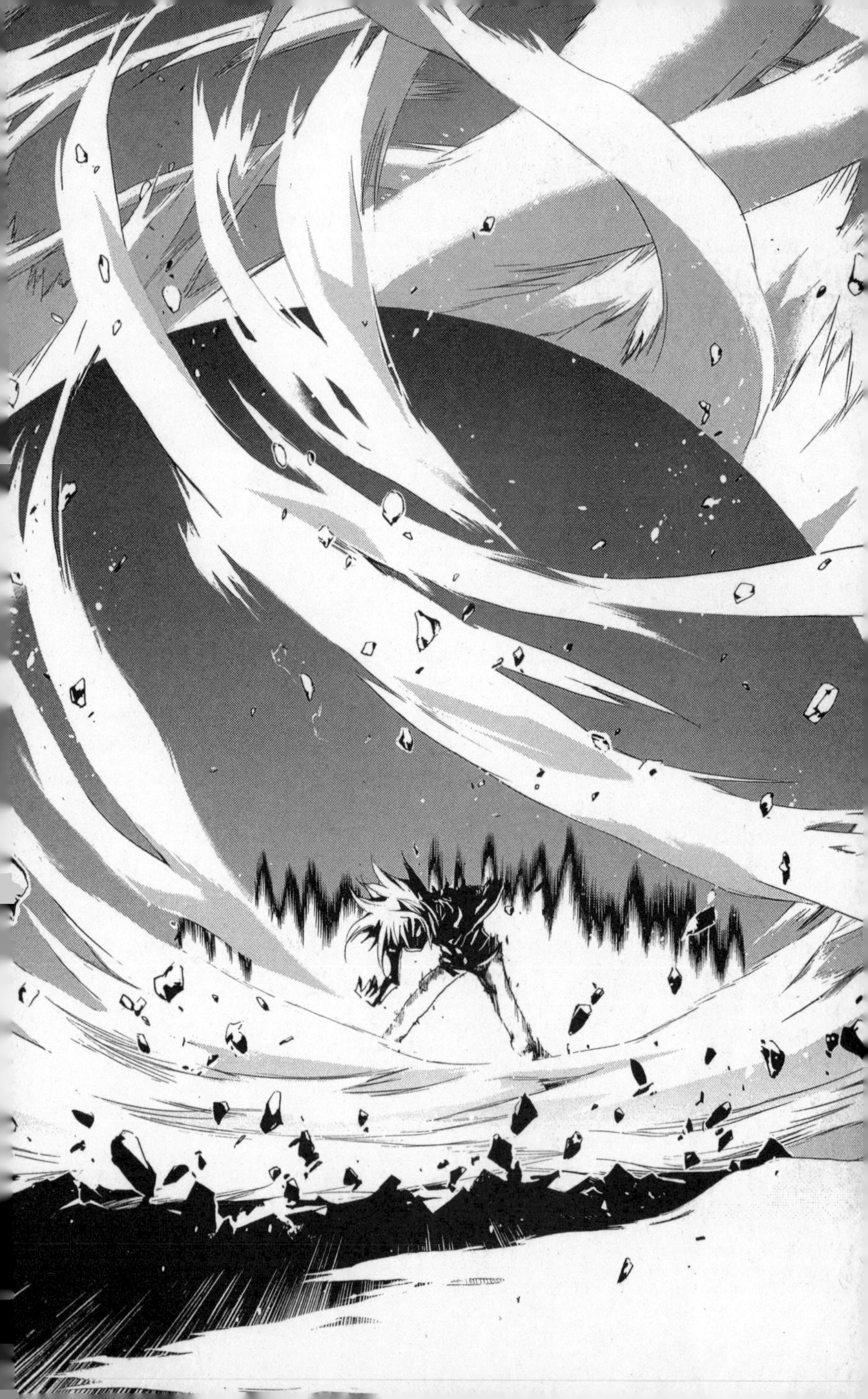

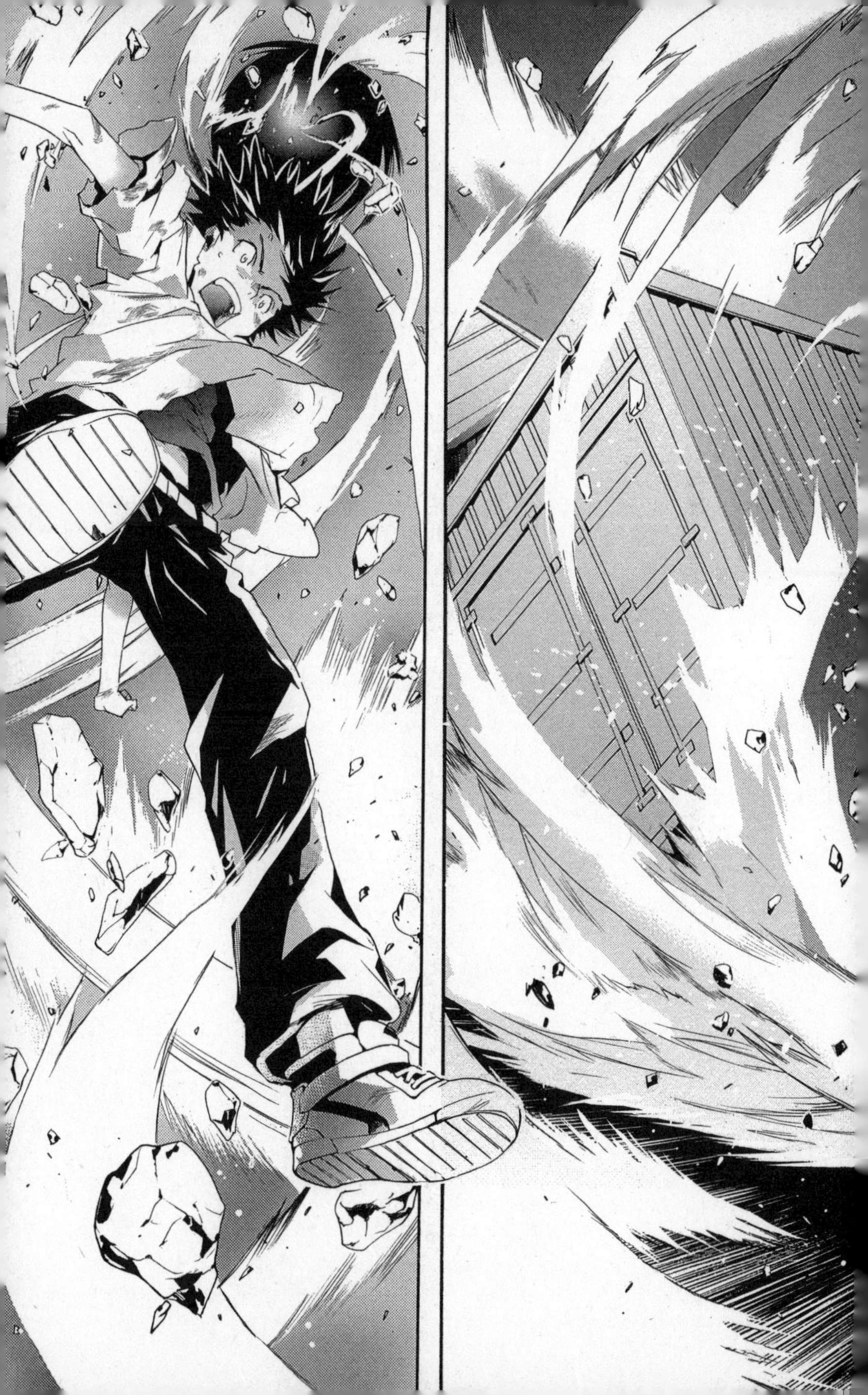

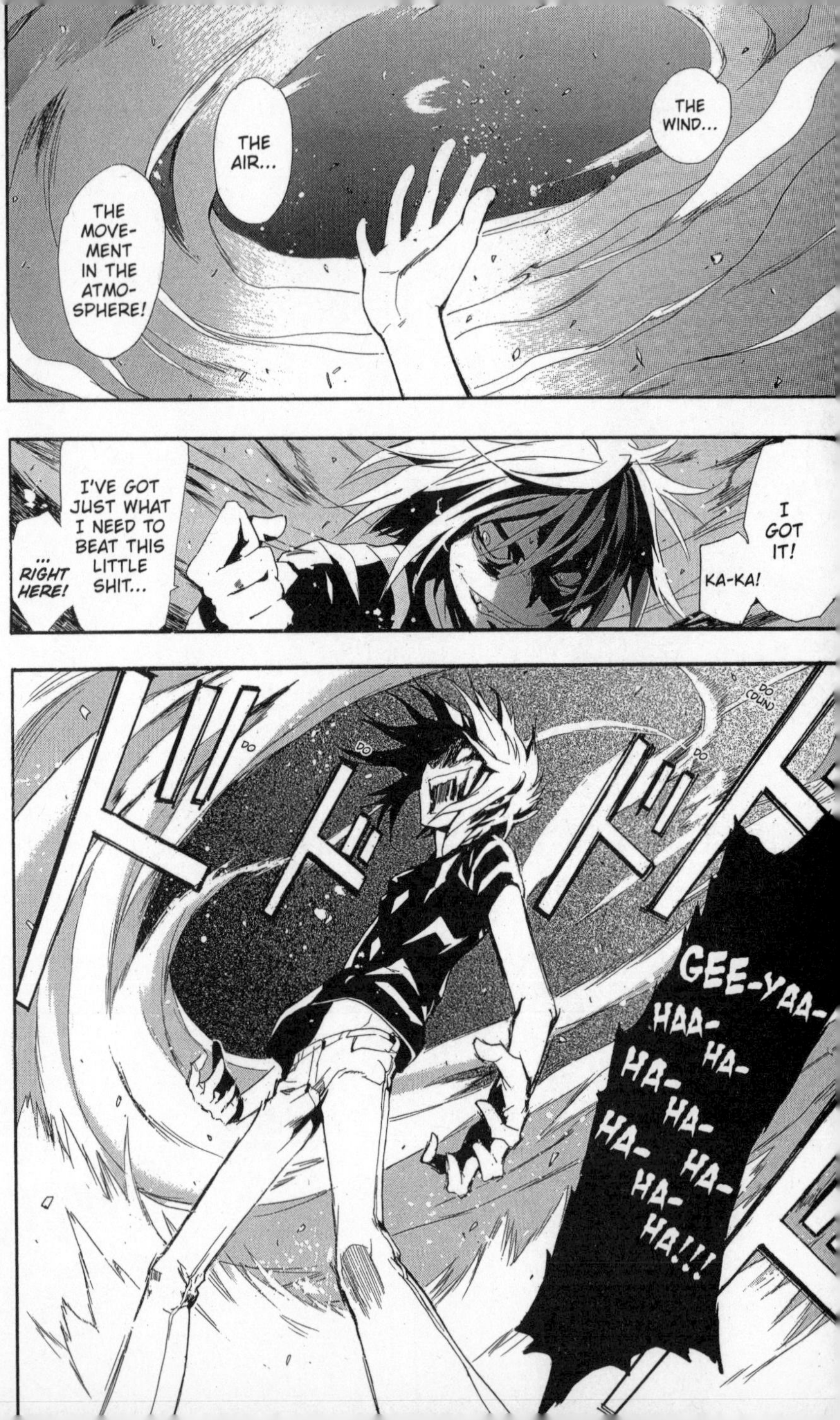
THE WIND...
THE AIR...
THE MOVEMENT IN THE ATMOSPHERE!
I GOT IT!
KA-KA!
I'VE GOT JUST WHAT I NEED TO BEAT THIS LITTLE SHIT...
...RIGHT HERE!
DO (DUN)
DO
DO
DO
GEE-YAA-HAA-HA-HA-HA-HA-HA-HA-HA!!!

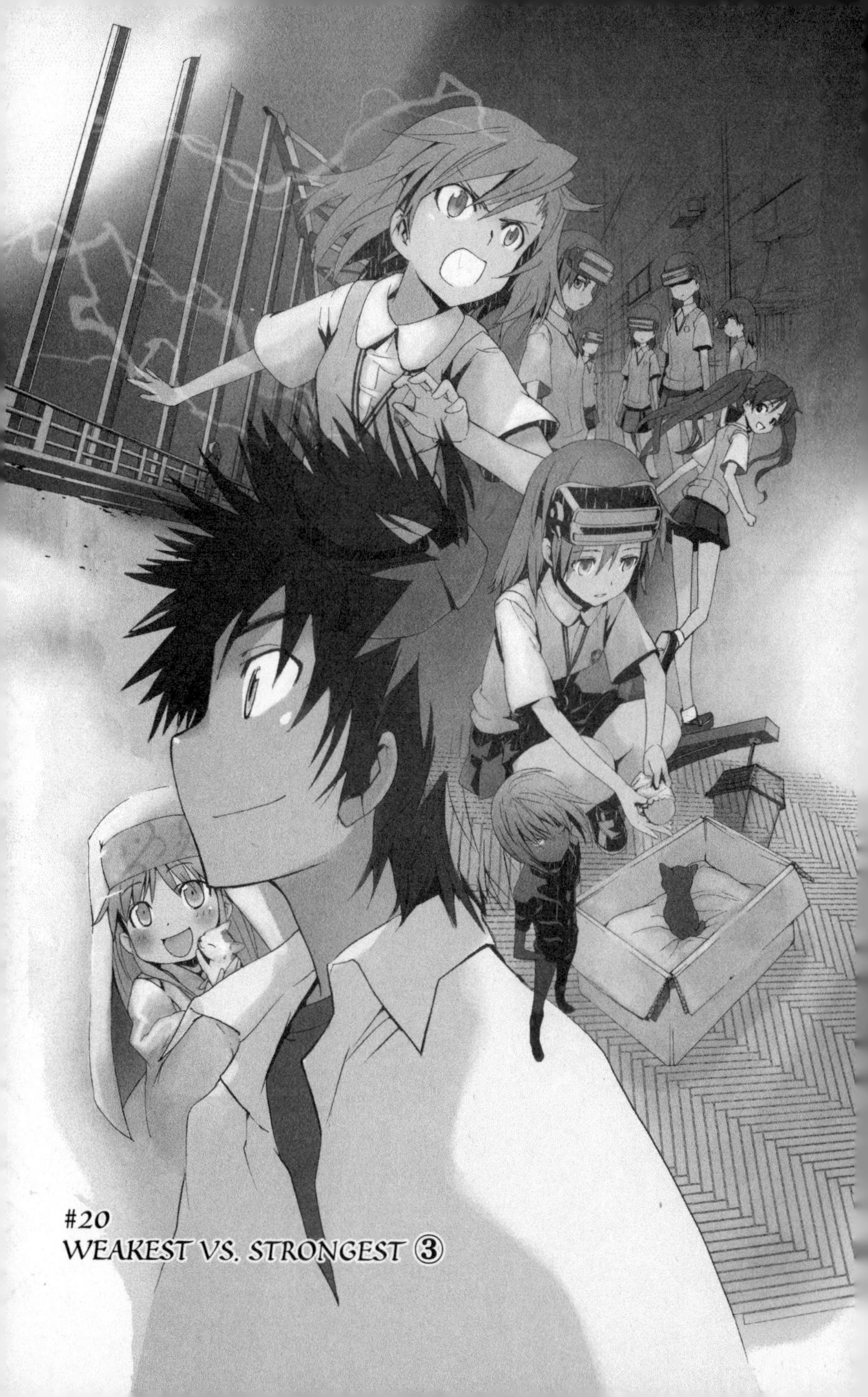

#20
WEAKEST VS. STRONGEST ③

A Certain Magical Index

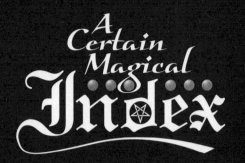

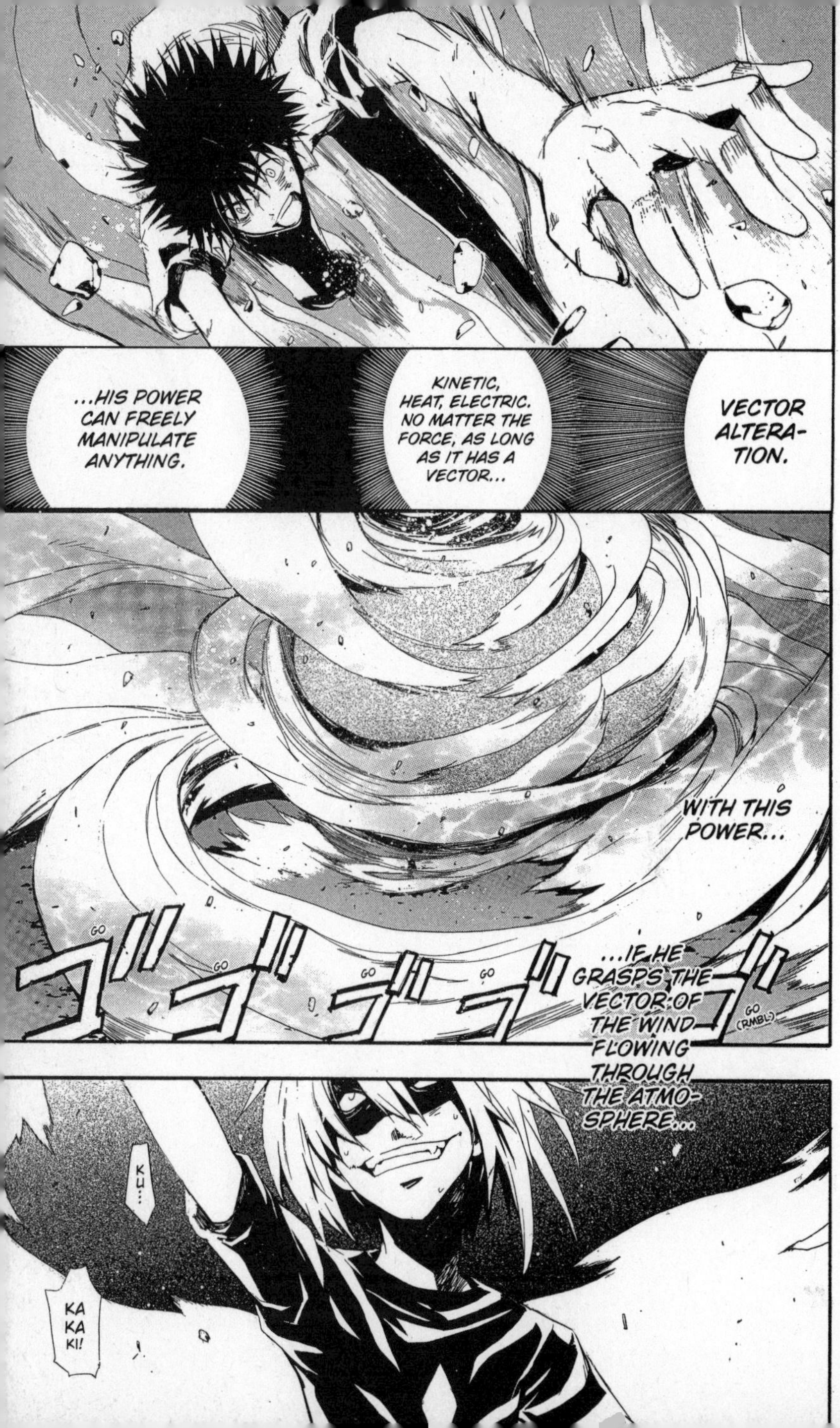
VECTOR ALTERATION.
KINETIC, HEAT, ELECTRIC. NO MATTER THE FORCE, AS LONG AS IT HAS A VECTOR...
...HIS POWER CAN FREELY MANIPULATE ANYTHING.
WITH THIS POWER...
GO (RMBL)
...IF HE GRASPS THE VECTOR OF THE WIND FLOWING THROUGH THE ATMOSPHERE...
GO
GO
GO
GO
KU...
KA KA KI!

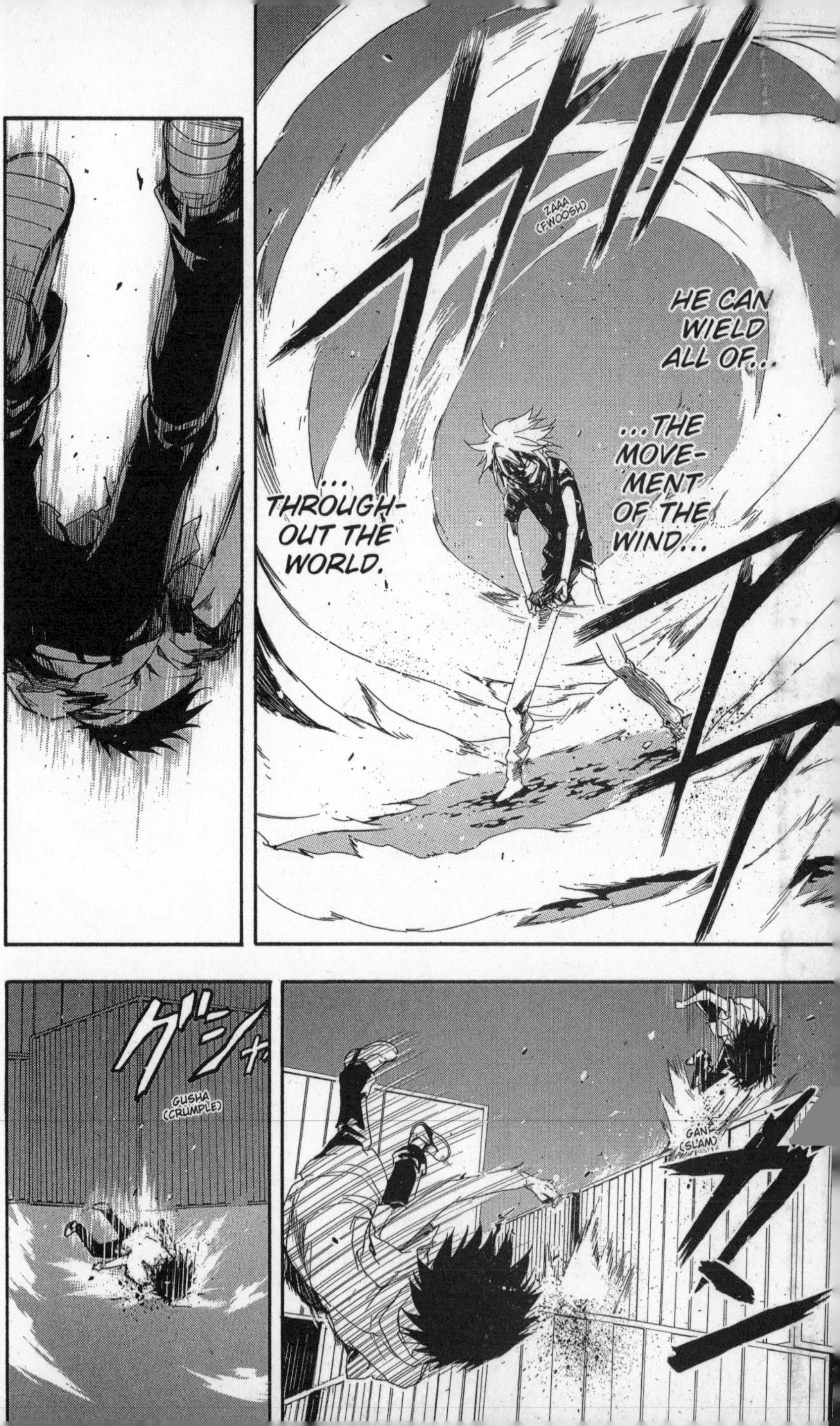
ZAAA
(FWOOSH)
HE CAN WIELD ALL OF...
...THE MOVE-MENT OF THE WIND...
...THROUGH-OUT THE WORLD.
GAN
(SLAM)
GUSHA
(CRUMPLE)

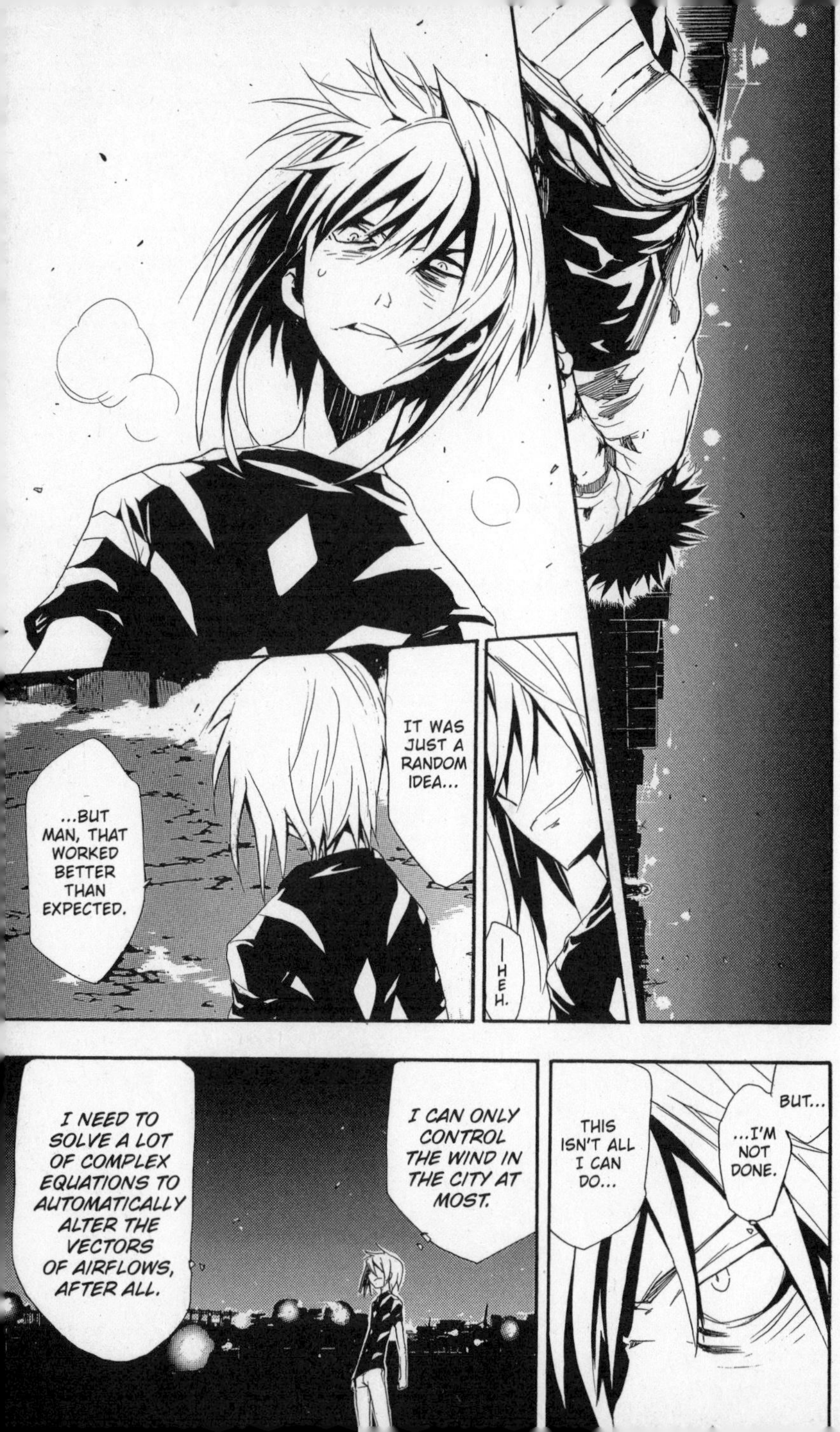
HEH.
IT WAS JUST A RANDOM IDEA...
...BUT MAN, THAT WORKED BETTER THAN EXPECTED.
BUT...
...I'M NOT DONE.
THIS ISN'T ALL I CAN DO...
I CAN ONLY CONTROL THE WIND IN THE CITY AT MOST.
I NEED TO SOLVE A LOT OF COMPLEX EQUATIONS TO AUTOMATICALLY ALTER THE VECTORS OF AIRFLOWS, AFTER ALL.

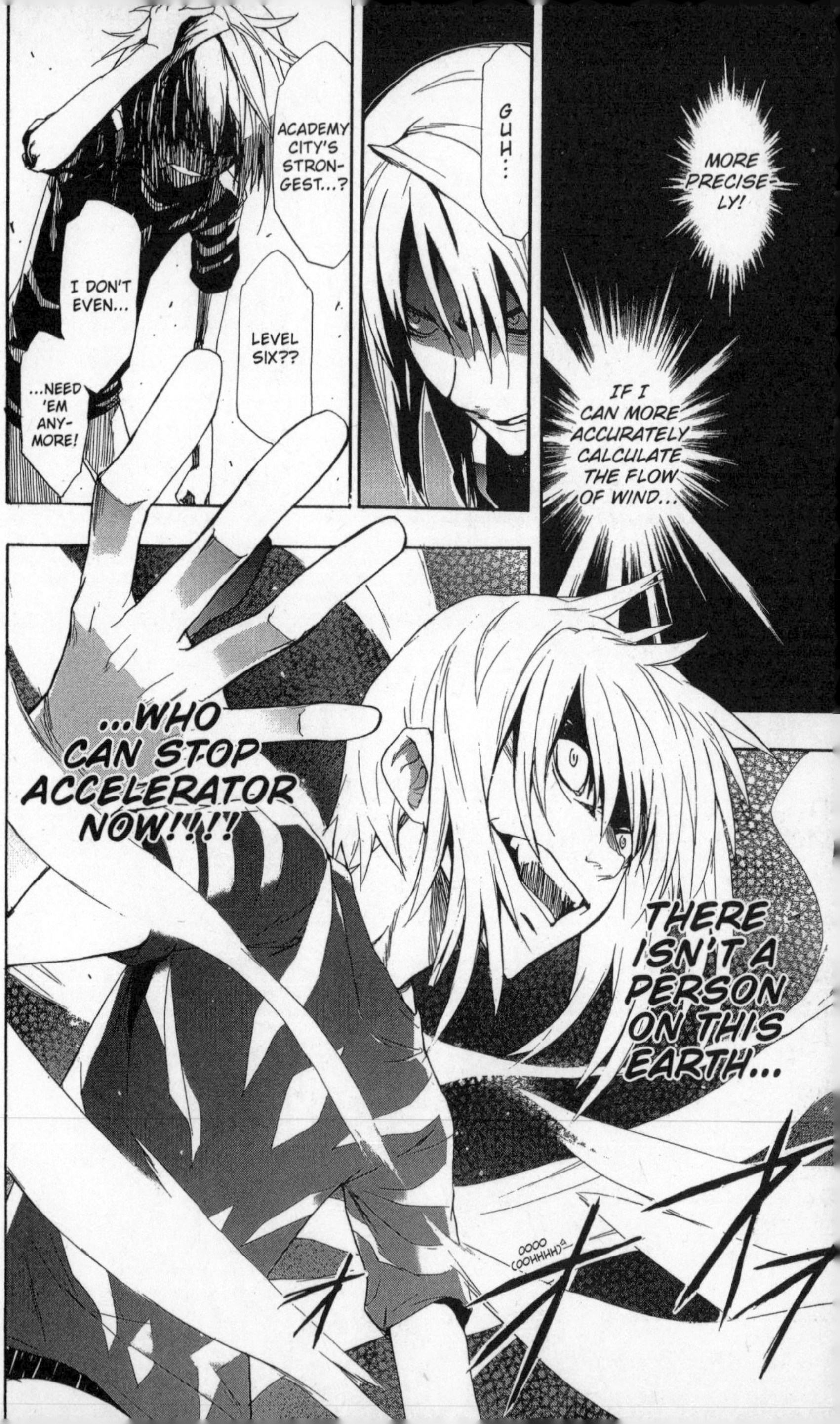
MORE PRECISE-LY!
IF I CAN MORE ACCURATELY CALCULATE THE FLOW OF WIND...
GUH...
ACADEMY CITY'S STRONG-GEST...?
LEVEL SIX??
I DON'T EVEN...
...NEED 'EM ANY-MORE!
THERE ISN'T A PERSON ON THIS EARTH...
...WHO CAN STOP ACCELERATOR NOW!!!!
OOOO (OOHHHH)

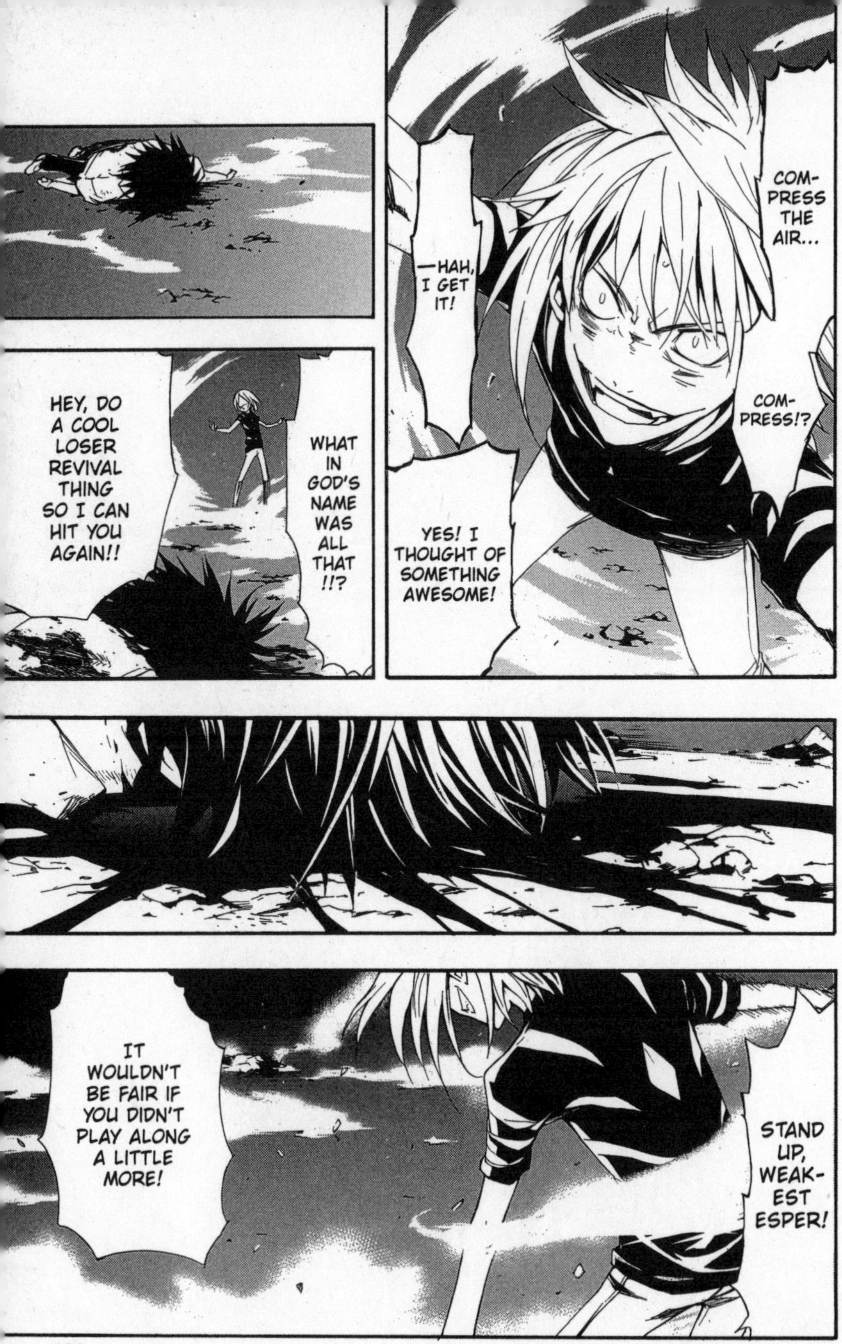
COM-PRESS THE AIR...
—HAH, I GET IT!
COM-PRESS!?
YES! I THOUGHT OF SOMETHING AWESOME!
WHAT IN GOD'S NAME WAS ALL THAT!!?
HEY, DO A COOL LOSER REVIVAL THING SO I CAN HIT YOU AGAIN!!
STAND UP, WEAK-EST ESPER!
IT WOULDN'T BE FAIR IF YOU DIDN'T PLAY ALONG A LITTLE MORE!

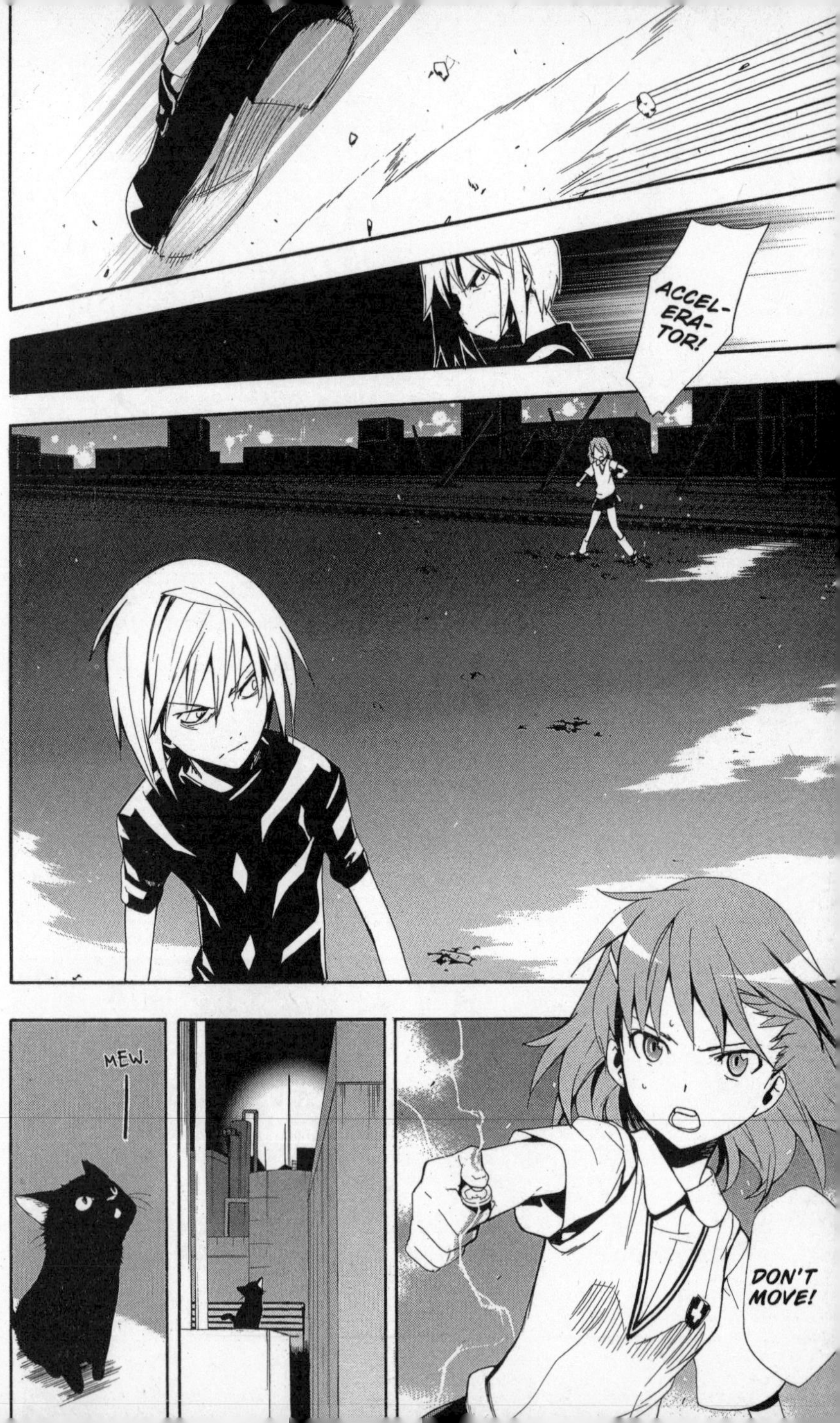
ACCEL-ERA-TOR!
DON'T MOVE!
MEW.

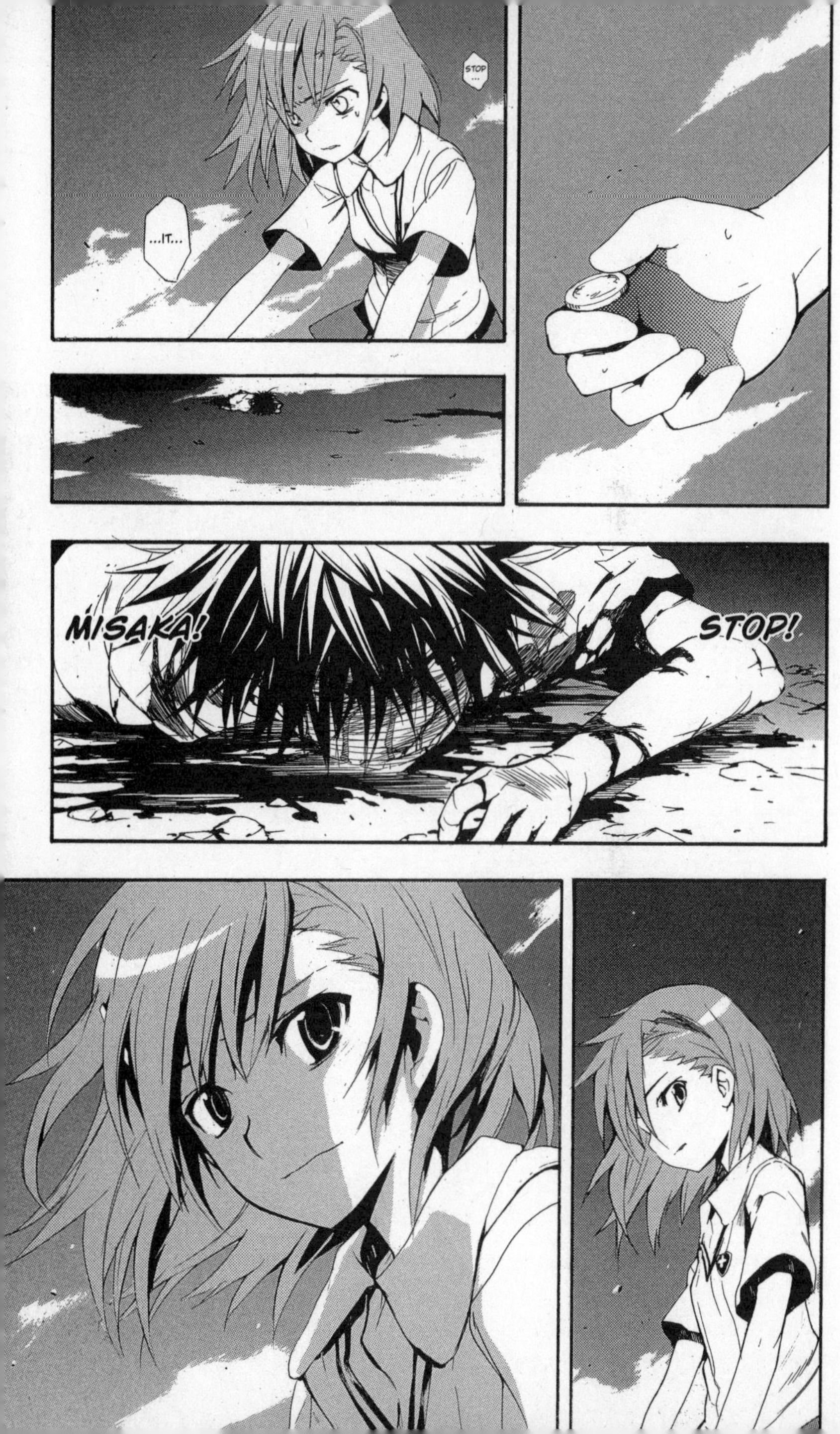
STOP ...
...IT...
STOP!
MISAKA!

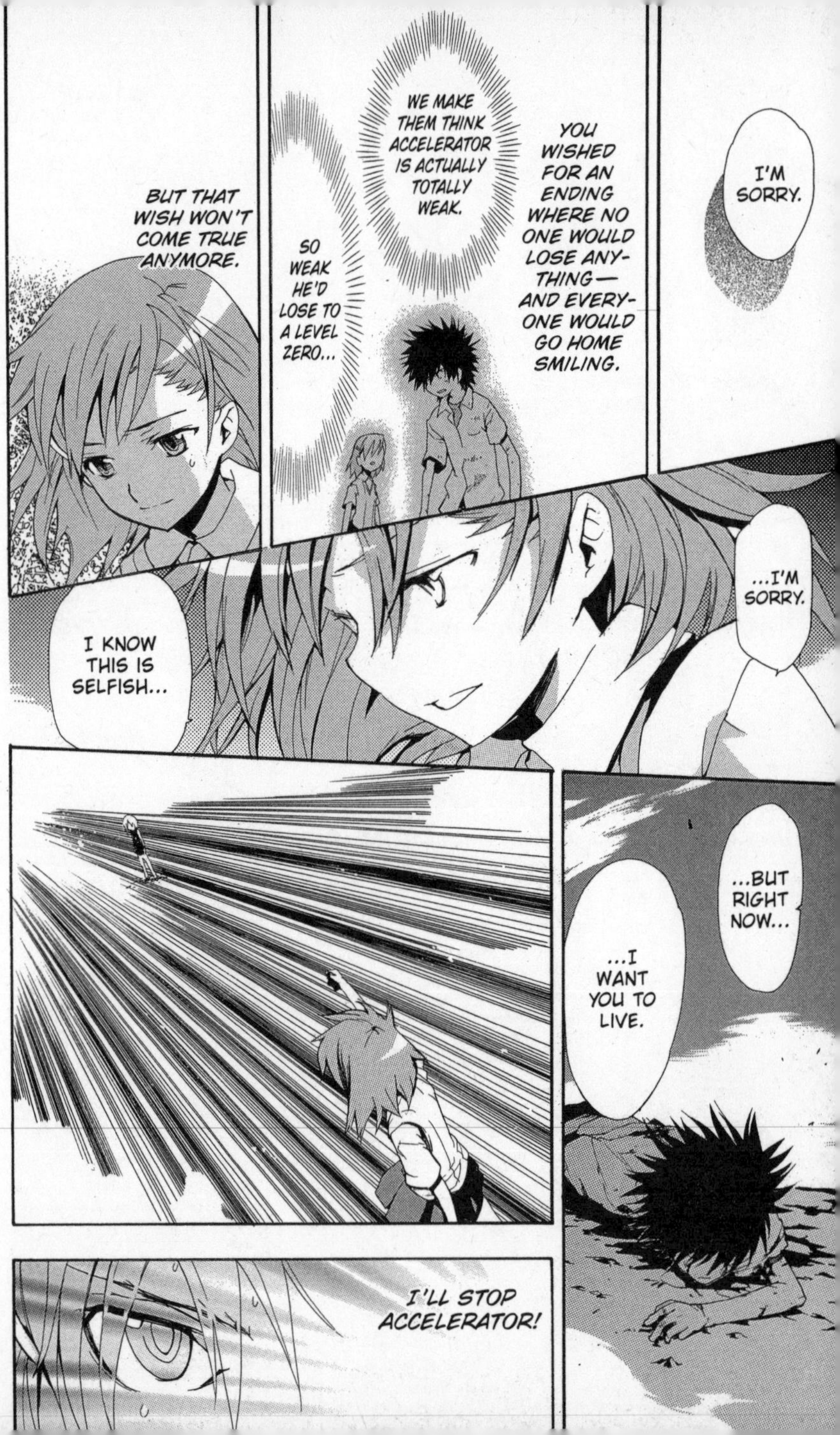
I'M SORRY.
YOU WISHED FOR AN ENDING WHERE NO ONE WOULD LOSE ANY-THING— AND EVERY-ONE WOULD GO HOME SMILING.
WE MAKE THEM THINK ACCELERATOR IS ACTUALLY TOTALLY WEAK.
SO WEAK HE'D LOSE TO A LEVEL ZERO...
BUT THAT WISH WON'T COME TRUE ANYMORE.
...I'M SORRY.
I KNOW THIS IS SELFISH...
...BUT RIGHT NOW...
...I WANT YOU TO LIVE.
I'LL STOP ACCELERATOR!

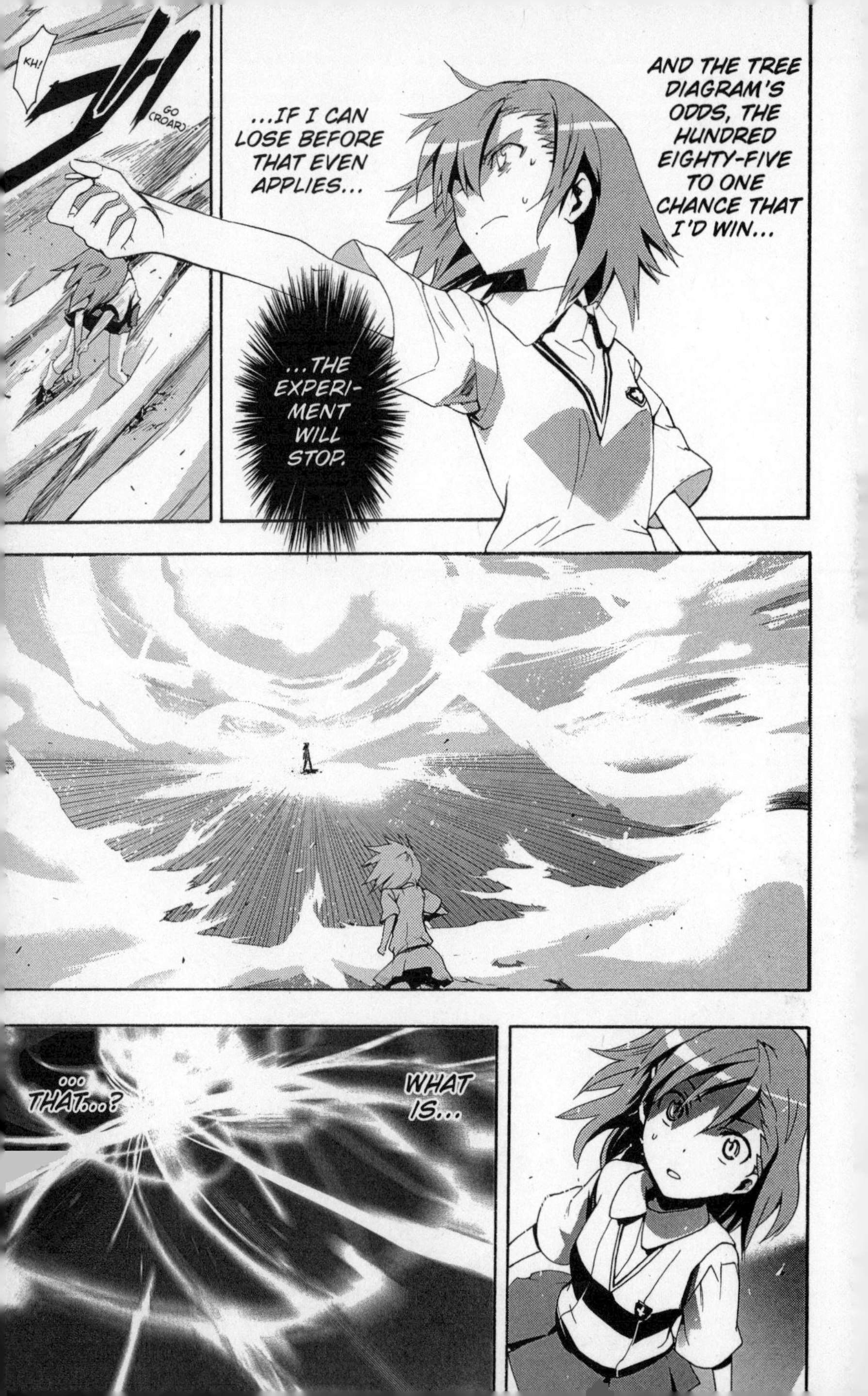
AND THE TREE DIAGRAM'S ODDS, THE HUNDRED EIGHTY-FIVE TO ONE CHANCE THAT I'D WIN...
...IF I CAN LOSE BEFORE THAT EVEN APPLIES...
...THE EXPERI-MENT WILL STOP.
KH!
GO (ROAR)
WHAT IS...
...THAT...?

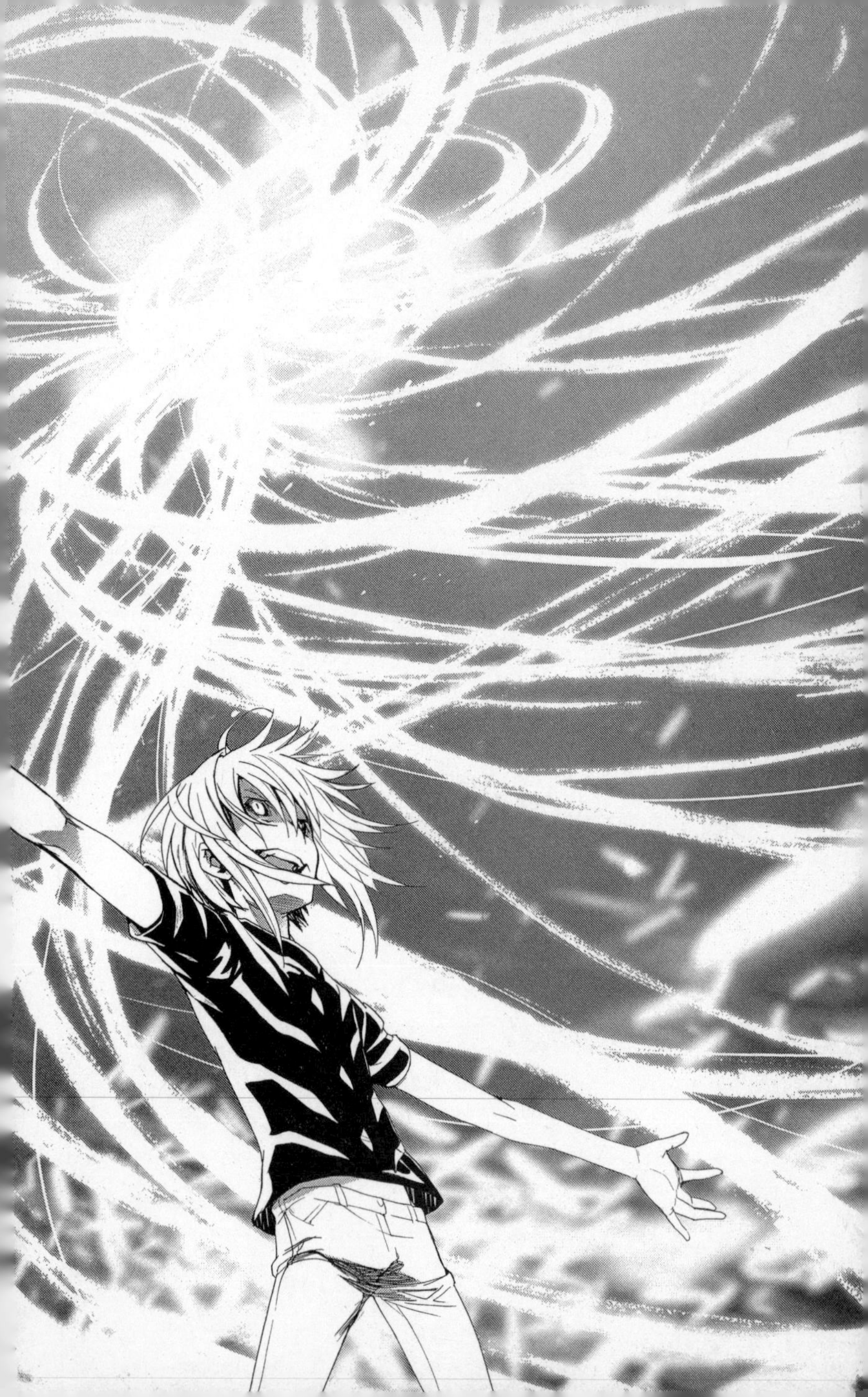

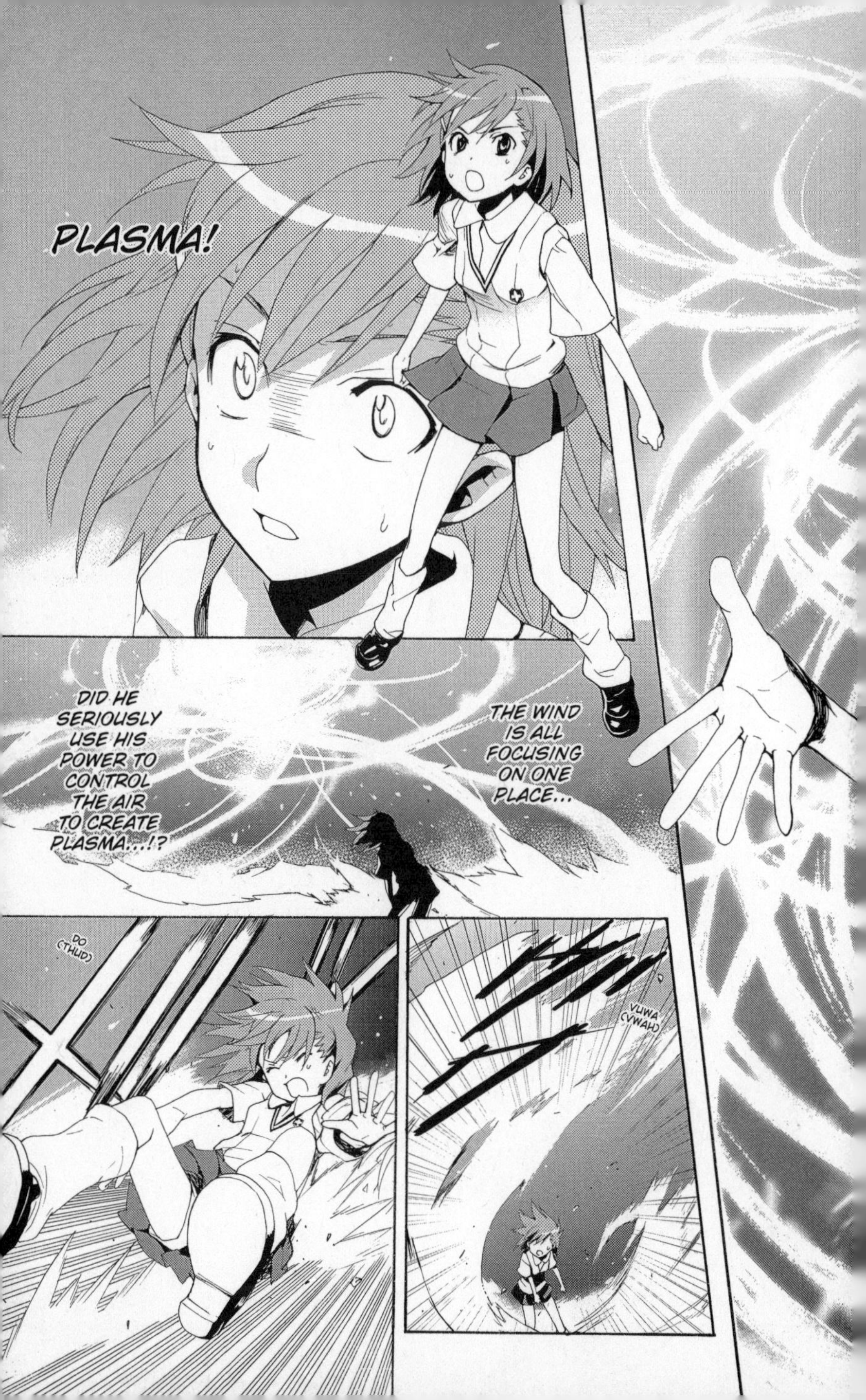
PLASMA!
THE WIND IS ALL FOCUSING ON ONE PLACE...
DID HE SERIOUSLY USE HIS POWER TO CONTROL THE AIR TO CREATE PLASMA...!?
VUWA (VWAH)
DO (THUD)

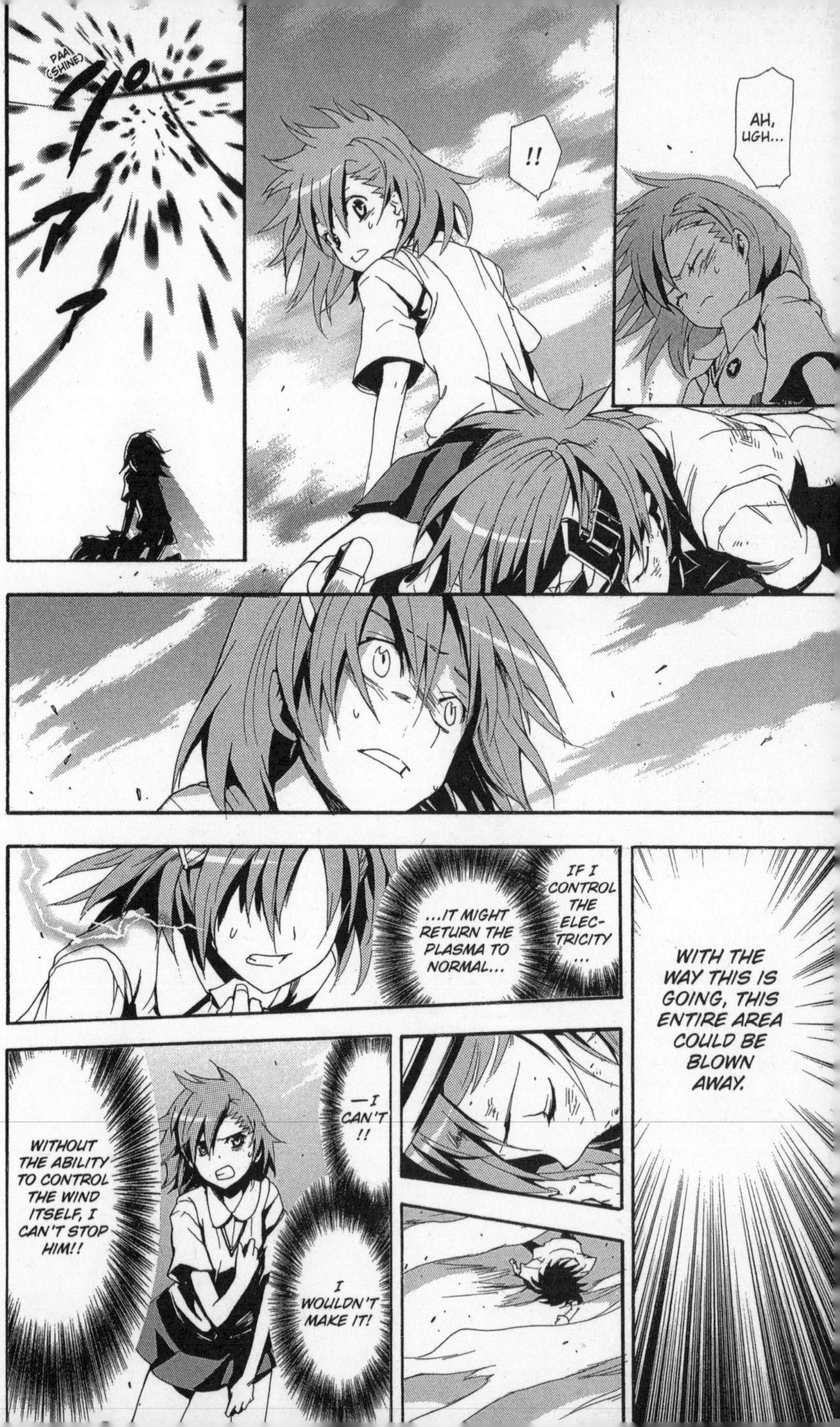
AH, UGH...
!!
PAA (SHINE)
WITH THE WAY THIS IS GOING, THIS ENTIRE AREA COULD BE BLOWN AWAY.
IF I CONTROL THE ELEC-TRICITY ...
...IT MIGHT RETURN THE PLASMA TO NORMAL...
—I CAN'T!!
WITHOUT THE ABILITY TO CONTROL THE WIND ITSELF, I CAN'T STOP HIM!!
I WOULDN'T MAKE IT!

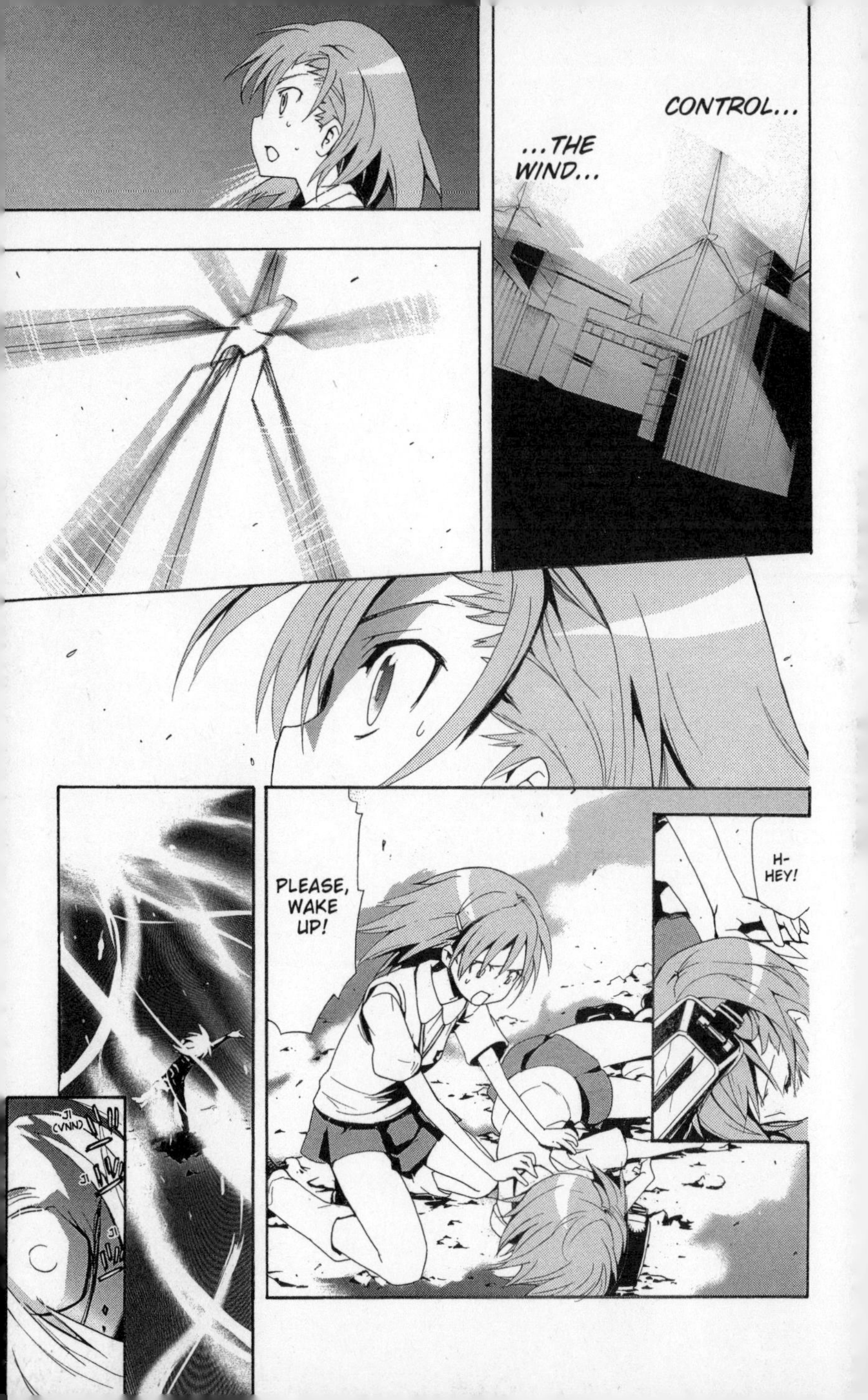
CONTROL...
...THE WIND...
H-HEY!
PLEASE, WAKE UP!
JI (VNN)
JI
JI

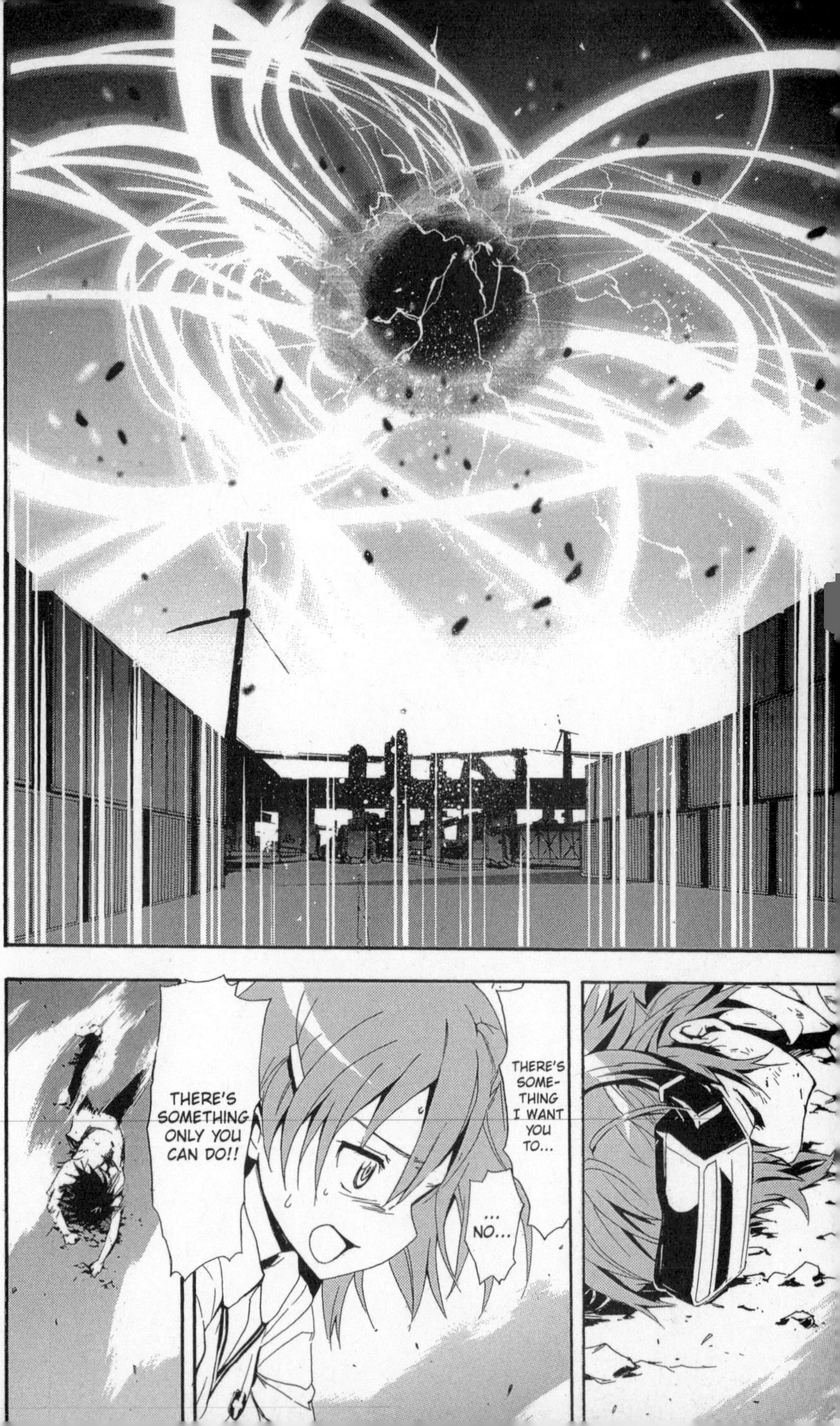
THERE'S SOMETHING I WANT YOU TO...
THERE'S SOMETHING ONLY YOU CAN DO!!
...NO...

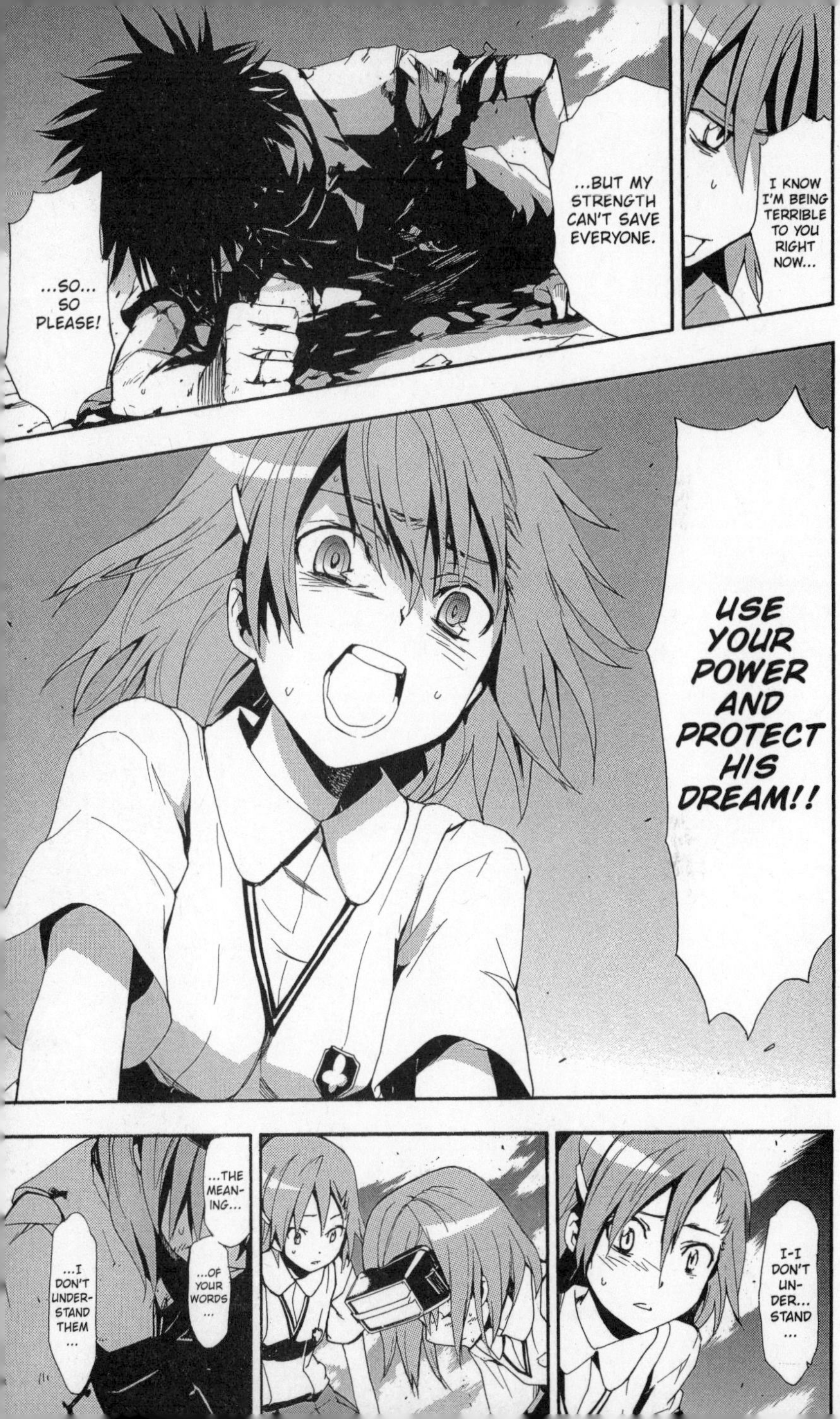
I KNOW I'M BEING TERRIBLE TO YOU RIGHT NOW...
...BUT MY STRENGTH CAN'T SAVE EVERYONE.
...SO... SO PLEASE!
USE YOUR POWER AND PROTECT HIS DREAM!!
I-I DON'T UN-DER... STAND ...
...THE MEAN-ING...
...OF YOUR WORDS ...
...I DON'T UNDER-STAND THEM ...

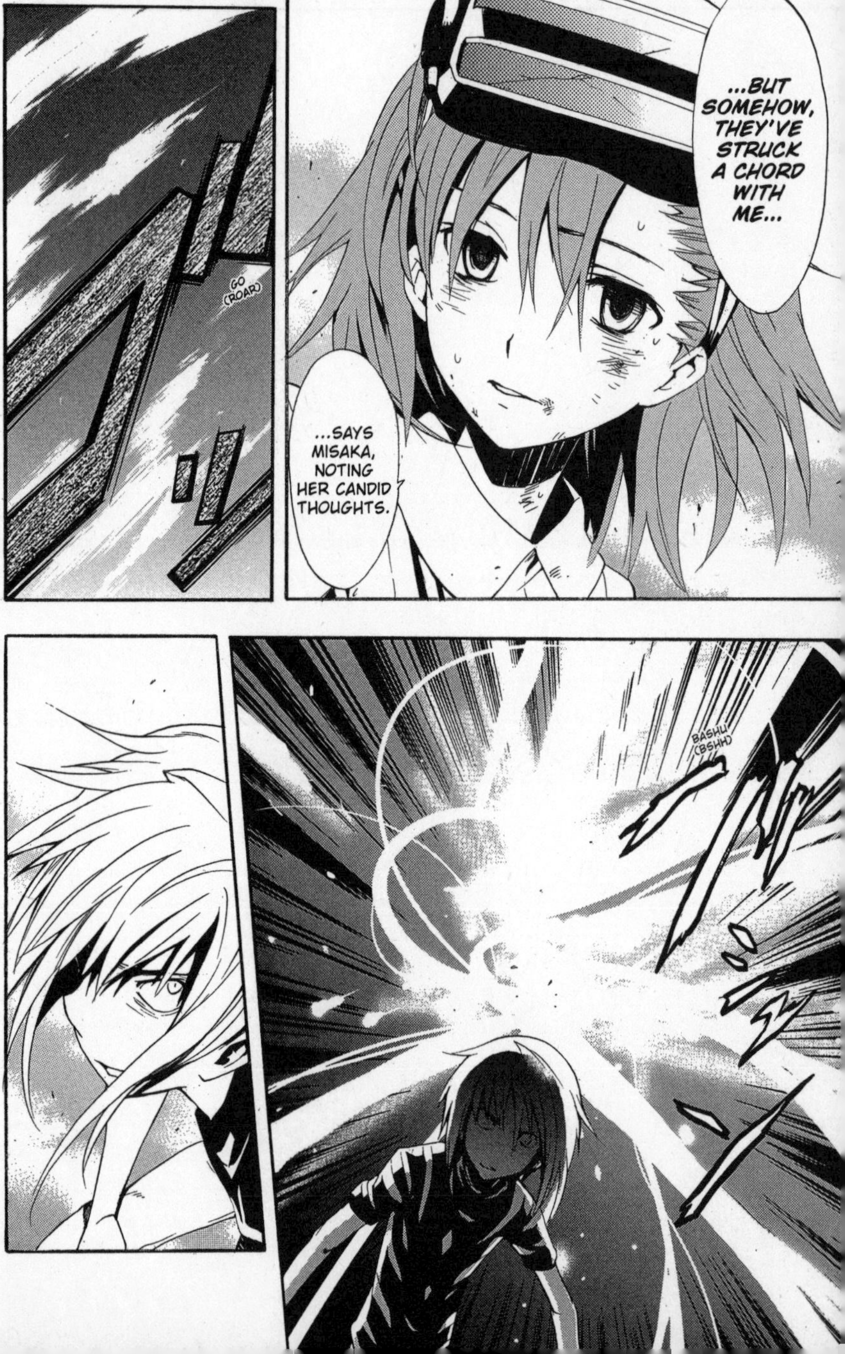
...BUT SOMEHOW, THEY'VE STRUCK A CHORD WITH ME...
...SAYS MISAKA, NOTING HER CANDID THOUGHTS.
GO (ROAR)
BASHU (BSHH)

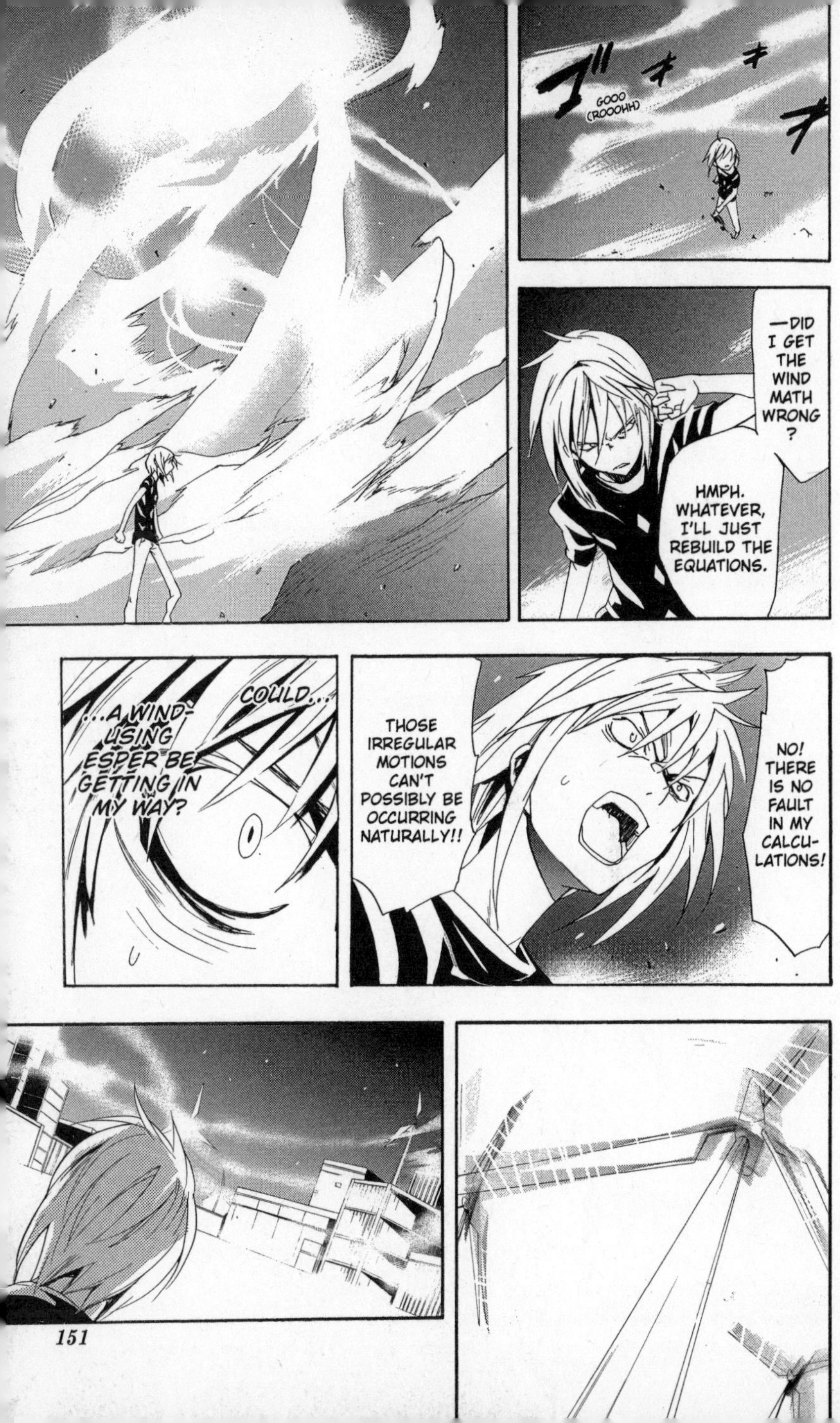
GOOO (ROOOHH)
—DID I GET THE WIND MATH WRONG?
HMPH. WHATEVER, I'LL JUST REBUILD THE EQUATIONS.
NO! THERE IS NO FAULT IN MY CALCULATIONS!
THOSE IRREGULAR MOTIONS CAN'T POSSIBLY BE OCCURRING NATURALLY!!
COULD...
...A WIND-USING ESPER BE GETTING IN MY WAY?

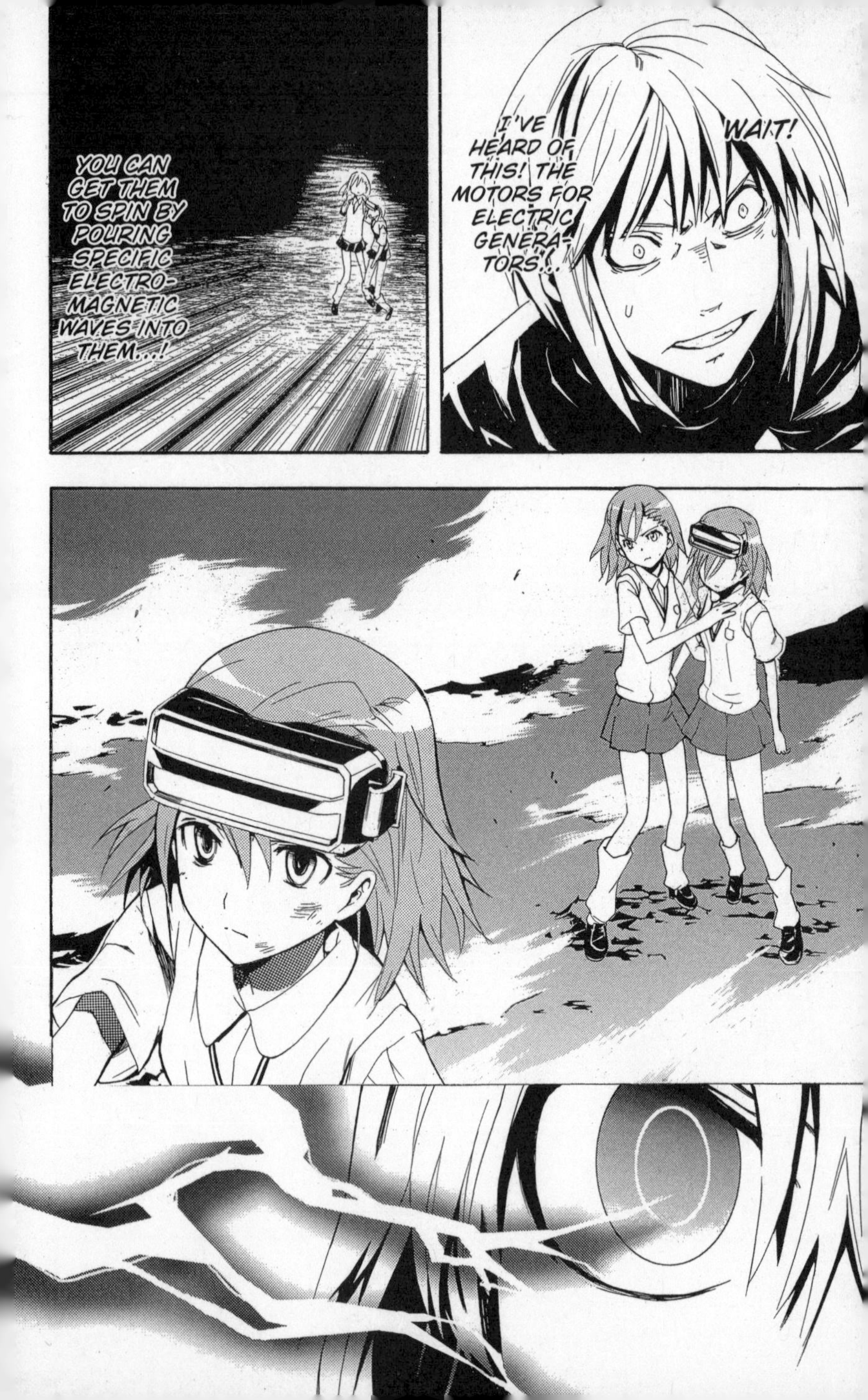
WAIT!
I'VE HEARD OF THIS! THE MOTORS FOR ELECTRIC GENERATORS...!
YOU CAN GET THEM TO SPIN BY POURING SPECIFIC ELECTROMAGNETIC WAVES INTO THEM...!

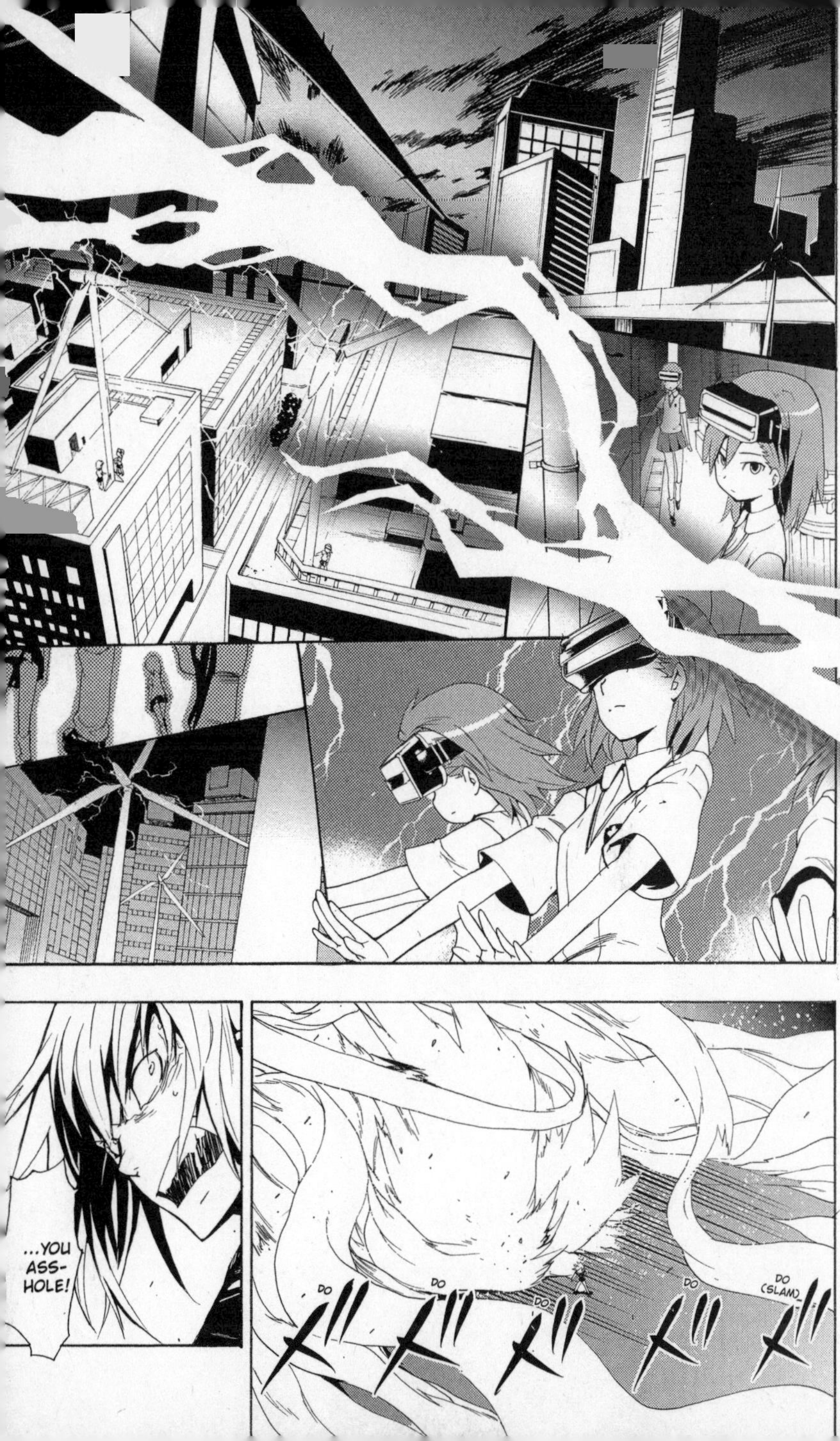
DO (SLAM)
DO
DO-
DO
DO
...YOU ASS-HOLE!

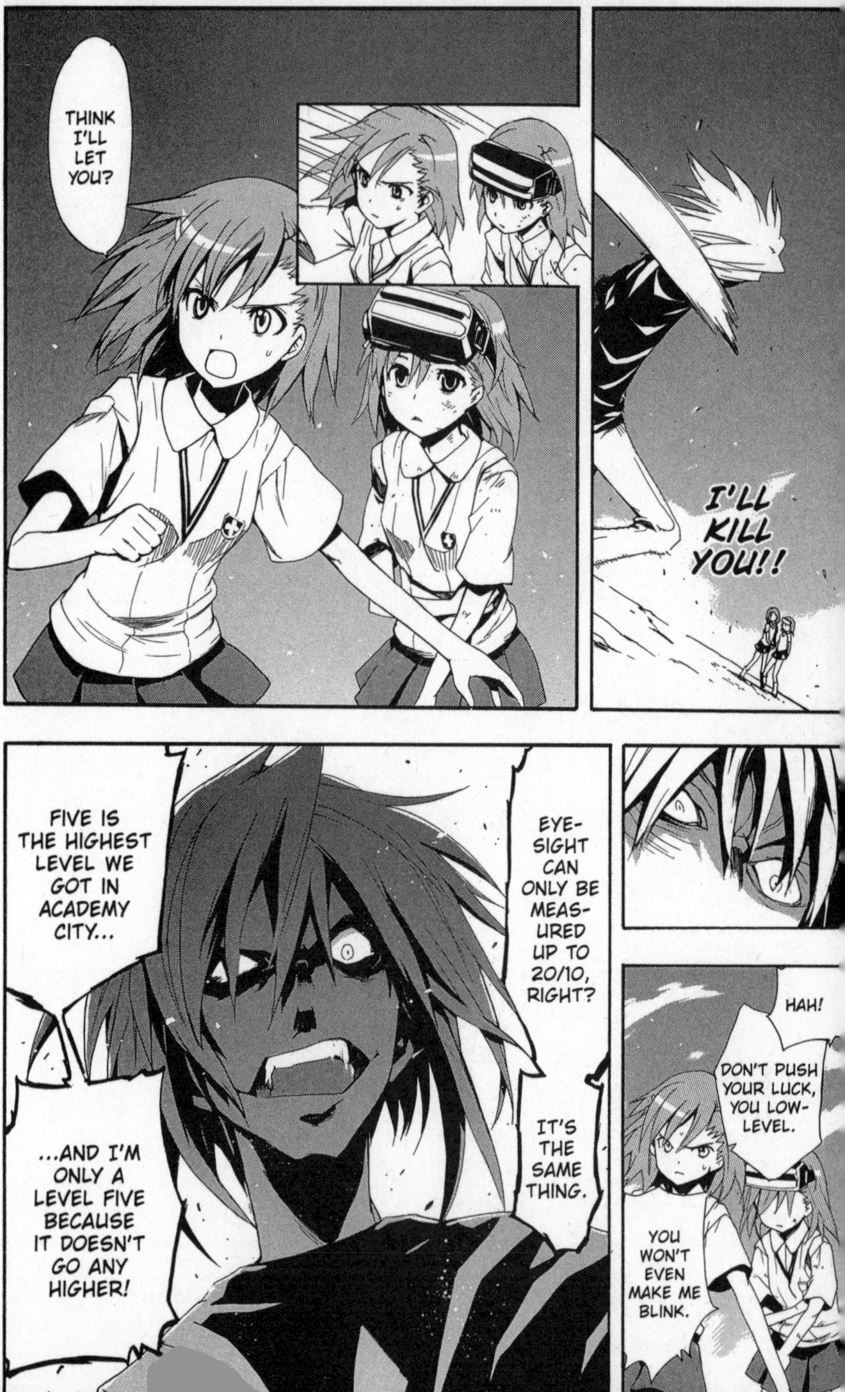
I'LL KILL YOU!!
THINK I'LL LET YOU?
HAH!
DON'T PUSH YOUR LUCK, YOU LOW-LEVEL.
YOU WON'T EVEN MAKE ME BLINK.
EYE-SIGHT CAN ONLY BE MEAS-URED UP TO 20/10, RIGHT?
FIVE IS THE HIGHEST LEVEL WE GOT IN ACADEMY CITY...
IT'S THE SAME THING.
...AND I'M ONLY A LEVEL FIVE BECAUSE IT DOESN'T GO ANY HIGHER!

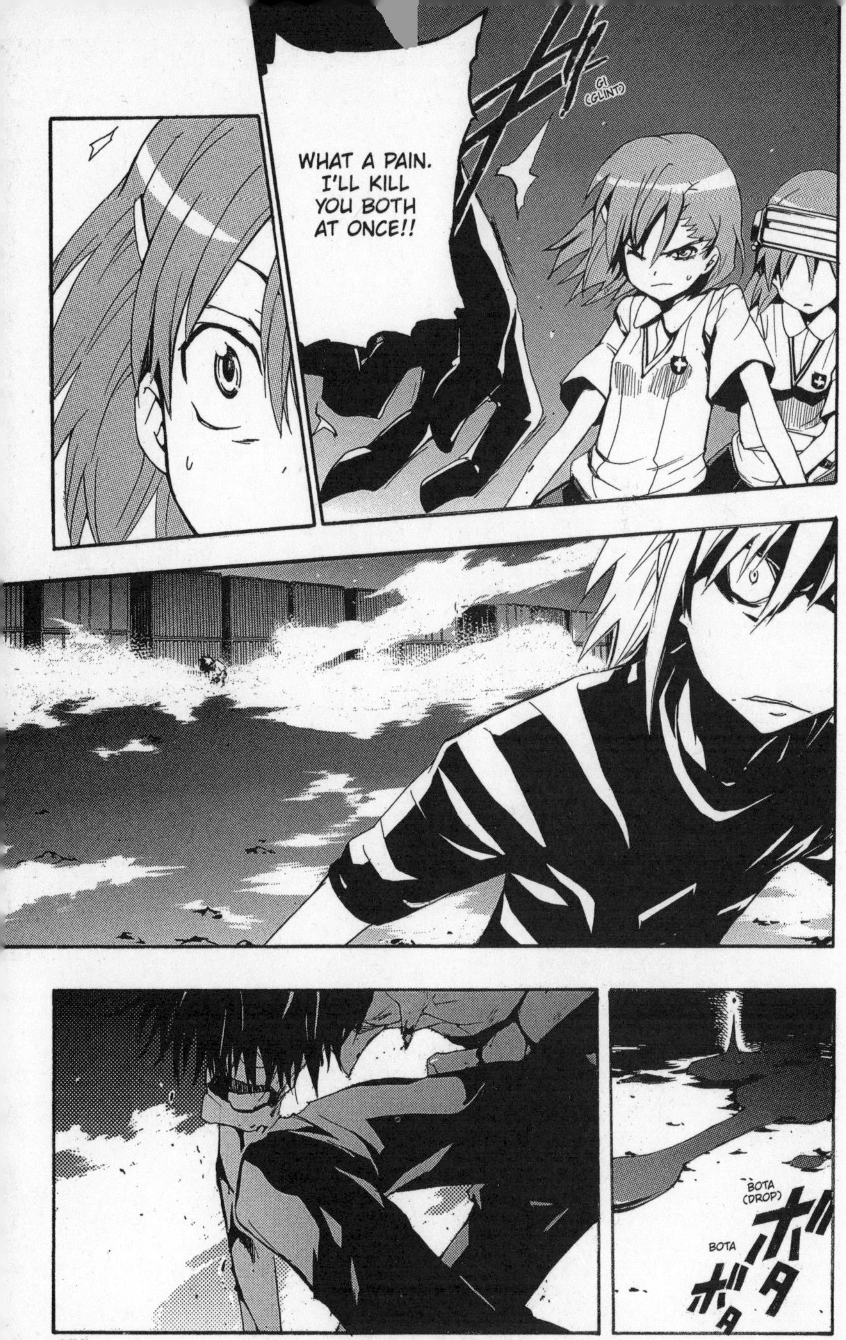
GI (GLINT)
WHAT A PAIN. I'LL KILL YOU BOTH AT ONCE!!
BOTA (DROP)
BOTA

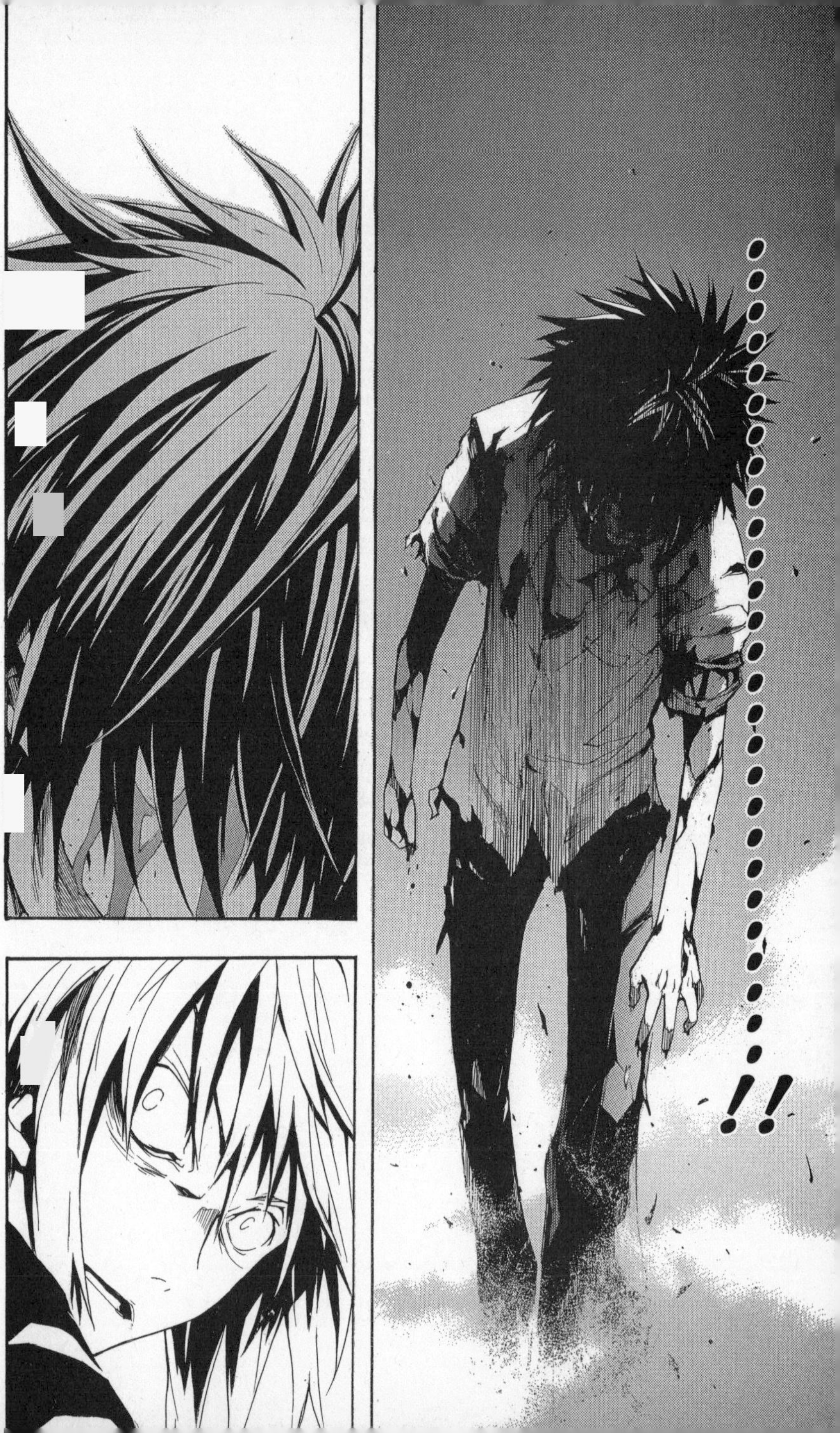
......!!

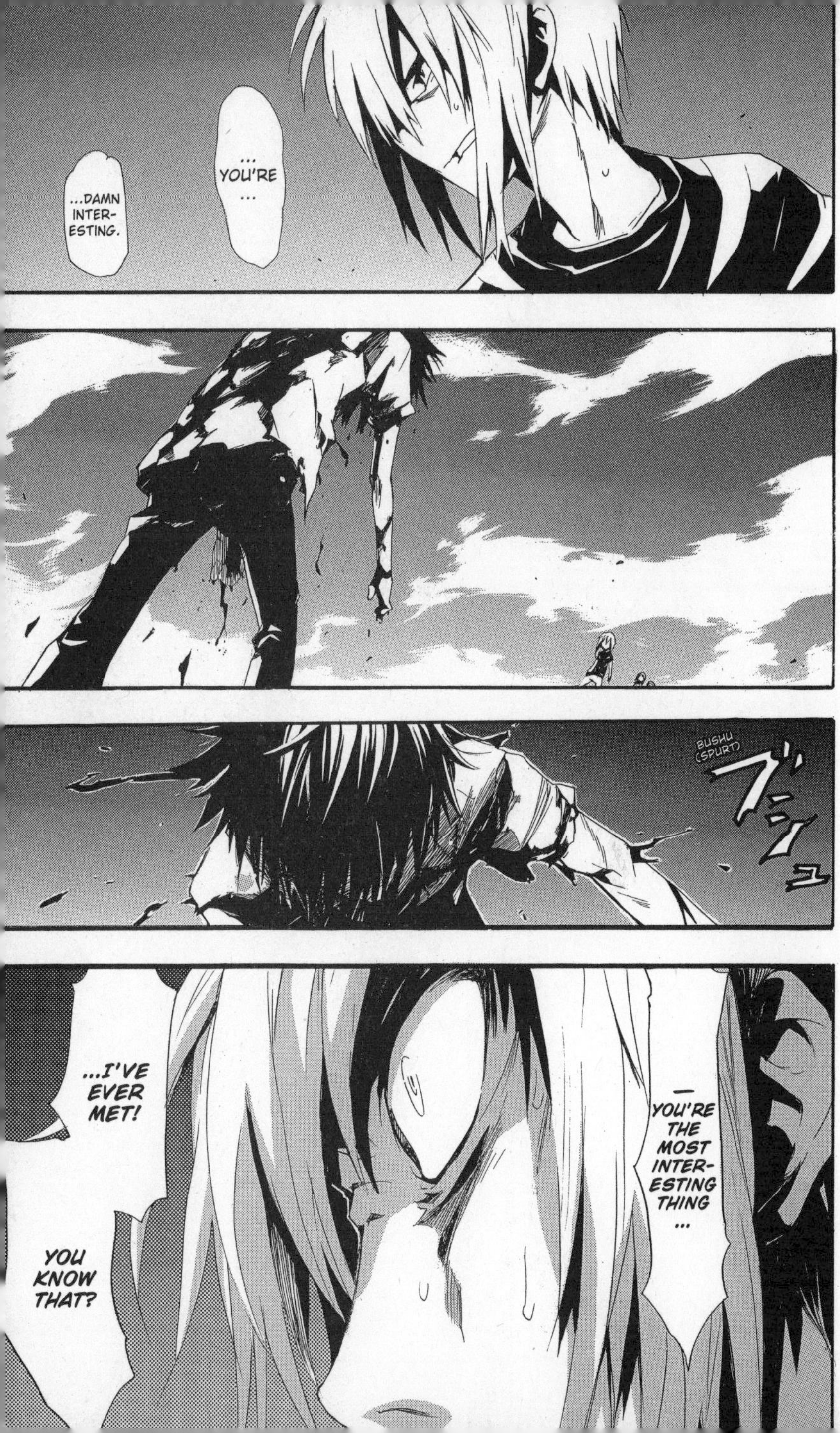
... YOU'RE ...
...DAMN INTER-ESTING.
BUSHU (SPURT)
ブシュ
— YOU'RE THE MOST INTER-ESTING THING ...
...I'VE EVER MET!
YOU KNOW THAT?

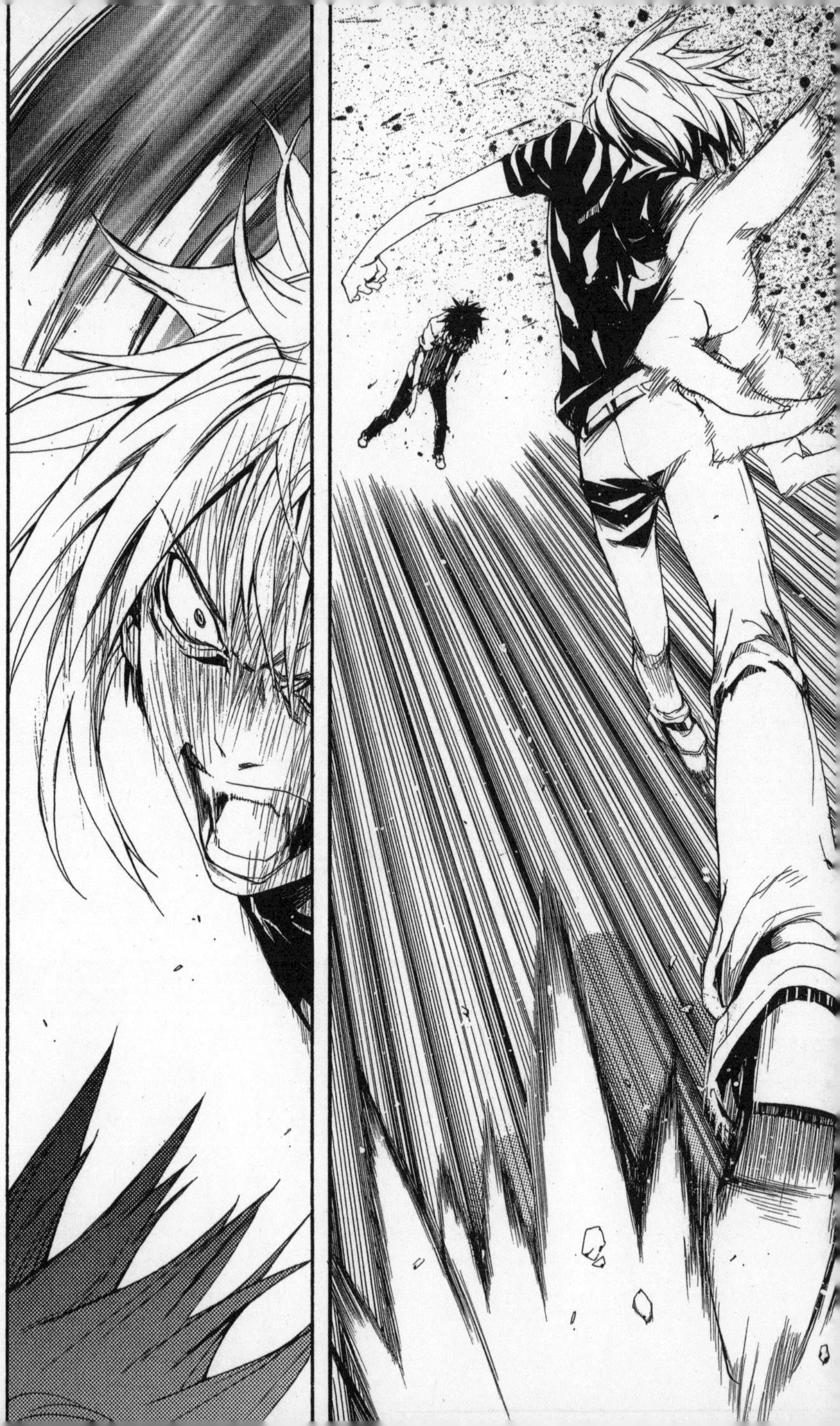

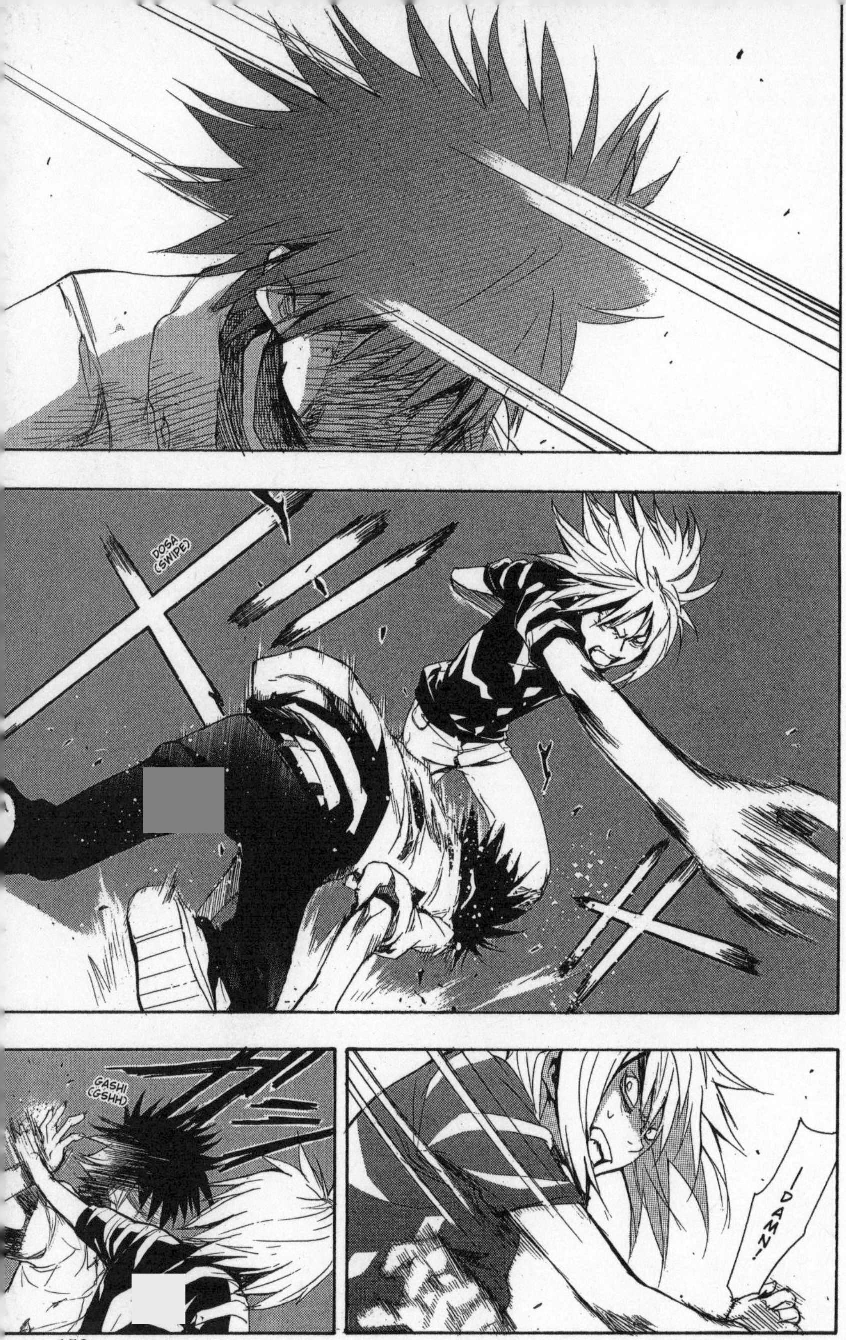
DOSA
(SWIPE)
DAMN...!
GASHI
(GSHH)

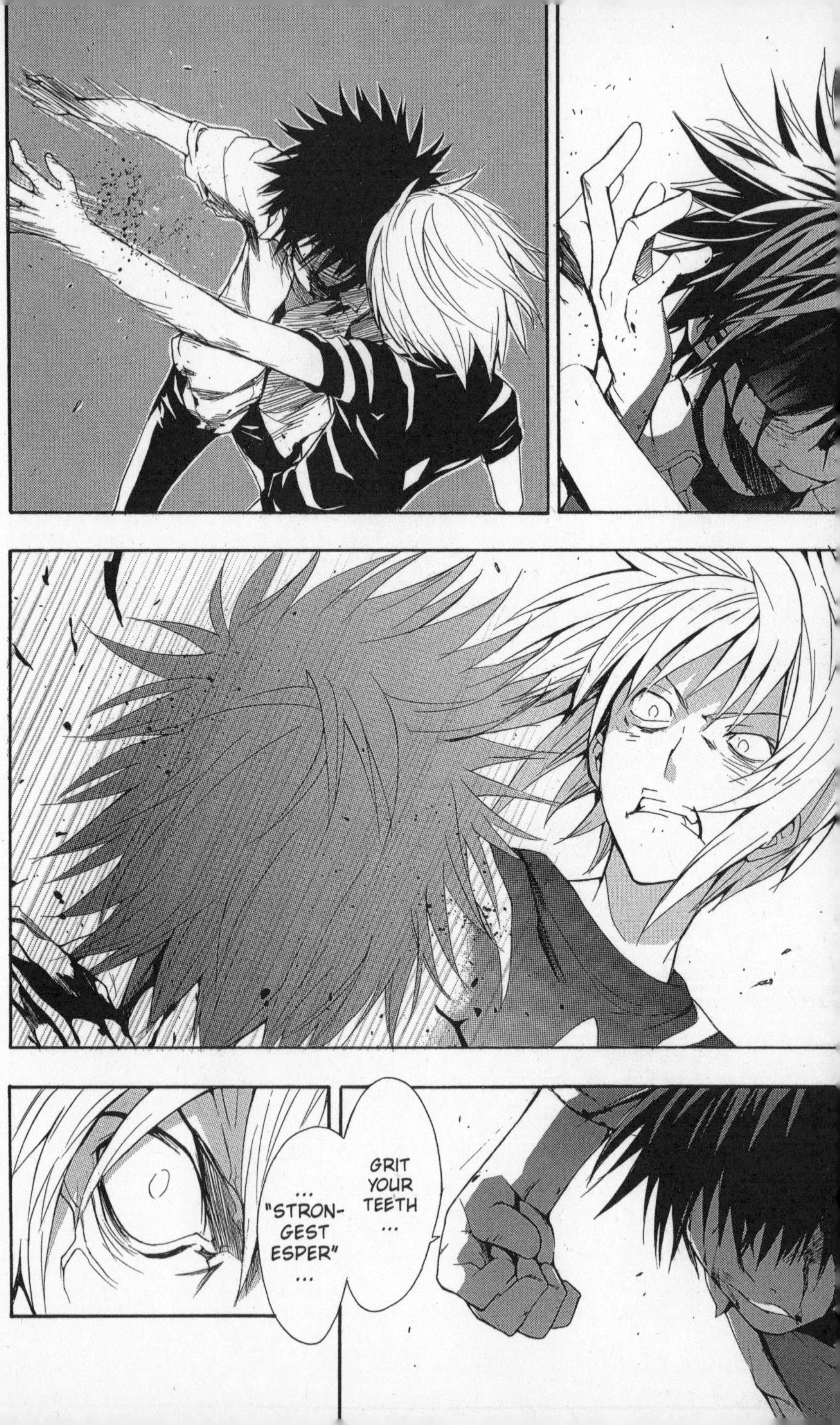
GRIT YOUR TEETH ...
... "STRONGEST ESPER" ...

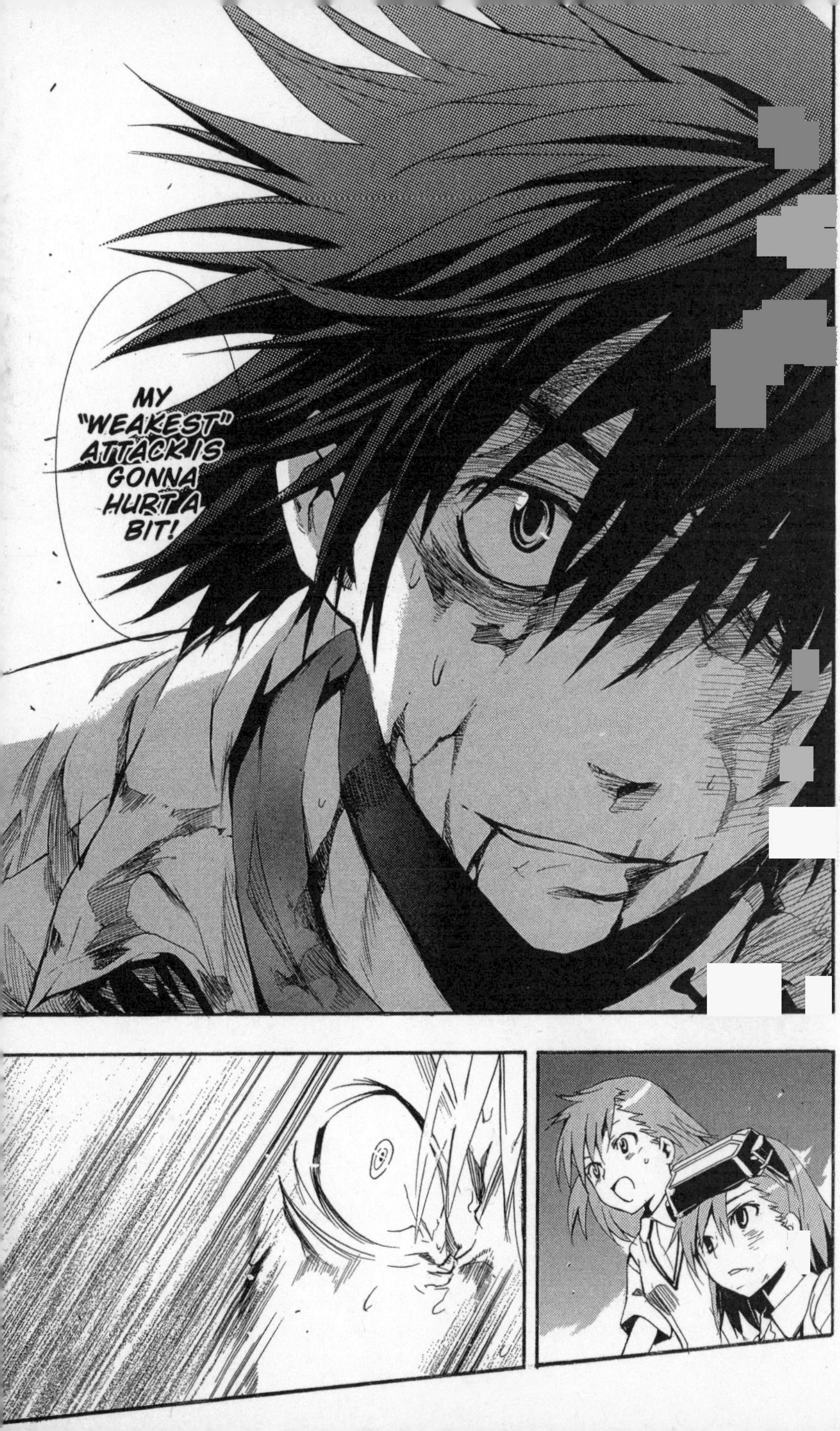
MY "WEAKEST" ATTACK IS GONNA HURT A BIT!

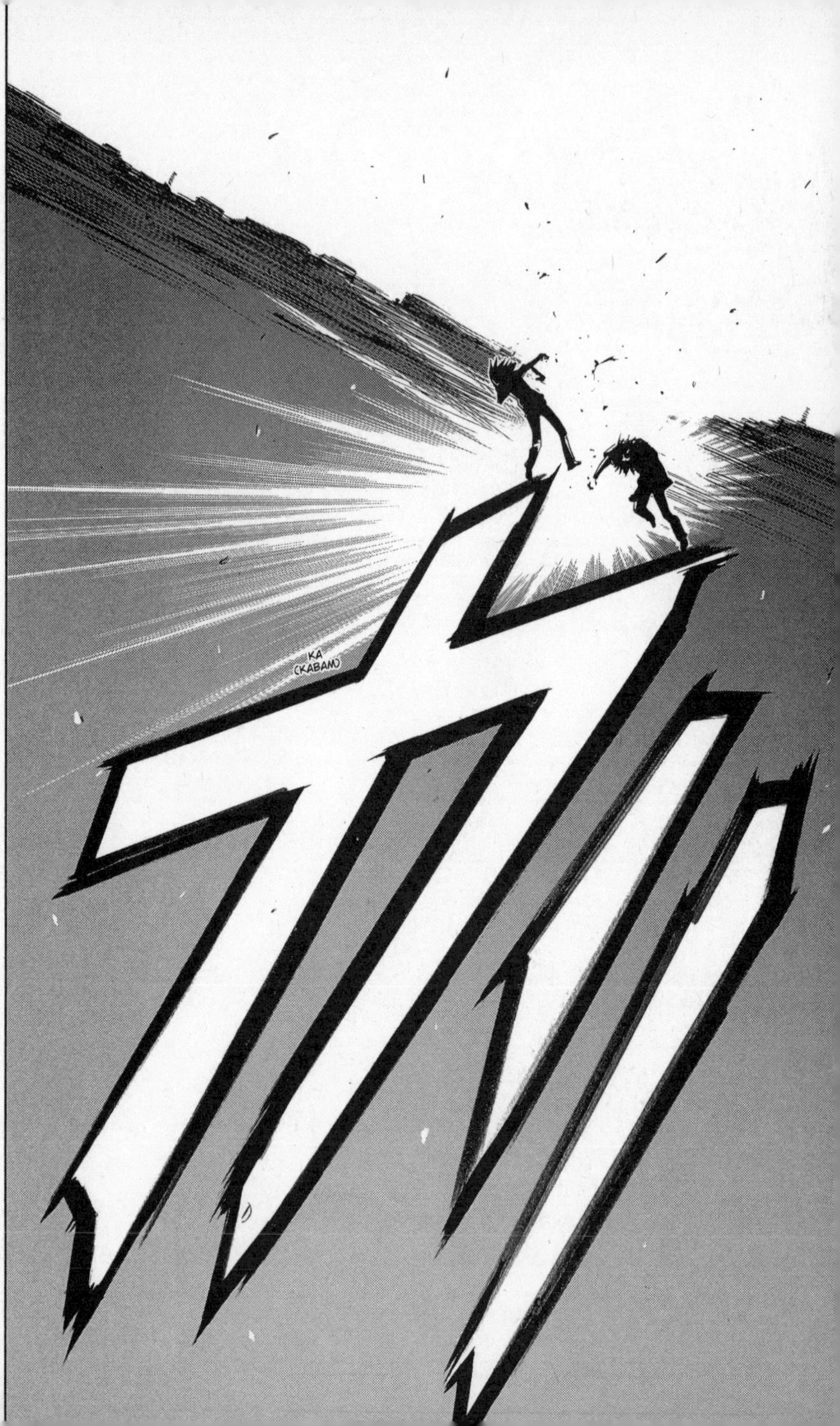
KA
(KABAM)

#21 EPILOGUE

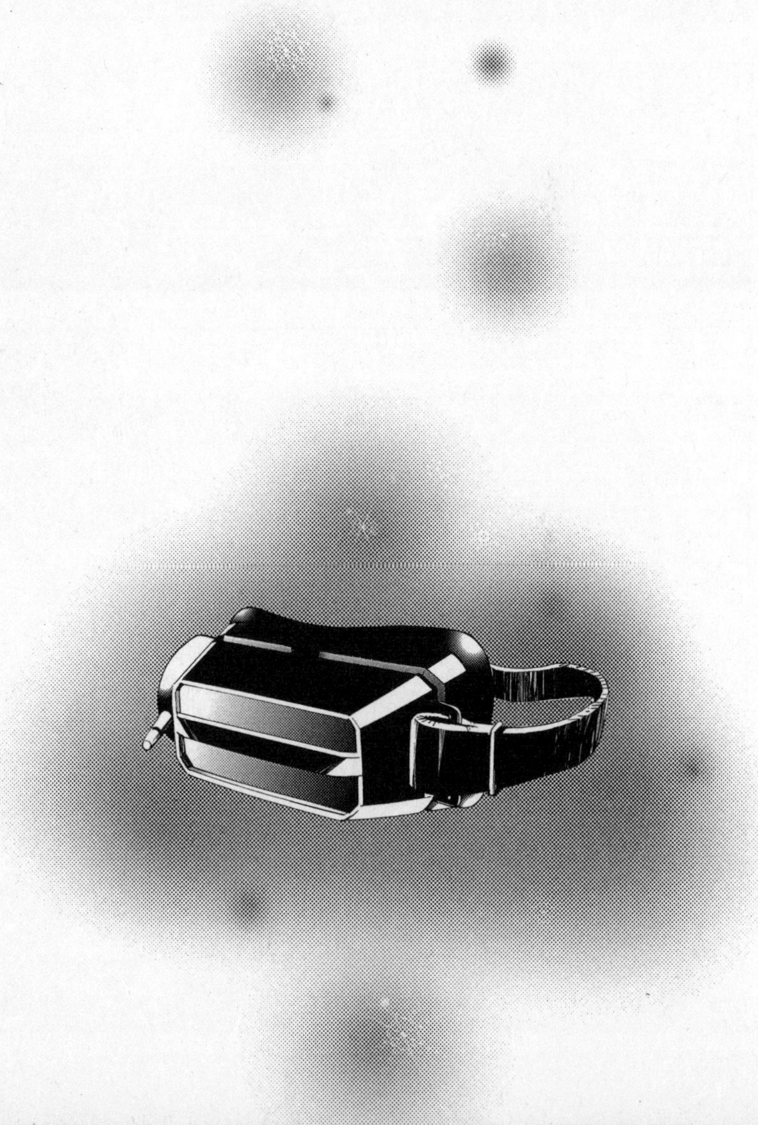

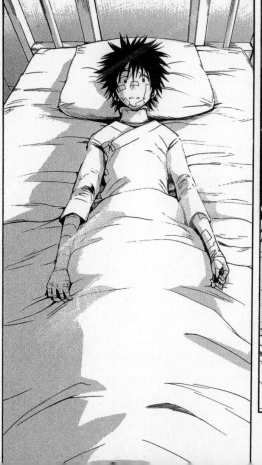

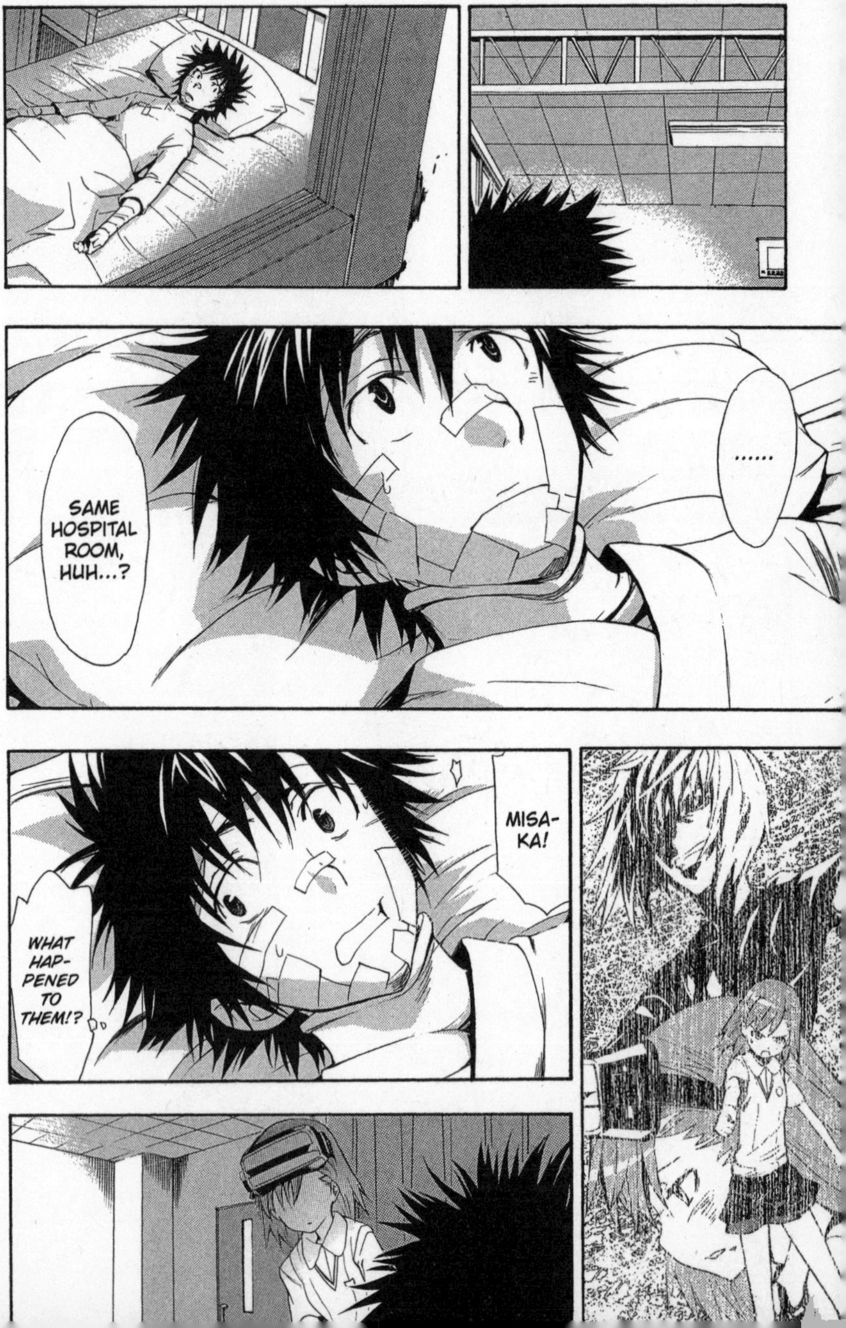
......
SAME HOSPITAL ROOM, HUH...?
MISA-KA!
WHAT HAP-PENED TO THEM!?

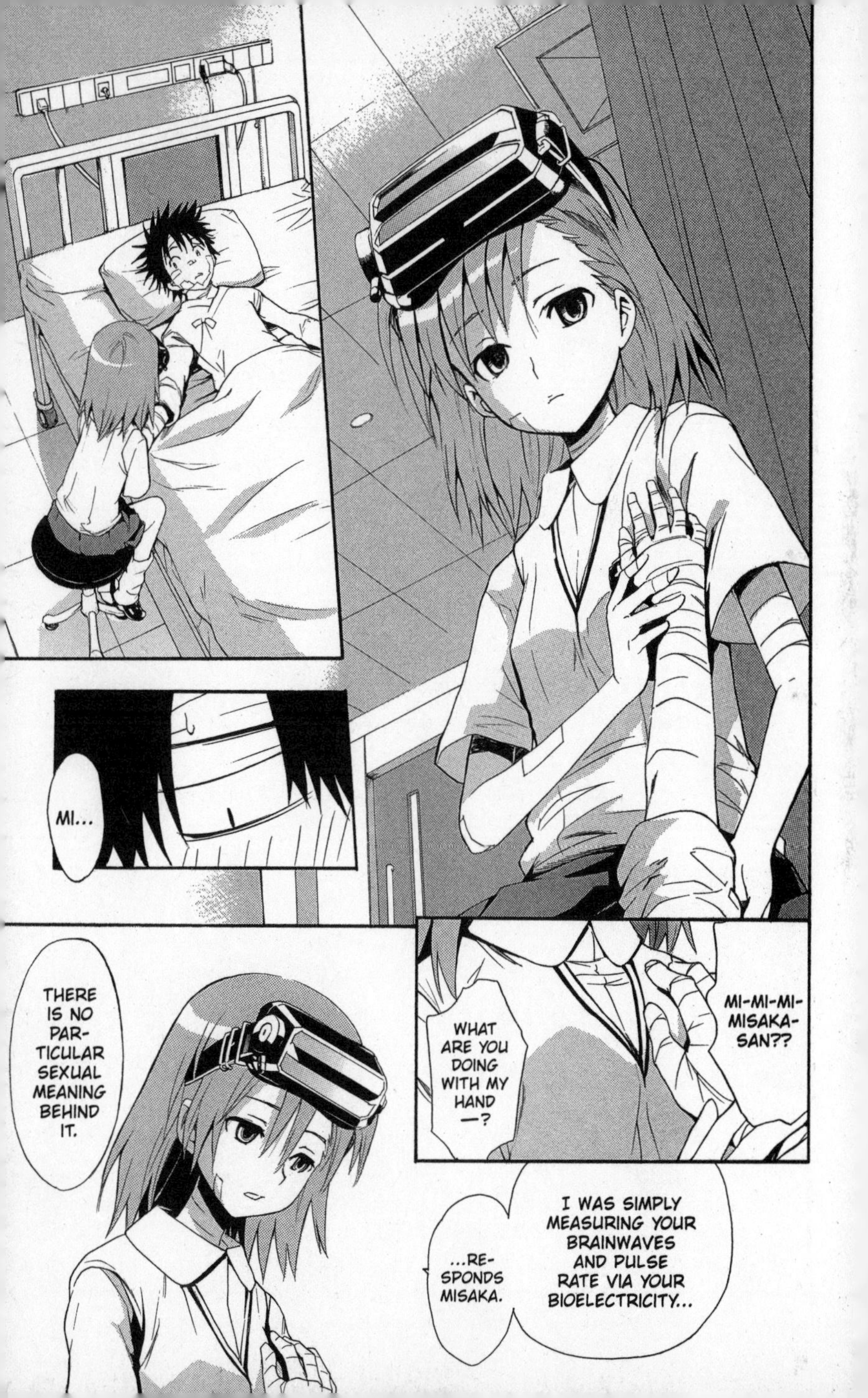
MI...
MI-MI-MI-MISAKA-SAN??
WHAT ARE YOU DOING WITH MY HAND—?
I WAS SIMPLY MEASURING YOUR BRAINWAVES AND PULSE RATE VIA YOUR BIOELECTRICITY...
...RESPONDS MISAKA.
THERE IS NO PARTICULAR SEXUAL MEANING BEHIND IT.

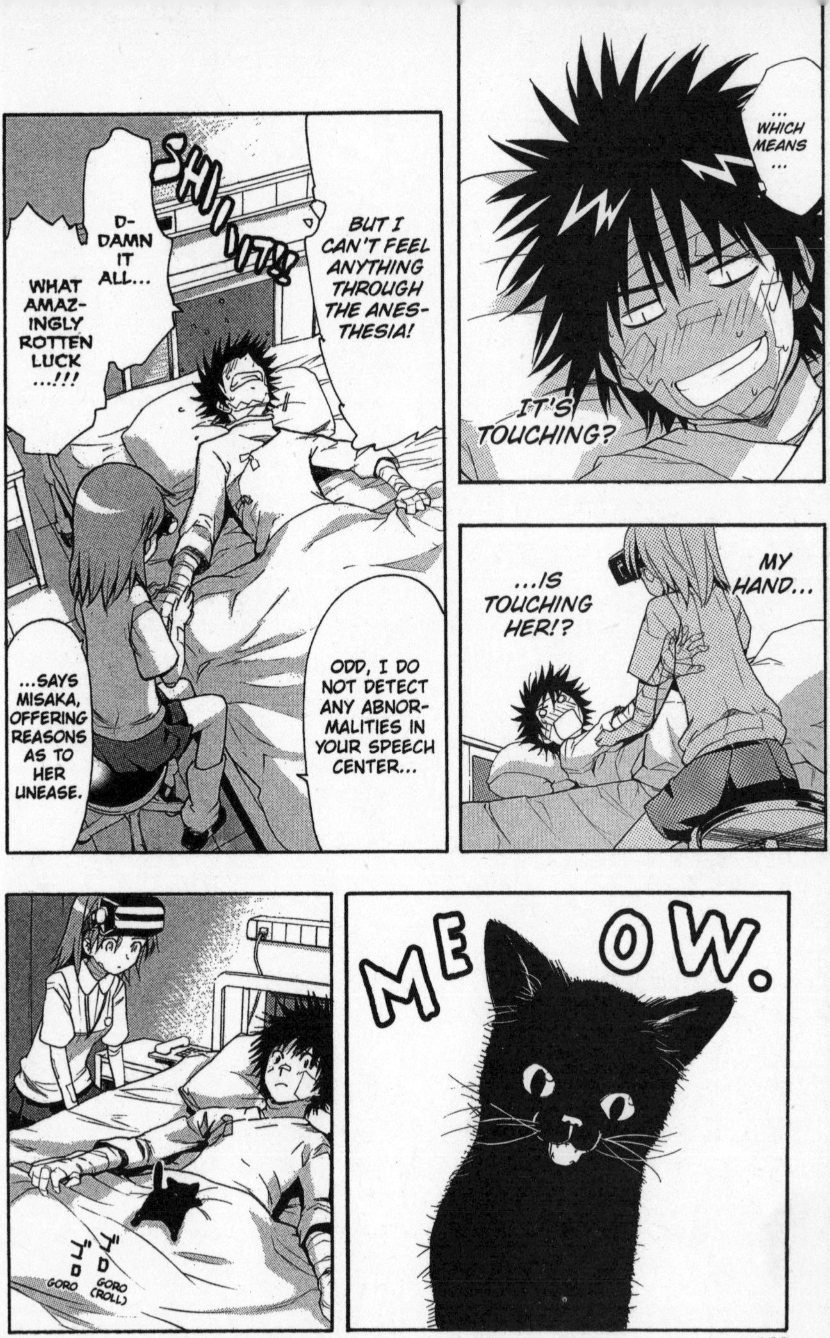
...WHICH MEANS...
IT'S TOUCHING?
MY HAND...
...IS TOUCHING HER!?
BUT I CAN'T FEEL ANYTHING THROUGH THE ANES-THESIA!
SHI-IT!!
D-DAMN IT ALL...
WHAT AMAZ-INGLY ROTTEN LUCK...!!!
ODD, I DO NOT DETECT ANY ABNOR-MALITIES IN YOUR SPEECH CENTER...
...SAYS MISAKA, OFFERING REASONS AS TO HER UNEASE.
MEOW.
ゴロ GORO (ROLL)
ゴロ GORO

I GUESS WE BOTH MANAGED TO GET HOME, HUH?

... WELL ...

MISAKA CANNOT YET RETURN TO THE SAME WORLD AS YOU...

... DECLARES MISAKA BLUNTLY.

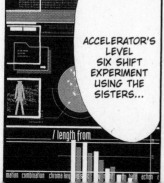

ACCELERATOR'S LEVEL SIX SHIFT EXPERIMENT USING THE SISTERS...

/ length from

HUH ...?

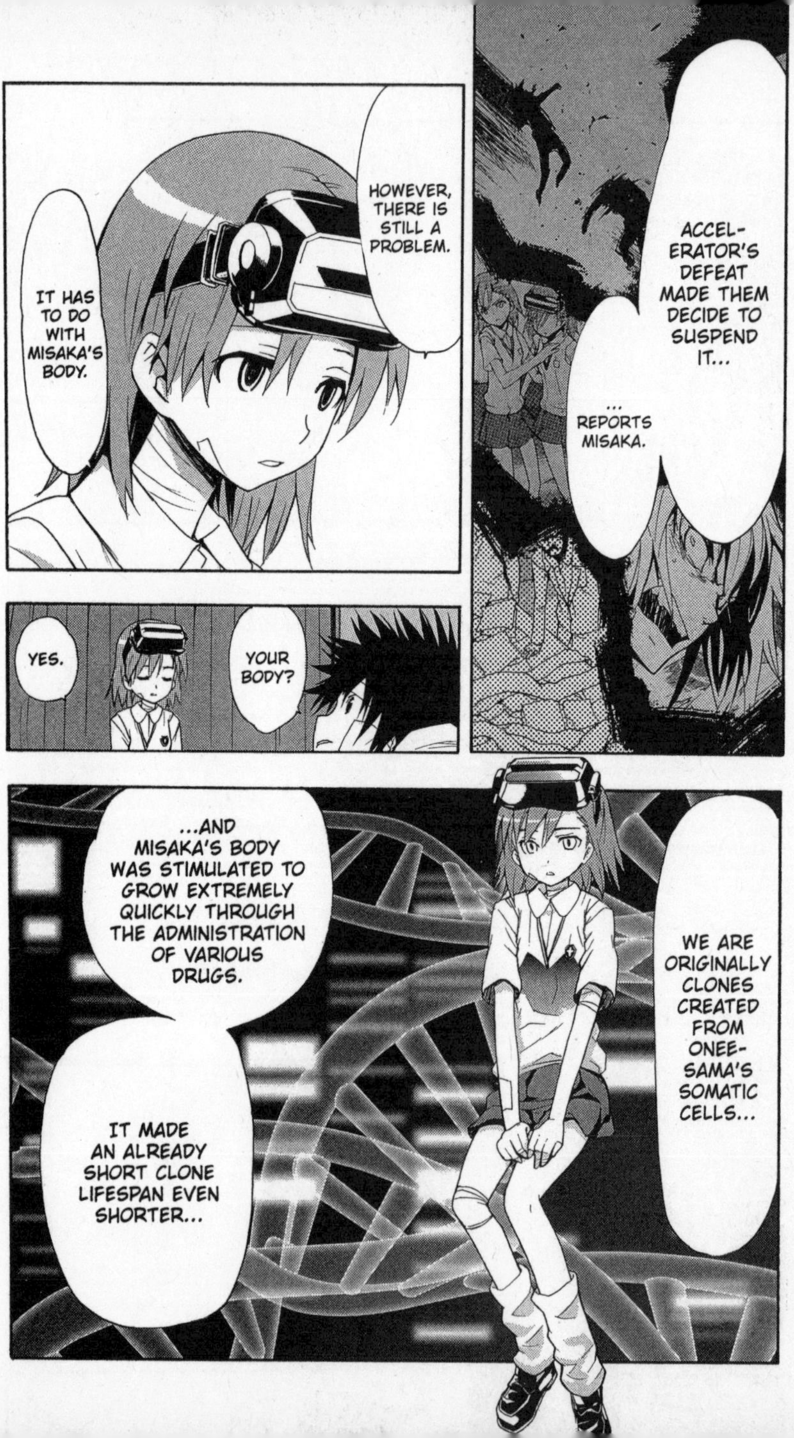
ACCEL-ERATOR'S DEFEAT MADE THEM DECIDE TO SUSPEND IT...
... REPORTS MISAKA.
HOWEVER, THERE IS STILL A PROBLEM.
IT HAS TO DO WITH MISAKA'S BODY.
YOUR BODY?
YES.
WE ARE ORIGINALLY CLONES CREATED FROM ONEE-SAMA'S SOMATIC CELLS...
...AND MISAKA'S BODY WAS STIMULATED TO GROW EXTREMELY QUICKLY THROUGH THE ADMINISTRATION OF VARIOUS DRUGS.
IT MADE AN ALREADY SHORT CLONE LIFESPAN EVEN SHORTER...

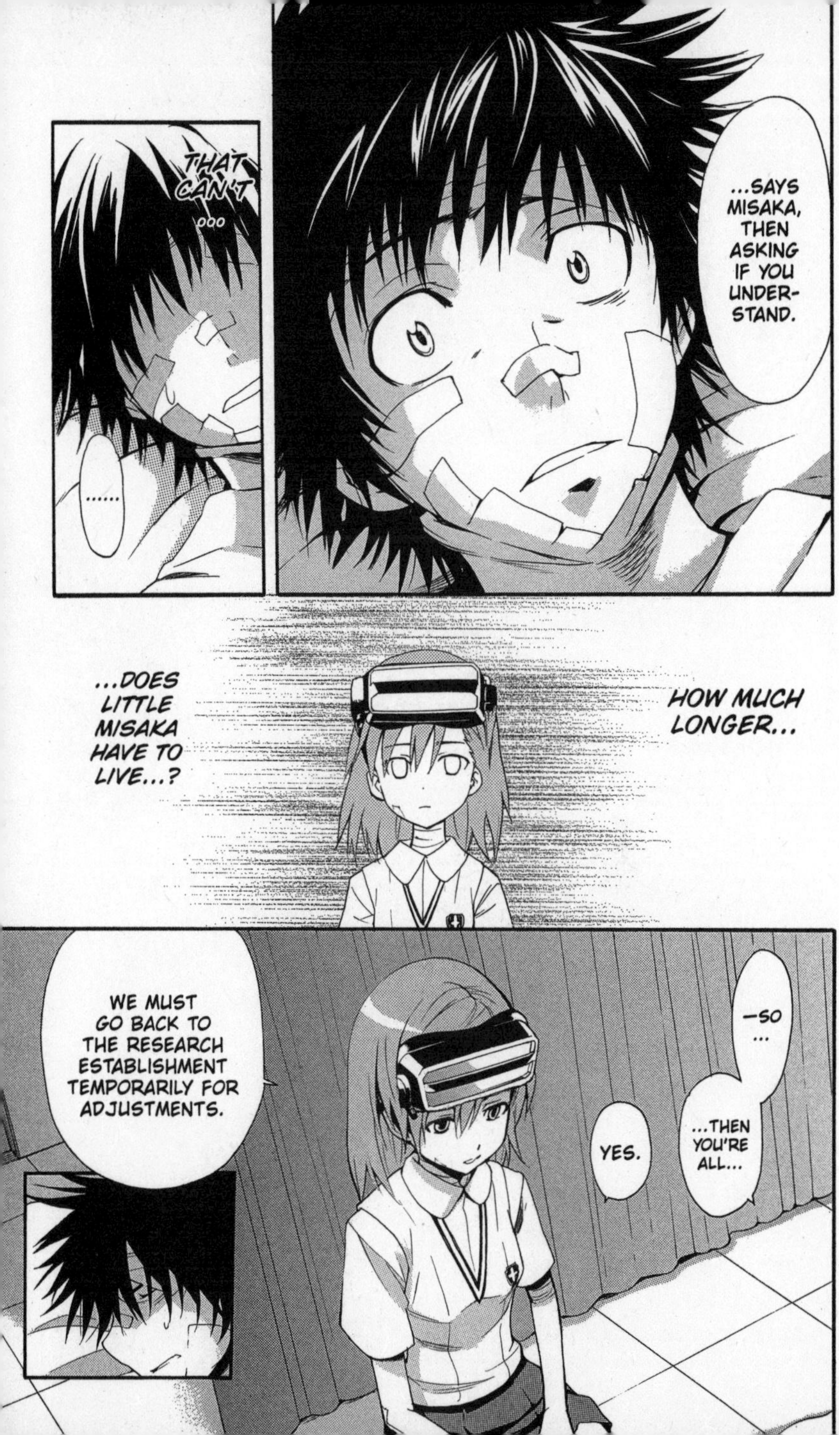
...SAYS MISAKA, THEN ASKING IF YOU UNDERSTAND.
THAT CAN'T...
......
HOW MUCH LONGER...
...DOES LITTLE MISAKA HAVE TO LIVE...?
—SO...
...THEN YOU'RE ALL...
YES.
WE MUST GO BACK TO THE RESEARCH ESTABLISHMENT TEMPORARILY FOR ADJUSTMENTS.

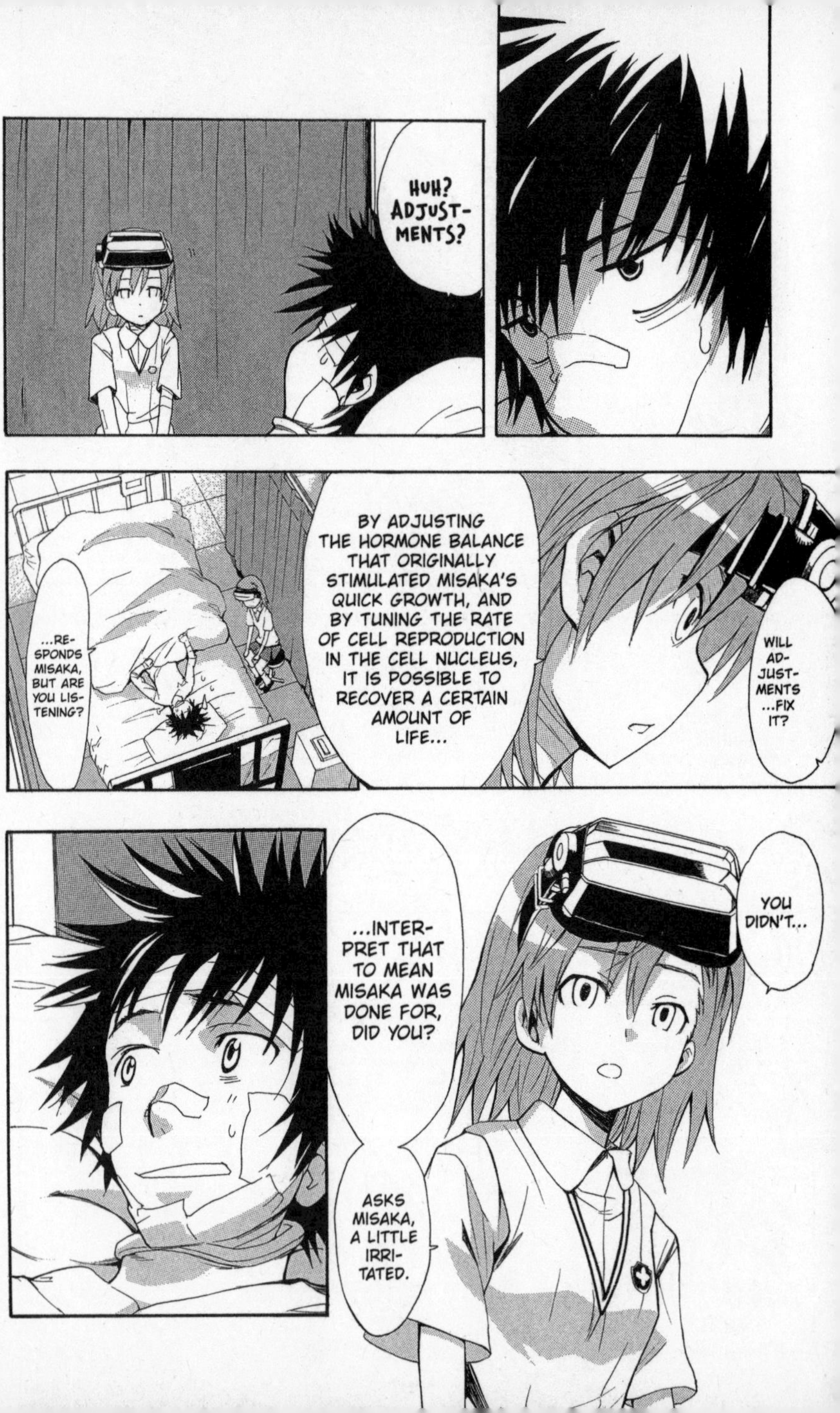
HUH? ADJUSTMENTS?
WILL ADJUSTMENTS ...FIX IT?
BY ADJUSTING THE HORMONE BALANCE THAT ORIGINALLY STIMULATED MISAKA'S QUICK GROWTH, AND BY TUNING THE RATE OF CELL REPRODUCTION IN THE CELL NUCLEUS, IT IS POSSIBLE TO RECOVER A CERTAIN AMOUNT OF LIFE...
...RESPONDS MISAKA, BUT ARE YOU LISTENING?
YOU DIDN'T...
...INTERPRET THAT TO MEAN MISAKA WAS DONE FOR, DID YOU?
ASKS MISAKA, A LITTLE IRRITATED.

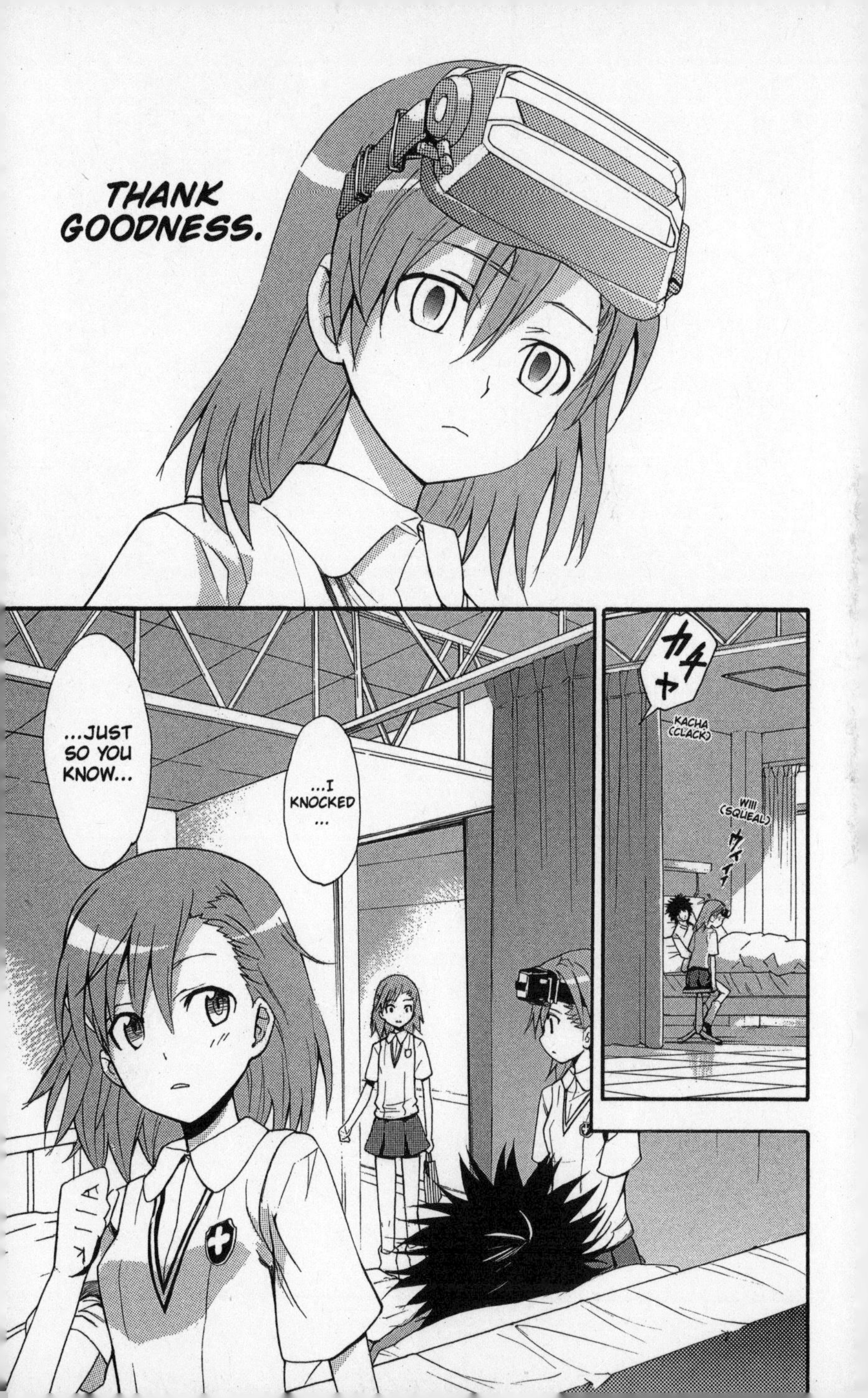
THANK GOODNESS.
カチャ
KACHA (CLACK)
WIII (SQUEAL)
...JUST SO YOU KNOW...
...I KNOCKED ...

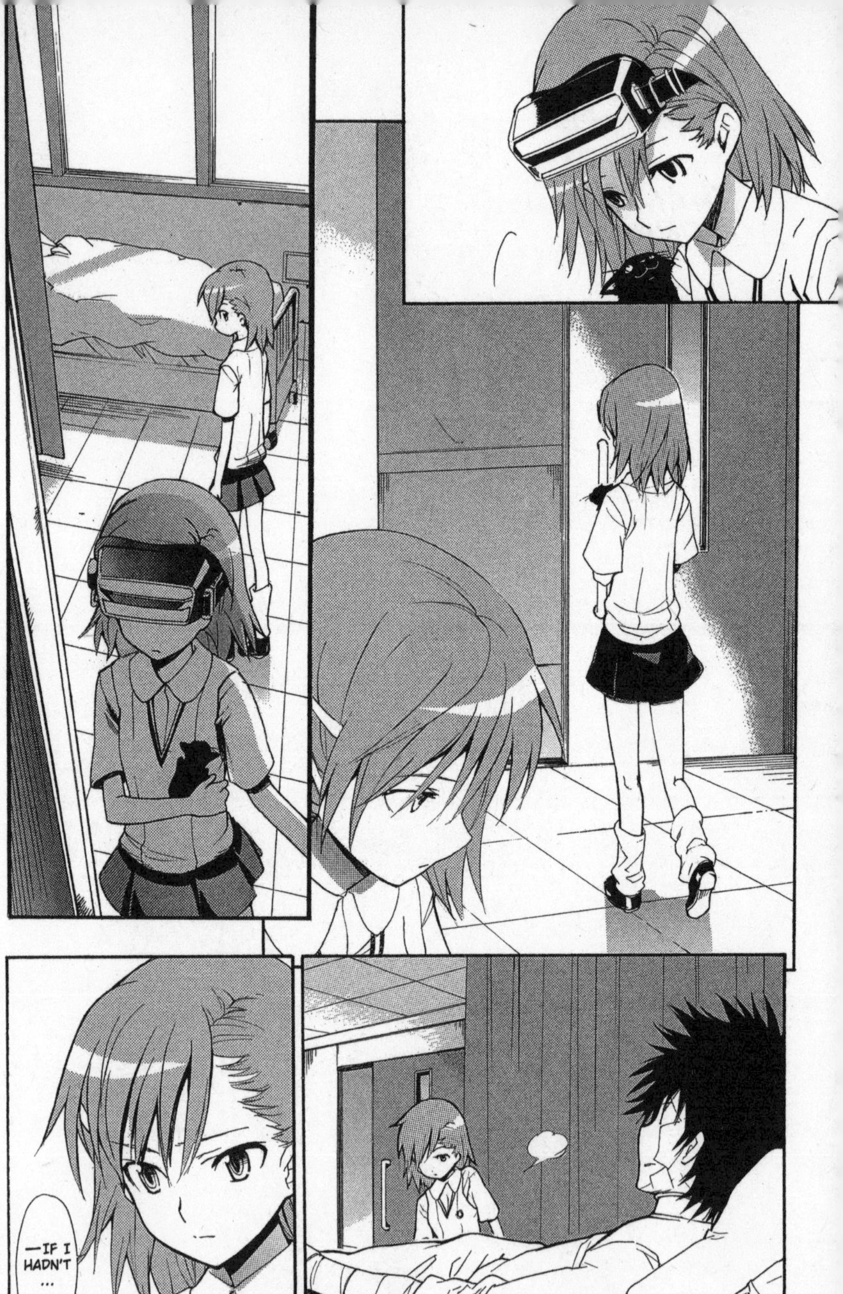
—IF I HADN'T ...

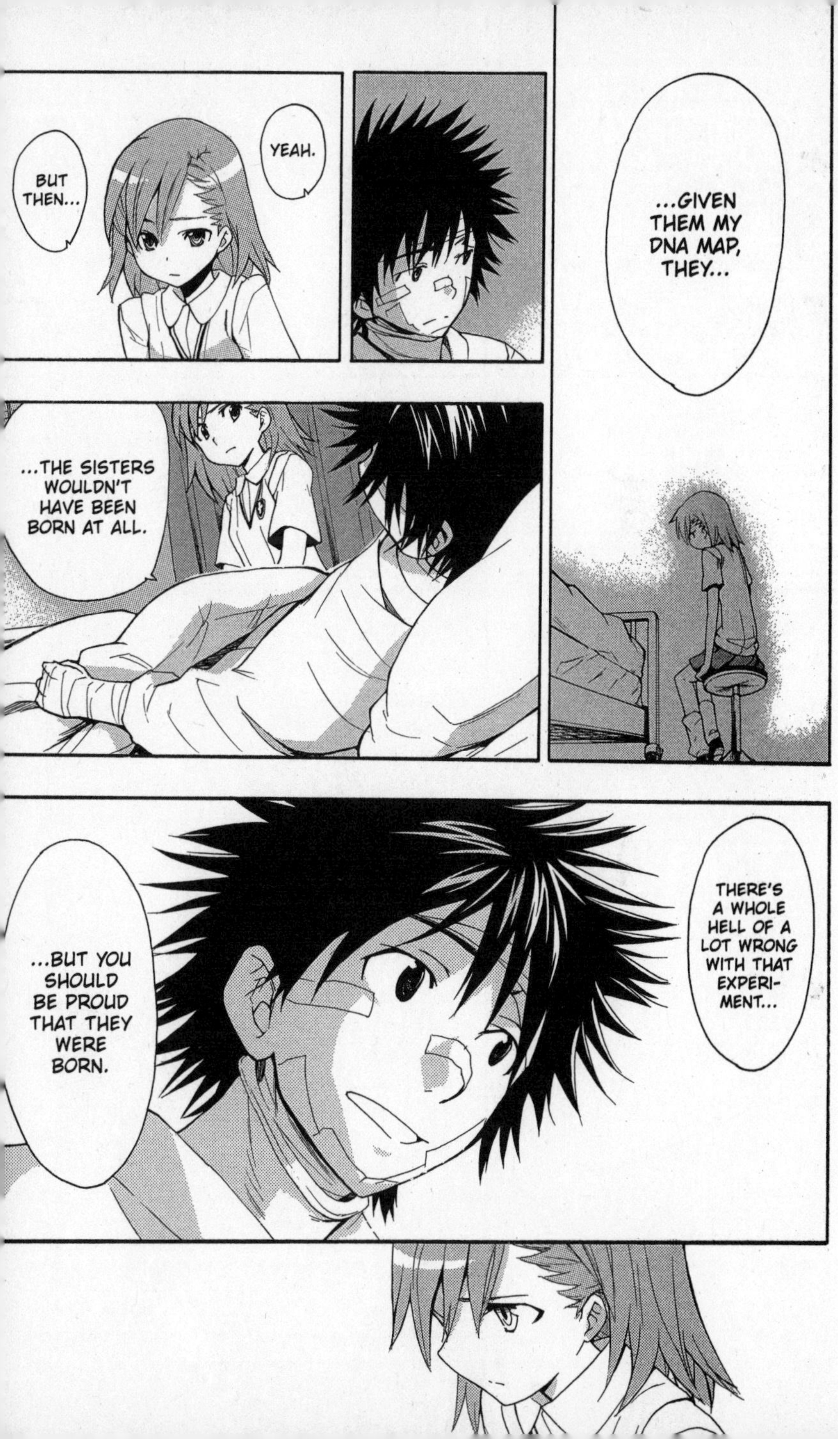
...GIVEN THEM MY DNA MAP, THEY...
YEAH.
BUT THEN...
...THE SISTERS WOULDN'T HAVE BEEN BORN AT ALL.
THERE'S A WHOLE HELL OF A LOT WRONG WITH THAT EXPERI-MENT...
...BUT YOU SHOULD BE PROUD THAT THEY WERE BORN.

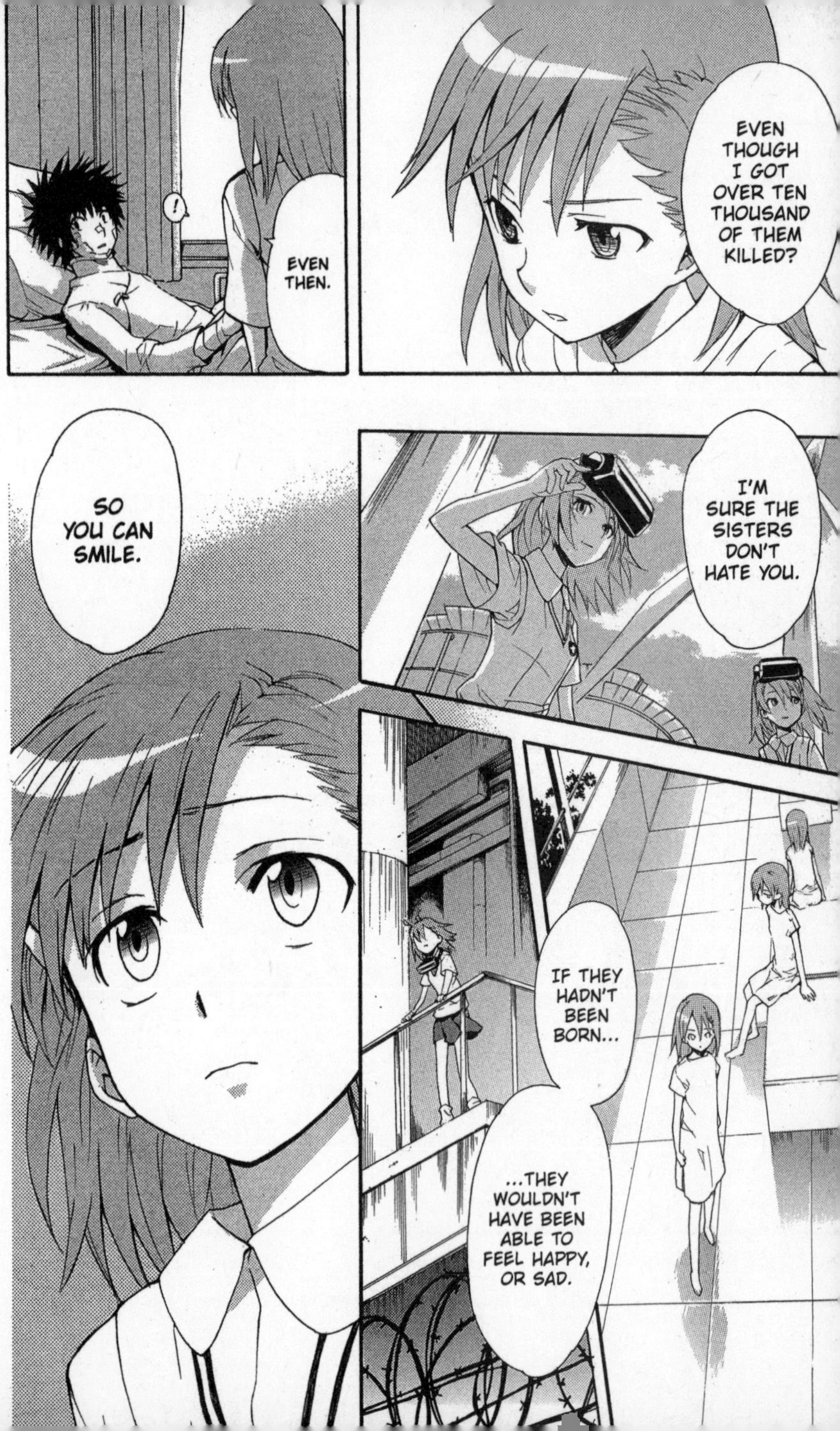
EVEN THOUGH I GOT OVER TEN THOUSAND OF THEM KILLED?
!
EVEN THEN.
I'M SURE THE SISTERS DON'T HATE YOU.
IF THEY HADN'T BEEN BORN...
...THEY WOULDN'T HAVE BEEN ABLE TO FEEL HAPPY, OR SAD.
SO YOU CAN SMILE.

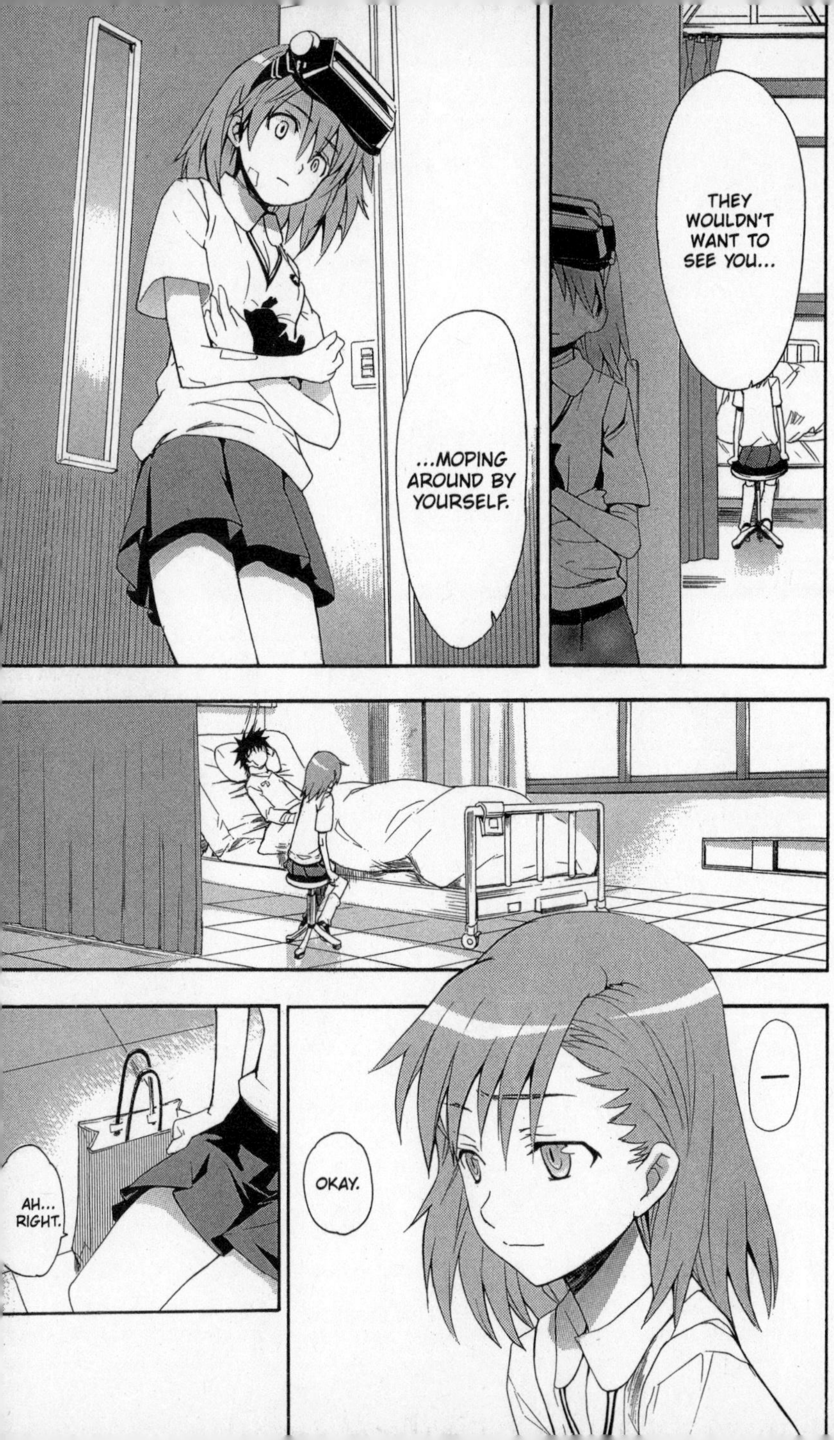
THEY WOULDN'T WANT TO SEE YOU...
...MOPING AROUND BY YOURSELF.
—
OKAY.
AH... RIGHT.

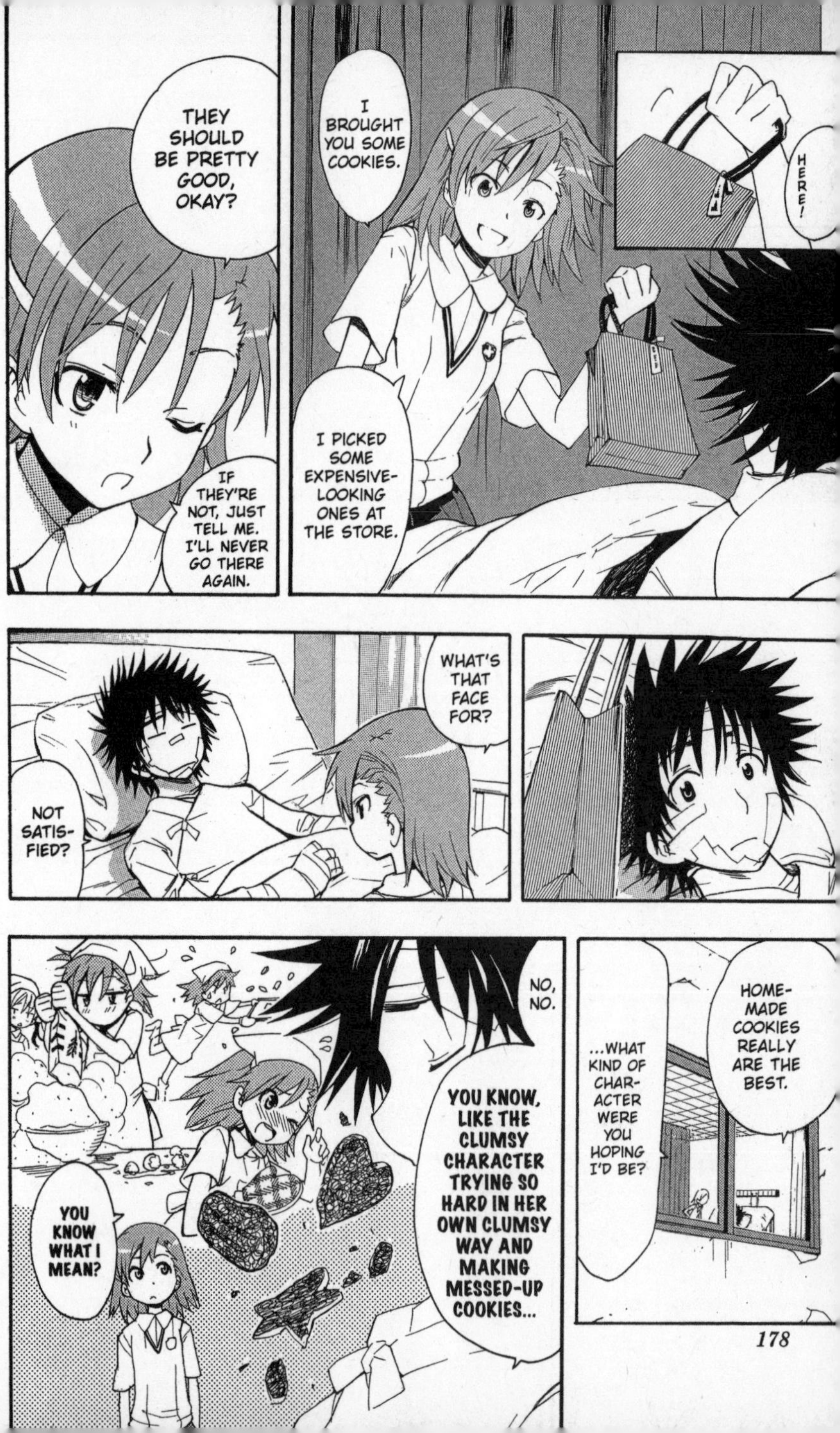
HERE!
I BROUGHT YOU SOME COOKIES.
I PICKED SOME EXPENSIVE-LOOKING ONES AT THE STORE.
THEY SHOULD BE PRETTY GOOD, OKAY?
IF THEY'RE NOT, JUST TELL ME. I'LL NEVER GO THERE AGAIN.
WHAT'S THAT FACE FOR?
NOT SATISFIED?
HOME-MADE COOKIES REALLY ARE THE BEST.
...WHAT KIND OF CHARACTER WERE YOU HOPING I'D BE?
NO, NO.
YOU KNOW, LIKE THE CLUMSY CHARACTER TRYING SO HARD IN HER OWN CLUMSY WAY AND MAKING MESSED-UP COOKIES...
YOU KNOW WHAT I MEAN?

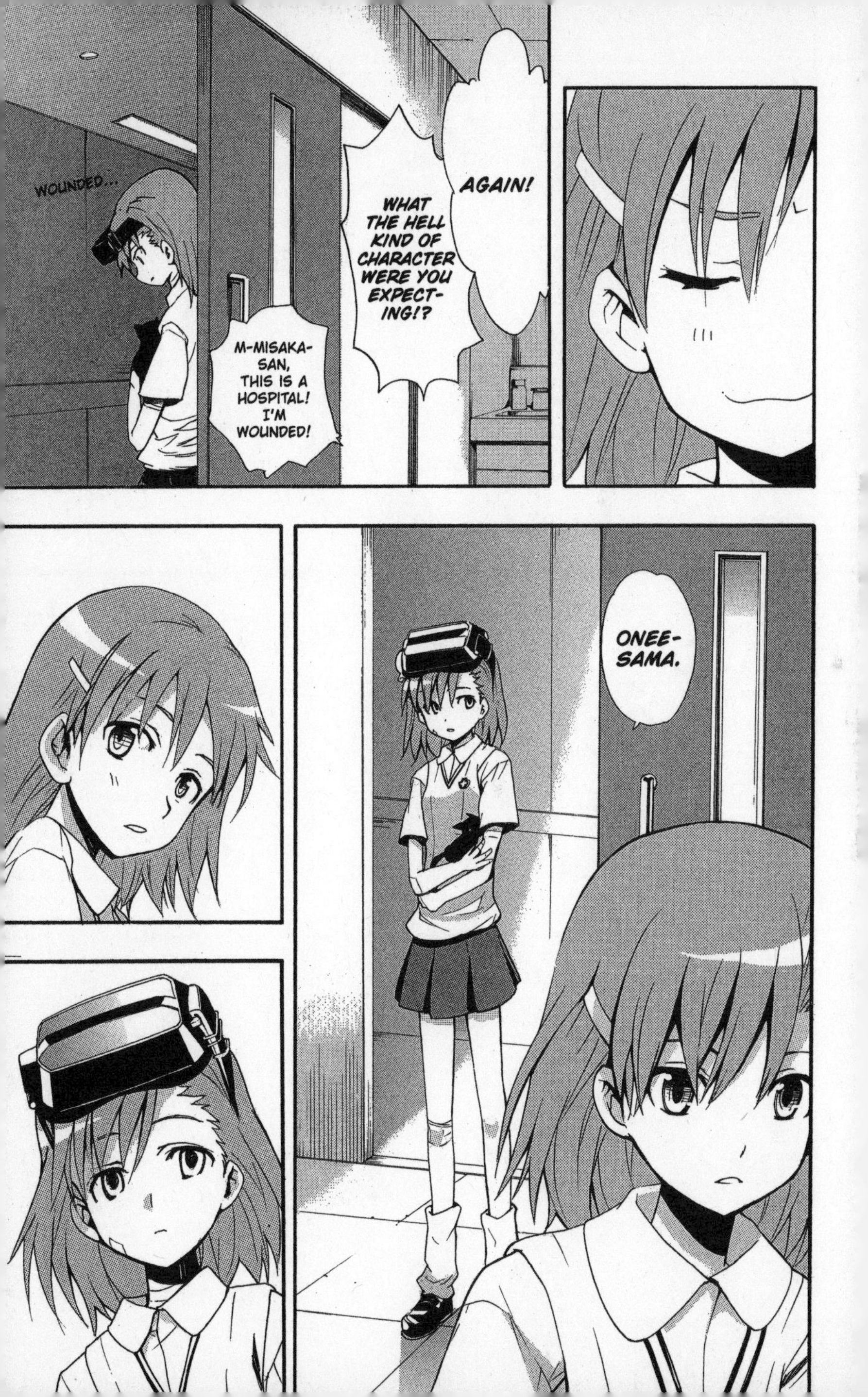
AGAIN!
WHAT THE HELL KIND OF CHARACTER WERE YOU EXPECTING!?
M-MISAKA-SAN, THIS IS A HOSPITAL! I'M WOUNDED!
WOUNDED...
ONEE-SAMA.

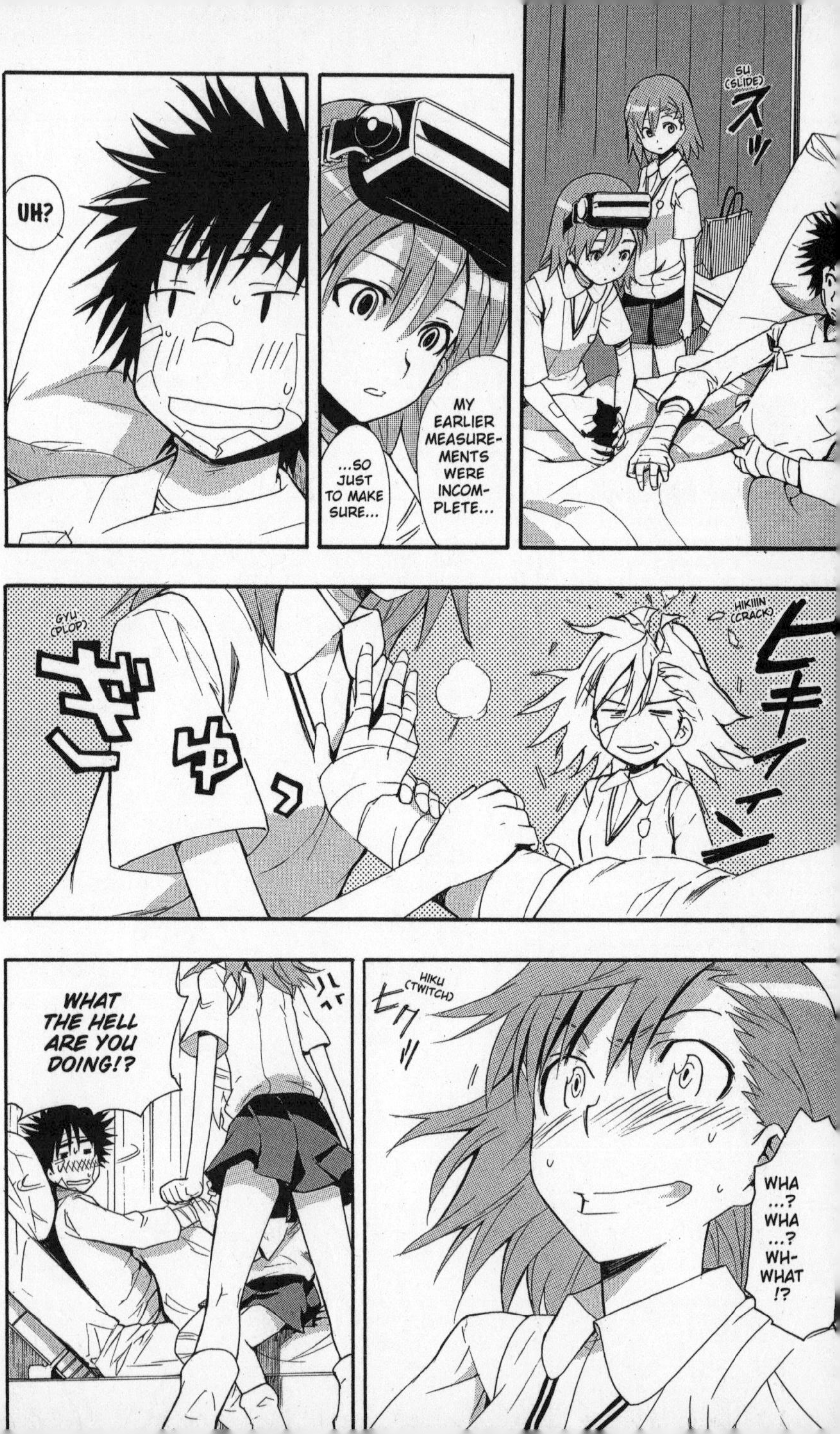
SU (SLIDE)
スッ
MY EARLIER MEASUREMENTS WERE INCOMPLETE...
...SO JUST TO MAKE SURE...
UH?
HIKIIIN (CRACK)
ヒキィィン
GYU (PLOP)
ぎゅっ
HIKU (TWITCH)
ヒクッ
WHA...? WHA...? WH-WHAT!?
WHAT THE HELL ARE YOU DOING!?

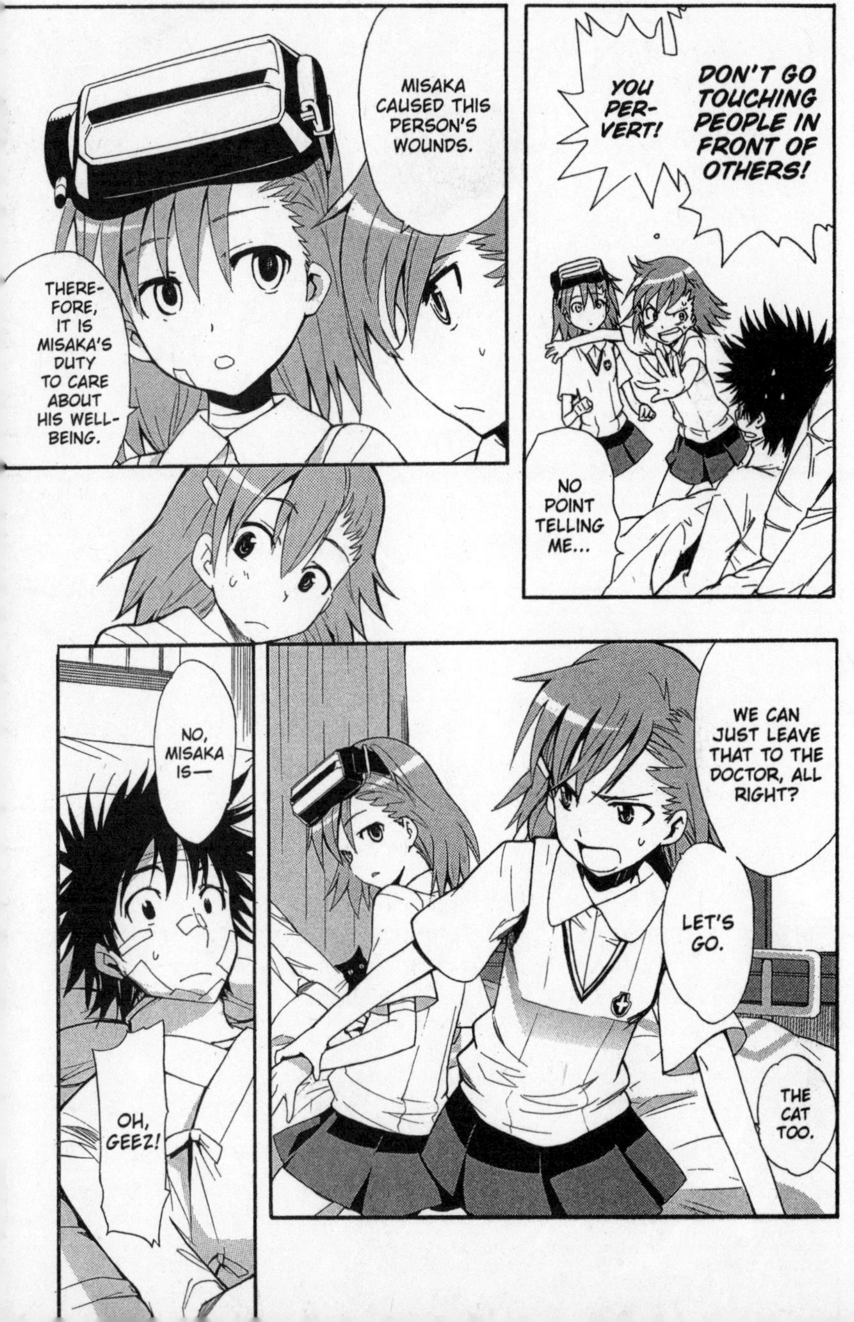
DON'T GO TOUCHING PEOPLE IN FRONT OF OTHERS!
YOU PERVERT!
NO POINT TELLING ME...
MISAKA CAUSED THIS PERSON'S WOUNDS.
THEREFORE, IT IS MISAKA'S DUTY TO CARE ABOUT HIS WELL-BEING.
WE CAN JUST LEAVE THAT TO THE DOCTOR, ALL RIGHT?
LET'S GO.
THE CAT TOO.
NO, MISAKA IS—
OH, GEEZ!

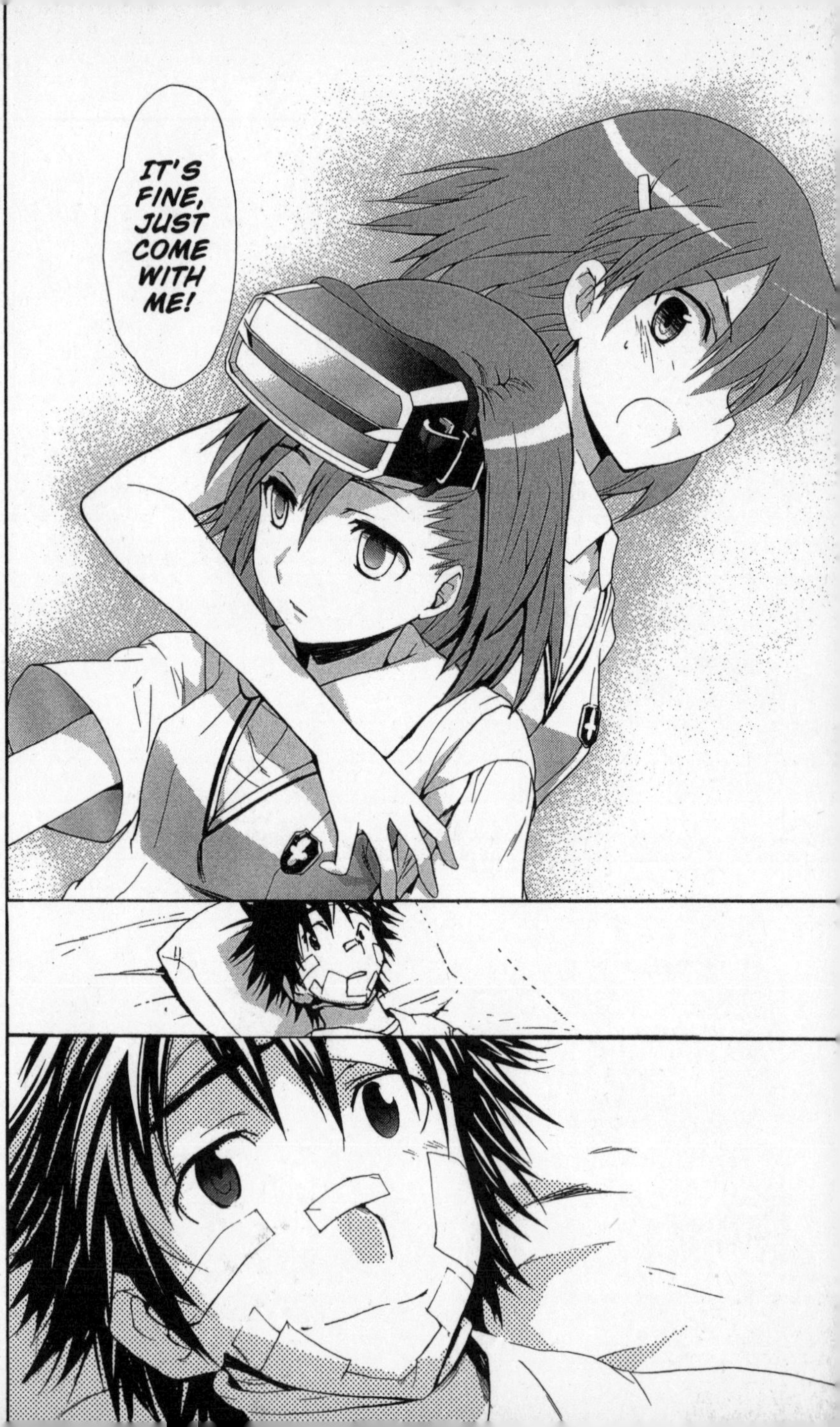
IT'S FINE, JUST COME WITH ME!

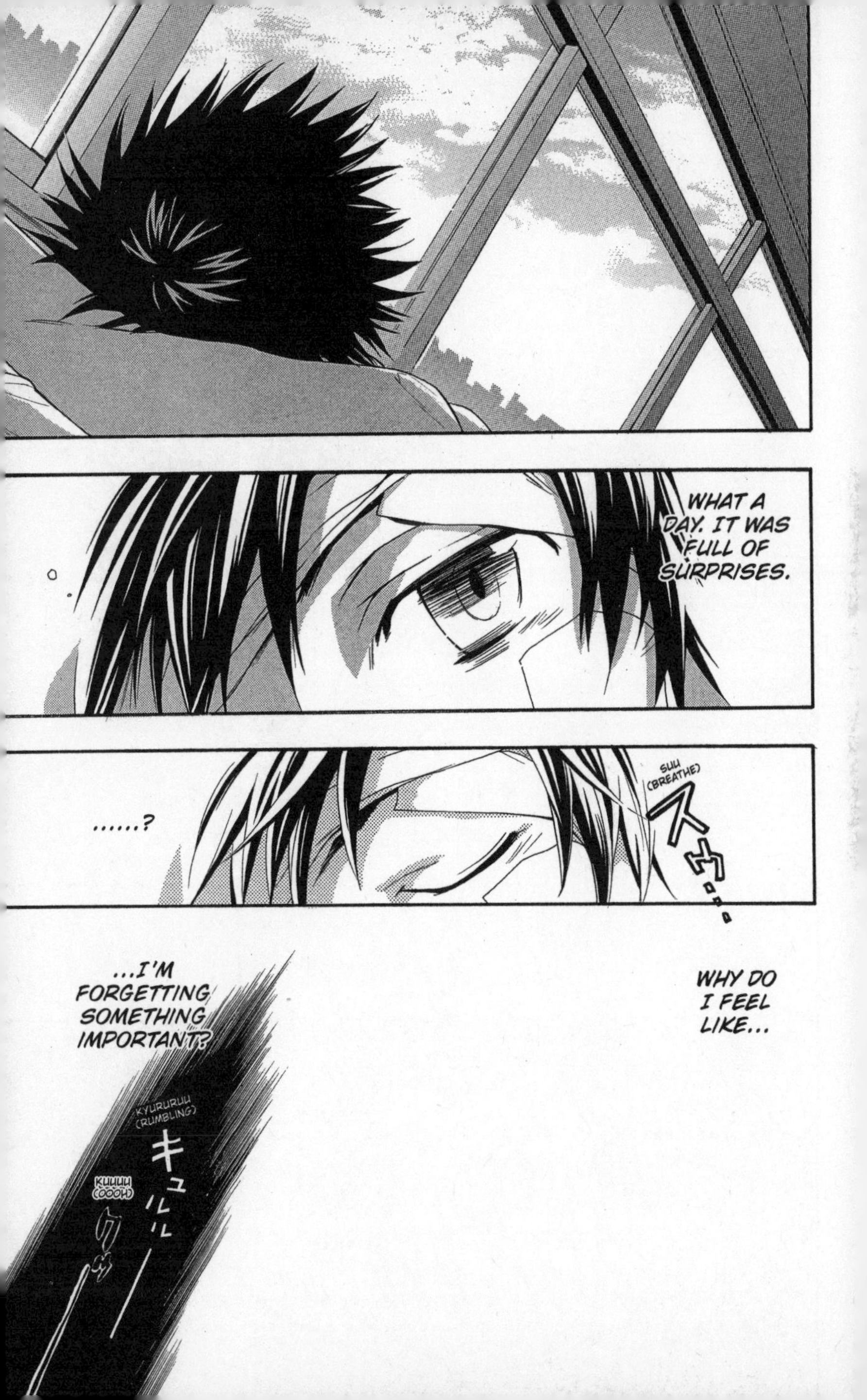
WHAT A DAY. IT WAS FULL OF SURPRISES.
SUU (BREATHE)
......?
WHY DO I FEEL LIKE...
...I'M FORGETTING SOMETHING IMPORTANT?
KYURURUU (RUMBLING)
KUUUU (COOOH)

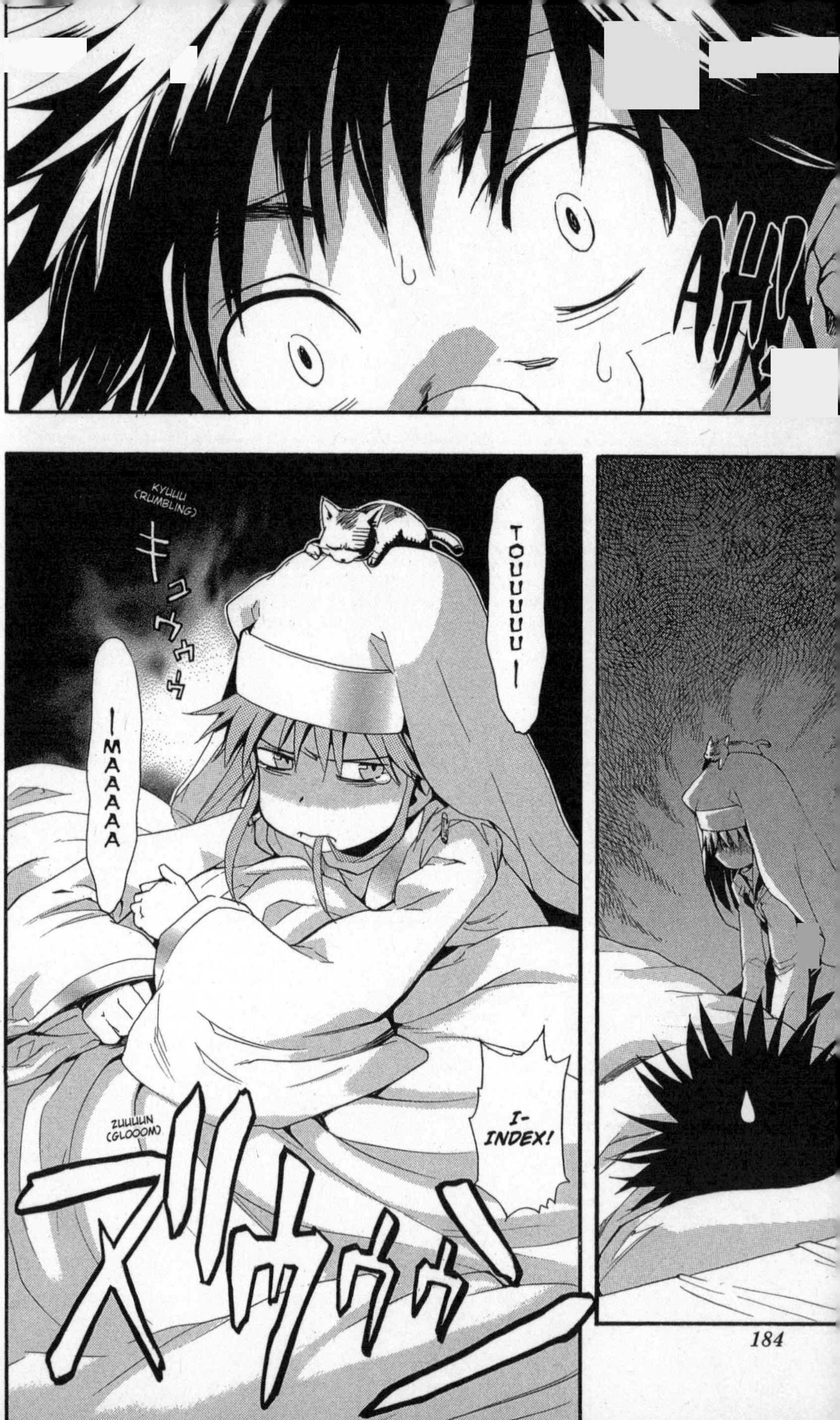
AH
TOUUUUUU!
KYUUU (RUMBLING)
IMAAAAA!
I- INDEX!
ZUUUUN (GLOOOM)

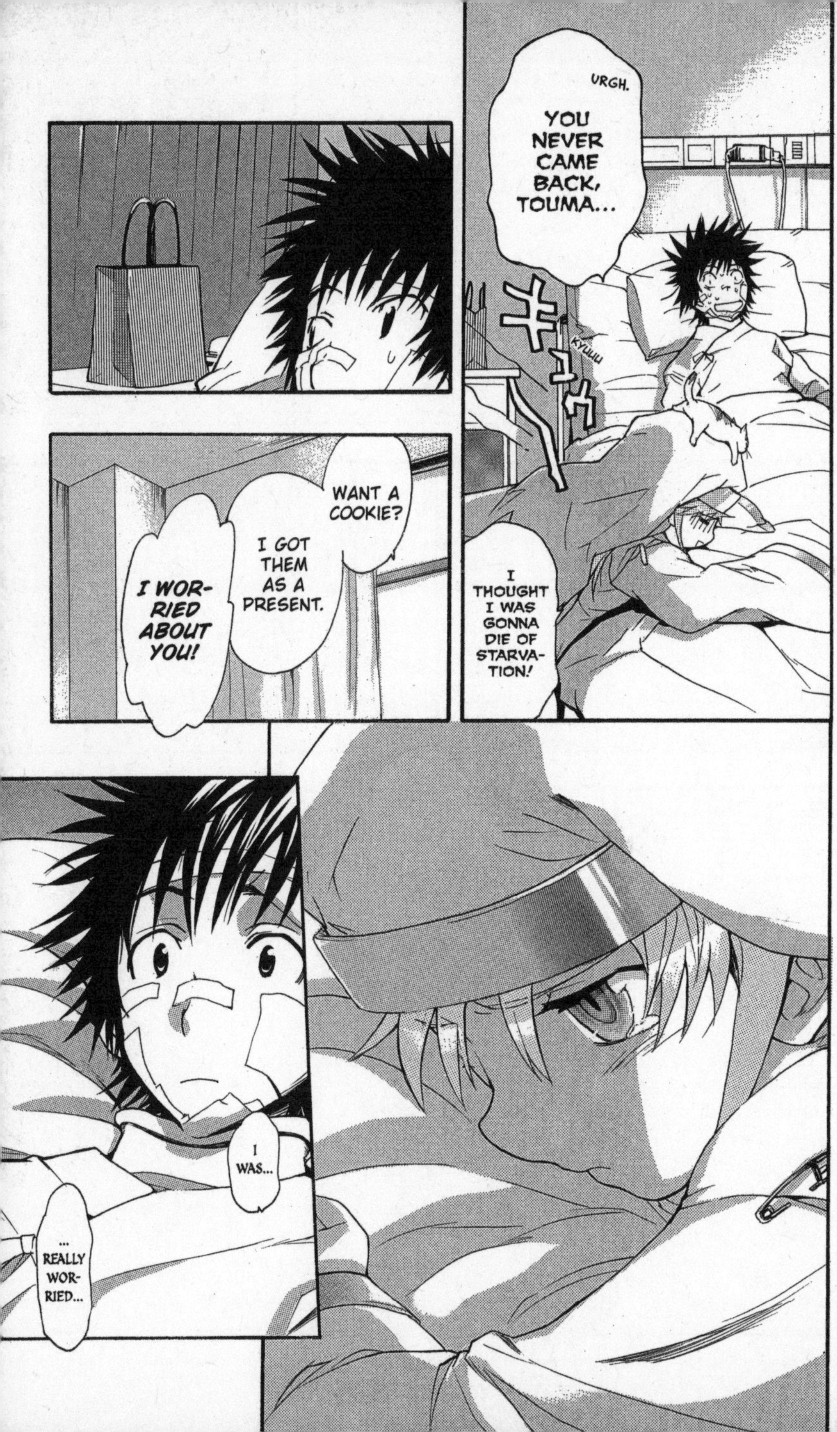
URGH.
YOU NEVER CAME BACK, TOUMA...
KYUUU
I THOUGHT I WAS GONNA DIE OF STARVATION!
WANT A COOKIE?
I GOT THEM AS A PRESENT.
I WORRIED ABOUT YOU!
I WAS...
...REALLY WORRIED...

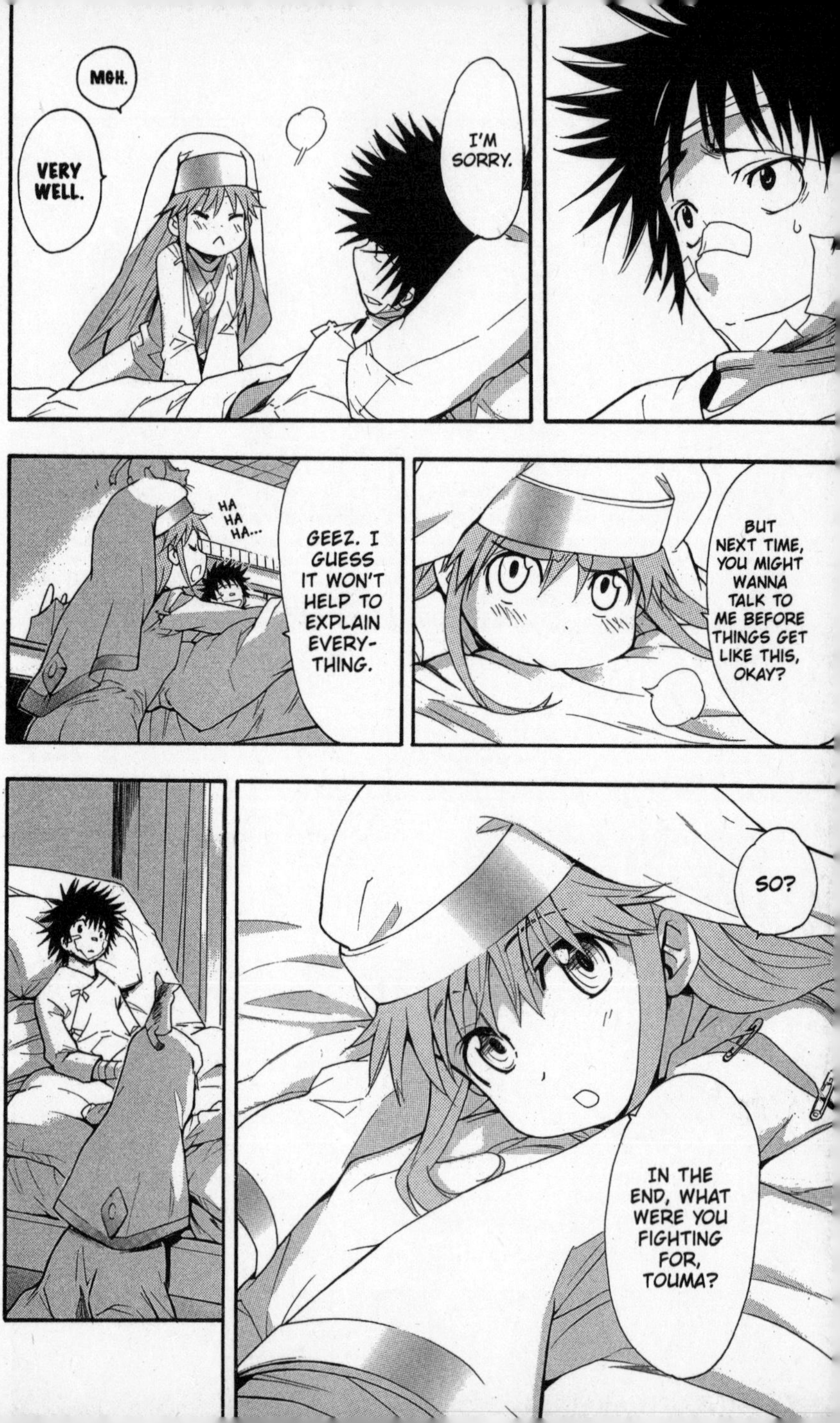
I'M SORRY.
MGH.
VERY WELL.
BUT NEXT TIME, YOU MIGHT WANNA TALK TO ME BEFORE THINGS GET LIKE THIS, OKAY?
GEEZ. I GUESS IT WON'T HELP TO EXPLAIN EVERY-THING.
HA HA HA...
SO?
IN THE END, WHAT WERE YOU FIGHTING FOR, TOUMA?

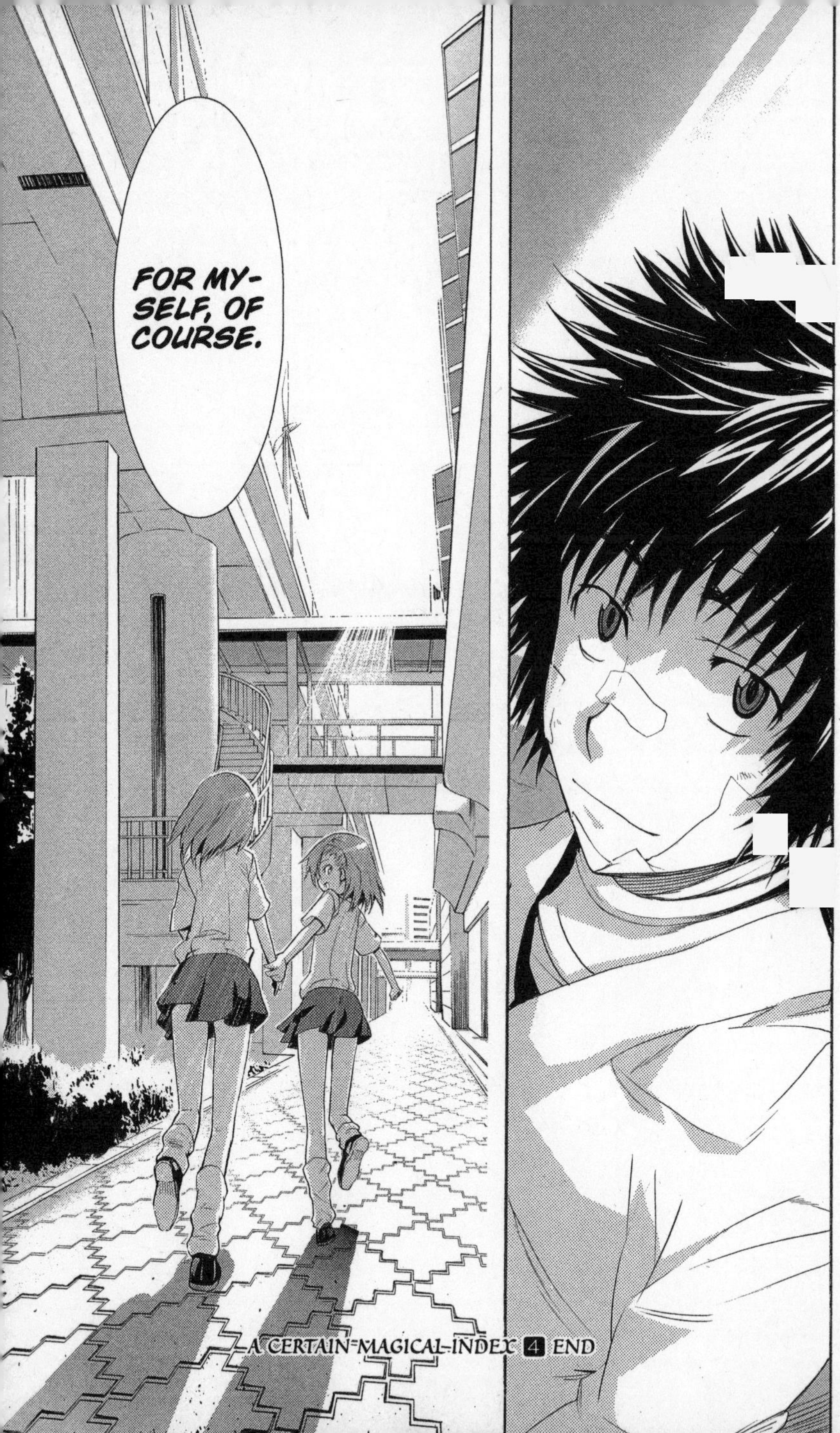
FOR MY-SELF, OF COURSE.
A CERTAIN MAGICAL INDEX 4 END

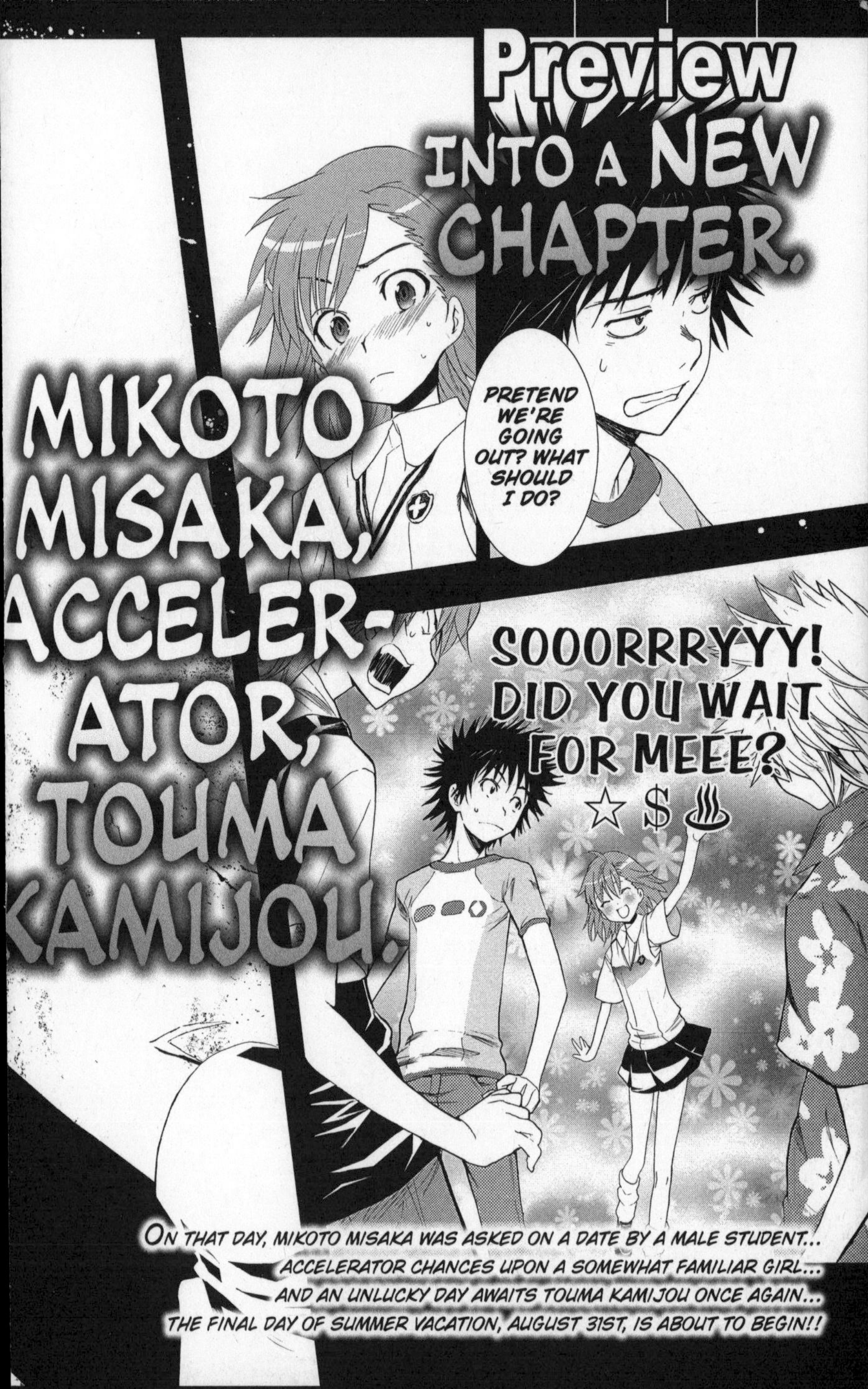
Preview
INTO A NEW CHAPTER.
PRETEND WE'RE GOING OUT? WHAT SHOULD I DO?
MIKOTO MISAKA, ACCELER-ATOR, TOUMA KAMIJOU.
SOOORRRYYY! DID YOU WAIT FOR MEEE? ☆$♨
ON THAT DAY, MIKOTO MISAKA WAS ASKED ON A DATE BY A MALE STUDENT...
ACCELERATOR CHANCES UPON A SOMEWHAT FAMILIAR GIRL...
AND AN UNLUCKY DAY AWAITS TOUMA KAMIJOU ONCE AGAIN...
THE FINAL DAY OF SUMMER VACATION, AUGUST 31ST, IS ABOUT TO BEGIN!!

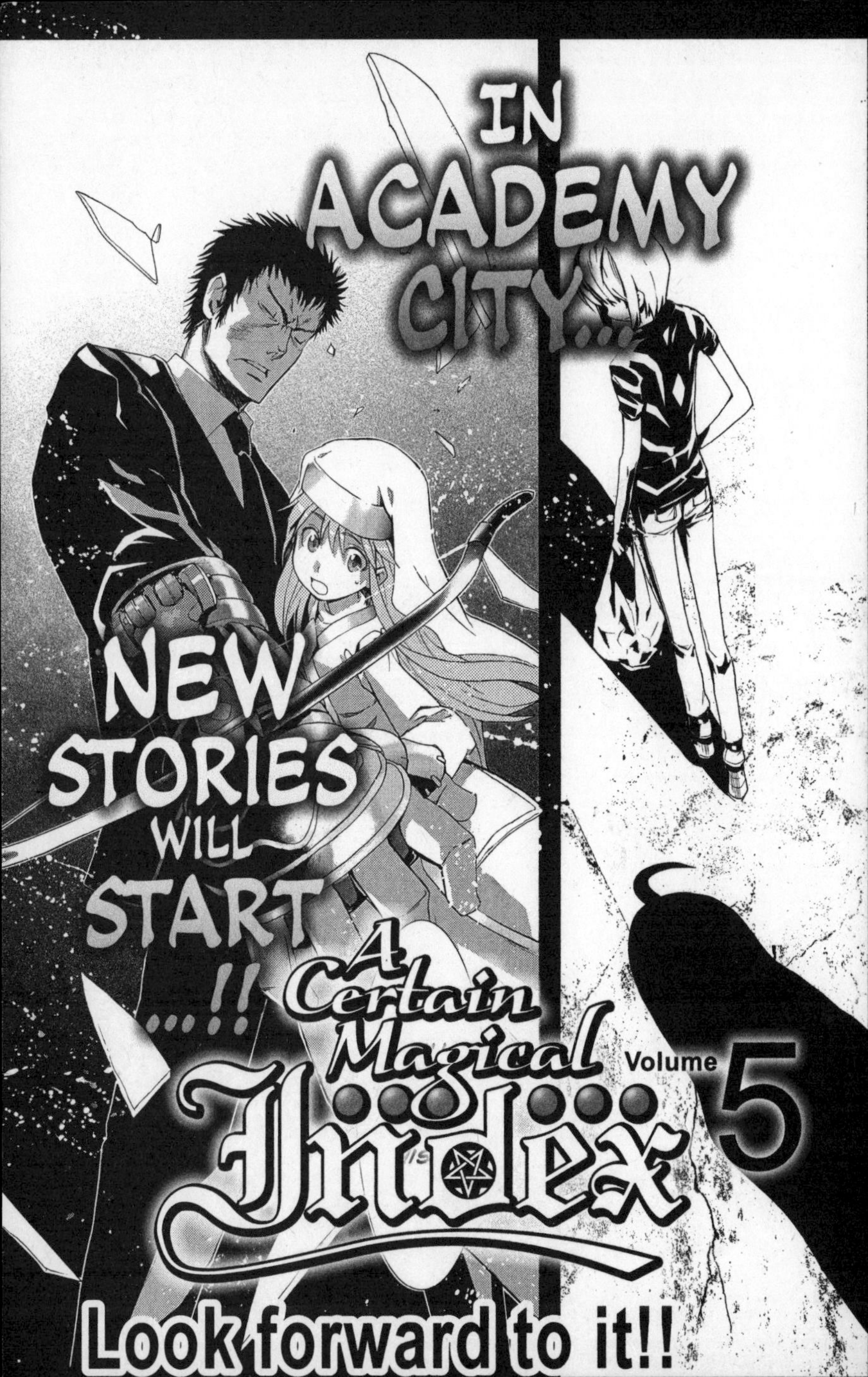
IN ACADEMY CITY...
NEW STORIES WILL START...!!
A Certain Magical Index
Volume 5
Look forward to it!!

WELCOME TO IKEBUKURO, WHERE TOKYO'S WILDEST CHARACTERS GATHER!!

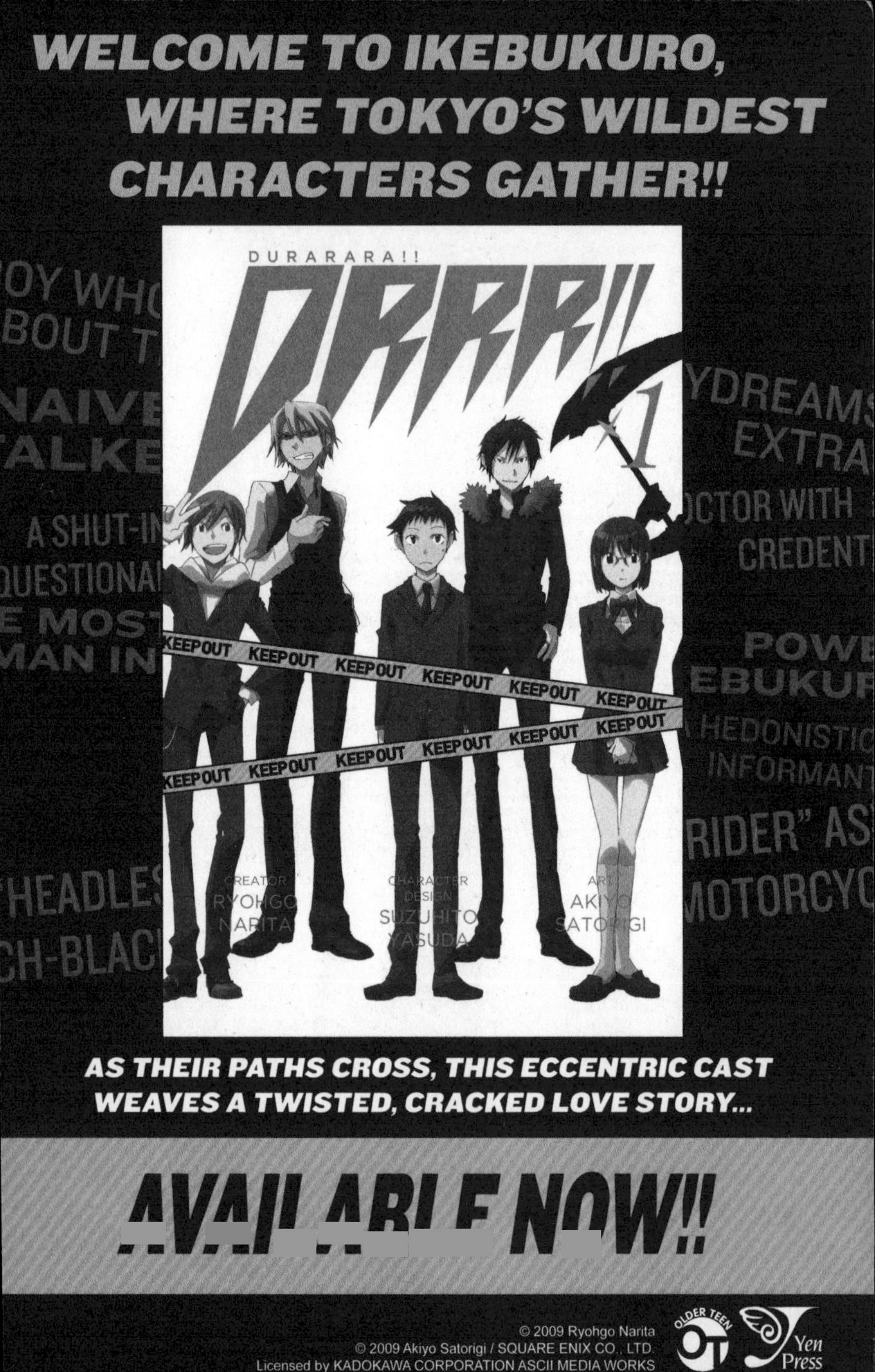
DURARARA!!
DRRR!!
1
KEEPOUT
CREATOR
RYOHGO NARITA
CHARACTER DESIGN
SUZUHITO YASUDA
ART
AKIYO SATORIGI

AS THEIR PATHS CROSS, THIS ECCENTRIC CAST WEAVES A TWISTED, CRACKED LOVE STORY...

AVAILABLE NOW!!

The Phantomhive family has a butler who's almost too good to be true...

...or maybe he's just too good to be human.

Black Butler

YANA TOBOSO

VOLUMES 1-21 IN STORES NOW!

A CERTAIN MAGICAL INDEX ❹

KAZUMA KAMACHI
KIYOTAKA HAIMURA
CHUYA KOGINO

Translation: Andrew Prowse

Lettering: Brndn Blakeslee & Lys Blakeslee

TOARU MAJYUTSU NO INDEX Vol. 4
© 2009 Kazuma Kamachi
© 2009 Chuya Kogino / SQUARE ENIX. CO. LTD.
Licensed by KADOKAWA CORPORATION ASCII MEDIA WORKS
First published in Japan in 2009 by SQUARE ENIX CO., LTD.
English translation rights arranged with SQUARE ENIX CO., LTD.
and Hachette Book Group through Tuttle-Mori Agency, Inc.

Translation © 2016 by SQUARE ENIX CO., LTD.

Yen Press
Hachette Book Group
1290 Avenue of the Americas
New York, NY 10104

ISBN: 978-0-316-34597-2

10 9 8 7 6 5 4 3 2 1

BVG

Printed in the United States of America